IN SEARCH OF
CANAAN

IN SEARCH OF

CANAAN

Black Migration to Kansas
1879-80

ROBERT G. ATHEARN

THE REGENTS PRESS OF KANSAS
Lawrence

© Copyright 1978 by the Regents Press of Kansas
Printed in the United States of America
Designed by Yvonne Willingham

Library of Congress Cataloging in Publication Data

Athearn, Robert G
In search of Canaan.

Bibliography: p.
Includes index.
1. Afro-Americans—Kansas—History. 2 Kansas—
History. I. Title.
E185.93.K16A8   978.1'004'96073   78-2343
ISBN 0-7006-0171-6

FOR

CLAIRE ATHEARN
who knows why

CONTENTS

LIST OF ILLUSTRATIONS

ACKNOWLEDGMENTS

The first thing that should be said in the way of acknowledgments is that my wife, to whom the work is appropriately dedicated, not only did all the things that academic wives do, or are alleged to have done, in aid of her husband's research, but in this case she was the discoverer of the topic. While working alongside me on another projected book—she was examining old newspapers at the Kansas State Historical Society, Topeka—she ran across news items dealing with the 1879 black rush into Kansas, and thanks to her high degree of intellectual curiosity, she began to take notes. She then urged me to continue the "dig," in the belief that this was a worthwhile topic, and after I became aware of how little western historians knew of this movement, I agreed to undertake the writing job. One might say that in this instance we reversed our family roles: she planted the seed; I delivered. The blame for any imperfections in the result may be laid at my door.

Next in order are thanks due to Nyle Miller and Joseph Snell, of the Kansas State Historical Society, two old friends who went out of their way to be of help. Librarians across the country came forward, as all librarians do, and gave us every assistance. Thanks go to libraries at the universities of Maine, Missouri, Kansas, Kansas State, Texas, and Colorado, as well as to Baylor University, Louisiana State University, and Fisk University. A number of public libraries provided information, among them the New Orleans Public Library, the Memphis Public Library, the Kansas City Public Library, and the Houston Public Library. In addition to the State Historical Society of Kansas, similar societies at both Columbia and

St. Louis, Missouri, and in Mississippi, Tennessee, and Minnesota are due the warmest of thanks. The Library of Congress also offered its facilities.

My colleagues Matthew Downey and Clifford P. Westermeier offered assistance, as did Frederic J. Athearn, the contributor of citations from Texas newspapers. Professor Charles Nilon, University of Colorado Department of English, watched the project with interest and gave periodic advice and encouragement. So did Professors William Unrau, Department of History, Wichita State University, and Benjamin F. Brown, Department of History, University of Kansas. Many long hours and no small amount of devotion to the project were given by Carolyn Dill, Ruth Major, and Carol Watson of my department, three wonderful ladies who did the typing and offered suggestions; I owe them much. Finally, I want to acknowledge financial aid from the University of Colorado's Council on Research and Creative Work.

Short portions of the study have appeared in the *Record,* a publication of the Friends of the Library, Washington State University, Pullman (Vol. 34 [1973], pp. 2–21), and in the *Prairie Scout* (Abilene, Kansas: Kansas Corral of the Westerners, Inc., vol. 3 [1975], pp. 87–99).

IN SEARCH OF
CANAAN

The husbandman has found a land which . . . is destined at no distant day to become richer and fairer than Canaan.

—*Caldwell* (Kans.) *Commercial,*
May 6, 1880

PROLOGUE

In the years that immediately followed the close of the Civil War, Americans turned their eyes westward and resumed an old fascination with frontier settlement. The bitter memory of fratricidal conflict would not be effaced for their generation and for longer, but there was some solace to be found in keeping busy in a national sense, of working hard, of building—and forgetting. It was toward the unfinished task of settling such acres as could be settled in the apparently limitless public domain that the agrarian frontiersmen, both native and immigrant, again turned, and in full cry they made their assault upon the last of the nation's many Wests.

The high-plains country, long known as the Great American Desert, resisted and stubbornly held to its ungracious title by dealing farmers blow after blow, in the form of dry years, grasshopper invasions, and bitter winters; but unrelentingly the invading army of determined plowmen edged westward. Speaking native European tongues, or perhaps in the twanging accents of New England, and wearing the unromantic garb of field workers, they took up the challenge of the surveyors, and square by square, they began to cultivate the sections of prairie land marked off for their use by a government that itself had some doubts about the presumed agricultural bounty it had offered to settlers.

One explanation of the phenomenon lay in the force and persistence of the westward thrust, a characteristic that had permeated the American experience at every level for generations. But now, more than ever, the promotional aspects of western settlement were revealed as the hawkers of glad tidings beckoned to the easily convinced and talked of green pastures to the timid, entreating both groups to venture forth into America's gardenland where nature's bounty—to use a favorite phrase—awaited only the husbandman's magic touch. Land agents, railroad propagandists, and local governmental agencies exceeded themselves in denouncing the concept of the desert, in praising the new frontier's exceptional fertility, arability, and livability.

As the invasion mounted, statistics became impressive. During the 1870s, for example, Nebraska's population soared from about 123,000 to almost 453,000, and by the end of another decade the numbers had passed the magic million mark. Kansas did even better. As early as 1880 that state had nearly a million residents, and well before the decade ended, the total was increased by another fifty percent. The rush was no mere accident; Kansas leaders, as those in other western states, assiduously sought to attract settlers by every known means. In 1874 the Jayhawker legislators amended the laws concerning military service to exempt those whose religious beliefs opposed such duty, and in so doing, the lawmakers appealed directly to German-Russian Mennonites, who were then considering emigration from their homes in southern Russia. This was but a single instance of efforts made to put out the welcome mat, to encourage agrarians who wanted a new life and who, perhaps, were dissatisfied with their present homes to try their luck on cheap lands in the free atmosphere of the West.

The Mennonites, who came under increasing pressures from the Russian government, were by no means the first people who desired to leave a degenerating situation in search of a better life, as witness the earlier emigrations from Europe, dating back to the eighteenth century. But now, in post–Civil War America, one did not have to point to European political turmoil to find unhappy men and women who sought relief through emigration. The American South, suffering from the throes of Reconstruction, was a place where talk of fresh chance, of land ownership, and of political participation fell upon receptive ears. A large number of the listeners were former slaves.

Black settlers were not unusual in the West, for they had filtered into the new communities for some time. Kansas, in particular, had felt their presence after the Civil War as organized migrations had established black towns such as Nicodemus, but in the spring of 1879 there was added to this normal development a rush of southern Negroes that was, in many respects, unique. Mass movements were not new in American history—the Mormons had demonstrated that—but the hegira to Kansas and neighboring states was different in that it was sudden, unplanned, and therefore

4

disorganized, and it was leaderless. While there were both political and economic reasons behind the flight, there were also emotional, often biblical, overtones that gave the phenomenon a millenarian flavor. There was talk of the promised land; there were references to Egypt and the Jews and hints of a potential Elysium on the high plains, which added another dimension to the more ordinary aspirations associated with land, education, and political freedom.

The political ramifications of emancipation that unsettled the South for years after Appomattox and the "redemption" of the area by Democrats as a result of the compromises of 1877, developments in which southern Negroes saw their hopes for participation at the polls fade away, have been dealt with most recently by Nell Irvin Painter in her *Exodusters: Black Migration to Kansas after Reconstruction.* As she suggested, it was here that the former slaves were caught in a dilemma not of their own making and here that they suffered mental and physical indignities seldom experienced in the past.

Suspicious of their old masters, and therefore frequently unwilling to risk their new-found freedom in an uncertain wage relationship, many of them abandoned the farm for nearby cities. For example, there were thirty-five hundred fewer blacks in Alabama in 1866 than before the war, yet their numbers in such cities as Montgomery, Mobile, and Selma increased by between thirteen and twenty-five percent. This shift occasioned a loss of labor that was serious, as was evidenced in the depopulation of South Carolina's rice fields in 1866, a decline that resulted in a drastic reduction in the production of that foodstuff.[1]

The southern response to this truancy was the enactment of legislative codes so strict, and aimed so directly at blacks, that northerners were not far wrong in their suspicions about a massive reenslavement program being under way south of the Mason-Dixon line. So thorough were the codes that to say these people were second-class citizens was to assign them a higher rank than was the case. While blacks could own property, make contracts, sue, and be sued, they could testify only against members of their own race in court. Interracial marriage was prohibited, as was free movement from one community to another, and even the privilege of remaining out after a specified hour at night was denied. Occupational restrictions generally limited blacks to agricultural endeavor, and here strict contracts kept them in bondage for the duration of the agreement, usually a year. Any number of petty offenses brought fines, and those who were unable to pay were farmed out by local sheriffs to plantation owners who would pay the fines and thus acquire cheap labor.[2]

At the end of the war, many blacks refused to return to the fields

5

under a wage or sharecropping system, and their tendency to cluster in the cities produced a stalemate that some of their leaders sought to resolve through migration. During the 1870s, in particular, a revival of overseas colonization, as witnessed in an earlier Liberia movement, swept the southland. The year 1877 saw the organization in South Carolina of the Liberian Exodus and Joint Stock Company; neighboring North Carolina produced the Freedmen's Emigrant Aid Society; and in other states, similar groups sprang up. During the following two years, two small vessels transported a few American blacks to Africa, but their efforts barely touched the large reservoir of dissatisfied freedmen who wanted to leave the South and who now sought alternatives to a trans-Atlantic crossing.

During these postwar years an increasing number of discontented freedmen began to consider moving their families to some part of the United States where the former master-slave relationship had been minimal or nonexistent. In the late 1860s Benjamin "Pap" Singleton, a former slave who had spent his early years in Tennessee, undertook to induce members of his race to migrate to Kansas, where he planned to found some black colonies. His circulars drew some seven thousand responses, but most of the interested parties, as well as other thousands in the South, could not answer the call because they had no money with which to pay for the westward passage or for the land after they reached the new country. Those who were able to go were those who had achieved some kind of success at farming in the South and who had acquired funds enough to afford such a move. In this respect they differed little from white pioneers who headed west under the same conditions and for the same reason: to better their economic position.

Meanwhile, those who were shackled to their situations through poverty tried to cope with the conditions of southern life that now faced them. However, the future appeared to hold little promise of social, economic, or political participation in the post-Reconstruction era, and as they contemplated their lot, a sullen resignation seeped into the minds of landless workers who once had grasped at the straws of a meaningful freedom. Then, in the spring of 1879, what appeared to be one last wisp of hope drifted southward from Kansas, that special place where the martyred John Brown had come to fame.

Word spread across the southern farm country, and into the minds of those who labored over cotton or sugar crops, that the day of reckoning was near at hand, that the Lord had answered black prayers with the offer of deliverance in a western Eden. In this vast state where Brown had caused blood to flow in his righteous wrath, there was said to be land for all, and land especially for poor blacks who for so long had cherished the thought of a tiny patch of America that they could call their own. The soil was said to be free for the taking, and even better, passage to the prairie Canaan was rumored to be available to all, or almost all. A mere four dollars would buy deck space on a river steamer that put the pilgrim ashore at St. Louis, a city that stood only a width of a state away from the sacred soil of Kansas. Once there, the black brotherhood could stand together, could work the land, *their* land, in the manner of other Americans, and could thereby achieve that true freedom so far denied them.

Thus began a pell-mell land rush to Kansas, an unreasoned, almost mindless exodus from the South toward some vague ideal, some western paradise, where all cares would vanish once the beckoning gates were reached. In a narrower sense it spoke of black emigrants who sought their share of frontier farms, but in the main it told more about a nation whose wounds had been bound but had not yet healed. The southern problem, agonizingly long of solution, simply had erupted and overflowed. Kansas, an almost sacred ground in the eyes of earlier crusading abolitionists, seemed to be one logical place to catch the spillover of the southern outflow. Other northern states, whose residents expressed sympathy for the former bondsmen but who had no desire to provide new homes for them, spoke highly of the Kansas movement and of its enlightened residents who appeared to accept the fleeing blacks as part payment of the great national debt owed them but not yet fully paid.

Kansans expressed their thanks for these and other compliments and braced themselves for the onslaught.

1

AND WALK INTO
JORDAN'S TIDE

As darkness blanketed the city on a raw March evening in 1879, an Anchor Line packet boat, dimly bearing the name *Colorado,* felt its way through swirls of large wet snowflakes and gingerly touched the riverside wharf. With lines secured and the vessel made fast, the crew could go ashore to investigate the night life of St. Louis, another eight-day run from Vicksburg now at an end. Cabin passengers would have no trouble finding cabs to carry them quickly over muddy streets and into warm, waiting hotels. The unloading of crates and barrels consigned to wholesale houses could wait for daylight.

But part of the cargo was moved ashore that night. The deck passengers, who had paid four dollars apiece for passage and who had furnished their own bedding and food, fell somewhere between the categories of people and things. Two hundred in number, they were black southerners from far down river who were now bound for an unseen land of promise to the north. Tired, hungry, and frightened, they were told to go ashore. Obediently they groped for land, jostling each other in the darkness; and clutching their few ragged belongings, they sought any shelter that could be found along the cold, wet embankment.

A local newspaper reporter, whiling away a dull evening at his office, learned that one of the river steamers had landed with a strange and unexpected cargo. He sauntered through the gaslit night, mildly curious. As he neared the river he heard a low hum of voices, but there were no campfires or any sign of light. The huddled, shivering strangers, he learned, were from some of the river counties in Louisiana and Mississippi.

9

When asked why they had come, they gave vague answers about having seen promising circulars that spoke of Kansas as a land of opportunity, a place that seemed far away and still undefined on a cold spring night.

Kansas? Pencil poised, the questioner asked for some elaboration. Well, they said hesitantly, there was talk that someone, presumably the federal government, was passing out forty-acre farming plots to former slaves in that new country. And that was not all. Each recipient was to be given mules, plows, rations, and other necessities with which to start a fresh agricultural life—merely for the asking. No, they were not sure, but it all sounded exciting; and fearing that indecisiveness might spoil the main chance, they had sold their belongings for whatever the goods would bring and had joined the rush toward the Vicksburg waterfront. Now, it began to appear, the wish had been the father of the thought. There was no welcoming committee at St. Louis, no governmental representative waiting to escort them to their new farmsteads, no one who seemed to know anything about the latest bonanza in the West.

Here they were, without a cent and with no hope for tomorrow, muttered one of the men. He thought they could not be worse off. That brought denial from some of the others, who said pointedly that they could be worse off. They could be down South. The assertion generated vigorous nodding among those within earshot.

What was so bad about being down South? the reporter asked. His question brought a flurry of answers. Cotton paid only about eight cents a pound, and the planters tended to fix their own prices, volunteered a self-appointed spokesman. "You've got to give the planter a bale or 400 pounds even, and furnish your own bagging for every acre," he explained, pointing out that this did not always leave much for the sharecropper.

That was part of it. Then there was the store system, so much complained about in company towns across the country. "We've got to pay fifteen to thirty-five cents a peck for meal, and if we get it on time, we've got to pay double, not only for that but for calico and other things, and when Christmas comes round and the old women and children ought to be getting something, there ain't nothing to get."

As the old man shook his head over the hazards of the credit system, another grim-lipped refugee commented upon a general complaint that had gained wide circulation throughout the North in post-bellum days. These people were frightened, he explained; their lives were filled with personal insecurity: "I know, within the last three years, of seventy-five men who left their houses at night, and were never found until the buzzards found them in the fields or in the valleys." The reporter made note of it, without comment. A few days later, when such arrivals made the matter more

10

newsworthy, his paper—which was of Republican persuasion—would advise such newcomers not to linger in Missouri, where "a Missouri Democrat would rather kill a nigger than eat his breakfast any day." But there was no editorializing that night. The journalist wrote a straightforward account of what he had seen, and then called it a day. The next morning his fellow townsmen, who toyed with their breakfasts without entertaining any murderous thoughts, noticed a story that told of strangers on the shore. They learned that two hundred southern Negroes, en route to Kansas, had arrived and that they were "dead broke."[1]

The news item failed to excite any of the local Anglo-Saxon humanitarians. During the previous month the *Belle of Memphis* had unloaded over a thousand bales of cotton and about a hundred blacks of both sexes and all ages. These passengers had straggled through the city and had disappeared from the streets, part of the group having moved into vacant houses, causing no trouble at all. They were not tramps, the press had explained; rather, they were squatters who either would move on or perhaps would find work in the city.

Thus, when the latest group appeared, there was no rush to the waterfront, soup kettles in hand and hearts filled with compassion, to render first aid. Floods, earthquakes, and tornadoes—natural disasters that left hundreds homeless through violence—were much more compelling reasons for municipal turnouts. But there was no violence, disaster, or excitement in this happening.[2]

The morning was quiet. A handful of tiny fires dotted the river bank, around which were gathered women and children, a few of the latter nursing at their mothers' breasts. Some of the men warmed themselves; others wandered aimlessly up and down the levee, making small talk and munching on large chunks of bread purchased by the few who had any money. When asked about their plans, they were evasive because they had no plans or because they suspected the motives of interrogators.[3]

Aside from the curious, the first person to show any particular concern for the refugees was Charlton H. Tandy, who admitted that their arrival was a complete surprise to him. As he walked among them, along the snow-covered levee, he saw that some of his people were hungry and without proper clothing, particularly the children who "were bare-footed and just as they came off the cotton-fields, in their cotton clothes, very ill-prepared to meet the weather we then had in the city of Saint Louis."[4] Alarmed, Tandy went into action. First, he gathered together a number of the single men and led them into the city, where they were farmed out to families of his acquaintance. As he puzzled over the plight of the

11

others, a chance conversation gave him an idea. Why not try the Mullanphy Board? asked a former secretary of that charitable organization.

Tandy knew of its existence; almost everyone in St. Louis did. Thirty years earlier Bryan Mullanphy, the only son of a well-to-do merchant, had been sitting in a local saloon, having a friendly drink with one of his friends, and apparently the conversation had turned to the plight of poor emigrants—many of them Irish—who were stranded in the city on their way to the mines of California. Bryan, either worried about the fact that he had no children to receive his inheritance or engulfed by a momentary flood of sentimentality found at the bottom of a glass, suddenly asked the bartender for a scrap of paper, and upon it he dashed off the terms of his will. Within two years he was dead, and the public learned that he had left a half-million dollars to aid travelers who were stalled at the "Gateway to the West."

Tandy, as well as most others, assumed that the fund was intended for emigrants, the bulk of whom were from Europe and were white. Yet, there were cases on record where money had been advanced to colored settlers who, in the past few years, had filtered out of Tennessee and Kentucky, bound for Kansas homesteads. Therefore, the suggestion, coming from a man who had served on the Mullanphy Board, appeared to have merit. It was worth a try. Losing no time, he headed for the board's offices, located at 307 Locust Street, and sought an interview with Theodore Laveille, a former innkeeper who now received $2,000 a year to manage the daily affairs of the agency.

The meeting was brief and devastating. No, said Laveille, there were just too many applicants; their numbers soon would exhaust the small funds available. When the amazed applicant collected his wits and offered a meek objection, Laveille cut him down, remarking that he did not wish to discuss the matter—and good day.

Angered but unwilling to take "no" for an answer, Tandy sought out the board's chairman, Frederick Hill, who remarked that as he interpreted Mr. Mullanphy's will, these strangers were not entitled to any assistance. He did not say that succor was reserved for distressed members of the white race; he merely left a strong implication that this was so. A lesser man than Tandy would have doffed his cap, shrugged his shoulders, and consoled himself with the fact that this had been going on for a long time. Instead, he went to the attack, insisting that he have an audience with the board itself. Hill told him to come back at three o'clock, when the gentlemen, as it happened, were to hold a regular meeting. Perhaps they would hear him.

At the appointed time, Tandy turned up, with twenty-five ragged refugees in tow, and encamped his little band in the board's waiting room. Here they sat for two hours, hoping that the matter of black refugees would come under discussion; but it did not, and the members prepared to adjourn. Recognizing one of the members, Tandy leaned over the railing that divided the room and asked if he could speak to the board.

"I don't know, Mr. Tandy, whether you can or no; I will speak to the gentlemen and see if they will hear you," the man responded. For a third time the cause appeared to be lost, but Tandy, now having crossed his Rubicon, plunged on. Silently he stared into the eyes of the other man, radiating grim reproach. After a few moments of awkward silence the board member blurted out: "Gentlemen, we must hear what he has to say."

Somewhat annoyed, but impressed by the appearance of a small mob in their modest quarters, the board members reluctantly concluded that they had better listen. Told that these people were stranded and that it had been Bryan Mullanphy's intent to help such unfortunates, they argued that while this was true, previous cases had been few in number and the attendant expense proportionately small. Here, on the other hand, were upwards of two hundred people, with no assurance that they were not merely the advance guard of an army of indigents. It would just be too expensive.

There was another argument. To help the poor was a commendable act; to assist honest plowmen in their quest for western farms certainly was in accordance with the American dream. But as one of the businessmen pointed out, this was a different situation, and it was not right for St. Louis to export a lot of paupers to Topeka or to any other city.[5] One had to think of the brothers in neighboring municipalities. In the end they gave Tandy one hundred dollars, with instructions to use it for food.

The small bequest did not solve the problem, for it did not answer the basic question of what to do if the trickle of blacks became a flood. Even as the Mullanphy Board issued its ration money, the *Grand Tower* was thrashing its way up river, and on it were said to be another five hundred refugees. Worse, rumor had it that another nine hundred waited at one of the Louisiana landings, clamoring for passage.

The businessmen of St. Louis watched the advance on an imaginary battle map with growing apprehension. Once more they reaffirmed their belief that it would be cruel, not only to Kansas, but to the refugees themselves, to direct this flood toward Kansas. That remained the principle. But, reasoned the thinkers, there were practical considerations. Local resources were not geared to cope with an invading army of indigents. If more hungry hundreds appeared, even such a social service as providing soup lines would gobble up the remaining funds.[6] Thus, the only logical conclusion appeared to be the discovery of some means to halt the infiltration.

The men of the Mullanphy Board were not alone in their dilemma. Mayor Henry C. Overstolz, described as being "much at sea" over the problem, paced his office floor and foresaw a civic crisis comparable to the occurrence of some natural disaster, such as flood or plague. As an ordinary, rational human being, his inclination was to help the needy, provided they were few and not too needy. But as he remarked, to do so would not only establish a precedent; it would advertise St. Louis as a mecca for those waiting down river. He wanted to stem the tide, not swell it.

As the mayor pondered his problem, it grew. A local newspaperman, watching the levee seethe with migrant blacks, called the movement "Africa's Exodus." Only three days had elapsed since the *Colorado* had made port. "To put the question fairly and squarely, St. Louis is threatened with the influx of thousands of Negro families who are absolutely without means," the paper elaborated.

No one had to qualify the situation with the words "fairly and squarely" for Henry Overstolz. It was threatening, no matter how one viewed it. But he was a man of action, the elected leader and protector of his people. Prussian-born, he had lived in America for most of his fifty-seven years, having made so much money at merchandising, and then in lumber, banking, and insurance, that he had retired twice before the age of fifty. Also, he had married wisely, selecting as his mate Philippine Espenschied, a daughter of one of the oldest and best-known wagon manufacturers in the West, and she, in turn, had presented him with six children. So the German, who had worked his way up the ladder of success in the New World, to be head of an insurance company and president of the Fifth National Bank of St. Louis, and then, in the American tradition, to political rewards for such financial leadership, was not likely to be without an answer when the hour of trial faced his city. In fact, a local historian remarked, only four years later, so great was the mayor's power that it might have been dangerous in the hands of a lesser man, but he was said to have wielded it carefully and only for the public good. And that was just what Overstolz wanted historians to say. He knew that if he were to be remembered as a leader, he had to be firm in the present crisis. Thoughtfully stroking his heavy mustache, the stocky burgomaster pondered the problem and then undertook a little research.[7]

Thumbing the city ordinances, the mayor recalled that one of them provided for fines against any railroad bringing paupers to the city; the law applied to steamboat companies, as well. Municipal officials had the power to require a one-thousand-dollar bond from any steamboat or railroad company to ensure against such an occurrence; that amount of money could support a goodly number of paupers, provided they did not stay too long. So, concluded the mayor, the law should be invoked against riverboat companies. But his legal advisers held up a collective staying hand and advised caution. The steamboats were common carriers, as were the railroads. The migrants had paid their passage, which was all that the transportation company could require of them.

Frustrated, the mayor tried another tack. It was an administrative rule of thumb that whenever public coffers were threatened and nothing in the municipal rule book applied to the emergency at hand, the ancient health problem was a reliable standby. In this case he could unsheath it for temporary use with apparent justification, for yellow fever had ravaged river towns with particular intensity in the recent past. Surely, people in rags must be potential disease carriers. So Overstolz sent out a hasty call to members of the City Board of Health, requesting an immediate special session.

Board members were understanding. They agreed that the approach of the *Grand Tower,* with its rumored cargo of civic problems, indeed called for action. One of them suggested that it was possible to stop the vessel and to quarantine its passengers, hold them for a few days, and then persuade them to go back home. His colleagues were more cautious. They pointed out that it would be costly to feed this great number and, worse, that once cared for, the inmates might elect to stay and take advantage of the free boardinghouse, confining as it might be.

Another problem vexed the Health Board. Supposing it interned and fed the unwanted visitors, hoping that they would then return home, where could people who were too poor to buy food find passage money? Capt. John P. Keiser of the Anchor Line, which did much business with both local and southern merchants, showed his firm's civic spirit by offering to return the unwanted goods, free of charge. The board was pleased and thought the offer most generous, but there was no assurance that the emigrants could be prevailed upon to return, and there was no legal manner by which force could be used. All right, said one of the nettled members, if these people could not be coaxed or forced into going back, how about shipping them on up the river to Wyandotte, Kansas? If they wanted to go to Kansas, help them; it would cost only about three dollars a head, a very good investment considering the complications of the problem. It was an attractive idea, but it was set aside for the time being on the ground that Wyandotte might lose its municipal temper and ship the whole lot back on the first available steamer.[8]

Still searching for an answer, but finding none, Mayor Overstolz did the best he could—he made a gesture. On March 15 he issued a public proclamation, warning impoverished blacks to stay away from St. Louis and advising them to remain in their southern homes. While this was fruitless, since a large percentage of those to whom it was directed could not read, and if they could, they were not likely to see the mayor's manifesto, it would please southern planters who were losing their field hands at a critical time of the year. As the city fathers knew, these were very good customers.

City folks were both curious and puzzled by those who swarmed in and, like locusts, threatened the economic garden by the river. Caught by surprise, they tried to understand the reasons behind this unexpected thrust in their direction. Apparently it was a combination of hysteria and bonanza, a drive powered by terror from behind and golden dreams ahead. The "pull" factor, however, seemed to be the more powerful of the two. The rush upon Kansas was compared to that at Leadville, Colorado, during the same year; in each case, sudden affluence was the end in view.

"It is worse than the Leadville excitement," wrote one who had visited the waterfront. "Outrageously absurd as it is, the children of Africa down there, with an ignorance as dark as their skins, have somehow got it in their heads that if they will come up to St. Louis they will be transported free of charge to the fertile plains of Kansas, and when there the Government will provide them with land, several hundred dollars, a mule and a plow." He was dismayed to see some of them walk to the nearest railway station and confidently ask for the pass that they supposed awaited them. "Then they learn that they have been 'fooled.' But still they hope that in some mysterious way they will be transported to Kansas and all will come out 'hunky-dory.' "[9]

Slowly, word filtered back to the levee: there were no free railroad tickets to Kansas, and it was doubtful that other reported fringe benefits existed. That brought a murmur of angered disappointment from those who had come north aboard the *Colorado*. One of the old men arose and gained their attention. He explained that the reported pot of gold at the Kansas end of the rainbow did not exist, and he asked if the disappointed emigrants from the South wanted to return. The answer was a sullen, determined no, and with that the old gentleman agreed. Together, he promised them, they would go forward and "walk into Jordan's tide."[10]

The *Colorado* group generated both interest and sympathy among newsmen who wrote their stories with a warmth that avoided excessive sentimentality. They talked of the "poor creatures" who had crawled beneath tarpaulins along the levee, trying to escape the wet and cold of night, and of sitting around tiny fires with the strangers, listening to accounts of hardships down South that surpassed any of the stories written by Harriet Beecher Stowe.[11] Then came the *Grand Tower,* in the predawn darkness of the sixteenth, pouring ashore between five and six hundred more men, women, and children. This time, newspapermen, in search of human-interest stories, were harder to find along the waterfront. Southern merchants and St. Louis businessmen, with furrowed brows and annoyed countenances, formed the welcoming committee. Why have you come? and Why don't you go home? they asked. Then, as if to anticipate their own questions, a spokesman read the mayor's proclamation to the pilgrims, warning that the city of their choice was absolutely without funds to support them or to send them on to some more promising place. Not only was there no work to be had, but those who arrived without money or friends surely would experience "much suffering and destitution," read that coldly official document.

The question of why they had come went without a satisfactory answer. When St. Louis and other cities to the west asked it, the responses were vague and varied. The overriding theme was traditional among most settlers along the American frontier—to better one's condition, particularly economic. But there were variations. Some talked of financial trickery among the southern whites, of petty persecutions, and, now and then, of discrimination by local law officers. When questioners suggested that denial of the ballot had sent these people fleeing, the responses were disappointing. A number of them said that this was true, and they showed resentment; but a great many others displayed a frustrating lack of interest in politics, admitting that they never had tried to vote.

If these colored agrarians were not all driven away from the South, then what were the attractions up river, particularly in Kansas? Newspaper reporters and businessmen at St. Louis, seeking answers to this puzzler, suspected that propaganda was involved. Occasional references to leaflets or broadsides sent one of the newsmen in search of evidence. All he could find was a small circular signed by a T. W. Raymor, a colored emigrant agent of Vicksburg, that warned against listening to anyone making false promises of free transportation to Kansas or free land upon arrival. Disappointed at his findings, the reporter concluded that even though Raymor had sounded a warning, he had made an implied promise. Even supposing that the victims had reached this happy conclusion, the danger of leading them astray was not imminent if one accepts the same reporter's estimate that only one in five hundred of the newcomers could read.[12]

More satisfied was the correspondent of a New York paper, who

17

chatted with the field hands and then revealed to his readers that bull-dozing—political intimidation—was the reason for flight. He said that the southern Negro, tired of such practices, simply had decamped. Republican newspapers readily accepted this view because it fitted their preconceptions perfectly. During the coming months it was their favorite answer to the repeated question, Why have you come?[13]

Perhaps the most realistic answer came from an irritated old lady who responded to the query in exasperation, saying that she just did not know why she had left home. Advised that Kansas was big and flat and that it would take money to get started, her annoyance grew. Heatedly she said that if she had known there were no trees there, she never would have listened to all the talk. She had something in common with the city fathers who puzzled at the movement. She, too, wondered why.[14]

St. Louis Negroes were less inclined to ponder the origins of the movement. They knew something of southern political conditions, but they knew also that they were in no position to do much about it. Following Tandy's lead, they offered to help, much in the manner of volunteer firemen who respond to an emergency, by giving what aid they could and as fast as possible. Private homes were opened, and quarters, often already overcrowded, were shared with their thinly clad countrymen from the waterfront. The overflow crowded into small churches, with pallets scattered on the floors to provide dry beds for the night. In near-military fashion these places of worship were converted into command posts, where strategy sessions were held and plans were laid to combat the deepening crisis.

On March the seventeenth, as local Irishmen marched through muddy streets chanting the praises of the Lord's chosen people, a handful of His troubled children gathered at one of the churches to talk about some of the less blessed. Charlton Tandy, now regarded as a leader, presided. One by one the speakers rose, but most of them were more inclined to point the finger at southern oppressors, who were accused of driving these black Jews from Egypt, than to offer concrete aid or even helpful suggestions.

John H. Johnson, a young Negro attorney and a clerk at the local custom house, was sympathetic. He had talked with some of the arrivals and they had complained vehemently of political, social, and economic oppression. But as a member of the resolutions committee, just organized, he shared Tandy's view that the call was for action, not vindication. He proposed the creation of a Committee of Fifteen, which would be charged with the task of raising money for relief. The group was appointed, along with a number of subcommittees that included some local preachers, and to start the ball rolling, a hat was passed. Returned to the chairman, it yielded fifty dollars.[15]

Three nights later a large gathering of blacks, along with a few whites, again met in one of the churches, Tandy presiding. Apparently the money-raising program had stalled, or Tandy was still embittered at the parsimony of the white community, for he opened the meeting with a bitter attack upon the Mullanphy Board. A mere hundred dollars, he scoffed; why, he had known of cases where a single white family had received three times that much to reach its western destination. What kind of justice was that?

Others were in an equally grim mood. One angry man proposed a group of stinging resolutions that condemned southerners for their past actions, but he overshot his mark, carrying on at such lengths that there were cries from the floor commanding him to sit down. Disorder mounted. Someone suggested, as a diversionary tactic, that the minutes of the previous meeting be read, a motion that was carried amidst the hurling of random imprecations and the noisy singing of "Hang Jeff Davis on a Sour Apple Tree" by a group of dissenters who directed their displeasure at no one in particular.

The turmoil subsided momentarily when James Milton Turner rose and asked for recognition. He was one of the black community's best-known members, and he commanded respect, if not affection. Although he was not yet forty, he had risen from slavery, had attended Oberlin College, and had served in the late war, having been wounded at Shiloh. After the war he taught school in Kansas City, and in the spring of 1871 he was appointed Minister Resident and Consul General to Liberia, partly, it was said, because in 1870 some twenty thousand Negroes had cast Republican votes at his advice. It was now less than a year since he had come home from Liberia, and as a man reputed to be the first Negro to be awarded a diplomatic post, he was something of a local celebrity. When he asked to be heard, the crowd listened.[16]

Turner was a moderate. Attacks upon the white establishment struck out at the group from which he had received all his political rewards. But discounting any such debts, he was not inclined toward extremism, and he saw no point in the resolutions proposed from the floor by the appointed Resolutions Committee. John W. Wheeler, who was also well known to the black community, rose to support Turner's position. Negroes, he said, could not afford to array themselves against the whites, and he thought that nothing would be gained by assuming a militant stance. His people needed help, and he preferred that they should ask for it, not demand it. Wheeler, who would be remembered as one of Missouri's more flamboyant

Negro editors, often was vehement in his writings, but his social and economic views were basically conservative, as he indicated on that March evening.[17]

But moderation was not popular that night. There was excitement in the air, the thrill of togetherness, and had anyone thought of it, the clenched fist might have been raised in defiance to the established order. As it was, apparently fists were in evidence, for reporters wrote of renewed argument, increased disorder, and "then supreme confusion that promised to end in a free fight." At the critical moment, just as name-calling and angry gesticulations threatened to dissolve into a donnybrook, one of the white women in the audience, who was known for her sympathy and good works among the Negro residents, arose and asked for order.

In the manner of the old-fashioned schoolma'am, she scolded the unruly audience, shaming them for such disgraceful conduct and sharply demanding instant reform. Sheepishly, like naughty children, they subsided. The most extreme of the impromptu resolutions were withdrawn. As the "official" proposal, they adopted one in which the South was criticized in less revolutionary tones for bulldozing, Ku Kluxism, intimidation, and degradation. The meeting was closed by passing the hat, which yielded fifty dollars, and the chastened participants quietly went home.[18]

By the time that members of the St. Louis black community and a handful of concerned whites had gathered on that tumultuous evening, the problem at hand was approximately ten days old. While the movement had not yet reached flood proportions, by then an estimated fourteen hundred southern Negroes had reached the city, some of whom had continued by rail or Missouri River steamer, having enough money of their own to pay the required fare. On that morning the *City of Vicksburg* landed, bringing an additional forty refugees, who were in worse circumstances than their predecessors. Without money and clothed in rags, they possessed nothing in the way of household goods except a few cracked dishes, pots, kettles, and pans and some blankets and quilts. A determined but somewhat discouraged delegation of their countrymen met them at the Anchor Line wharf and took them to St. Paul's chapel, which was located at Eleventh and Christy avenues. When a polite inquiry was made, suggesting that perhaps they would like to return home, there were no affirmative responses. With a shrug of their collective shoulders, the committeemen set about farming out the latest batch of arrivals to anyone who would volunteer shelter.

By now about a thousand of these arrivals remained in the city, perhaps ten of whom each day found some kind of employment. Private homes had taken as many as possible; the rest crowded into the churches, where they lined up before the soup kettles by day and slept together on the floor at night. The others drifted about town looking for work or just loafing on street corners, uncertain as to how they should pass the time.[19]

For those who had money, the problem was solved. Saloons and gambling joints along Christy Avenue, operated by enterprising members of their race, did a thriving business. Not only were local palaces of pleasure open to visitors, their proprietors were even willing to accept talented strangers into their ranks. Travelers who were ignorant of the big town's opportunities were enlightened by representatives who were so aggressive that they even boarded incoming vessels and explained new fields of economic endeavor to prospective clients. For example, when the *John B. Maude* arrived—a steamer named after a prominent and highly respectable St. Louis merchant—it was met by a delegation of local blacks who awaited it "for the purpose of getting women to accompany them to their haunts of vice." The boarding party was repulsed, but the counter-attack was not a complete success. A few aggressive invaders dodged past the defenders and made their pitch, to which several of the female pilgrims listened and then went ashore to turn a penny.[20]

Editors puzzled over the membership of the hegira. They were not by nature a migratory race, wrote one. They preferred to live in the poverty of the southern cotton fields rather than to venture north in search of a better living, and as a rule, they bore much abuse from their old masters, who understood this tendency to remain rooted. It therefore followed, he concluded, that stories of political terror and economic injustice toward southern blacks must be true.[21]

As documentation for this thesis, the case of Curtis Pollard was cited. His was a story that might have dovetailed into *Uncle Tom's Cabin* without further editing. Pollard, who was then sixty-nine, had farmed in Madison Parish, Louisiana, for the past fifteen years. During Reconstruction years, when the federal army supported black aspirants to office, he had served in both houses of the state legislature. His departure for the North had come quite unexpectedly; while helping some of the emigrants haul their worldly goods to the *Grand Tower,* then tied up at Delta, Louisiana, he had been compelled to take passage himself. A band of men, brandishing cocked guns, accused him of encouraging the others—a charge that he denied—and ordered him aboard. Leaving his teams, as well as a weeping wife and children behind, he had borrowed the four-dollars fare, and now he was a transient in St. Louis, without funds and fleeing to some undecided and unknown destination. The South was rid of another accused agitator, or in the local parlance, a "smart nigger."[22]

21

Stories such as Pollard's generated sympathy among white residents, but they were reluctant to open their purses or to accept the black immigrants among them. Evidence indicates that the desire to get them out of town overshadowed any philanthropic impluses that spoke of supporting them for any length of time. Even the Mullanphy Board was moved from its intransigence. While at first it refused to grant more than the one hundred dollars intended for food, it now decided that the founding father must have intended to aid black as well as white emigrants, and somehow $187.50 was produced to buy seventy-five boat tickets to Kansas. Tandy later recalled that, eventually, the board donated about $450.[23]

The transients had no argument with their hosts. While a few may have found friends in St. Louis and concluded that the place had possibilities, most of the arrivals had started for the land of promise—Kansas—and that is where they wanted to go. A number of northbound packet boats stopped at St. Louis after mid March, some bringing as many as five hundred blacks; others, no more than a handful. Those who had any money at all went on by rail or by Missouri River steamboat; the remainder either waited for the next steamer or simply were stranded, without funds. Less than a week after the *Colorado*'s arrival, arrangements had been made to send forward its leftovers, as well as those who had arrived later on the *Grand Tower,* the *Maude,* and other boats. Passage was secured on the Missouri River steamer the *Joe Kinney,* which was bound for Wyandotte and points beyond and was scheduled to sail on the twenty-first.

Of those who wanted to go, about three hundred had the necessary $2.50 deck fare; another one hundred fifty presumably were without any funds. The Transportation Committee, made up largely of prominent men from the city's Negro community, provided money. As is sometimes the case in the administration of welfare funds, the screening process failed to separate the needy from the greedy. An undetermined number—probably quite small—failed to make an accurate report of financial status in accepting free passage. There was a moment of embarrassment when one old fellow with $800, who had sworn that he was penniless, dropped his pocketbook and the contents spread over the deck. Shamefacedly admitting the size of his bankroll, he surrendered $2.50 and joined the ranks of paying passengers.

There were administrative lapses. Willis Carter, presumed to be one of the group's leaders, collected money from sixty or seventy travelers with the promise that he would obtain the necessary tickets. Then he passed them out at random, some of the recipients having paid nothing at all. Those who had entrusted him with their money set up a loud clamor, accusing Willis of chicanery and even of downright theft. It looked for a time as though the self-appointed ticket agent, surrounded by the angry mob, would come to bodily harm. Only the intervention of the boat's officers and members of the Transportation Committee prevented blows from falling. Getting the misspent money back was like trying to unscramble eggs, and after fruitless appeals, those in charge were forced to take up a subscription for passengers who had paid but had received nothing.

Then came the next excitement: boarding. The wharf, to which the *Joe Kinney* had come for its passengers, became the scene of a momentary camp meeting, with chanting, singing, and the sound of joy taking on a near-religious fervor. This was the day of jubilee; next stop, the promised land. It was also a moment of relief, the end of waiting. "Nearly all were merry," wrote a witness to the happiness, "the committeemen because they were ridding themselves of a part of their burden; the refugees because they imagined their fondest hopes were soon to be realized."

They filed across the gangplank, this strange ragged army, which marched upon some unseen objective, cheerfully unconcerned about the problems that lay ahead. "Some carried bundles of clothing, crockery, baskets and boxes of eatables," noted a local scribe, "while others, divested of all but wearing apparel, and possessing none too much of that, moved along freely and joked with those who were burdened." Mothers anxiously watched their progeny, fearful of losing some of the smaller pilgrims in the rush to get aboard. But one young woman came aboard, head bent down and crying; she had buried her child only that morning.

It was six in the evening before loading was completed. Roustabouts, shouting "All aboard for Ka-an-sas!" having called out their final warnings, now began to take in lines preparatory to sailing. Passengers crowded along the portside railings and took a last look at St. Louis. Suddenly one of them began to sing, and the crowd joined in:

Oh, Kansas! sweet Kansas!

We's boun' fur de happy lan' ob Kansas.

They were still singing as the *Kinney* cleared the wharf, and with stacks smoking and paddles slowly foaming the mud-colored water, it splashed off into the gloom.[24]

2

THE SPIRIT OF ST. LOUIS

For the local committeemen, who had voluntarily assumed the task of caring for the transients, there was to be no rest. Before that Saturday evening was over, some of them may have wished that they were aboard the *Joe Kinney* as it disappeared up the Missouri, bound for the "happy land." As it was, they barely had time to wave farewell before whistles were heard from down the Mississippi, warning that more work was at hand.

It was the *Halliday,* with several hundred more migrants from the South. Their appearance was not, however, as discouraging as it might have been. Many of this latest group had an ample stock of household goods, even mules, wagons, cows, and calves. Better yet, a number of them had enough money for rail or boat fare to Kansas City.

The local reception machinery was once more put into motion, and beds were laid out in local churches to provide a place for those who were in need. When the *Annie P. Silvers* arrived the next morning, the reception committee heaved a collective sigh of relief. It brought only two Negro families, both of which were promptly cared for.[1]

During the following week the Reverend John Turner, one of several local ministers involved in the work at hand, set about collecting money to buy boat tickets to Wyandotte for another four hundred hopeful Kansas settlers who were becalmed at St. Louis. The Mullanphy Board reluctantly produced enough for seventy-five passages, and by beating the bushes among other charitable institutions, Turner found enough money to pay for another one hundred fifty. The *E. H. Durfee,* of the Kansas City

Packet Company, was engaged for the trip, and on March 29 Turner and Capt. George G. Keith supervised the loading.

Once again there was some difficulty about collecting money from those who had funds, and in some cases, local committeemen were obliged to become quite firm. When the solvent and the insolvent were sorted out, some three hundred boarded the boat, only seventy of whom paid their own fares. Another hundred, who could not be provided for, were turned away, and they went back uptown to await further action from their sponsors.

It was morning before the *Durfee* was ready to clear for Wyandotte. The passengers had remained on the boat all night, sleeping wherever they could or conversing quietly with one another to pass the time. But at dawn there was renewed excitement and a murmur of anticipation. As the sun rose, hawsers were cast loose, and with the ringing of bells and the throb of the stern paddles, another boatload of southern emigrants moved out into the Missouri River. Those who saw off the latest contingent were satisfied with their work, and they presumed that others would take up the cause when the group reached Kansas. It was an assumption that was to disturb both black and white residents of that young state, for it was even less prepared to cope with the rush than had been the surprised municipality of St. Louis.[2]

Although the prominent members of St. Louis' black community who had worked so hard to help their distressed countrymen from the South drew great personal satisfaction from their endeavors, they now began to doubt that they could keep up the good work for any length of time. Local sources of financial aid were limited and were beginning to show signs of exhaustion. But the flow of humanity from the South gave no indications of abating.

The second week of April confirmed fears that the problem was far from solution. The *Colorado* returned with twenty-five adults and a few children, swelling the total on hand to about one hundred fifty. Funds were available to send all of these forward, but after that there would be no more money for others. Then came the *Grand Tower,* carrying two hundred fifty, or all that could be crowded aboard the already over-burdened vessel. The latest arrivals would have to shift for themselves, remarked a local newspaperman. Some of them were able to do that. They had a little money, but this small reserve had cost some of them dearly. Simon Mitchell, of Vicksburg, admitted that he had sold his house, worth $400, for $6.00, and a spring wagon, valued at $40.00, had gone for $4.50. Others, who told similar stories, complained that what little they had was diminished by new demands from riverboat officers.

For example, until now no charge had been made for dogs, but these arrivals had to pay $1.00 each for canine transportation, and children, who had been traveling free, now were assessed four dollars each.[3]

Behind the *Grand Tower* were the *Halliday,* the *City of Vicksburg,* the *John B. Maude,* and the *Annie P. Silvers,* each carrying a few more deck fares. They deposited another 186 hungry travelers on the levee. Few of this latest group had money to take them any farther, but they were under the impression that it made no difference, since the fares would be paid in some way or other. The newcomers sat around camp-fires, on temporary benches made from kegs and planks, waiting for someone to provide food, shelter, and travel funds. The Reverend John Turner and twenty-four other St. Louis blacks, who constituted the hastily assembled committee that had aided the first refugees, now faced a real dilemma. The group, known locally as the Committee of Twenty-five, was out of money and in debt. In desperation, Turner sent out another appeal: "Help us! in God's name."[4]

Those to whom the request was directed were sympathetic, but were somewhat nettled by the situation. Local contributors understood that employment was to be had on an Iowa railroad project, and thirty dollars a month was offered to prospective workers. When this information was relayed to the migrants, they sulked and said that they did not know where Iowa was. Besides, they had been told that Kansas was the promised land —no one down South had said anything about Iowa—and that was where they were going; no other place interested them.[5]

So they clung to the waterfront, cold and uncomfortable but stubbornly determined to reach Kansas. Canvas walls were hastily erected to ward off the raw wind that swept the river. A few camped on a Star Line wharf boat, awaiting the next Missouri River packet bound for Kansas. Two of the women found brooms and swept the deck clean where it was not occupied by the baggage. Fires were lighted on the levee, and those who had anything to cook brought out their fry pans; the others simply gathered around and warmed their hands. Before long, Turner found a few groceries, which the women now prepared. A cluster of children jumped rope nearby, cheerfully unaware that their elders had problems.[6] As Turner watched the scene, he wondered how long he could find food for these troubled people. Fortunately, help was on its way. During the early days of April, Charlton Tandy and James Milton Turner made separate trips to Washington, D.C., to plead with the president and other officials for federal aid. Although neither of the men had any success, their presence in the East was noted by the press, and through interviews they put their case before the public. Tandy, for example, spoke before a crowd of ten thousand at New York's Cooper Institute. The aged, tottering politician Thurlow Weed was on the platform that night, denouncing the treatment accorded to southern Negroes, and when the hat was passed, it gathered $350. Tandy's appearance before both houses of the Massachusetts legislature, as well as a speech at Fanueil Hall in Boston, generated more publicity. At St. Louis, the financial waterspout took on new life, and a few dying droplets turned into a small trickle.

A Zanesville, Ohio, sympathizer shipped off two boxes of clothing and $32.50 in cash, with the comment, "May the Lord's blessing go with it and make it as the widow's oil." From Decatur, Illinois, came word that $157.35 had been collected and that it would be along shortly. A theological seminary at Oberlin, Ohio, sent three barrels of used clothing, as did the Second Congregational Church of that city, the latter group saying that it had $5 left over after paying shipping charges, and it, too, would go into the mail. Promises of aid came from a literary society in St. Paul, Minnesota, as well as from individuals in Philadelphia, Cleveland, Indianapolis, and smaller cities. A resident of Buffalo, New York, who had no money to send, offered the advice that Dakota, not Kansas, was the "promised land."

Northern Negroes also responded. Mrs. Anna Douglass of Burlington, Iowa, sent a box of clothing; and John A. Brown, principal of a Negro school at Dayton, Ohio, calling the exodus a "providential act," promised to give all the aid possible. "God bless the movement," he added.[7] Before long, small amounts of money were coming into St. Louis from all over the country. The Reverend Moses Dickson, pastor of the Eighth Street Baptist Church, reported that he had received $186.50 during the last three days of April alone.[8]

Those who contributed were curious to know the seriousness of the situation, how many indigents required help, and where their money was going. The *St. Louis Globe-Democrat,* a Republican journal, tried to answer the question. While a head count was hard to establish, it was estimated that by mid April 6,250 blacks had arrived, 2,300 of whom had been able to pay their own fares to Wyandotte. About 350 remained in St. Louis, awaiting transportation, of which 65 were ill enough to require medical attention. To help the needy, $1,969 in cash had been collected, supplemented by clothing and supplies valued at $850. By that date the Committee of Twenty-five's finance committee was out of funds and owed $41 for groceries and $599 to the Missouri River Packet Company for transportation. The committee's headquarters, located at 618 North Levee Street, also was used as a clearing house for transients who were looking for jobs in the city or were awaiting a chance to move on. "We contracted a big debt there," one of the committeemen later testified.[9]

By now, leaders of St. Louis's black community had concluded that relief operations were being handled inefficiently and that a more permanent, more efficient organization must be developed. A less complimentary interpretation, suggested by some of the dissidents, held that there was money to be made in this sudden and unexpected transient business. The finger was pointed at J. Milton Turner, secretary of the finance committee, who was charged with failing to acount properly for some of the funds that he had collected in the name of charity. Outraged at the implication, or unable to make proper explanations, the accused resigned and went into business for himself. On April 14 he and seven others incorporated the Colored Immigration Aid Society. Its announced purpose was to raise funds for the establishment of Negro colonies in the West and to assist Negroes in their efforts to leave the South. Shares priced at a dollar minimum were offered to the public.[10]

The secessionists called a meeting for Saturday evening, April the nineteenth, at the Lindell Hotel. At that time J. Milton Turner, who presided, announced that the Committee of Twenty-five had conducted its business in a "very random and irresponsible" manner, that it now was totally disorganized, and that it could not even get together to perform its duties. Listeners were told that the other Turner—the Reverend John—having plunged his committee into debt, was anxious to turn over both the work and the liabilities to the new group. Some two thousand dollars had been expended, explained J. Milton Turner, and now he, in turn, demanded an accounting of its disposition.

Clearly, continued the chairman, a new and nationally organized effort was called for, not only because of the St. Louis situation, but also to answer the demands of a growing dissatisfaction among southern Negroes. He revealed that there was the prospect of getting fifty thousand acres of land in Texas from a railroad company, but he did not regard that as any solution to the problems of his people. Blacks were leaving Texas; why should others want to go there? Before adjournment the organizers decided that their executive committee should have an all-white advisory board in order to give the work a wider base in the community. A meeting was called for Monday evening, to further perfect organizational details of this newest black-colonization project.

St. Louis was treated to, not one, but two, meetings. J. Milton Turner's Colored Immigration Aid Society held its meeting at the Lindell, as scheduled, but only nine or ten people attended. Turner casually mentioned that he had received $20 or $25—he had forgotten which—from "a gentleman named Thomas." Then came questions about money raised by the Committee of Twenty-five. Charles Stark spoke up and said that he had been made treasurer of that group and had received $206.95. Turner was surprised. He thought the figure was nearer $2,000. No, said Stark, only a little over $200. As a matter of fact, because the chairman had gathered in recent contributions, he had received little or nothing lately.

Meanwhile, St. Paul's Chapel, at Eleventh and Christy avenues, was the scene of a rival strategy session. The Reverends John Turner and Moses Dickson had issued a call to the faithful of the Committee of Twenty-five, but only a dozen had shown up. However, the meeting proceeded. The little group first considered financial matters, and after hearing from Moses Dickson, of the finance committee, that not $200 but only $25 constituted the funds on hand, it turned to even more serious considerations. J. Milton Turner's recent legal move, to incorporate a rival relief organization, now threatened the establishment. This dictated the severest kind of action.

In a proper parliamentary manner it was moved that the name of J. Milton Turner be stricken from the rolls of the Committee of Twenty-five. The motion also mentioned the touchy subject of money, revealing that the accused was known to have received contributions but that he had not surrendered any of it since April 11. As the instigator of the motion took his seat, the fray began; the ensuing debate reached violent proportions in a matter of moments.

The Reverend John Turner, ignoring his role as presiding officer, took the floor and announced that if J. Milton Turner and his group "wanted to go off and set up a kingdom for themselves they could do so," but he did not propose that the secessionists should break up the present work. That was too mild a stand for John Wheeler, who was known for more extreme positions in local civic matters. He openly accused Milton of betrayal and called him the "Judas of the Committee." The charge was a little strong for other participants, some of whom recognized both Milton's political power and his prestige in the Negro community. Wheeler's blast set off "a red-hot debate, amounting to a tip-top wrangle," reported a local newspaper.

When the flames of contention finally burned low and the orators had exhausted their supplies of invective, it was concluded that no matter what one thought of J. Milton Turner, the Committee of Twenty-five had outlived its usefulness and that a more permanent organization was needed. Thus the Colored Refugee Relief Board, with offices at 903 Morgan Street, came into being.[11]

Although Wheeler's words were harsh, there was some truth in them.

The announced purpose of Turner's Immigration Aid Society—to be financed by charitable contributions—was to send Negro farmers into what he described as the "rich and growing West." Granting that charges accusing him of mishandling funds may have been exaggerated, or may even have been without foundation, it is easier to show that he saw some financial benefit to be derived from the business of immigration. John H. Johnson, who had known Turner from boyhood, agreed with Sen. Henry W. Blair, who later said of the undertaking: "It looked like a scheme to raise funds to purchase lands in Kansas that are to be sold out afterwards on the installment plan."

Circumstances appear to have governed Turner's attitude toward the exodus. At first he charged southerners with "extortion, murder, rapine, arson and barbarous outlawry" and urged Negroes to leave the South. But when it became clear that his immigration plan was a failure, he opposed the exodus, asserting that the South was the true home of the Negro and that there he should remain.[12]

The running battle of the blacks was well covered by local reporters, who were amused at the sudden interest in philanthropy shown by some members of the St. Louis Negro community when eastern money in support of the cause began to appear. The resulting publicity, however, caused some concern among business leaders. If the word spread throughout the disaffected plantation areas of the South that not one, but two, St. Louis committees were raising money to help westering immigrants, the whole movement might be accelerated, rather than slowed. The split also was regarded as being detrimental to the case of the refugees. Civic leaders who worked in behalf of these unfortunates in both St. Louis and at Wyandotte, feared that eastern philanthropists now would hesitate, not knowing the proper place to send their contributions. They suggested that J. Milton Turner's group disband.

The *Missouri Republican,* a leading St. Louis newspaper whose politics were Democratic, lamented the fact that the flow continued. About two percent of the arrivals had died, it reported, and another ten percent were sick. Like it or not, the municipality would have to fight the spread of disease, and if it did not want to absorb a large group of indigents, it would have to provide for some means of getting them out of town, preferably to Kansas, to which place these people stubbornly insisted that they wanted to go. The editor was annoyed at the nation's Republican press, particularly the newspapers of New England and the Middle Atlantic States, for publicizing the exodus and for calling it a significant event. He noted that while these journals expressed sympathy for the southern Negro and talked loudly of tyranny in Dixie, none of them had invited the refugees to its city. Instead, he said, they usually applied Horace Greeley's advice, suggesting, "Go West, young black man," go west to Kansas, "where John Brown's soul is doing perpetual guard duty."[13]

Fears that the influx of colored immigrants would continue to clog the levees at St. Louis were justified. By late April it was estimated that between 8,600 and 9,000 had arrived since the movement began, only about 2,400 of whom had been able to pay their fares to Kansas.[14] If these figures were at all accurate, this meant that since the estimate at mid month, approximately 2,500 more had arrived, most of whom had no money to continue their travels. Missouri River packets continued to carry away all who could buy tickets and those for whom passage was supplied by contributions. On April 14 the *E. H. Durfee* left for Wyandotte with 300, and five days later the *Joe Kinney* took another 250. That left behind some 60 or 70, most of whom were sick.

The relief was only temporary; new arrivals from the South came in daily, sometimes in driblets, at other times in substantial numbers. John Turner's Colored Refugee Relief Board contracted with the Missouri River Packet Company to provide passage to Kansas at $3.00 per head for adults and $1.50 for passengers between the ages of twelve and twenty-one, smaller children being carried free. The company also allowed as many transients as could be accommodated to live in its wharf boats until they were ready to go on. A correspondent from an eastern newspaper mingled with wharf-boat residents, observing their daily lives with fascination. Roustabouts piled baggage and household goods onto the decks, while relief committee members brought in supplies of firewood and food to be prepared on the adjacent shore. At night the campers moved around in the firelight, some carrying on animated conversation about joyful days ahead, while others joined in group singing or dancing. At last, when the excitement had subsided, they lay down and slept on the shore or scattered about on the bare boat decks.[15]

Supplying this small army of emigrants kept members of the Relief Board busy. On the evening before the *Joe Kinney* sailed, for example, Moses Dickson and some of his helpers arrived at the wharf with 300 loaves of bread, 258 pounds of meat, 4 barrels of crackers, 2 barrels of beans, and 1 barrel of corn meal to be distributed among the passengers on their way to Wyandotte.[16] John H. Johnson later estimated that between seventeen and twenty thousand dollars were thus expended that spring and summer, most of which came from New York, Philadelphia, Boston, and other outside sources.[17] Up to June 9, said Johnson, almost 74,000 rations, worth about ten cents each, had been distributed. By then the board had received 350 packages of clothing—hats, boots, shoes, caps—

valued at $4,329.10, almost all of which had come from the East. In addition came garden seed, farm implements, and even soap, pins, and needles.[18]

As the weather warmed, some of the problems facing the stream of arrivals and their sponsors were modified. Now it was a matter of food, clothing, and transportation, without the complicating factor of cold, wet weather. But as the numbers swelled and as the physical problem of handling growing numbers of bodies increased, both white and black St. Louis worried. Charlton Tandy later revealed that, according to records kept by the Relief Board, over twenty thousand Negro men, women, and children passed through St. Louis in the "Exodus year" of 1879.[19] How many more transients, who did not require or obtain assistance, entered and left the Gateway City is a matter of conjecture.

By and large the Exodusters, as they came to be called, were peaceful and law-abiding; they caused law officers almost no difficulty. Most of them were confused and frightened, and they were herded in docile groups to places of food and shelter. Far from being a danger to public order, the strangers continued to serve as the victims of St. Louis Negroes, who enticed them into saloons, gambling houses, and brothels and stole their baggage under the guise of caring for it in the name of the relief committee. Before long, charges of more serious misconduct were heard.

On the evening of March 30 a local Negro named Henry A. Green attended one of the meetings held at a local church in behalf of the refugees, and in answer to appeals for help, he volunteered to take Sylvia Ann Craxton, aged eleven, home to sleep with his own children. Later that evening the child was found wandering around the city, in a daze, and upon being questioned, she said that she had been raped. On May 6 Green came up for a trial, and after brief testimony and only a few minutes of deliberation by the jury, he was found guilty and was sentenced to twenty years in the penitentiary.[20]

While problems such as these disturbed the city fathers, the main difficulty was financial and to some degree emotional. Later in April, for example, a group of St. Louis businessmen met to ponder the problem of expediting the movement out of their city. The Reverend John Turner, representing the Relief Board, suggested that the flow be turned in the direction of the Neosho Valley, in southeastern Kansas, to which place emigrants could be sent by rail for $3.75 a head.

"I don't think much of that," said Meyer Rosenblatt, collector of the city of St. Louis; "you might as well send them to Wyandotte." He argued that Wyandotte was not only located "right in the heart of the promised land," it was also on a main transportation route, where both

33

rail and boat services were available. He preferred the speedier means of travel. "Don't send them by the circuitous route of the river; too much time is wasted and money expended in doing so," he argued. "Get old emigrant cars for $120 each. A great number of persons can be crowded into them, and the transportation will be more rapid while the expense will be less."

Rosenblatt's desire to get the job done quickly, cheaply, and by the most direct route met with the disapproval of some Kansans. Businessmen from Wyandotte who attended the meeting were not enthusiastic about his choice of destination for the emigrants. One of the reasons that they had come to St. Louis lay in the hope that some city other than theirs could be found as the main target for the westward thrust.[21] But despite their objections, Wyandotte continued to be the next stop for the black emigrants.

During these weeks, black committee members experienced further frustrations. In mid May, Charlton Tandy returned from his eastern junket, where he had sought political support and financial contributions. At a meeting held in the Eighth Street Baptist Church he told his listeners that the black schism was not confined to their city. Upon reaching Washington, D.C., he had sought out Frederick Douglass, the great Negro emancipationist, hoping to use his influence in getting an audience with the president. Although Tandy had met Douglass several times in St. Louis, he was now given a frigid reception. "I don't know you, sir; you had better get some old time Abolitionist to introduce you," said Douglass, who flatly refused to cooperate. Tandy then turned to another of his race, Professor Richard T. Greener, of Howard University, who performed the requested service.

When Tandy's acceptance by the "old-time Abolitionists" throughout the East became apparent, Douglass sent word that he was ready to receive the emissary from St. Louis. Tandy told his supporters at the Baptist church meeting that he had replied, "Go to the Devil," and the audience erupted in loud cheers.

This annoyed J. Milton Turner, who had become the gadfly of the relief group that he had left. He now jumped to his feet and delivered a highly eulogistic speech in behalf of Douglass. The chair tried to quiet him, saying that a resolution offered by Tandy—one that strongly censured Douglass—was not debatable; but Turner drove on, unwilling to yield. After considerable confusion and turmoil in the heavily packed church, a development that had become a regular occurrence at these meetings, it was ruled that Turner would not be heard. The complainant merely turned up the volume and ignored the dictum until he was drowned out in the uproar of protest. To restore peace and to prevent a possible outbreak of fisticuffs, it was decided that the motion should be tabled. Satisfied that he had achieved a standoff, Turner sat down.[22]

Squabbles among individuals were merely scattered oratorical fire-fights; the main battle centered about the question of coping with the influx. Local Negroes, who were prominent or who sought prominence in the new situation, were concerned primarily with feeding, housing, and supplying further transportation for their brothers from the South. City fathers, on the other hand, wanted either to turn back the flow or to divert it elsewhere—at a minimum cost.

In June, Thomas C. Bedford, of Vicksburg, filed a suit against the Memphis and St. Louis Packet Company (popularly known as the Anchor Line), asking ten thousand dollars in damages and alleging that the company's vessels had broken the law concerning overloading. When questioned at St. Louis, company president John A. Scudder, whose vessels normally carried only freight, explained that it was all due to a misunderstanding; he thought that he had permission from the authorities to carry as many as three hundred passengers. Of more interest to residents of St. Louis was the remark, made in connection with the story, that "this suit grows out of the late exodus of Negroes from the South."[23] By inference, the crisis had passed.

At times it appeared that this might be the case. During the late spring an old and unused foundry was converted into barracks to provide the immigrants with more suitable housing. A newspaper reporter, visiting the place during the first week of July, found only a dozen refugees there, four of whom were sick.[24] By now, a nationally known relief agency, the Western Sanitary Commission, had joined the work, and it attempted to provide emergency relief services at the old foundry. However, this latest volunteer group was obliged to give up very shortly, being out of funds, and the facility was therefore closed. Newcomers again resorted to camping along the river banks or in wharf boats of the Missouri River Packet Company. James Yeatman, president of the Sanitary Commission, expressed regret at having had to retreat from the battlefront, but he was obliged to admit that the task was just too formidable. He had entered the work thinking that the movement would be of short duration and that those who were in distress could be helped for a relatively small amount of money. He was wrong on both counts. After having expended six thousand dollars, Yeatman discovered that the flow of newcomers had not abated and that there were no indications that it would. The only solution that he could offer was to inform southern Negroes that no more help could be expected in St. Louis and that if they came, they would be on their own.[25]

St. Louis businessmen must have nodded their heads in assent. They had been saying the same thing for weeks. When Yeatman complained that he had appealed in vain to city authorities for help in carrying on his work, no apologies were forthcoming. Philanthropic efforts, financed from the outside, were welcome, but money from local Caucasian sources was increasingly hard to come by. Funds expended merely seemed to generate the arrival of fresh hordes from the South. Gradually the St. Louis business community was hardening its attitude to such a degree that critics must have thought it downright misanthropic.

3

THIS MACEDONIAN CRY

The passengers who boarded Missouri River steamboats for the last leg of their migration to Kansas had no desire to stop anywhere short of that announced goal. Some of them landed at Kansas City, because they had no other choice, but most of them preferred to avoid that place because of its open hostility to the exodus.[1] Wyandotte, just across the river, was regarded as a sanctuary. It was located on the magic soil of Kansas, a state whose very name was possessed of a special meaning to the pilgrims who sought this near-mythical land of promise.

As the *Durfee* neared Kansas City early in April, a local newspaper trumpeted the sour notes of hate and suspicion that the emigrants so earnestly had hoped to avoid. The *Times* warned that "five hundred penniless and destitute Negroes" were headed upriver. It accused St. Louis of having secretly paid the passage of what it termed "this cargo of human rubbish," and it wondered why the western Missouri metropolis should receive and care for "the paupers and thieves of St. Louis." Garrison the town, a reporter advised the residents of neighboring Wyandotte. Fend off this dangerous and undesirable army of indigents.[2]

If Kansas City was militant, Wyandotte was merely puzzled by the development. Observing the arrival of ragged, hungry Negroes by the hundred, one of the white residents commented that it looked "like the alm houses of the Mississippi Valley had been searched to get them together." The little Kansas town, of some five thousand residents, was totally unprepared for such a sudden and unexpected influx, but its residents recognized human need when they saw it, and they made strenuous efforts to

37

prevent suffering. Taking a cue from St. Louis, Wyandotte opened its churches, and all available means of shelter were offered to protect the strangers from the cold, driving spring rain. About three miles north of the city lay the village of Quindaro and the old Freedmen's University buildings, some of which now were put to use as temporary barracks. The university, founded by the Reverend Eben Batchley in 1857, had declined after the Civil War and had been taken over by Negro residents of the town, particularly by members of the African Methodist Church.

The Quindaro safety valve was helpful, but only to a degree. It diverted part of the flow, but "still they come," said one of Wyandotte's civic leaders. "We shall certainly be swamped. We are not panic stricken, although the shrill whistle of every boat which comes causes us many anxious thoughts." In his eyes the sudden presence of an army of sick, unwashed, poverty-stricken human beings was the equivalent of an invasion, and thus, as a "war measure," as a public necessity, he thought that the state of Kansas had the responsibility of aiding one of its beleaguered cities.[3]

By the early days of April the *Fanny Lewis* and the *Joe Kinney* had deposited some 600 Exodusters; then came the *Durfee* with another 450. Back to St. Louis went the *Joe Kinney* after yet another load, and so the rotation continued until, by mid month, an estimated 1,700 to 2,000 were camped at Wyandotte's doorstep. "For the sake of God and humanity can you obtain free transportation for four hundred colored refugees on the K.P. & Santa Fe roads," begged Mayor J. S. Stockton, of Wyandotte, in a telegraphic appeal to Gov. John St. John at Topeka.[4] The little Kansas town was approaching the bursting point.

Meanwhile, as the numbers mounted steadily, the complexity of the situation grew. The sick were nursed by volunteers from the community, local doctors donating their services, and even patients who were ambulatory were watched with deepening concern as fear spread that they might be carriers of yellow fever. Each day brought reports of deaths among them, and even their dead bodies presented local authorities with fresh problems. By mid April the city and county authorities at Wyandotte were locked in an administrative impasse, the county claiming that it had exhausted its quarterly funds for the burial of paupers, and the city stoutly maintaining that it could afford to bury only its own dead.[5]

Although the Wyandotte city fathers stated bravely that they were not inclined to panic, the avalanchelike proportions of the movement upon their city put them in a frame of mind that approached such a condition. Then, to irritate an already maddening situation, the *Kansas City Daily Journal* goaded them by inferring that their whole philanthropic effort was shallow. R. M. Tunnell answered for the Wyandotte relief committee, grimly explaining that his group was making every effort to aid these sick, hungry people, and it was also doing everything in its power to find work for those who were strong enough to be employed. It was particularly discouraging to hear that a local farmer had tried to hire one of the young Negro boys for summer field work, offering to supply him with clothing, board, and room, but to no avail. The former southern field hands wanted at least fifty cents a day, nothing less, and until such wages were forthcoming, they proposed to wait and draw free rations at Wyandotte. Meantime, said Tunnell, fresh bread was being supplied daily, and rations of meat were issued when they could be procured. What was needed most was money for transporting these people to their desired destination, but cash donations were few. Only six dollars had been offered by mid April.[6]

After studying their plight, the civic leaders of Kansas City and Wyandotte concluded that possible solutions to the problem resembled the three "R's"—relief, rehabilitation, or removal. Sheer numbers were drowning the relief efforts; for the same reason, rehabilitation was out of the question. The apparent answer lay in distributing the human backlog thoughout Kansas, fragmenting it into segments that would be small enough for the little communities to the west to absorb them. But that would take time and money.

The situation called for energetic action. The flow of immigration had reached flood stage, and the two cities, particularly Wyandotte, were being inundated. Mayor George M. Shelley, of Kansas City, appealed to the secretary of war, George McCrary, asking that a portion of the Fort Leavenworth reservation be set aside as a temporary abode for these people and that government rations be issued to them. McCrary neatly sidestepped the request by explaining that Congress, then in session, was the proper source of money for emergency rations and that Shelley should look to that body for assistance. The mayor understood that he had been turned down. Adrift in the no man's land of congressional debate, his application was bound to die of old age, for the southern congressmen, whose constituents were suffering from the loss of black labor on their plantations, would kill any measure designed to aid the fleeing refugees.

Wyandotte tried another approach. In an appeal addressed to "the generous citizens of the United States," a civic committee asked the American public for contributions enough to meet the emergency. A brief statement, sent to newspapers across the country, explained the problem and concluded with the plea: "In the midst of this general suffering and great need for immediate aid we send this Macedonian cry for immediate assistance."[7] Reporters who mingled with the refugees readily admitted that indeed they were in dire need. Early arrivals from the South camped along the levee, living in tents, rough board shelters, and tin shacks, in which they huddled together, trying to stay dry and warm. Some begged door to door for food, while others sat mutely awaiting help. One old lady expressed the prevalent feeling of forlorn hope among them when she explained that the Lord would provide. "He brought us out of slavery, and He will take care of us in Kansas," she calmly informed a resident of Wyandotte who visited the waterfront bivouac.

"They expected to be received with open arms and placed immediately on Government land," wrote another observer, in puzzlement. Corvine Patterson and Henry Reed, both local Negroes, urged municipal authorities to allow these people to remain. The idea found some support among white community leaders, principally the Northrup brothers, who were local bankers. Some of the immigrants did stay, establishing little communities along the river bottom, one of which was first named Juniper Town, and later Mississippi Town because of the large numbers from that state; and out of that beginning came a permanent black settlement at the mouth of the Kaw (Kansas) River. Rattlebone Hollow, north of present Kansas City, and Hogg's Town, at its extreme western limits, also grew from squatter seeds sown in this year of the Exodusters.[8]

With each passing day, more arrivals swelled the refugee camps at Wyandotte, and rapidly the feeling of panic, so recently denied, came closer to realization. It was bad enough to listen to criticisms from neighboring Kansas City, but when Topeka chimed in, irritations in Wyandotte mounted sharply. The Topeka *Commonwealth* openly accused Wyandotte of not wanting the Negroes because it was a Democratic town and the influx might alter its political complexion. Those river-town Democrats were more afraid of the possible infection of Republicanism than of the threat of yellow fever, taunted the Topeka editor. The *Wyandotte Herald* lashed back angrily, saying that much had been done for these unfortunates and that politics had nothing to do with the situation. It was not that the city was opposed to black immigrants; it just did not want so many of them. As to politics, the editor remarked, Republican skirts were far from clean on the issue of race prejudice.

As Topeka chided Wyandotte, other Kansas towns expressed their sympathy for these foot-loose people, inferring that it was the duty of all Kansans to lend a hand; however, few of them made offers of material aid. With some irritation the Wyandotte paper recorded a recent meeting at Lawrence, where a resolution of sympathy was passed. The document stated that "we regard the exodus of the colored people of the South as a legitimate result of the injustice practised upon them, and since so many of these people reach Kansas in poverty and suffering we should be untrue to our history . . . if we did not extend to them a cordial welcome, and so far as we are able to do so, relieve their distress, and aid them to find homes on the free soil of Kansas."

Fine, growled a frustrated Wyandotte editor. In principle there was nothing wrong with such high-flown sentiments. But Topeka had no conception of the complexity of the problem. Those who had been dumped ashore, he said bitterly, were a lazy, shiftless lot, composed largely of aged infirm men, decrepit women, and little children. The few among them who were young and strong were inclined toward indolence. His town was not a manufacturing center or a place with any visible sources of material wealth, he continued, with mounting annoyance; it was more a residential suburb of Kansas City than an economic entity. Under the circumstances it appeared obvious to him that the contest into which the little city had been thrust was an unequal one, and viewed in that light, Wyandotte had done more than its share. Was it not time for high-minded men in other Kansas towns to do likewise?[9]

Wyandotte's principal moral burden was the struggle with its conscience. It was difficult to talk about such recent historial events as "Bleeding Kansas" and "the spirit of John Brown" without showing at least an outward sympathy toward the newcomers, if for no other reason than the fact of their color. Yet, the sudden intensity of the movement, as well as its unexpected volume, quickly turned open-handedness to thoughts of economic survival. Even Wyandotte's older Negro population reacted negatively. V. J. Lane, editor of the *Herald,* later testified that "they were as much opposed to it as the whites; and while there are a few of these Mississippi and Louisiana negroes still there [in 1880], they do not associate or affiliate with the older negroes. There is as much difference between them as there is between the day and night, and the regular negroes there do not want anything to do with them."[10]

During the week of April 17 to 24, at a time when some seventeen hundred refugees were encamped on the outskirts of the city, the waning philanthropic impulses of downtown businessmen finally expired. In this case, forbearance foundered on an ancient Anglo-Saxon rock: the distaste for those who accept charity in preference to honest labor. A representative from the coal mines at Higginsville, Missouri, had offered to take fifty men and their families and to pay the miners from one to three dollars a day, but there was only a grudging and tentative acceptance among prospective employees. When the time came for departure, they made excuses, and finally they declined to go. None of those questioned about their decision wanted to live in the old Slave State of Missouri; they preferred Kansas, where they still believed that free land, farm equipment, and provisions awaited them. Nor did they want to be separated from the main group.

About the time that word of this refusal to accept alternatives spread throughout the business community, word came that the *Durfee* once more was on its way from St. Louis, bearing another boatload of Exodusters. To make matters even worse, two St. Louis Negroes who represented the Relief Committee of that city, visited Wyandotte in order to investigate the condition of the refugees. They brought the unwelcome news that the *Joe Kinney,* with more than two hundred additional immigrants, probably would be sent upriver about the twentieth of the month. The men sent back word that the residents of Wyandotte were very much excited and did not want any more of these people.[11] As a further frustration, local contributions, which were calculated to alleviate the situation, still hovered around the six-dollar mark.

Tensions mounted and tempers grew taut. An eastern correspondent described the mood of local merchants when he wrote that the unfortunate proprietor of a drugstore, in front of which the itinerants were inclined to lounge, had discussed the situation "with frenzy in his eye" and had threatened to leave town unless matters improved. The reporter put his finger on the central problem when he said that "all Wyandotte waxes warm over the injustice of being obliged to bear the whole burden alone." The emotional heat increased until Mayor Stockton, labeled by a local editor as "wishy-washy," was forced to act. On April 18 he issued a proclamation, addressed to any and all steamboat lines or transportation companies, threatening legal action should they continue "importing destitute persons to our shores."[12] No one down river paid him any attention.

"Immigrants continue to arrive," warned a Wyandotte dispatch of the nineteenth; "the people are tired of receiving them." The story explained that the end had come; no more would be allowed to land. Two days later, when the *Durfee* steamed into view, carrying another 240 black passengers, an official delegation stood waiting on the shore. When he was told that he could not unload them, Capt. George Keith objected angrily and then shoved off. He landed near the Plankinton & Armour packing plant, in Kansas City, amidst loud protests from officials of that city. But there being no municipal ordinance to cover the emergency, the authorities were obliged to accept the unwelcome travelers. A money-raising campaign was quickly launched, and within a few days the whole lot, except for one family, was shipped off to Manhattan, Kansas.

Meanwhile, Wyandotte's decision to put a freeze on black immigration remained firm; but there were some vexatious leaks in the municipal iron curtain, and the flow merely subsided to a dribble. One of the townsmen remarked that threats were being made openly by one of the local judges, and this was a dangerous augury. Worse, he said, were the threats of vigilante action and the possibility that these unfortunate people were "likely to be wiped out by the violence of public antipathy in Wyandotte."[13]

This was more than alarmist talk. On the evening of April 24 a mass meeting was held at Dunning's Hall, where it was resolved that since warnings and waterfront confrontations had failed to stop the flow, a committee of public safety be appointed to "act in any manner they see fit" in dealing with the crisis. When a more level-headed participant suggested that this was too strong a stand and that the final vote be delayed, he was howled down. The motion passed, heavily. Those who opposed such drastic action met in a rump session after the others had gone home; they agreed to work within the law and to utilize their elected representatives to solve the problem. These men, including editor V. J. Lane of the *Herald,* were not opposed to fending off the exodus, but they feared the implications and the possible results of mob action.[14]

As Wyandotte's civic leaders gathered in troubled caucuses, uncomplimentary rumors about the city's lack of humanitarian qualities spread throughout the land. Chicago papers retailed the story that Wyandotte was ready to assess a headtax of five dollars on each of the unwanted transients in order to keep them away. "Scurrilous lies," shouted the *Wyandotte Gazette* in an anguished denial. Even more annoying was the tale, widely broadcast from nearby towns, that Wyandotte's local volunteer Rifle Club was ready to turn back further attempted landings at gunpoint. Pure prevarication, said the *Herald,* vowing that its town never would act in violation of the laws of the land or at the expense of humanity.[15]

Apparently it was money, rather than cooler heads, that stayed impending violence; for when most of the newcomers were shipped off to Ellis, Kansas, at a dollar a head, the town returned to near-normal. "Wyandotte breathes more freely," sighed the *Gazette.* Even better, it added, reverberations of the protest had reached down river as far as St. Louis. The exporters of blacks from that city now agreed to pay the fare of those aboard the *Kinney,* on its next trip, clear through to Leavenworth.[16]

Mayor Stockton wanted to make sure that nothing would go wrong with this proposal. In his role as president of Wyandotte's Relief Committee, he telegraphed to his opposite numbers at St. Louis and asked for a parley. He and several of his associates from the Wyandotte business community arrived in the Gateway City on the twenty-seventh and made straight for Barnum's Hotel, where a conference had been arranged. The visitors assured their hosts, particularly the Reverends John Turner and Moses Dickson, that Wyandotte wanted to do its part, but it was simply the wrong city for philanthropy on such a large scale. It could not accommodate that many paupers; furthermore, the states of Kansas and Missouri ought to lend aid in problems of such magnitude. If any city was the chosen spot, surely it was Topeka, said Stockton, for it was headquarters for the Central Immigration Board of Kansas. Wyandotte's emissaries were effusive in their praise of Kansas, and of Topeka, in particular. The St. Louis group listened politely, then promised to get in touch with the Central Relief Board of Topeka and to redirect the traffic to places suggested by that body.[17]

Wyandotte's salesmen for the promotion of reverse immigration were successful. Early in May, one of the town's papers published the good news that the *Joe Kinney* had passed on up the river to Leavenworth with three hundred refugees, stopping at Wyandotte only long enough to unload forty-two hundred railroad ties. A week later it was announced that except for those who had obtained work or had rented farms in the neighborhood, all the remaining black transients had been shipped to Topeka via the Kansas Pacific Railway and had been deposited with the Central Relief Board in that city. "The exodus is over practically for the season, and entirely so as far as Wyandotte is concerned," announced the *Gazette* triumphantly. This civic achievement having been accomplished, the temporary barracks, thought by many to have been inadvisedly constructed, were torn down, and the material was quickly sold. Wyandotte could now advertise: "No Vacancies."[18] There remained only a few lingering apprehensions that rival neighboring towns might take reprisals for the recent action, but Wyandotte's more resolute businessmen assured each other that the action had been necessary and that growing western municipalities were made strong by resolution, not by pusillanimity.

Leavenworth, the next stop up river, had its own worries, but instead of thinking in terms of economic reprisal, it took a lead from Wyandotte's book and endeavored to keep the stream of westering blacks moving, rather than trying to halt or reverse it. In mid March, when news of the first large landings at St. Louis reached Leavenworth, its press had taken the view that the flight of these poor people from their southern homes was a gross outrage, one that not only would deprive the plantations of their needed labor but also would overburden young Kansas communities with objects of charity. Charges by the St. Louis press that Kansas did not want

Negroes were quickly denied. The young state simply did not want large masses of indigents, said the *Times*. It was not a matter of race prejudice. On the contrary, Kansas "extends an invitation to men of all races and nationalities to come and make their homes with her; we invite white men, black men and yellow men and men of every other color, only asking that they shall know what they are doing, and come prepared to take care of themselves till they can gain a support from their farms."[19]

Its conscience purged by statements of racial equality and good will toward all men, Leavenworth turned to the practical realities of its new situation and took stock. As the newly devised Wyandotte by-pass began to function effectively, pressure upon Leavenworth increased sharply; by riverboat and rail came fresh parties of blacks. When eight carloads of them, attached to a Missouri Pacific freight train, rolled into the city, the usual stories of hunger and sickness appeared in print. Of 132 newcomers, 21 were ill, principally from pneumonia. They were a "seedy lot," remarked a Leavenworth newspaper, forgetting its avowals of toleration, and there was "not a good field hand among them." The city council's response was a hastily raised fund to send these undesirables on to some other city. There were smiles of relief when the rumor passed that Jay Gould was hauling part of them westward over his Kansas Pacific Railway for nothing.[20]

But in the meantime, immediate attention to the sick and hungry was required, a matter that does not appear to have deeply concerned the white people of that busy river town. As had been the case in other cities, the black population became involved in attempts to solve the problem, its members offering what little aid they could give. Typically, they were divided in their opinions about the wisdom of the movement. William D. Mathews, who was well known in the community, foresaw disaster if the hegira continued in its present form. Remarking that in the previous year a railroad at Cincinnati had offered him a job as an immigration agent among southern blacks, he explained that he had declined because he thought it was not in the best interests of his people to bring them north unprepared for their new life. All that could come of it, he concluded, would be an increase of prejudice against them in the North and West. He agreed with Frederick Douglass that the place for the Negroes was in the South, where, in time, they would become the ruling element. John L. Waller, a former slave, offered sharp dissent. "This is a Revolution, but a peaceable and quiet one," he wrote to Kansas Governor St. John. These people had been robbed of their liberty in the South, he argued, and he quoted Patrick Henry to the governor: here and now was the place to stand firm.[21]

The leaders of Leavenworth's business community were not interested in the philosophical theories of early revolutionaries. They had no time to theorize. Overnight they had been presented with a problem, the solution to which had to be practical and immediate. More-thoughtful members of the community agreed that colonization of penniless and unprepared people far out on the western prairies was destined to end in failure and suffering. But their notions about alternatives did not include keeping these newcomers around. Faced by the problem of feeding destitute, hungry strangers, Mayor W. M. Fortescue asked Governor St. John if the state had made any arrangements to care for them. Equally important, he wrote, had the governor's office formulated any plans to send "into the interior the refugees arriving in our State"? Meantime, he promised, he would do the best he could in providing temporary assistance until they could be sent westward.[22]

The mayor, against whom no charges of being wishy-washy would be leveled, was good to his word. When the *Joe Kinney* arrived, early in May, its black passengers were not allowed to land. Fortescue, cash in hand, carried out his "forwarding" promise by handing Captain Keith $250, along with the suggestion that Atchison was a more appropriate destination for his cargo. True, Leavenworth was in debt, and it had no means of financing such civic enterprise; but this was a special occasion, one in which the city administration, supported by contributions from local businessmen, acted in what frequently has been termed the "best interests" of the municipality. When the *Joe Kinney* reached Atchison, its reception was far from friendly. Bitterly recalling that the unwelcome passengers had been deflected from Leavenworth, an Atchison business-man dourly remarked that "they sent them on up to us; we thought that was a pretty sharp trick on their part." Lamenting the failure of his city's warning system, he explained that the steamboat "came up very quietly and got a good many ashore before we knew of it. Some parties went down to try to induce the captain to load them up and take them away again, but could not prevail upon him to do so."[23] Apparently, ready cash for a continued voyage was not forthcoming, or perhaps Captain Keith had ascended the Missouri River as far as his resources and his patience would take him.

Atchison's concern over the unexpected and unexplained influx typified that of river towns from Kansas City northward. In March, at a time when the local press proudly announced the arrival in Kansas of some twenty-five hundred "intelligent and thrifty" white immigrants in the course of a single day, there was sympathy for the few Negroes who were already struggling for an existence in agricultural colonies to the west.

But as the *Atchison Daily Champion* pointed out, Kansas was a new state, one that needed capital, not labor, and it was hoped that the driblet of impoverished blacks then entering the state would not increase. The paper praised the efforts of Wyandotte, condemned the southerners roundly for their treatment of the former slaves, and called upon Congress to discourage a major movement of these unhappy people out of the South.[24]

The circumstances surrounding the arrival of some three hundred destitute blacks aboard the *Joe Kinney* hardened Atchison's attitude. "They consisted principally of old men, women, and children," complained city attorney H. C. Solomon, "and were in a state of the most abject poverty, with no means, ragged, filthy, and dirty. They were taken charge of by the city authorities." Fear, rather than philanthropy, motivated this action. As Solomon explained, some of them had measles, and the dread of cholera always was present; consequently most of their old clothing was burned.

When asked about the attitude of Kansans, in general, toward the black settlers, Solomon spoke frankly: "I am positive that it is the universal sentiment, not only in the city of Atchison and the county, but in the northern part of the State of Kansas, where they have come in in large numbers, that they are a detriment to the State, because they are paupers; they do not produce anything, and the large portion of those who are able to work will not work." As had been the case at Wyandotte, the crisis at Atchison produced instant legislation. Called together to devise some means of turning away "detrimental" immigrants, the city council quickly passed an ordinance prohibiting railroads, boat companies, and all transportation companies from bringing paupers into the city.[25]

The policy of restriction generated complaint. The Reverend R. De Baptiste, pastor of a Negro congregation in Chicago who visited Atchison, admitted that aid was being given, but not in any spirit of brotherhood. He decided that part of the reason was because "they have a Democratic administration there, in the city of Atchison, and they were not inclined to show them any great friendship or kindness." Had it not been for the churches, he said, these people would have been without shelter.[26]

Defenders of Atchison's civic spirit were annoyed by suggestions that too little had been done for the black transients. They pointed the finger at members of that race who had lived in and around the city for some time and who now showed very little disposition to help their troubled brothers. "We thought that perhaps it would be as well to have the colored people, who were in large numbers there [at Atchison], take charge of them," the city attorney later told a congressional committee. "They at first refused to have anything to do with them, so the mayor and city council met in special meeting and appointed a committee of citizens to take charge of them. The colored people who resided in the town were finally induced to open their churches, and they were put in there temporarily, and provided for by the city."[27]

Amidst a growing public clamor against the black surge and despite the restrictive immigration regulations devised by the city council, the movement into Atchison continued. The city's older Negro population displayed an increasing resistance through studied indifference to the problem, while the whites wrestled with their consciences and loudly proclaimed that the question of race was not involved. Edward Mills, a local grain dealer and member of the city council, insisted that if these people were as hard-working and as capable as the white immigrants, he would welcome them with open arms; it was not a question of color, but one of economic condition among the Exodusters. H. C. Park, editor of the Democratic *Daily Patriot,* represented the more inflexible view. When asked what he thought of the movement, he said that he did not think that there was a man, woman, or child in Atchison who wanted it. He did not go out of his way to deny race prejudice, but he argued that beyond this, there simply was little or no demand for farm labor in the neighborhood. Attorney Solomon agreed that little work was available, pointing out that this was the oldest and most heavily settled part of Kansas, where the steady white immigration over the years had more than supplied what extra farm labor the area required. The result was that nine-tenths of the blacks who arrived immediately became objects of charity. Even those who earlier had gained an agricultural foothold had experienced great difficulty, Park said. "We have in our county a little colony, you might call it, of colored farmers who have been there for a good many years, and I think it has not proved a success by any means."[28]

For a few there were jobs to be had in the towns. Green Smith, for example, arrived from Vicksburg with the May rush into Atchison and found a position in a local grain elevator.[29] He had read one of the circulars being handed around among field hands in Mississippi, and after reading of new opportunities in Kansas, he had decided to move. While his new home had not proved to be a land of milk and honey, he admitted that conditions here were better than those at Vicksburg. This was one of the ironies of the situation, and the dilemma into which small Kansas business communities were pushed. When the Green Smiths wrote letters to relatives in the cotton fields, unhappy southern Negroes took hope, sold out, and joined the rush. By finding work for the arrivals, Kansans merely aggravated their own problem; but when they made no effort to find places for them, they were criticized by humanitarians for being heartless, selfish, and racially prejudiced.

This was part of the reason that some of Atchison's residents, Republicans as well as Democrats, took a calloused view and opted for exportation. Before the flow began, they assumed a loftier position and had expressed great sympathy for a benighted people, but when the dikes broke and the great wash of humanity hit their city, self-interest rose to the top, as cream rises on milk, and businessmen closed ranks to save themselves from the flood. Criticism of their efforts to lend at least temporary assistance simply hardened their resolve to pass along the burden.

Added to this was the frustration that Atchison's city fathers experienced when they tried to persuade the Exodusters to leave town, if for only long enough to find work on nearby farms. They were reluctant to leave their own kind, those with whom they had come north, and they preferred any menial job in town to leaving the others. Even at harvest time, when jobs were available at $1.50 a day, they were generally reluctant to move into the country. It was not surprising, therefore, that the white community accused them of being lazy.[30]

Faced by stubborn black resolve to go west together, the residents of Atchison concluded that perhaps this was the best of all solutions; it appeared to please everybody. The inevitable committee was appointed, to work with the overseer of the poor, and in the city attorney's words, "that committee took measures to send them out to the interior of the State, and also to get them out of the State, if possible." One of the councilmen, who once had served as general passenger agent for the Central Branch of the Union Pacific running westward from Atchison, admitted that "we shipped a great many out on that line of road, and gave them a free ticket if they had nothing to buy their tickets with—to get rid of them." This final act of philanthropy was financed at public expense.[31]

A number of interior towns were the recipients of these shipments, in varying numbers and with widely divergent responses by those communities, but it was Topeka that bore the brunt of the load. This was the capital, the official residence of Gov. John Pierce St. John, the fifty-six-year-old chief executive officer of Kansas, who was a prohibitionist and a man deeply concerned with the problems of human relations. It was to him and to his office that Kansas mayors turned in search of help in solving their new-found and unexpected problem.

4

FORTRESS TOPEKA

John St. John was mentally and emotionally prepared to answer the call. As a lawyer, politician, and humanitarian, he blended perfectly into the intellectual landscape of "bleeding Kansas," where a little more than two decades earlier John Brown had attracted national attention. Even though that old fanatic long since had been swung to martyrdom, Kansans were aware that his spirit still hovered over them and that his misson was still theirs. Unconsciously, the more avid humanitarians among them awaited the emergence of another torchbearer, hopefully one whose political antennae were tuned to their particular set of signals.

In addition to the fact that St. John was on the "right side," from the viewpoint of reform-minded Kansans, he had all the qualifications of birth and breeding that the voters regarded as essential. As an Indiana boy who had struggled alone since the age of twelve to gain an education, achieve membership in the Illinois bar, and finally earn a lieutenant colonelcy in the federal army during the Civil War, he exemplified fulfillment of the nineteenth-century American dream. Horatio Alger, a contemporary, easily could have used St. John's success story as another example of "risen from the ranks" in one of his numerous accounts depicting opportunities in the land of plenty.

In 1869, after practicing law briefly at Independence, Missouri, St. John packed his books and followed the westward movement toward a younger part of the country. The residents of Olathe, Kansas, who watched the newcomer hang out his shingle, remembered him as a strong-featured young man whose bristling handlebar mustaches accentu-

51

ated piercing eyes and whose general bearing spoke not only of a war veteran mature beyond his years but of one who understood his goals and was determined to achieve them. That he quickly entered the political arena surprised no one in Olathe; it was almost expected of any young lawyer in a small western town.

The choice of Kansas as a place to carve out a career was, in his case, correct. St. John's espousal of the antiliquor crusade and his enthusiasm for women's rights rang all the correct bells in a society whose heritage found many of its roots in New Engand, a place where moral indignation sprang forth from the soil full blown and righteously angry. As a candidate for political office, he found his Huguenot background to be another asset; it reassured voters that his French blood bore no papist taint.

Armed with membership in the G.A.R., with impeccable moral and religious equipment, and with Republican party credentials, Olathe's latest political knight-errant presented himself to his neighbors and asked for their blessings. They responded by sending him to the state senate in 1873, and five years later their faith was vindicated when Kansas voters made him governor.[1]

No one who knew St. John personally or even by reputation was surprised at his sponsorship of the beleaguered blacks. Any young and ambitious member of the Republican party of 1879, especially one whose humanitarian qualities were advertised as his political stock-in-trade, would have shown little hesitation in extending the welcome mat to hungry, ragged blacks fresh from southern plantations. To condemn southerners for their treatment of that race, to accuse them of reenslaving the Negro despite the North's valiant efforts to "reconstruct" the South, was the hallmark of sincere and heartfelt Republicanism during the postwar years. Consequently, to receive these refugees with open arms was natural, for it was assumed that their flight stemmed from persecution, prejudice, and cruelties beyond the imagination of even Harriet Beecher Stowe, that they had just escaped from the dark ages, where ignorance and barbarity reigned. To lend succor was not merely an act expected of an enlightened people; it also had overtones that hummed with vibrations from earlier religious and moral crusades and held much promise of higher rewards. It was comforting to think that the leader of the new crusade was named St. John.

The governor's enemies contended that his sympathy for the helpless and impoverished legions at his doorstep was sired by political expediency, that the newcomers were to be used as shock troops in a counterattack against a new and dangerous alliance of Greenbackers and Democrats, the rising power of which threatened Republican dominance; and therefore, the whole business was said to have been born more of cynicism than out of sympathy.[2] An outrageous lie, said his supporters; and they cited St. John's earlier experiences with racial intolerance to show that his present attitude was sincere. The reference was to a wartime experience. When young Captain St. John had come home on leave to Charleston, Illinois, in 1862, he brought with him a Negro servant, who lived in the captain's home during a brief period. For this the officer was indicted under the so-called Logan Black Law, an act passed in 1853 to prevent the immigration of free Negroes into the state. Although St. John was not convicted of the charge, his political supporters in Kansas later argued that the experience nevertheless had left its mark upon him.[3]

The battle over the governor's motives in the matter of the Exodusters came out into the open on April 20. On that evening, Topekans met at the local opera house, and St. John was in the chair. He did more than preside; he led an emotionally charged audience, which created the Freedmen's Fund, subscribed over five hundred dollars on the spot, and passed a resolution pledging further aid to the black unfortunates. The governor's activist role pleased his followers, but it failed to convince his opponents that his action had philanthropic roots. They sought some assurances that the bill for his political ambitions would not be left on their doorsteps. That Topeka did not intend to support a large black population became clear when the resolution, which promised immediate aid to the suffering, emphasized as its long-range goal the transportation of refugees "to places where they may enjoy rights and privileges with all other citizens." Presumably, Kansas towns further west could expect to be called upon to do their duty.[4]

Although the mass meeting ostensibly was called to help alleviate a burning social problem, it created others. A fairly substantial group of Topekans opposed the influx, and some of them pointed the finger at St. John, accusing him of aggravating the situation by welcoming the blacks. The whole thing was rigged, they said. After St. John and others had made what one critic called "inflammatory speeches," the governor reached into a pocket and drew out a list of committee members that had been made up in advance and in anticipation of the committee's creation. Just as quickly, St. John's brother-in-law was named superintendent of the new organization. Another instant appointment was that of Judge N. C. McFarland, who was instructed to take the money just collected and make straight for Wyandotte, where help was needed. The "Judge," whose title was honorary—"titles are a plenty out there," he confessed later, when referring to Kansas—left for Wyandotte the next day, and by that evening he had furnished arriving blacks with one hundred loaves of bread and fifty pounds of bacon. Part of the money that he spent came from the purse of Susan B. Anthony, who attended the mass meeting and encouraged subscriptions by offering ten dollars to support yet another cause.[5] It was not just a handful of unhappy small merchants who opposed St. John's program of aid. Milton H. Case, a successful attorney who became Topeka's mayor in the spring of 1877, argued that such a small city as his—he guessed its population to be fourteen or fifteen thousand—could not accommodate a large number of indigents of any color. He agreed that most of the relief money had come from outside and that the question was not so much one of a drain upon municipal finances as that of confusion arising from excessive numbers. A moderate amount of city money had been spent on these people, he conceded, but not for relief; it had been used to send back home a handful who wanted to go. The mayor hastened to add that half-fare rail tickets were available for such a purpose.

Although Case had been unable to serve in the Union Army during the war, due to lameness, he had taken an active role in recruitment and was thoroughly dedicated to the cause. His enthusiasm did not have an abolitionist background; he had been, however, a strong advocate of the nonextension of slavery into the territories. In consequence, his views on the subject remained moderate, and in 1879 he was unwilling to march under the banner of St. John. Unlike the governor's followers, Case took little stock in the atrocity reports coming out of the South. True, he said, the refugees were quick to make allegations of murder, violence, and maltreatment by southern whites, but when they became disillusioned with Kansas and wanted to go home, they frequently admitted that their stories often were tailored to meet the expectations of the listeners.[6]

If Topeka's press was any reflection of public sentiment, popular feeling in the matter was mixed. The *Commonwealth,* a liberal Republican journal, so far as the Exoduster question was concerned, became an important spokesman for the St. John group. The day before the mass meeting it ran an editorial entitled "The Duty of Kansas," in which the editor held that the state had a responsibility to care for the newcomers. This should be no financial burden, he argued, for if the plight of these people became known around the country, money would pour in from all over the North. Meantime, he suggested, Kansas should perfect an organization to implement the program of aid. There was precedent for it, he reminded readers. For two years the people of Topeka and of Shawnee County had given a certain amount of assistance to Negroes moving westward. He referred to those who had come out of Kentucky and Tennessee in search of Kansas farmlands, some of whom were located in little colonies farther west.[7]

George S. Irwin, editor of the *North Topeka Times,* represented what might be called the conservative Republican businessmen's view. He thought that Topeka had exceeded its resources for philanthropy, that what he called "this relief business" was merely encouraging the movement, and that there was no real reason for the Negroes to leave the South. Typically, he denied any personal racial prejudice, arguing that regardless of color, these were people who could not care for themselves. Despite his denials of bias, he admitted that in all probability the newcomers could not expect to find equal opportunities for their children in the Kansas schools. In some districts, school boards already had excluded them. Even in Topeka the schools were not mixed; educational facilities were separate and, it was hoped, equal.[8]

As a result of the formation of a temporary relief committee at the April 20 meeting, Topeka indicated that its doors were open to the refugees. After Judge McFarland had spent some of the money raised that night to feed the refugees at Wyandotte, the remaining funds were used to transport some six hundred of them to the capital. Since the city was totally lacking in housing for them, the county commissioners gave permission to use buildings at the fairgrounds as a temporary abode. Far from meeting the emergency, the move simply created further difficulty, for upon hearing of Topeka's hospitality, some seven hundred additional blacks, a portion of them ill, arrived and waited for public aid.[9]

As it had been in Missouri river towns and at St. Louis, resident Negroes of Topeka tried to help their brethren. On the evening of April 28 a group of them met and formed their own relief organization. Among them were the Reverend T. W. Henderson, editor of Topeka's *Colored Citizen;* A. D. De Frantz and Columbus Johnson, both of whom had been active as founders of earlier Kansas Negro colonies; and John Milton Brown, himself a refugee from Mississippi who earlier had settled at Topeka. As members of an "establishment" of their own, they sought to stem the flow of indigents by printing and distributing pamphlets throughout the South that would disabuse plantation Negroes of their quixotic notions regarding Kansas. While they were sympathetic to the migrants, nevertheless Topeka's black community understood that great numbers of them might threaten their own economic security.[10] They were willing, however, to do what they could to aid those who had arrived and who were in need.

The average Kansan, black or white, was prepared to help the needy, regardless of color; but serious objections arose to opening the floodgates and to encouraging movements such as the one under way. Some of St. John's critics felt that he had shown great recklessness on this score at the recent mass meeting. The governor that evening "threw the doors of the state wide open, and said he wanted a million of them to come in."[11] Judge McFarland's enthusiasm for the strangers was equally annoying to businessmen. The "Judge" admitted that the initial influx was large, but, he said, there was no need to worry; Kansas easily could absorb two or three times the numbers witnessed in the initial assault.[12] It was talk such as his that tended to crystallize the opposition.

Local pressure against the exodus movement now began to build rapidly. The county commissioners, who had allowed the fairground to be used as a campsite for a month or six weeks, quite suddenly served an eviction notice, explaining that the place was in need of repair. The ad hoc relief committee accepted the decision and commenced construction of some temporary barracks on the north side of town. This simply moved the problem from one part of town to another, and it quickly became clear that this solution was not acceptable. Militant businessmen, acting as a self-appointed committee of public safety, tore down the partially constructed buildings and threw the remains into the river.[13] The action was explained away on the ground that local businessmen thought the barracks, in that location, would lower the value of their property. Topekans continued to insist that there was no racial prejudice among them.

Undaunted, the relief committee moved out of town, but within the charter limit, and commenced yet another set of barracks. These were little more than shanties, each having four compartments in which all the walls were lined with bunks. Twenty people were crowded into each compartment, where they slept and cooked. A nearby commissary building supplied provisions, and a small hospital, run by a white doctor who received his pay from the committee, cared for the sick.[14] Into these military-style quarters came a small army of confused, hungry migrants, still thinking of a new life on a government-granted farm situated in the land of the free. For a few, the first bloom of anticipation had faded, yielding to growing doubts and that gut-shrinking feeling that perhaps the wrong decision had been made.

But others, exhibiting cheerfulness and optimism, settled in to await further directions. The Lord had done very well by them so far, they assured each other, and there was no reason to doubt Him now. Kansans who watched this strange-looking crowd of emigrants long remembered them for their happy childlike chatter and their penchant for bright clothing. "The women were dressed in the gayest of colored dresses, red, purple, black and blue shining cloth," recalled one of the pioneer women in later years. "Their hats, if they had any, were also dressed with feathers and ribbon of many colors, and generally set high on their heads, for all the women wore their hair in rolls. Some had shoes, and those not lucky enough to possess a pair were just as jolly and gay as the rest." The men were dressed in old clothes, patched and pinned around them, some of which were hand-me-downs from a better day. All styles and shapes of coats were in evidence, frequently set off by battered stovepipe hats whose owners were barefoot. Most of the children appeared in long shirts that resembled nightgowns, and a few of them in pants, but none had shoes.[15]

The arrival of increasing numbers of Negroes in Topeka and the municipality's apparent willingness to receive them, as evidenced by the creation of a temporary relief committee and the construction of temporary housing facilities, put the city into the "Exoduster business" in a big way. But despite the mushrooming problem, St. John and his followers had made their commitment, and they proposed to honor it. That they were prepared for a lengthy siege was indicated in May when the Kansas Freed-men's Relief Association asked for incorporation under state law, its stated purpose being to aid "destitute freedmen, refugees, and emigrants coming into this state." A board of directors, consisting of thirteen members and headed by St. John, constituted its governing body. J. C. Hebbard, the forty-eight-year-old clerk of the Kansas House of Representatives, became the organization's first secretary, for which he received $100 a month. N. C. McFarland, who had acted as superintendent for the temporary body, ran the group's day-to-day operations. Despite inclusion of the phrase "and emigrants coming into the state" in the incorporation document, the main aim of KFRA, as it became known, was to help distressed blacks. Secretary Hebbard later remarked that upon occasion, white emigrants applied for aid in continuing their westward passage, but very few, if any, ever received it. The association resembled the Mullanphy Board of St. Louis—in reverse.[16]

According to the *Commonwealth,* which was the Relief Association's unofficial spokesman and St. John's unfailing supporter, there was much need for an organization dedicated to aiding the black immigrants. It reported that on the day after incorporation, 180 more arrivals were crowded into the limited housing facilities. Some of them were sent on by rail in order to relieve the congestion, but many were so sick and frail that they could travel no farther. Those who were not sick waited patiently as Relief Association representatives found food for them. "Young and old were seated on the platform, eating canned goods, spare ribs, corn bread, and whatever could be obtained," commented a newspaperman who talked with some of the arrivals. Apparently, not all of them were penni-less, for they were warned against having anything to do with men who claimed to be agents of the state or federal governments, who might solicit a fee for locating the newcomers on lands. Such men were frauds, said the *Commonwealth;* avoid them, and go straight to J. C. Hebbard, who was legitimate.[17]

As a rule, the clergy, both black and white, quickly accepted the situation and tried to be of assistance. As always, there were exceptions. Early in May the Reverend Joshua A. Barratt, of North Topeka, announced that he would give a public address entitled "Shall We Either Directly or Indirectly Encourage the Filling of Kansas with Paupers?" The notice was challenged immediately by an unidentified member of the Relief Association, who wrote a letter signed "Incorporator," in which he argued that there was a greater demand for black labor in Kansas than could be supplied. The scheduled lecture took place on the night of the thirteenth at the North Topeka Baptist Church, and despite inclement weather, a large crowd turned out. In a last-ditch effort to dilute the minister's criticisms, St. John's group suggested that Barratt give equal time to a Negro so that the audience might have both sides of the story. When he declined, the *Commonwealth* quickly charged that the minister was racially prejudiced because he would not allow a Negro to speak in his church.

The controversial lecture revealed something of the split suffered by the community. After Barratt warned his audience that every dollar given in support of the Exodusters would cost Kansans fifty times that much in the future, he openly attacked the Relief Association, calling it a mere money-making scheme, one in which officers drew large salaries but from which the Negroes got very little. Perhaps feeling that he had gone too far with his accusations, he concluded the effort by asking all his supporters and friends in the audience to stand up. The *Commonwealth* was happy to announce that only about one-third of those present arose, an assertion that generated a joint letter from three members of the audience who said the correct figure was *two*-thirds.

The *Commonwealth's* editor was very much annoyed by the attack upon St. John's group. "A clergyman, by virtue of his position, has no right to make charges against the best citizens of the State, without some shadow of proof," he told Topekans the following day. It was outrageous to think that St. John, McFarland, Hebbard, and other philanthropic men, who were giving their time in order to aid the distressed, should be accused of participating in a scheme to make money from so worthy a cause. Barratt was accused of being an unimaginative man who advocated the building of a wall around Kansas that would prevent the state from growing. This touched upon sensitive civic nerves, for the idea of stifling growth was one that was much frowned upon in the burgeoning West of that day.[18]

It was necessary to talk in general terms when attacking the Reverend Mr. Barratt, not only because he was a man of the cloth, but also because of his position in the community. He moved to Topeka in 1868, and there he remained for the next forty-eight years, evangelizing, organizing Baptist churches in the area, and becoming one of the most "marrying and burying" preachers in the town's history. It was he who had organized the North Topeka Baptist Church, at which the controversial meeting was held, and he was its pastor for a decade. During those years he did not accept a penny in salary. Frail and almost blind, he went about his work in a busily cheerful manner, but when aroused, his evangelical determination rose to the surface, and he spoke his mind openly. Since he combined a business career with his religious endeavors, he was, in effect, a part of the Topeka commercial community, and this, in itself, allied him with a number of local merchants who viewed St. John's efforts as somewhat visionary.

Barratt and his supporters took the position that Kansas had all the laborers it needed and that any more would constitute a surfeit that would lower wages. They countered arguments that current relief measures were financed from outside the state with the contention that after such temporary funds were exhausted, the state would have to continue its support of these people. This was what Barratt meant when he said, at the evening meeting, that every dollar spent would cost fifty later on. Worse, he argued, there was evidence to show that the welfare program was attracting many who might otherwise have stayed home. Some of the Exodusters openly admitted this to Barratt when he put the question to them.

More annoying yet was the fact that, despite St. John's insistence regarding the willingness of these people to work, they did not always find it convenient to take jobs. In testifying before an investigating committee, Barratt himself later described an incident to support such a claim:

> A colored lady, some time since, passing my gate, stopped to lay a bundle off her head on my gate-post. I saw her standing there, and asked her "Where did you get that bundle?" She replied, "Well, mister, if you want to know, I'll just tell you. I went down to the relief house last Saturday, and they wanted to know if I had labor. I told them I had been laboring. They told me they would not give me anything because I was laboring; and then I concluded I would not labor for that cause; so I did not work this week. And I went down this morning and told them I hadn't anything to do and could not

get anything, and I wanted some things, and they gave me all this."
She opened her bundle and showed me what she had.

The sanitary problem was another argument used to discourage the movement. St. Louis and other cities had employed it; now it was Topeka's turn. One member of the city council told Barratt that after one carload had arrived, they stood in front of his home "and they attended to their natural wants there." Residuals of nature's calls dotted other parts of the city. The rail cars upon which that particular group had arrived lay on a siding for a day and a half after arrival, and Barratt reported that "at that time the side-track was so filthy for two hundred yards that it was impossible for a lady or almost any man that cared for himself to walk along it." Nor were the barracks, to which these people were taken, models of sanitation. Barratt thought the quarters dirty and a breeding place of disease. "It is a pretty hard place," he said.[19]

The Reverend Mr. Barratt's outspoken stand on the Exoduster issue drew fire from other members of the local clergy, both black and white. The Reverend Joseph Cook countered with a public lecture in which he charged that the exodus was due to extortion, pauperization, and murder in the South. At another meeting, held at the North Topeka Methodist Episcopal Church, an enthusiastic crowd rocked the building with a thunderous rendition of the song "Hold the Fort." A well-known local Negro, the Reverend John Milton Brown, publicly thanked Barratt for the part that he had played in producing such a large turnout at this gathering—it was almost an indignation meeting—after which he explained that he had traveled over much of Kansas, and he could assure his listeners that concern about overemployment was absolutely groundless.

Brown later admitted that much of the excitement in Topeka had arisen from fears that the city's finances would be exhausted in its efforts to feed Negro itinerants. He denied that the Relief Association had made any effort to attract southern Negroes to Kansas, but rather its function was to care for those who came of their own volition. But before the movement was over, Brown himself became the author of a statement that the association had cared for as many as twenty-five thousand Negroes from different southern states.[20] Barratt and his followers had predicted a figure of similar magnitude, one that in itself suggested serious problems for a city whose population was not that large.

Because the movement grew to such proportions, it was St. John, above all, upon whose doorstep the blame was laid. From the outset, some of Topeka's more cautious philanthropists had declined to have any official connection with the Relief Association. One of them openly admitted that the group was apt to be criticized, and he excused his declination on the ground that he would be in a better position to defend the organization if he were not a card-carrying member.[21] For St. John, however, there was no escape hatch. As an avowed reformer, one who had espoused the cause of humanitarianism as his major and temperance as his minor in the curriculum of public life, he was as irrevocably committed as any martyr.

In the true spirit of the crusader, St. John did not shrink from the challenges ahead. As the movement gained strength in April and May of 1879, more than three thousand letters poured into his office, some from southern Negroes who asked for information about the land of promise, others from supporters who praised his efforts. Overnight he became one of the nation's leading advocates for the advancement of the black man, a fighter who was no mere theorist, but one who was in the cockpit, actually carrying on the never-ending battle for human rights. Hundreds of people throughout the North sent their reassurances on scrawled penny postal cards, on cheap paper, and in the shaky handwriting of the aged, or on embossed letterhead stationery denoting personal means or influential firms, most of which pledged some kind of financial aid. Others merely offered their prayers.

Encouraged by such outpourings and possibly quite flattered by his sudden ascent to national prominence, St. John responded. "I am glad to know that the great heart of the loyal North is right upon this question," he said to his newly acquired following, "and I can assure you that Kansas, though yet in her infancy, will do her whole duty." Recalling wartime days, he promised that services of the former slaves would be remembered: "We have not forgotten that these same black men fed our boys and piloted them through the swamps and jungles of the South when fleeing from Southern prison-pens to a free North; and now that they, after years of oppression and abuse are compelled to flee from the same country and seek shelter in our midst, let us be true to them, as they were faithful and true to our boys in the past." When Missourians read these words, they reacted sharply. "Low partisanship" and "namby-pamby sentimentalism," commented the Democratic *Missouri Republican,* of St. Louis.[22] Missouri, an old Slave State, was perfectly willing for St. John and Kansas to have all the refugees who came up from the South. Most of the money that St. Louis had raised in behalf of these people was spent on transportation. It wanted them to keep moving.

There was some disposition among Topekans to use contributed funds for the same purpose: to pass along the overflow to towns farther west. F. W. Giles, of that city, objected to the practice, arguing that the money should be used to buy plows and teams "and [to] lead this army of wealth producers to the unoccupied lands in thousands of acres, laying everywhere around us." But, he cautioned, they should not be sent into the desert—western-most Kansas—where certain failure awaited them: "Every mile that these destitute people may go toward the interior diminishes to them the probabilities of the comforts of necessities of life, and if they go on to Government lands unaided by capital there, a fearful suffering must be theirs before another May day greets us." Why not encourage landowners in eastern Kansas to furnish capital and tools to these workers and thereby get a return on their investments through cultivation? asked Giles.[23] It might have been pointed out to him that this was exactly what white southerners had done with their lands and thereby had created a situation of dissatisfaction among the tenant farmers.

St. John had no argument with the idea of black settlement in rural Kansas. He was convinced that his state had plenty of untilled government and railroad lands in the western part of the state, but he said that it was impossible for anyone, black or white, to take up these acres without some financial backing. He estimated that it would require from $150 to $300 per family to do this. However, the governor concluded, unless these people were willing to become tenant farmers, they would have to take their chances in the arid part of the state, for by 1879 the line of settlement was slowly moving through that area.

St. John was more concerned over ideological than practical matters. He agonized over the conditions that were alleged to have placed these people at his doorstep, constantly returning to the arguments that they had been dealt with unfairly, robbed of their earnings in the South, and that they had fled only when conditions became unbearable. His more realistic Republican friends must have winced slightly when he persisted that "as for Kansas, I think I speak the sentiment of the people when I say that they shall never be turned from our doors for want of bread. As for myself, I believe that God's hand is in this work and that the present exodus from the Southern States is one of the means used by Him to forever cement the American Union and to render secession in the future impossible." In his mind, and in that of a good many eastern humanitarians, the war was yet to be won, and Republican party leaders were aware that such beliefs still packed a political punch. St. John, clinging to his beliefs, ignored the fact that of the three thousand who had arrived by early May, about two thousand were, in his words, "comparatively destitute." Kansas could bear the burden, he insisted.[24]

The Reverend T. W. Henderson, editor of the *Colored Citizen,* of Topeka, was more conservative on the question than was the governor.

Editorially he advised southern members of his race not to leave their homes without some financial resources. He would be happy to have as many as one hundred thousand Negroes in Kansas, he wrote; but only those who could sustain themselves should undertake the move, only those who would be a burden to no one. Part of Henderson's concern stemmed from the condition of those who made up the hegira. Most of them were old and inclined to infirmity. Kansas was a place for the young and vigorous, he cautioned; chances there for the elderly were much diminished.[25]

The practicality of such views was lost upon Topeka's more enthusiastic humanitarians. Triumphant sounds of the crusaders' trumpets continued to reverberate from the *Commonwealth*'s editorial offices. Negro emigration was not new, the paper reminded its readers; for some time, Topeka had served as a distributing point for black immigrants coming out of Tennessee and Kentucky. And now, with the heightened tempo of things, that city had not faltered, as had some of its less worthy neighbors, but rather it had gladly assumed its responsibilities. "As we have stated some time since, it is a part of the penalty we have to pay for our sins as citizens of the United States, which we have been guilty of towards the black race," proclaimed the editor.[26] It was a sentiment that must have made old William Lloyd Garrison, now in his last year of life, glow with pride.

Pleased also was Governor St. John, for the *Commonwealth* was his mouthpiece, his pipeline to the national press and to the hungry eyes of thousands across the country whose hearts beat just a little faster at the prospect of taking up old cudgels that had presumably been laid aside after Appomattox. These were the days of May, days in which black legions of poor overran the redoubts of Kansas conservatism, cheered on by determined crusaders who marched under St. John's flying banners. But by June, as the first waves became an army of occupation, even the governor began to entertain second thoughts. He had not changed his views about the worthiness of these people; they were, he maintained, sober and hard-working American men and women who wanted no more than an opportunity to be gainfully employed. But pressure was growing at home. Important business figures, and hence men of some political consequence, talked louder now about the economic consequences of the flood. As numbers mounted, financial aid from other parts of the country failed to keep pace, and this began to worry the governor. "It seems to me that the people of the North do not fully comprehend the magnitude of this movement, otherwise they would certainly take a greater interest in the matter," he complained to a correspondent in Washington, D.C. By then, on the ninth of June, the association had given aid to about four thousand destitute Negroes. Much of the money that had been spent had come from such open-handed places as Cleveland, Ohio—some sixteen hundred dollars, in fact—but, lamented St. John, the shame of it all was that New York City had failed, and "so far as I know, has not yet contributed as many cents." Quantities of old clothes had been sent to Topeka from across the land, but that was not enough. What the Relief Association needed was cash.[27]

Another thing was needed, said some of the exasperated civic leaders: fewer Exodusters. By early June, even St. John was beginning to admit it. The thought was in his mind as he sat down to acknowledge a contribution of sixty-one dollars received from Negro troops of the Twenty-fourth Infantry, then stationed at Fort McIntosh, Texas. The money was appreciated, he told one of its officers, but he hastened to advise that Kansas had all the migrating Negroes it could handle for the time being. It would be best, he thought, if refugees did not come to his state "in large numbers wholly destitute, for if they do, in the course of time, it would be impossible to provide for them." The enlisted men of the regiment were not apt to leave for Kansas in the near future, unless they deserted, but apparently St. John now thought it wise to spread the word to all points south of Kansas that he was not in the business of recruiting.[28]

He took the same stance when writing to Joseph M. Kern, of the St. Louis commercial firm Sells & Company. Kansas never had done anything either to encourage or repel the black immigrants, he argued; it simply had tried to aid the destitute. Ordinary dictates of humanity had been the sole mover of such actions. The source of the trouble, said St. John, lay elsewhere. "It seems to me that the best way to stop the exodus of the colored people from the South is to cease charging them from $7 to $10 per acre rent and from 20 to 25 cents per pound for bacon and $1.00 to $1.50 per gallon for 40 cent molasses and 20 to 25 cents per yard for 6 cent domestics and like fabulous prices for other articles that the colored people are compelled to have."[29] Since Sells & Company did a heavy trade in such goods with southern buyers, St. John hoped that his message would reach the offenders who practiced such deceit upon Negro buyers.

By July of 1879 even the *Commonwealth*'s crusading spirit was beginning to falter. Quoting a letter from the Brooklyn *Eagle,* in which the writer said that the black movement was a calamity to be submitted to with Christian forbearance, the Topeka editor agreed that in the crisis, Kansas had done its duty nobly. He thought that Americans who had sent money to aid in the cause paid only what was due from a nation whose earlier conduct toward the Negro had not been without fault. The

real culprits in the whole affair, charged the *Commonwealth,* were the
southerners who had continued their injustices toward the blacks. When
they reformed, the flights from the South would cease. This would be
desirable for all, it was argued, especially for Kansas, a state that did not
want any kind of immigrants who were without some means of self-
support.[30]

The newspaper's retreat from an earlier position of rigidity faithfully
represented the changing views of St. John. In late July the *Missouri
Republican* said that the Kansas governor already had hinted strongly
that the sending of any more southern Negroes to Kansas would be a
cruelty to them and a burden upon the white community. Agreed, said
the St. Louis editor, but he predicted that the governor would find that
it was much easier to start such a movement than to halt it and that the
governor had not seen the last of this problem.[31] St. John understood this.
At the end of July he wrote:

> We have already received and cared for between four and five
> thousand of these people here in Kansas. The labor market has been,
> I will say, overstocked with them. It is utterly impossible to obtain
> employment for them now. The funds of the association are about
> exhausted, and to send more of them here in addition to the number
> that are already here and must be provided for, would be a cruel out-
> rage upon the black man, and will necessarily result in much suffering
> on their part for the want of food or the opportunity to earn it.[32]

Those who had predicted the labor glut—the Reverend Mr. Barratt was
one of them—found some solace in being right. Southern newspapers also
made note of the admission and hastened to spread the word in their
respective areas.

Aside from growing difficulties at Topeka, St. John was faced by
other complications. In the middle of July, for example, the association
sent ten adults and four children to Wichita, and most of them were
returned as fast as they could be rounded up and put on the train. Wichita's acting mayor minced no words in rejecting the Topeka exports. "Our
city will prohibit the introduction of any more exodus by quarantine. Shall
return all that will come," he telegraphed. Childish conduct, the Topeka
Commonwealth cried out in righteous indignation, "so ridiculous as to be
laughable." What really angered that newspaper was the *Wichita City
Eagle's* suggestion that the Topekans were making money out of the
movement. Nonsense, was the angry response; Topeka had raised over
six hundred dollars to aid these people. What other Kansas town had done
so much?[33]

About the time that the *Commonwealth* was chiding Wichita for its cold and heartless attitudes, word came from Kansas City that another 150 refugees had arrived there and that they would be sent to Topeka. The Relief Association acted instantly by sending a representative to Kansas City on the afternoon train with instructions to have them sent on up the river.[34]

St. John and his friends must have conceded privately that, as the St. Louis paper predicted, once the movement had commenced, it was hard to stop. Publicly they were obliged to pursue the course that they had initiated, with minor changes in direction and emphasis. While they stuck by their guns, arguing that Kansas, in general, and Topeka, in particular, had an obligation to care for the needy, regardless of color, they accentuated their efforts to find homes and employment for the black immigrants somewhere beyond the environs of Topeka. Not only had the group received more refugees than it had bargained for, but its appeal to humanitarian hearts and purses had exceeded all expectations and had converted a small slide into an avalanche. The rest of the nation, particularly the Northeast, finally had awakened to the possibilities of the great crusade being carried on by a lonely warrior and his followers in faraway Kansas.

The *New York Tribune* now praised Kansas, assuring its readers that any other state would have panicked, but these courageous people had persisted, and as a result, black emigrants were settling down on new western lands.[35] John Brown, Jr., of Put-in-Bay, Ohio, offered to enlist in the great cause now being refought on the land where his father had campaigned. Although he was now fifty-eight, Brown announced that if the call came, he would not be found wanting.[36] From Rollin, Michigan, came word that another old campaigner was ready to serve. Elizabeth Comstock, described as a "kind, motherly old Quaker lady," then in her sixty-fourth year, wrote that her interests had been awakened by reading newspaper accounts about the new movement in Kansas. As a minister in the Society of Friends and a zealous worker in the field of Christianity who had spent the last twenty-five years of her life relieving suffering humanity, she felt that here indeed was a cause worth joining. She proposed to start collecting old clothing, bedding, and what she called "more substantial metallic sympathy" for these unfortunates. She felt sure that her many friends on both sides of the Atlantic would honor her requests. All that she now required was a set of directions from General St. John, and she would march. Alongside her would be her old friend Laura S. Haviland, a former abolitionist, then seventy-one years old, who already had taken up her station on the Kansas battlefield.[37]

It was at this point that Governor St. John began to think that he had painted himself into a political corner. Just when he had begun to retreat in the face of heavy criticism in Kansas, the bugles of the Christian soldiers were heard on a faraway hill, and he was not at all sure that he wanted to be saved by them. By September, he said, Topeka had seen some seven thousand Exodusters, and although it could be argued that these easily could be absorbed into the white population of Kansas, that mix was not occurring.[38] Rather, the black immigrants tended to cling to Topeka, or at least to other small Kansas towns, and their numbers appeared to be larger because of this concentration. Increasingly, St. John believed that while his original stand had been correct from a humanitarian point of view, it now had begun to reveal some serious political limitations. Looking hard at his political future, he tried to retreat, but too late. The descent upon Kansas of eastern enthusiasts for his cause engulfed him in a sea of flattery and assurances that he was indeed presidential timber. He should have known better than to have listened to such siren songs. As a temperance advocate and as a crusader for women's rights, he faced no insurmountable political problems in Kansas, but his venture into black philanthropy was not one that promised very big returns in a basically Anglo-Saxon frontier agricultural community. The voters illustrated that point by returning him to private life in the election of 1882.

5

KANSAS—BLACK ON WHITE

Kansas, in the late 1870s, was riding the crest of a land boom the exciting reverberations of which were felt as far away as Europe. The westward rush was so great in the spring of 1879 that the *New York Times* thought the day not far off when Kansas would be "the empire State of the trans-Mississippi country."[1] Kansans beamed with pleasure at such praise and told each other that the state's Board of Agriculture indeed was doing a great job of advertising agricultural opportunities. It pleased them even more when Missourians grudgingly acknowledged the Kansas board's spectacular success and resolutely voted funds "to be expended in attracting immigrants" to their own state. Even Missouri's inclination to question the fertility of Kansas lands was swept aside with a generous wave of the hand by those who lived beyond the Missouri River. As true champions, they ignored the lamentations of lesser lights, and in those wonderful booming years that saw an army of immigrants sweep westward across Kansas, there was room enough in prairie hearts to forgive jealous Missourians.[2]

The Kansas immigrant crop bloomed early in 1879. By late February, settlers were arriving at the rate of one thousand a week, and during the next month the rush reached flood proportions. The Atchison, Topeka and Santa Fe Railroad dispatched entire train loads of them westward. Both the Kansas Pacific and the Hannibal and St. Joseph lines experienced unusual demands for passage.[3] By mid March the magnitude of the land rush was attracting national notice. A dispatch from Kansas City told of three thousand people passing through that gateway to the West in a single day. Six hundred of them were from Bucks County, Pennsylvania. The Pennsylvanians attracted particular attention, for they were rated as top-grade immigrants who were "filled by a spirit of confidence and contentment, very different from the hopeless and almost reckless aspect of many emigrants, and they brought with them to the new country all their household goods." Within a few days the arrival of yet another group of Pennsylvanians, accompanied by ten carloads of belongings and some four hundred thousand dollars in cash, generated murmurs of approval from the Kansas press.[4] This was the type of newcomer that quickened the pulses of land agents who awaited them in Kansas.

On April 11 a Kansas City paper logged the arrival of another twenty-five hundred prime specimens identified as "white emigrants."[5] In reporting figures that indicated an enormous jump in acreage taken up, a Washington, D.C., dispatch commented: "As far as we know none of the colored emigrants have taken any of this land, though reports indicate that at least 8,000 have gone to Kansas from the South within the last few months."[6] An Emporia paper suggested who some of these new landowners were when, in September, it estimated that forty thousand Germans had settled along the Atchison, Topeka and Santa Fe line in the preceding five years.[7] It was estimated that in the nine months preceding July 1879, over two and a quarter million acres of land had been taken up in the state under homestead and preemption laws, a figure that could be translated into a population gain of between seventy and eighty thousand people.[8] These statistics, published for the edification and pleasure of Kansans, gave no hint that the place was becoming overcrowded. On the contrary, an Olathe newspaper proudly announced that "we have plenty of room for all creation."[9]

Not quite all of creation. The Kansas business and professional community had serious reservations about the probable success of black settlers, and while the objection understandably was not widely publicized, it existed. Those who lived in eastern Kansas, where the brunt of the burden first was felt, and whose sentiments perhaps were molded by proximity to the old Slave State, Missouri, tended to be more outspoken in the matter. When some of them were questioned, at a congressional hearing in 1880, their opinions emerged.

A. A. Harris, a Fort Scott, Kansas, attorney who had lived in that city for nine years, represented the feeling of his class. He was convinced that western conditions made it impossible for the Exodusters to improve their situation by migrating to Kansas, and although his neighbors were willing to help out in individual cases of suffering, they would not, could not, give aid to large numbers of indigents. He predicted that "the people of Kansas will let them alone severely. They do not want them to come there. . . . They have as much as they can do to feed themselves, and they are not going to feed a large number of helpless people."

When pressed, the average Kansan denied any racial prejudice, but Harris, upon interrogation, would not corroborate the denial. Although there was plenty of land for sale in his neighborhood, he admitted: "I think that the men who own the adjoining lands would not want colored people to buy them and settle on them." When asked if white farmers could not employ black labor, the attorney explained that farming was practiced in the frontier tradition—by members of the farm family. Even if a farmer wanted to hire a black, he said, it would be inconvenient, for there were no separate quarters for the workers such as were found in the South. When asked if itinerant farm laborers did not "live in," he admitted such was the usual practice, but in the case of the blacks there was reluctance to live with them or to eat at the same table. John Milton Brown agreed that his fellow blacks did not fit easily into the frontier agricultural mold. The trouble was, he said, "that the people in Kansas do not run their farms in the same way as the people of the South; they have not large plantations, with houses, or cabins, already built upon them, specially in order for the persons to live in who are employed upon their farms."[10]

The Fort Scott attorney might have mentioned a recent event in his city to further document the feeling of that city. A Negro, charged with assaulting a twelve-year-old girl, was taken from the local jail in March of 1879, and escorted by thirty masked men supported by a mob, he was hung to a lamp post. Then, to celebrate the act, a fire made from dry-goods boxes was kindled in the street, and the body was incinerated. "Kansas, with all her Radicalism and pretended love for the Negro does not hesitate to lynch a Negro culprit or to remonstrate against the immigration of the Negro into their state when they discover he is a nuisance," chortled the *Memphis Weekly Appeal*.[11]

John Davis, a Junction City, Kansas, editor who also farmed, confirmed the agrarian objection to Negro immigrants. Those farmers who had tried the experiment, he said, were unhappy with the result. Negroes who ventured out from the small towns usually would not stay and work on a farm for any length of time. Although he did not say it, they became lonesome for their own kind, and in addition, the situation in which they now found themselves did appear not to vary materially from that of the South. They were still agricultural workers, living at a subsistence level, in "the bleak and arduous land of Kansas," as a St. Louis newspaper expressed it. Thus, said Davis, the experiment not only was unsuccessful, but the general movement tended to diminish white immigration into Kansas and to slow the needed flow of capital into that state. S. J. Gilmore, the Kansas Pacific's land commissioner, told Governor St. John much the same thing.[12]

Yet another argument held that black farm hands simply had no place in the western agricultural picture. It was admitted that they could grow cotton in the South successfully, where the hoe culture still predominated and where sharecropping had replaced the earlier gang labor or slaves. But, as one Kansan explained, his state was new, and its farmers as yet had but little means. "Not one in ten is forehanded enough to be able to afford to keep help." He appealed to another popular belief when he pointed out that Kansas farmers did much of their work with machinery, and he contended that the Negroes did not know how to work with it.[13]

More serious than the problem of supplying them with farm labor was finding jobs for them in the small towns. The presence of unusual numbers of blacks in the towns, as well as the pressure to put them to work, thereby saving the community from paying out doles, irritated whites who wanted the work. It was not difficult, by playing on racial prejudices, to convince people that the blacks were absorbing all the jobs. For example, a Topeka doctor erroneously told investigating congressmen that the Negroes had largely displaced white labor in Kansas, had driven it out, and therefore the exodus was a "positive detriment to the state." This, he said—and again without foundation in fact—had materially lessened white immigration into Kansas.[14] The latter point touched a sensitive area; at that time Kansas was making great efforts to solicit white settlers. T. C. Henry, a real estate broker and one of the largest landholders of central Kansas, questioned his friends at Abilene about the desirability of black labor. Their feelings on the matter, he discovered, were "very decided upon this point." He told Governor St. John that it would be unfair to present residents, as well as to those who might come later, to glut ordinary labor outlets in the small towns. A Junction City paper, in advocating a larger white immigration, spoke for the promoters when it remarked that "we . . . cannot content ourselves with the growth produced only by natural increase and the Negro exodus."

While Henry was not always willing to admit the presence of grasshoppers or the existence of drouth in his western agricultural paradise, he did so now. Some of the white farmers were in need of relief to keep them alive, he reported to the governor, and in view of that situation he could not see the wisdom of allowing dependent classes to increase.[15] It was a difficult admission for this well-known land boomer, but he felt that his community was in a delicate financial condition, one that could take no further risks.

St. John and his followers talked in bold terms about their responsibility and that of Kansas in the matter of rescuing these victims of southern cruelty. Political opponents of the governor, as well as those who really had no very strong antipathy toward him, felt constrained to keep silent on the question on the ground that open opposition to the black arrivals might be politically inexpedient as well as contrary to current humanitarian trends. To be put in a position of defending southerners was unpopular in an era of Republican "bloody shirt" waving, one in which loud cries were heard across the land that the war had been lost and that the southern Negroes had been reenslaved.

Yet, a good many Kansans privately agreed with a remark made by Sen. James H. Lane, in 1861, that "our prejudices against them are unconquerable."[16] Much had happened since then, but even in 1879 Mayor Milton H. Case of Topeka openly admitted that his state would just as soon not have the Exodusters. When a member of the Senate investigating committee asked him if there was dissatisfaction in Kansas over the black movement, Case answered in the affirmative.[17] Sen. Preston B. Plumb, of Kansas, sensed dissatisfaction among his constituents, and he, too, opposed the influx of blacks. He used the argument that there was a deficiency of timber and a lack of building material for settlers, a contention that was denied by Negro leaders in the movement, and one that did not square with accounts found in the promotional literature of the day. Black farmers would suffer in Kansas, he contended, not only because of climatic conditions, but also because they tended to congregate in the towns, "places fraught with evil." His position was picked up and given wide circulation by southern newspapers.[18] From its distant listening post the *Times* of London concluded that "the preponderance of testimony there [in Kansas] indicates that she does not want the Negroes."[19]

As the westward flow of blacks heightened, attracting increasingly wide notice, those who had approved it or were at least accused of contributing to the development joined St. John in a retreat from their earlier hard line. The railroads, targets of all kinds of charges by westerners, strongly denied stories that their land agents had originated the whole movement. The Kansas Pacific and the Missouri Pacific frequently were pointed to as the leading culprits. They denied it. S. J. Gilmore, land commissioner for the Kansas Pacific Railway, insisted that it was the practice of his department to discourage from coming all persons who did not have from three hundred to five hundred dollars with which to make a start.[20] Thomas Nickerson, president of the Atchison, Topeka and Santa

Fe, said that his road had done no more than to offer black emigrants the same rail rates as those given the whites. Privately he admitted to St. John that "I have no doubt that the 'Exodus' of colored people into Kansas has seriously interfered with the sale of our lands and with our efforts to bring a good class of population into Kansas." Nevertheless, he offered to raise money to help those already there who were in distress.[21] A. S. Johnson, Nickerson's land commissioner in Kansas, warned prospective black settlers that government lands for some 250 miles west of the Missouri River already were taken up and that the latecomers would have to settle in an arid, sparsely settled treeless land. He called western Kansas "the extreme frontier, outside of civilization," a place where "coal is gold," and he concluded that "it is absolute folly to send them out on the frontier." This, at a time when he and fellow land commissioners from other roads were advertising the same area in superlatives. Johnson concluded that the movement of blacks into Kansas should be terminated. The state had done more than its share, he said, and its people had absorbed as many as they could. It was time to call a halt.[22]

There was tacit agreement with this view in a large segment of white Kansas society. The problem was how to act in such a situation without appearing to be selfish and unkind. Even more difficult to justify was the contention that Kansas was a land of milk and honey for white farmers, but one that would be a veritable hell for blacks. The *New York Times* spoke more frankly than had Kansas editors. Admitting that the exodus was slowing up, the newspaper saw little prospect for a revival of the movement. With all its resources, said the editor, Kansas was not the promised land, and its population was not inclined to give the impoverished newcomers a very sincere welcome. Then the editor touched upon a point that was becoming an extremely sensitive issue in Kansas, one that provided St. John with a growing dilemma. "Nothing less than a persistent use of the forcing process will enable the professional philanthropists who have the matter in charge to renew the movement with anything like its original vigor,"[23] remarked the New York paper. It was the presence of professional philanthropists, such as the Comstocks and the Havilands, and their efforts to make Kansas a black haven that irritated Kansas community leaders. These volunteers, many of them Quakers, simply assumed that Kansas was an open playing field and that since their cause was right, there would be no objection to their efforts. As St. John observed the growing antagonism between these groups, he realized even more just how complicated his political position had become, and desperately he sought a way out of the problem.

By the end of 1879 the Kansas governor was in full retreat. Writing to Horatio N. Rust, a Chicago philanthropist, St. John admitted that "there is not only no room for more but some of those already there must be got rid of."[24] By "got rid of" he meant diluting the growing blackness of Kansas by sending some of its Negroes to Nebraska, Colorado, and outlying states, as well as by diverting to other places any newcomers. The Kansas Free Land Association was in full agreement. Its directors actively sought means of diverting black immigrants "to other States in more need of laborers, and where the people are better able to care for such as are in destitute circumstances." The inability of the Kansas Freedmen's Relief Association adequately to care for the arriving indigents spurred the diversionary activities of the Land Association, the management of which showed increasing concern over the detrimental economic effect threatened by the Exodusters.[25] The Topeka *Commonwealth,* apparently sensing the tightening of public opinion on the question, doggedly reasserted that Kansas welcomed all who wanted to come, but it warned that they must make their own arrangements for getting there.[26]

While concern over the financial condition of immigrants cannot be said to have commenced in this exodus year, it rose to new heights and became a public issue among Kansans at that time. Nor had there been any noticeable resentment over the arrival of Negroes before then, primarily because their numbers were comparatively insignificant. In 1860 the Territory had a population of 625 free Negroes and two slaves. Ten years later the figure stood at 17,108, and within another decade, thanks in part to the exodus movement, the number jumped to 43,107. After that, the rise slowed; by 1890 there were 49,710 Negroes in Kansas. None of these figures represent a proportion as high as five percent of the total population. Prior to 1880 most of these people lived in eastern Kansas, near the Missouri River, tilling small farms or congregating in the towns.[27] They had arrived in a slow trickle, usually with some money. The few who were poor found work or were given a start by members of their race who were already established. In short, as a people they were not much different from the other immigrants.

The best known of the early Kansas Negro settlements were the colonies. There were a half dozen such settlements, the most prominent of which was Nicodemus, located a few miles east of Hill City, in the northwestern part of the state. Organized by a group of Topeka Negroes in 1877, Nicodemus challenged warnings that the arid land in the vicinity of the 100th meridian was a place that promised little success for farmers. Although it finally withered on the vine, as have many small western agrarian towns, for years it stood as a symbol of success among black farmers on the high plains. Today only a few families remain in this little community.

While the black colonies were led by members of their own race, white land boomers usually provided the inspiration for settlement. In the case of Nicodemus it was a white Indiana preacher named W. R. Hill, who laid out Hill City in the fall of 1876 and who sought additional population in order to build up his area. In July, 1877, about thirty Kentucky Negroes, who came via Topeka, provided the seed for the new colony near Hill City. In the autumn of 1877 another three hundred fifty arrived, strengthened by a contingent of one hundred fifty who came in March, 1878. Later that year, two more groups, one from Missouri and another from Kentucky, joined the others. The colony's name is commonly believed to have had biblical origins, but there is stronger argument for the claim that it commemorated a legendary slave who purchased his own freedom after arriving in America. Plantation Negroes were familiar with the lines:

> Nicodemus was a slave of African birth
> And he was bought for a bag full of gold;
> He was reckoned a part of the salt of the earth,
> But he died years ago, very old.

Hill took credit for originating the colony, telling St. John that he was its father and that the offspring was doing very well. The immigrants, he said, "were poor and had nothing in the start while at this wrighting [April, 1879] they are in fare circumstances." He had collected a five-dollar locating fee from each family, two-dollars of which he paid to the government as a filing charge. Although Hill is said to have taken little part in the government of Nicodemus, he had no intention of letting the newcomers acquire any political power. When asked about such a possibility, he was said to have remarked: "We will have to make concessions to the niggers and give them a few little offices, but when we get the county seat at Hill City, they may go to ——."[28] Despite this prediction, Negroes became a political force in the county, gaining a number of important offices.

Nicodemus was not the first of the black colonies. In 1875 a Tennessee mulatto named Benjamin Singleton started Baxter Springs, or Cherokee Colony, in Cherokee County of southeastern Kansas. This small, energetic former slave had interested himself in western colonization for his people since 1869, and his name became the most familiar of all in this work. Far from being Exodusters, these people usually had money with which to buy land, and Singleton himself was essentially a land promotor, although he never admitted that his motive was purely economic. He always insisted that not only had he advised his people against going west without funds, but that he would not permit any of them who did not have some money to join any of his ventures. Later, in 1878, along with two other blacks named A. D. De Frantz and Columbus Johnson, he founded the Dunlap Colony, southwest of Topeka, in Morris County. Also referred to as the Singleton Colony, it was a larger endeavor, having some eight hundred settlers as opposed to the three hundred of Baxter Springs. These black farmers bought land from the government at $1.25 an acre, paying down one-sixth in cash and the remainder in six installments at six percent interest. During the first few years there was considerable friction between the black community and neighboring whites, which was characterized by a refusal to allow blacks to use white cemeteries. By 1881 the animosity reportedly had abated.[29] The Dunlap Colony was later chosen as the educational center for Kansas blacks. Located there were the Literary and Business Academy, sponsored by the Kansas Freedmen's Relief Association, two primary schools, and a Quaker-sponsored industrial school.[30]

In 1878 an effort was made to establish a black colony in Hodgeman County, about twenty-five miles north of Dodge City. The most convenient rail connection was at Kinsley (Edwards County), on the Atchison, Topeka and Santa Fe line; contemporaries sometimes referred to the settlement as the Kinsley Colony. There were 107 members in the original group, all from Kentucky, who were reinforced by an additional 50 later in the year. Being about thirty miles from Kinsley, they tried to start a closer town of their own, named Morton City after Oliver P. Morton of Indiana, but the task of town-building, while trying to eke a living from the tough Kansas sod, was too much. After erecting a frame building, intended as a store, and a few sod huts, they abandoned the project.

These colonists took up some fifty homesteads and a few timber-culture claims, upon which they constructed dugouts and soddies to shelter their families. Typical of the settlers was Lafayette Green, who lived in a fourteen-by-fourteen-foot dwelling that was five feet underground and two feet above, covered with some pine boards to keep out the weather. By the spring of 1879 he had only eight acres under cultivation, six in wheat and the rest in corn and a little garden. Although well water was available by digging about twenty feet, Green had hit solid rock at thirteen feet, and he had to carry water a mile to make his coffee. Nor was his domestic life very happy. Green's wife was sick, and their six children were all back in Kentucky, where they would remain until he had enough money to send for them. The small piece of property that he owned in Kentucky had attracted no buyers, and he was afraid to leave his new location for fear of not complying with the provisions of the homestead law. Lafayette Green had been very anxious to go West; now he was there, trapped.

The others were not much more fortunate. Those who had mules plowed a few acres and managed to plant a small crop. Others knifed a single furrow into the tough mat that covered the land, and tried to grow corn in these slits. A few brave souls chopped out little circles of sod by hand and watched in vain for corn stalks to sprout from the prairie. Before long they encountered further difficulties. As other settlers before them had learned, a minimum amount of cash was needed in order to make improvements and to buy food. Part-time labor was the traditional solution to this problem, and one means of earning money was to work in nearby towns. However, in this case such settlements were too far away. Harvest-time wages paid by neighboring white farmers brought from seventy-five cents to a dollar and a half a day, but such work was seasonal, and these farms often were some distance away on a thinly settled frontier.

Distance, that deceptive western trap, assessed its penalties in other ways. Coal hauled by wagon from the railroad demanded from seven to ten dollars a ton, a price that was burdensome to the poor of any color. Blacks, along with neighboring whites, scouted the countryside for buffalo chips deposited by passing herds. These, along with brush, twigs, or even dried grass, were burned in a desperate effort to coax out a little heat. Cupboard staples were equally expensive to bring in from any distance, and so the small streams were searched—frequently with success—for small fish with which to supply farm tables. The forlorn resident would not have disagreed with a correspondent from the Boston *Herald* who called the Hodgeman County colony a failure.[31]

In point of time the black colonies of Kansas generally preceded the exodus movement, and the people who inhabited them either purchased their lands or took up government homesteads. Most of them had some funds with which to move; they were part of an orderly movement westward, usually organized by Negroes, and they took up their new homes as a result of a planned, group migration. Quite different from the Exodusters, they had not fled precipitously or in panic from their former homes. Moreover, they held themselves apart from the penniless field hands from the deep South who constituted the exodus, and as a rule, they did not welcome these strangers to their settlements any more than any people who are dirt-poor welcome impoverished, hungry kinsmen who will have to be fed.

The fact that the Kansas Freedmen's Relief Association spent part of its funds in an effort to locate some of its charges in colony-type settlements gave rise to a confusion that exists today, that the Kansas Negro colonies were, in part, the result of this sudden and precipitous movement. An example of KFRA's efforts was the Wabaunsee Colony, which was located fifty miles west of Topeka in 1879 on 1,280 acres of university land. It was decided to provide for thirty-one families, the association making the necessary down payment, with users granted nineteen years in which to pay the balance. Barracks to house the newcomers temporarily were built by the association. But even here, Negro capitalism participated. Isaiah Montgomery, who once had been a servant of Jefferson Davis's brother but who later had become a prosperous southern planter, bought a section of this land for his own use and employed nine Negro families from his Mississippi plantation. By the end of 1880 the Wabaunsee Colony was said to be self-sustaining.[32] The Little Coney Colony, located in southeastern Kansas' Chautauqua County, was the last to be sponsored by KFRA. In 1881 that organization assisted fifty-six families in procuring land and the initial necessities of life required to begin settlement. With this effort the period of Kansas black colonies came to a close.[33] Despite this association between the organized colonies and the exodus excitement, they were of separate origins, and it is even logical to argue that the exodus effectively killed the colony movement.[34] The black colonists themselves were the first to make the distinction between the two groups, and even today if one talks to the descendants of those Kentucky Negroes who settled Nicodemus, he will be told in terms of great clarity that they were as different as black from white.

By and large, Kansans had no objection to the arrival of black colonists, provided that they either paid for their land in the manner of other settlers or took government homesteads without asking their neighbors for financial assistance. That these people tended to settle in groups, creating a voluntary segregation, also was entirely acceptable. But when they came in droves, big-eyed with fright, tattered and hungry and as dependent as children, the white community objected. It was flattering to think that the word "Kansas" equated with "freedom," and that these people used it as a symbol for the negation of tyranny and oppression, but the proprietors of that great sanctuary became uneasy when they suspected that it was being used as a dumping ground for the black dissidents of the South. While they were accustomed to excessive advertising, as practiced by the land boomers, the exaggerations of promotional literature did not, in their view, sift out and select the more "desirable" immigrants.

As the Exodusters began to pour into Kansas in alarming numbers, it was only natural that questions were asked as to the state's sudden popularity among southern blacks. Incoming Negroes made vague references to posters, handbills, and other bits of advertising that they had seen or heard about. Efforts to find examples of such broadsides usually were unavailing, and as the movement heightened, so did the efforts of Kansans to lay hands on the source of this publicity. Perhaps the best known of the circulars was signed by one Lycurgus P. Jones, who enjoined his readers to "show this circular to none but colored men, and keep its contents secret," thus explaining, in part, why it had become a collector's item rather early in the game.

When a New Orleans paper finally produced a copy of this rare document, it made public the promotional efforts of Lycurgus Jones, who may have been an imaginary figure:

(Strictly Private)
Attention Colored Men!
Office of the Colored Colonization Society
Topeka, Kansas

Your brethren and friends throughout the North have observed with painful solicitude the outrages heaped upon you by your rebel Masters, and are doing all they can to alleviate your miseries and provide for your future happiness and prosperity. President Hayes, by his iniquitous Southern policy, has deserted you, while the Democrats who now have control of Congress, will seek to enslave you if you remain in the South, and to protect you from their designs, the Colonization Society has been organized by the Government to provide land by each of a family, which will be given in bodies of one hundred and sixty acres gratuitiously. This land is located in the best portion of Kansas, in close proximity to Topeka and is very productive. Here there are no class distinctions in society; all are on equality. Leave the land of oppression and come to free Kansas.

Lycurgus P. Jones President[35]

The Kansas press had no clues as to the origin of the circular. An editor from one of the river towns puzzled over it editorially, remarking that no such individual was known at Topeka and that no society of such a character had ever been organized there.[36] The Topeka *Commonwealth* called it an "infamous document" and charged that it had been broadcast throughout the South to make money for its senders. It was generally known, explained the paper, that interested parties in the South were selling ostensible information to prospective emigrants as to "how their claims against the government for the promised farms should be prosecuted." The Jones circular was believed to be a part of this promotional effort.[37]

Handbills distributed in a Louisiana parish carried a glowing message of free land and of implements, provisions, and other necessities available on ten years' credit. Pictorially represented were enormous potatoes, apples, peaches, and a prodigious growth of corn, all the products of an incredibly rich western soil. The tangible results of such bounty were suggested in views of black men who rode about in carriages, smoking cigars, while toying with enormous gold watch chains.[38]

During 1879 the Brenham, Texas, *Weekly Banner* several times published a letter said to have been written by a Texas Negro who had gone to Kansas, where, upon arrival, he was greeted by the governor, congressmen, and other officials. After this official welcome, went the story, the newcomer was given a homestead and a subsidy with which to work it. Not only was this typical, suggested the writer, but it was only part of the hospitality accorded to migrating blacks. Others, he said, were given mules to work the land, five hundred dollars in cash, and were put up in first-class hotels while they awaited completion of commodious homes then being built by a benevolent national government. It has been suggested that the letter was written as satire, to make even the most gullible black realize the improbability of such conditions in Kansas, but if this was the case, the intention was not realized.[39] Restless and anxious to move, a good many of the unread and emotionally aroused plantation Negroes were prepared to believe such stories. When these fables were passed on by word of mouth, the land of promise was made to glow even brighter on a far horizon.

For the illiterates—and there were many—chromolithographs bore the same enchanting message. One of them, called "A Freedman's Home," depicted a charming cottage, gabled and with dormer windows, set off by a commodious veranda. Through floor-length French windows embellished by filmy lace curtains, one could view the Negro family relaxing at the close of the day, their castle drenched in the rosy haze of a breath-taking Kansas sunset. The father, presumably just returned from the harvest field, reclined in an easy chair, reading the *New York Tribune,* while happy children romped on the carpeted floor nearby. In one version of the chromo the owner's wife reclined languidly on a sofa, listening to the melodious tinkle of a piano played by her daughter. Another pictorial interpretation of black life in Kansas allowed the viewer to peer beyond the parlor into the kitchen, where the lady of the house directed a corps of servants and cooks who were preparing the evening meal. Beyond the settler's home could be seen a grove of shade trees sheltering a few well-fed deer, who grazed contentedly and awaited their appointed time at the family table. In another sector of the view, turkeys flew by at easy range, making it almost unnecessary for the master to take his shotgun beyond the shade of the veranda in order to bring down another juicy variant to an already rich diet. In the background, responding eagerly to the healthy rays of western sunshine, towered a luxurious stand of corn, whose stalks appeared to groan from their burden of enormous ears. Yet another version of plains paradise depicted "Old Auntie" at rest on the veranda of her western home, knitting stockings as she gazed contentedly upon herds of buffalo and antelope that fed just beyond the rich wheat fields. Approaching the gate of Old Auntie's domain was a black hunter, who somehow had managed to shoulder an enormous deer carcass, after which he had added a whole string of freshly killed wild turkeys. Literally smothered in wild game, he obviously had as his destination Old Auntie's larder, which already must have been bulging.[40]

Chromos, letters purportedly written by contented black settlers in the West, and oral endorsements by those who said they had seen the promised land—all were used to induce discontented southern field hands to pack up and leave. Negroes representing themselves as government agents or railroad representatives scoured the cotton fields, looking for countrymen who had the means to move. One "agent," using a chromo as bait, told credulous villagers that he had but a few tickets for Kansas, and they would go to the first comers. More gullible buyers paid a single dollar for a small flag that presumably would entitle them to free transportation north, where, upon surrender of the flag, they would receive free land. So popular was this offer in one Mississippi community that farmers began selling cows for two dollars apiece and chickens at a penny each in order to raise money for the venture. Before the "land rush" was over, nearly a thousand blacks had gathered expectantly to wait for a train that never arrived.[41]

Some of the prospective emigrants did not even get a small flag, worth about one cent, as a memento of their experience. Confidence men, both black and white, "sold" group passages to hopeful settlers and then left the country. For example, one of them visited St. Landry Parish, Louisiana, where he organized emigration clubs, the memberships of which ranged between fifty and a hundred persons. Each family, depending upon its size, was required to advance between ten and fifty dollars to cover transportation costs. Consternation reigned among subscribers when their white Moses absconded with the money. "He was last heard of in the town of New Iberia enjoying a glorious drunk," reported a Baton Rouge paper.[42] Near Meridian, Mississippi, one Daniel McKennan performed a similar service for those who were inclined to move. While his transportation rates were much more reasonable—one dollar each for adults and fifty cents for children—the results were the same. When the time came for departure, important business elsewhere required McKennan's pres-ence.[43] Another form of fraud practiced upon gullible Negro farmers was that employed by "agents" who promised, for a fee, to escort household goods, livestock, or other belongings through to the Kansas destination and to meet the owners at the end of the trip. Usually the baggagemaster was never heard from again.[44]

In time, reports began to filter back to the South from those who had reached the prairie paradise, and the accounts were not flattering. Some of the recent migrants, now disheartened, wanted to come home. Boston King wrote to his former employer, Isey Richardson, a Mississippi planter, asking for help. "My family is sick," he explained; "all of them is under the wether and if there is any way you can assist me in getting back i will work with you until i pay it." King's complaints were basic: he was going broke in Kansas. Another southern Negro, a schoolteacher who had gone north, evinced his disillusionment in more general terms. He said that he had expected social equality in Kansas, but he had not found it. Nor had he found waiting the free farm, house, and mules that had been advertised.[45] One of the exodus women, when asked why she did not go to work on a Kansas farm or as a domestic in someone's kitchen, explained that Kansas farmers used machines of which she knew nothing and that the plains farmers were not particularly anxious to have black cooks.[46] Henry Watson, who stopped in St. Louis en route to his former southern home, vented his feelings about Kansas. When he got back he intended to make a speech warning all who would listen not to look up river for solutions to their problems. He promised to tell his friends, "Don't fool you'selves looking to Kansas, or after a bettah place 'n you got now."[47]

When the Voorhees Committee interrogated some of the black migrants in the spring of 1880, it listened to further complaints. Hender-son Alexander, a former slave who worked on a plantation near Shreve-port, Louisiana, was one of those who regretted picking up his belongings at the age of forty-five and moving to a new country. He admitted that the talk he had heard about Kansas was so favorable that he decided to join the movement. Far from destitute, he had savings amounting to about $750, enough to provide train fare for himself, his wife, their two children, and his mother-in-law. Leaving a reasonably comfortable home, he and a party of his friends, about eighty in all, arrived in southeast Kansas at Christmastime, 1879. Almost at once the Alexanders decided that they had made a mistake.

"They had no houses for us," he explained later. "They had one house there, and every one of us had to get in that one house. We was all lyin' round there in a jam, and was in an awful fix there; my mother-in-law was sick." The Alexanders then tried to rent a house, but they found that Kansans wanted to sell, not rent. Meantime, crowded and cold, the family suffered; the mother-in-law soon died. "I had on good clothes, a big overcoat and overshoes . . . , but I couldn't keep warm nohow to save my life," Alexander complained. "I was done cold all the time." Trying to be objective, he volunteered the opinion that "Kansas is a good place, but it didn't suit me at all. . . . It is prarie and the wind blows there pretty hard, and I don't know what to think of the country at all."

Puzzled over his situation, and anxious to learn of opportunities, Alexander questioned some of his white neighbors about opportunities in this land of plenty. "I axed 'em how much money could a man make here in a year. Some of 'em told me he could make a hundred and fifty dollars; and they axed me how much I made in Louisiana; I say, some years I cleared five or six hundred dollars, and some years four hundred, and I told 'em I cleared seven hundred and fifty dollars this year." The astonished whites told the recently arrived southern farmer that he should have stayed where he was, and asked him why he had come to Kansas. Somewhat puzzled himself, Alexander could only mutter, "A man is free now to go where he please."

But to go "where he please" proved to be something less than satisfactory. "I got disheartened," he confessed, "and I wrote to Mas' Foster axin' him could he make me a situation, because I didn't like that country [Kansas]. . . . My family was in disturbment, and that kept me in disturbment, . . . and I jess had to pick up and go 'way." So, back to the plantation of James Foster he went, a disillusioned pioneer who, like many an American infected by a westering urge, had found the adventure more rigorous and less rewarding than he had anticipated.[48]

Philip Brookings, a former slave who lived at Yazoo City, Mississippi, was another of those bitten by the "exodus bug." Apparently he was another victim of propaganda, a southern farmer who appeared to have suffered from no particular economic or political persecution, but one, rather, who just had the urge to move.

"Well, we got papers down there, now and then," he explained, "and every time we read them, it was all 'Kansas, Kansas, Kansas.' It looked as if a man could just play wild out there, doing nothing, all but. I had been worth right smart, and had got broke; and as everybody was going to Kansas, and every newspaper we would get hold of said 'Go to Kansas,' because we could make so much there, and do this and that there, I concluded I would shuffle out and go there. There was a prospect of getting hold of a big thing, you know." He admitted quite candidly that the

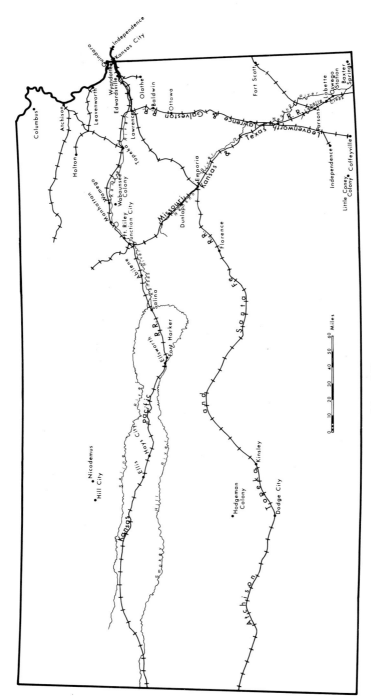

Map of Kansas

Life in the barracks at Topeka (1879) was austere and apparently boring, as witness the occupants, who seem to be waiting for something. *Courtesy of Kansas State Historical Society, Topeka*

Harper's Weekly showed its readers scenes such as this one depicting Exodusters preparing to leave Vicksburg. *Courtesy of Kansas State Historical Society, Topeka.*

ANOTHER STEP TOWARD CIVILIZATION.

Mr. Solid Brutus. "Why, Mr. Exode Cæsar, you are a Man and a Brother after all. So step into my parlor."

Of the numerous Negro conventions that met in the exodus year of 1879, the Vicksburg Convention was the only gathering that was managed by whites. *Harper's Weekly* for May 31, 1879, had some reservations regarding the sincerity of white southern planters. *Courtesy of Kansas State Historical Society, Topeka.*

reason he had "got broke" had nothing to do with racial prejudice or even southern economic conditions. He had a drinking problem, and it had destroyed him financially.

Brookings arrived in Kansas in January, 1880, and at once began to look for work. Finding none, he tried to survive until warmer weather, when farm jobs might be available. Fortunately, the early months of 1880 were relatively mild. Showing the abiding faith of his race, he attributed the lack of cold to heavenly intervention, remarking, "I suppose God Almighty knew how the poor negroes in Kansas was fixed, and so came between them and the north wind, or many a one would have been played out there before now."

In March, as the land began to thaw and farmers readied themselves for spring planting, Brookings scoured the countryside, making inquiries. All he heard was talk of hard times and little employment. "That is the result of you niggers coming out here; there is nothing here for white men to do; that is what makes it hard times," the farmers told him. Still hopeful, he pushed on, and talked to another farmer, who said he needed no help; he and his wife milked the cows and did all their own farm work.

Returning to town empty-handed, Brookings asked for help from "this refugee board," as he referred to the Relief Association, but he was told that he would have to live at the barracks if he wanted to be fed. When he declined to go, because the inmates there were dying at the rate of eight or ten a day, he was denied aid. Unwilling to return home, he stayed on, still hopeful. He tried to find work for another three months, most of that time being unemployed, but now and then getting a chance to earn a few pennies. "Finally I concluded it was time for me to light out of Kansas," he admitted. "I wanted to go home pretty bad."

But getting home was much more complicated than he had imagined. He had no money. Someone suggested that the Relief Association might be willing to provide aid for this purpose, and Brookings tried that source once again. "So I goes over, and blazed in there and spoke to a man, and says I, 'I cannot get anything to do; I want to go back,'" he told the Voorhees Committee; but the clerk showed little sympathy, saying that he had no funds for such purposes. When Brookings explained that he could not find work, he was told that he was not alone in that situation. "I stood there awhile, and by and by shuffled out," said the disgruntled applicant. The situation appeared to be impossible. "If I were back home I might get in a crop of cotton; but I cannot make enough here in the summer to carry me through the winter," he explained. "And in Kansas, if a man did not make money in the summer, he stands a darned poor chance in the winter. Let there come a few cold days, and they will run coal up to thirty cents a bushel."

About all Kansas had offered Philip Brookings was a chance to further reform himself. Drink, the demon that had undone him in the South, was out of the question for a man who did not have enough money with which to buy food. But now he would have given anything for one nip at the bottle. "In Kansas a man would need it if he could get hold of it," he remarked during a conversation on the subject of spirituous beverages, "for Kansas has the roughest wind you ever run across in *your* life." But even that solace was denied him. As he put it, "a man without money in Kansas totes a low head."

Supposing he made it back to Mississippi, would he keep his silence there, Brookings was asked? No, was the vehement response, he would not advise anyone to try Kansas. "If I see any of them that wants to break up and go to Kansas, I am going to use the best means in my power to coax them off from that notion; I will tell them that they might as well be in the middle of the Mississippi River when they could not swim a lick. I will tell them it will be a race which will they do first, starve to death or freeze to death."[49]

Washington Walker, a neighbor of Henderson Alexander's and a former member of the James Foster plantation, near Shreveport, was another of the "go-backers." But he did not return in bitterness. Walker, along with a great many southern Negroes and millions of westering whites, simply had thought that he could do better in the American West. By his own admission he was well treated in Kansas and was not particularly bothered by the cold, but he found the shift from cotton culture to corn farming a difficult transition. "I didn't think I understood that kind of farming," he commented. The experiment in testing more northerly climes cost him about six hundred dollars. His emigrating group consisted of ten members, all of whom returned. The others had not fared even as well as Walker, being obliged to husk corn at twenty-five cents a day. Their complaint was familiar: the cold and a lack of firewood.[50] They, too, were glad to return to the South, its limitations seeming to be much less onerous after viewing another part of the country.

Some of the Exodusters sought out the Negro colonies, hoping that fellow members of the race would welcome them. By and large, they were disappointed. William Nervis, who made his way out to Nicodemus, came away with the impression that it was a shabby little town in which there was no work for newcomers. There was no timber available for home building, and flat, forbidding plains country "gave him a chill" when he viewed it. Discouraged and sick, he made his way back to Wyandotte and took the first available boat down river. His view of Nicodemus was confirmed, in the spring of 1880, when a group of the town's residents petitioned Governor St. John for help, saying that they desperately needed clothing, provisions, and other supplies if they were to survive.[51]

Nor were Negroes in the white Kansas towns unreservedly enthusiastic about the migratory tendencies of their southern brethren. The *Kansas Herald,* a Topeka paper published by blacks, favored the movement as a matter of principle, but at the same time, it admitted, "we incline to the opinion that it is unwise for all the emigrants from the South to concentrate in this city." Indeed, continued the editor, the growing West was a fine place for home seekers, regardless of color, and he thought that there were many attractive places in other parts of Kansas to which the Exodusters might well go.[52]

Ministers of Negro churches, who usually took an active part in helping the arriving blacks and thereby witnessed a good deal of the suffering, found it difficult to share the *Herald*'s approval of the movement. One of them, in discussing the matter with reporters at Washington, D.C., described a recent trip to Kansas. Conditions there were deplorable, he said; he advised fellow members of his race to avoid the place if at all possible. Another, who lived in Fort Scott, Kansas, was much more outspoken in his opposition. "The man who tries to get our people to emigrate to Kansas," he wrote to a friend in Texas, "ought to be put in jail and stay there for five years." He regarded the whole movement as a cold-blooded, calculated fraud, of which the ignorant immigrant was the innocent victim.[53]

Kansas whites also voiced concern. Throughout the spring and summer of 1879 newspapers carried stories of drouth and of suffering among pioneers in the far-western reaches of the state. Referring to that area as "the frontier," a Kansas editor predicted that at least half of the present residents of western counties would have to be aided if they were to get through the coming winter.[54] But such admonitions to black frontiersmen were of no more avail than they ever had been when addressed to those who had made up their minds to go west. Once the movement gathered momentum, bad news was dismissed as ugly rumor, and happier accounts were accorded a degree of veracity. As if in answer to the warnings that spoke of difficulties in the plains country, the Exodusters sang a new version of "Dixie":

> Oh! I'se gwine to leave dis land ob cotton;
> Pork am sceerce, and I works for nothin';
> Away! Away! Away! Dixie land!

Dis Dixie's land what I was born in;
Tain't no place for raisin' corn in;
    Away! Away! Away! Dixie land!
Den I wished I was in Kansas
    Away! Away!
Wid Gideon's hand in Kansas land,
To lib and die in Kansas—
    Away! Away! Away up norf in Kansas.[55]

And so the flow continued. While many came in the hope of better economic conditions, others had even higher aspirations. One blind Exoduster, when asked about his motivation, explained: "Ise had a vision from de Lord, and he tells me to go to this yer Kansas and I shall git back my sight." Another, an old man suffering from pneumonia in Lawrence, Kansas, refused medical attention, saying to those around him: "Why bless you, chillen. De Lord has smiled on me, and I'll close dese old eyes in de land ob promise!"[56]

Considering the extraordinarily high hopes and the sometimes even childish expectations harbored by the Exodusters, it is surprising that the disappointment in Kansas and other plains states was not crushing. Yet, most of them stayed. Lacking adequate figures, we can only speculate about how many went home, but the available evidence suggests that perhaps the percentage was not as high as that of the whites who advanced westward and then retreated. A Mississippi tourist, visiting Manhattan, Kansas, in the spring of 1880, wrote that the Negroes were indeed disappointed in Kansas, but not to the extent that they were willing to give it up. "They have not realized what they anticipated," he wrote. "They are open in this expression—still I can't discover a prevailing sentiment to return. The older ones would like to return—the younger ones generally would not return. They all feel that they have made a leap, and must abide by it, as it is too far and too much trouble and expense to return."[57] John Milton Brown, of Kansas, agreed with that assessment. He admitted that the members of his race loved the southern soil and enjoyed its climate, but he added: "It is the greatest horror of their lives to mention the idea of their going back there to suffer what they have suffered in the past. They will not go back. They will die first."[58]

6

THE ELDORADO
OF THEIR FOOLISH DREAMS

Southern reaction to the sudden exodus of field hands was one of puzzlement mixed with resentment. The average white plantation owner or
businessman at first refused to believe that the movement was serious,
but when it developed into a rush and threatened to upset the local labor
situation, anger turned to concern and finally toward compromise.

During the first few weeks of the phenomenon the southern press took
a "good riddance" stand, maintaining that only the most shiftless of the
blacks were on the move and that they would not be missed. Memphis
expressed sympathy with the residents of St. Louis, who had taken the
first shock of the assault, one of its papers remarking that the migrating
blacks were without means, did not want work, and were indifferent as
to the future but were willing to take all the free food and clothing they
could get.[1] A foolish hegira, echoed other southern papers; a mindless
flight that would be of no help to its participants and one that would
benefit the South by ridding it of undesirables. In fact, said a correspondent of a Texas newspaper, southern whites should be happy over the
development, for, he argued, it was detrimental to a superior race to have
within it large numbers of an inferior race, particularly if the latter had the
ballot. He pointed to certain communities in Louisiana and Mississippi,
places where white residents appeared to be utterly without public spirit,
in order to demonstrate how an "inferior" people could act as a fungus
upon an otherwise healthy body politic.[2]

Let them go, let them find out for themselves, chanted the editors; the
flight of labor would cease once these people tried to make a living in a

cold, unfriendly land—the "Eldorado of their foolish dreams."[3] The southern blacks were utterly unsuited for northern industry and the northern climate, they asserted. One of them went so far as to predict that at higher latitudes the Negro race would be extinct within fifty years.[4] Less extreme was the prediction that ebb tide would be followed by flood tide, that within a few years the flow would be in the direction of the South, where the climate, the customs, and the general "take it easy" habits of the people were better suited to the nature of the Negro race.[5]

The "let-them go; good riddance" reaction did not conceal an underlying bitterness against the "ungrateful" migrants who were leaving hearth and home. Never, said a Louisiana editor, would southerners yield to the "insane demands of these clamorous tramps." By "insane demands" he meant the insistence of the blacks that they receive better economic treatment than the near-slavery of sharecropping and that they have some voice in the political life of the South. Maintaining that the blacks were the best-paid laborers in America, whose rights were in no way interfered with, he charged them with the desire to become "the rulers as well as the laborers." That, he said, would never happen.[6]

Despite this adequate return for their labor, complained the landowner, black laborers were irresponsible and inefficient. Too long, said one plantation owner, had these workers had their own way, cultivating the land in a makeshift way and impoverishing the white owners in the process. And now, said a Mississippi planter, these ingrates wanted to pack up and leave, abandoning the owners who had furnished them with work. In great disgust he charged that "of all the immigrants the Negro is the most improvident. He will rush anywhere for rations. If a boat should go along the river labeled 'To Hell—Free Rations' the Negroes would swamp it."[7]

From New Orleans came the prediction that Negro colonies were bound to fail because of an absence of white leadership. "When left to himself and withdrawn from the energizing influence of the white race the Negro is apt to degenerate rapidly," said the *Picayune*. "These colonies are excellent nurseries for habits of idleness and immorality. They are asylums for the drones who would avoid an honest day's work and live upon the fruits of more industrious people's labor." This mouthpiece of Louisiana's white establishment mounted a steady attack upon the exodus during the spring months of 1879, constantly sniping at it by means of sarcastic comments scattered throughout various issues.[8]

Yet another southern explanation of the difficulty was that the young Negro generation was at fault. Those holding this view argued that prewar blacks had been brought up in an atmosphere of discipline and work, that upon emancipation the former slaves had no great trouble getting along because they knew how to work and had continued to do so. But those who had been born since the onset of the war were said to be lazy because their indulgent parents had not required them to earn their keep. Wives of this new generation of men were charged with spending too much time indoors, rather than helping their mates in the field. Both sexes under the age of twenty-five were accused of idleness, of demanding excessive wages when they did any work, and of lacking any desire to accumulate worldly goods. "If wholly left to themselves it is a commonly accepted theory that the race would not improve but would gradually relapse into the aboriginal status," concluded editor George W. Lloyd of the New Orleans *Picayune*.[9]

Lamentations, hand-wringing, and philosophizing in the press probably did not affect the migrants' attitude to any degree; a great many of them were illiterate, and those who could read undoubtedly spent very little time digesting newspaper editorials. But the businessmen and community political leaders, whose views the editors appeared to be expressing, were in a position to take action. Since merchants and wholesalers did a considerable business with steamboat companies whose vessels worked the river between New Orleans and St. Louis, they were able to put pressure on the transportation firms.

Before the exodus was very old, charges were heard to the effect that riverboat captains were refusing to pick up migrating blacks at certain "hot spots" along the river and that merchants and planters had threatened to withdraw their patronage if they carried such cargo. The companies issued denials, quoting some of the captains as saying that they had not been hailed by anyone along the way, others explaining that their boats were filled to capacity and they could not take on more passengers without endangering the safety of the vessel. Management also denied any generally expressed threats on the part of merchants and planters to boycott companies whose boats carried migrating blacks.[10]

At the outset, some of the boat companies made their positions absolutely clear. For example, the Pool Line and the Bart Able steamers publicly announced that if Louisiana Negroes in the Red River Valley wanted to emigrate, they would have to walk, because "they did not intend to transport a single one of them."[11] Lines operating between New Orleans and St. Louis agreed to carry Negro refugees who had the necessary fare, but their schedules were limited, particularly with regard to stopping points. Captains carrying black passengers did not regard such places as Vidalia, Louisiana, and Natchez, Mississippi, as favorable ports of call. As one of them admitted, "By God, they have armed every white man there to mob the first captain that lands a boat there with colored people on board."[12] Steamers stopping at these places were extremely careful about the passengers they accepted. An Alabama editor who went up river in the spring of 1879 witnessed the tensions that had developed at such stopping places. As his vessel approached Natchez, he saw "hundreds of people" on the banks hailing it, but to no avail. When they reached Natchez, a great number of blacks tried to board the vessel, but the clerk turned them away, saying that he did not want any such passengers.[13] When another vessel, the *James Howard,* stopped at Vicksburg, a local planter threatened to hold the captain responsible if he took on more than the fifty deck passengers allowed by law. The captain confined his load to the legal limit. When the *Howard* reached Natchez, swarms of blacks, luggage in hand, poured onto its decks, but they were forced to go ashore at sailing time.[14] John Kemp, a schoolteacher from Greenville, Mississippi, was one of the lucky ones who made his way north on the *Howard.* He reported that crowds of Negroes lined the levees, most of whom, he thought, had no money; but money or not, the captain refused to stop when they hailed him.

The captains had an argument. Hundreds of would-be passengers waited along the river bank in places where there were no docking facilities. A great many of them were unable to buy tickets. Others misunderstood the whole situation. Alexander Yerger, a Mississippi superintendent of schools who traveled on the *Grand Tower,* talked with some of the blacks waiting at one of the landing points. They explained to him that they were trying to get to Kansas, where land was free, and that the *Grand Tower* was a government boat set aside for their use. They did not expect to be charged for their passage. Such beliefs were detrimental to the Anchor Line, testified one of its captains, because the impression was left among southern whites that the company was financially interested in the exodus. Yerger, as a witness to the movement, denied that this particular line refused transportation to anyone of any color who had fare money.[15]

Plantation owners, faced by a loss of labor in the critical planting period, did not always share the "good riddance" theme played by the newspapers. L. L. Tomkies, of Shreveport, Louisiana, openly admitted that he had tried to dissuade his field hands from moving. One of his employees had once lived in Missouri, near the Kansas border, and when the exodus began, Tomkies asked him how he had liked the northern climate. It was too cold, was the response, much too cold; he would never go back to such a place. With some encouragement from the owner, the former Missouri resident passed the word that Kansas was no place for a black man, that for about half of the year one had to melt ice in order to water the cattle. Tomkies felt that the story, spread among the workers, had saved some of his laborers during that spring of 1879.[16]

Matters were not so gracefully resolved in some of the other river communities. At Greenville, Mississippi, the mayor frequently ordered the dispersal of Negroes who gathered to plan for, or to participate in, the exodus. When A. K. McKelly of that city wrote to a St. Louis newspaper inquiring about the possibility of chartering a boat to take two hundred emigrant families to Kansas, he was arrested and held in lieu of $250 bond for inciting Negroes.[17] Arrests were made for more specific reasons. Merchants or planters who had advanced food and other supplies to neighboring black farmers were angered at the prospect of being left with bad debts. A Jackson, Mississippi, newspaper told of two field hands who had, in this manner, departed for Kansas. They were charged by a local merchant, returned for trial before a jury made up of two whites and four blacks, and convicted. At that point an angry mob of Negroes rescued the prisoners and set them free. Word got out that a mob of whites was on its way, determined to kill all those who had participated in the vigilante action. At a joint meeting of the races, hastily called, it was decided that the convicted men would be returned to the authorities. Tempers cooled; bloodshed was averted.[18]

While the southern press did not disguise the fact that the exodus movement had thrown some of the Negro cotton farmers into a near panic and that some of them were fleeing largely for this reason, it tried to stifle apprehension among the whites and to minimize fear among the blacks. During the spring months of 1879 the region's newspapers preached the southern-white point of view on their front pages and in their editorial columns. Whenever possible, papers quoted well-known southerners, especially when they expressed assurances that the movement was transitory and that its severest effects would be felt only briefly.

When Gen. P. G. T. Beauregard stopped at the Planters' House Hotel in St. Louis during April, he was at once interviewed on the burning question of the day. "Thus far it is only local, incited no doubt by disappointed local politicians," he remarked, "but the error will soon be discovered." He predicted that most of those who survived in Kansas would return home at the earliest possible moment. "Our Negro population is as well off as any laboring class in the world, and, if they could only be induced to work regularly and continuously, they and the planters would be mutually satisfied," he concluded.[19] Joseph E. Johnston, another former Confederate general, gave equal assurances that the movement was small

93

and insignificant. He thought that the Texas Negroes were relatively well off and that they would continue to prosper "if the Northern missionaries would only let them alone and not keep them all the time fermented and disturbed about taking them to some gigantic Eldorado where all is money, silk dresses and bliss." Soon, he said, the unhappy blacks would discover that the exodus was "all wind."[20] Meanwhile, a prominent Arkansas planter wrote that the Kansas "fever" was insignificant in his neighborhood, and he predicted that it would soon run its course.[21] A Mississippi planter reaffirmed that opinion, saying that fewer had departed the region than had been reported. A few families had left, he admitted, but in his view they were of the class that were "behind with their merchants for supplies, are shiftless and very poor workers, and scarcely ever accumulate anything, and hence from their very character are of little benefit to any community." The *Picayune,* of New Orleans, gave his letter a prominent place in its columns.[22]

Despite all disclaimers, southern planters were concerned. Although the press continued to discount Kansas and to predict that those who left the South would "sigh for the fleshpots of Egypt long before they reach the promised land," there remained an underlying feeling that all was not well in "Egypt."[23] The uneasiness pervaded all the way from Tennessee to the Gulf States. When a group of two hundred blacks left Tennessee late in March, a Memphis paper remarked that each grown laborer was worth at least $800 to the state, and hence it had lost over $150,000 by the departure of what it called "this advanced guard." The editor made an important admission when he asked, "What value will our lands possess when we no longer have laborers to cultivate them?"[24] Far from taking a "good riddance" attitude, Memphis openly admitted the danger to Tennessee's farm-labor supply, or what one newspaper called "skilled and valuable labor."[25]

Candid men in the deep South admitted that the exodus could hurt them. Four planters, interviewed by the *Picayune,* of New Orleans, in the early days of the movement, said that already some five thousand workers had left the enumerated parishes of Louisiana. As a result, they estimated that cotton production in that area would drop by fifty to sixty thousand bales. To stop the labor drain, they had reduced rentals and had minimized other obligations asked of the sharecroppers.[26] By circumstances, the restlessness among field hands had developed at a particularly awkward time for the landlords. In early March, 1879, a financial panic had closed the doors of several New Orleans banks. Other institutions retrenched and either tightened their loan policies or refused altogether to put up any more money, even on real estate security. Merchants, in turn, found it impossible to make advances on anticipated crops. Conditions in Mississippi were called "deplorable"; the state's credit system was said no longer to be functioning. Northern capital, frightened off by the disturbed political situation, had dried up. To make matters still worse, yellow fever had laid low a number of laborers.[27]

Prominent among the planters who sought to answer complaints of the cultivators was Col. Edmund Richardson, of Jackson, Mississippi. His agent, who called Richardson the "largest planter in the world," wrote to the St. Louis firm of Sells & Company, promising that rents would be lowered by twenty to twenty-five percent and that henceforth less would be charged for provisions. Furthermore, he said that money would be provided to send black representatives into Kansas, where they could see for themselves that the place was no paradise. The lien laws that had caused so much complaint would be revised; he admitted that they had been abused. The agent hoped that Sells & Company could persuade some of the arrivals at St. Louis to turn back. "If you can get any to return," he wrote, "I can speak for our interest; we will give them land already broken up, prepared for planting, good houses to live in, and let them have regularly every month twenty pounds of meat, one bushel of meal or a proportionate amount of flour, one plug of tobacco per week, and such clothing as they may need to keep them comfortable."[28]

While the black sharecroppers welcomed the prospect of lower rents— it would satisfy one of their great complaints—they preferred to become property owners. A New Orleans paper, recognizing this as one of the main problems, predicted that southerners would go a long way toward pacifying these tenants if they would sell them "their 40 acres, on a long term arrangement, thus binding them to the land." It also suggested that plantation owners form an organization that would have as one of its aims better conditions and more favorable arrangements for renters. Not only would such a group be self-regulating, but also it could put pressure on smaller landlords who habitually took advantage of the blacks. Something should be done to alleviate the general situation, warned the editor, or the South would continue to lose its laborers. High wages paid in western mines and the use of Negroes as railroad builders were cited as specific instances of attraction for dissatisfied field hands. At that time the Northern Pacific Railroad talked of employing some five hundred southern Negroes on its construction crews.[29]

So concerned were leading southern planters over the flight of the workers that they decided to meet and discuss the problem. The governor of Mississippi issued the invitation, asking for black as well as white participation. The stated object of the meeting, formally known as the

Mississippi Valley Labor Convention, was to "take steps to check the emigration of laborers to Kansas."[30] For this purpose the delegates gathered at Vicksburg on May 5. White management attempted to create an atmosphere of conciliation, brotherhood, and understanding; figurative olive branches decked the halls. In a further effort to reassure the blacks that all was well, the press published denials that the former slaves had anything to fear at Vicksburg. The whole aim, said one newspaper, was the desire of the white people to deal fairly with the Negroes, and it warned that northern newspapers surely would seize upon the situation to make their readers believe otherwise.[31]

The gestures went unanswered. The blacks were suspicious because it was patently clear which race dominated the proceedings. Among the various officers elected, the titles "general," "colonel," and "judge" abounded, suggesting that the establishment had the managerial situation well in hand. Henry S. Foote, the aging former governor of Mississippi, gave the keynote address. Faced by overwhelming numbers, the black leaders cautioned their delegations against voting on various issues on the ground that the convention was bound to fail and that when it did, the responsibility should belong to the planters.[32]

The white response to such suspicions was a collective cry of injured innocence and a plea that delegates refute the downright malicious and partisan falsehoods that were being circulated about white motives at Vicksburg. No laboring class in the world was better off, asserted one editor, explaining that this one had the full and almost unrestricted use of land and capital that belonged to others. Carried away by his defense of the system, he declared flatly: "There is no class legislation in Mississippi."[33] But he was unable to explain why farm laborers were departing in droves from this workers' utopia.

The Vicksburg opera house had been scheduled as a meeting hall, but when it overflowed, the meeting was moved to the more commodious Concert Garden. On the second day of the proceedings, Col. W. L. Nugent, of Jackson, presented five major resolutions to explain the reasons for the exodus: (1) the low price of cotton, accompanied by a recent partial crop failure; (2) an irrational system of planting; (3) the vicious credit system; (4) apprehension on the part of the Negroes, "produced by insidious reports circulated among them" that their civil and political rights were endangered; and (5) false rumors about rewards that awaited the blacks in Kansas. The committee making these recommendations took particular note of the fifth point, expressing astonishment that "the colored people could be induced to credit the idle stories circulated of a promised land, where their wants would be supplied, and their independence secured, without exertion on their part." Some five and one-half million acres of government land still were available in Mississippi, said the committee's chairman, land that could be secured for about eighteen dollars in fees when 160 acres were homesteaded. It puzzled him that anyone should leave when things were so attractive at home.[34]

A Jackson newspaper praised Nugent for his skillfully drawn resolutions, saying that they covered the whole question as well as renewing pledges of good faith in dealing with the Negro race. The editor candidly admitted that the pronouncements were intended to soothe the feelings of black sharecroppers, and while he hoped that they would be of help in this regard, he doubted that words would halt the flight of labor.[35] The prediction was born out; the Vicksburg Convention generally was regarded as a failure, simply because the various promises made were not fulfilled.[36]

Toward the middle of May a New Orleans black organization known as the Emigration and Relief Committee asked Henry Foote to address that group and to elaborate upon his stand at the recent Vicksburg gathering. There he had offered substitute resolutions regarded as favorable to the Negroes, but after a heated debate, they had been voted down. Convention participants, said the invitation, had failed to appreciate either the causes of the exodus or the seriousness of its probable results. Now the Emigration and Relief Committee wanted to hear more about Foote's stand, one that it called both "patriotic and practical."

On the evening of May 21 the former governor spoke to a group of some three hundred people at Lafayette Square, New Orleans. He said that he very much regretted the exodus, and he admitted that its rather sudden appearance had surprised him. He was critical of the Vicksburg Convention, holding that it had not correctly set forth the reasons for the flight of labor and that there could be no understanding of it at any meeting where there was not a free and uninhibited exchange of views. Even if only a small part of the injustices admitted at Vicksburg were true, he argued, the offenses were sufficiently serious to justify blacks' leaving the country. He accused congressional Democrats of attempting to pass legislation that would forever deny Negroes the ballot.

The *Picayune* was sharply critical of Foote's stand, and it accused him of being more anxious to learn why the recent movement northward had taken place than he was to find a cure for it. The newspaper contended that he assumed all whites to be wicked and filled with animosity toward the black race, that he thought it was impossible for the two races to live side by side. Foote was charged with making assumptions where he had no knowledge, particularly when he used New Orleans as an example of ill treatment of the Negroes. The *New Orleans Times* assumed an equally critical attitude toward Foote, calling him an old and scheming politician who had gone over to the blacks, one who had no right to criticize the white planters as he had done at Vicksburg.[37]

Late in May the leading cotton planters of Washington County, Mississippi, held a convention at Greenville and unanimously adopted a lengthy memorial designed for northern consumption. It was a remonstrance and a defense of the southern labor system as it existed, one that vigorously denied any mistreatment of the Negro, while at the same time criticizing those northerners who had attempted to interfere in local southern matters. Since the war, argued the memorial, black labor had been drawn into the Mississippi Valley, and very little of it had emigrated from that area. Of those who had left recently, many already were reported to be returning, a demonstration of the convention's belief that things were not so bad at home, which even the Negro was coming to realize.

The convention's memorial also spelled out the conditions under which the postwar blacks raised cotton. Arrangements with them were of three kinds: (1) a lease of land, payable in cotton; (2) contracts for work on shares, the landlord supplying land, teams, tools, and forage and the laborer providing his own subsistence, the resultant crops being divided according to prearranged terms; and (3) a simple system of wages paid to laborers. The Negro farmer was said to have had free choice as to the method selected.[38]

Further evidence of the wide unrest among blacks all across the South in the spring of 1879 and of the deep distrust that they had for resolutions emanating from white-sponsored meetings was seen in the number and the locations of gatherings that they called among themselves to discuss the problems of their race. In mid April a Little Rock, Arkansas, Negro convention passed a resolution favoring the emigration of its people on the ground that they were being denied their constitutional rights, and therefore, it recommended that they should leave the country.[39] During those same days, another convention met at the Free Baptist Church in New Orleans to discuss further the practicality of an exodus from the South. Here it was brought out that Louisiana Negroes had been talking of such a movement ever since 1874, ostensibly because of pressures that ranged from the threats to action by armed mobs against the Negro population. Delegates were told that blacks outnumbered whites more than two to one in some parishes, even though they never could carry an election in them, and that one way to be "free from shotguns" was to leave.[40]

98

One of the principal speakers at the New Orleans black convention was Pinckney Benton Stewart Pinchback, a very well known mulatto who had served briefly as governor of Louisiana (December 9, 1872, to January 13, 1873) when Gov. Henry Clay Warmoth was suspended from office during impeachment proceedings. This son of a white planter and his former slave was born free, his mother having been emancipated by his father, and he had been sent to Cincinnati when he reached high-school age, where he was given a secondary education. During the Civil War, Pinchback raised companies of black infantry and of cavalry. In 1868 he was elected to the state senate, becoming president *pro tempore,* and late in 1871 he served as lieutenant governor upon the governor's death. After serving briefly as governor during the Warmoth imbroglio, he ran for Congress and was declared elected, only to have his election successfully contested by a Democrat. In 1877 Pinchback left the Republican party, to support the aspirations of Francis R. T. Nicholls, who became the Democratic governor of Louisiana in 1879. Apparently as a reward for party loyalty, he became surveyor of customs at New Orleans, his last politically oriented position. Now, in 1879, speaking before the delegates at New Orleans, he pursued the Democratic line, advising his listeners not to leave, not to join this fruitless exodus, but rather to stay in the South, the home of the Negro. It was a position that the famed Negro abolitionist Frederick Douglass was to take, and for which both men would be sharply criticized by members of their race. Pinchback's listeners were in no mood for conciliation; on the contrary, they appeared to favor any action that would displease the South. When one member pointed out that the exodus could result in the loss of thirty-five congressional seats to the South—and hence, to the Democrats—there was applause, and the group closed its meeting with a determined rendition of "John Brown's Body."

New Orleans papers scoffed at the assembled blacks in their city, poking fun at the members who they said were not really delegates at all, since anyone who wanted to could attend. During the debates that ensued, said the *Picayune,* the chair threatened to call in the police to preserve order, a situation that the editor described as "rough and tumble" oratory. Aside from the local Negro Republicans, he said, the group consisted of "strays from the country who have come down here on various uncertain missions." Behind this critical editorial attitude lay the continuing fear of potential black political power. Only recently had the carpetbaggers returned north, surrendering the South's political apparatus to the white Democratic establishment, and now the new custodians of power did not want to be disturbed. The blacks, conceded the editor, were satisfactory laborers, and some of them might even make good neighbors, but he reassured his readers that these people were finished politically. "Black supremacy will not be tolerated here. The experiment has been tried, and the record of its failure is the foulest and bloodiest chapter of the State."[41]

Shortly after the meetings at Little Rock and New Orleans, a major black convention opened at Nashville, Tennessee. It was not a reaction to white-sponsored meetings, such as the one at Vicksburg, but rather a general gathering that had been anticipated by black leaders for several months. In its early planning stages, in meetings held at Washington, D.C., during February, there was little talk of emigration, and of course there was no mention of the exodus, which had not yet commenced. The main concern at that time was the desire to discuss the general condition of southern Negroes. At that time the Teller Committee, headed by Henry M. Teller of Colorado, was holding sessions at the capital in which testimony was being taken with regard to political abuses in the South, and the newspapers were filled with stories of the bulldozing of southern Negroes at the polls.[42] By the time the delegates gathered at Nashville on May 6, much had happened. Now, migration, as a solution to southern black problems, had demonstrated its political potency, and consequently it simmered near the top of the racial cauldron.

When convention chairman John R. Lynch, of Mississippi, opened the meeting, he denied that the exodus was a prime reason for the gathering. That movement, explained the prominent Negro politician, had not been anticipated when initial plans to meet were formulated, nor, he added, was it one of the chief objects before the delegates. That he was mistaken to a degree was shown when, in remarking that blacks should not leave the South unless they had a very good reason for doing so, he added that he would not advise them to stay if they were mistreated; at this admission, there was an outburst of applause from the audience. Further evidence that the exodus was an issue came when an Arkansas delegate proposed a resolution to the effect that blacks were an important element in American agriculture and that they should emigrate from the South to places where they might enjoy the fruits of their labors, as well as social and political equality. He proposed that one or two commissioners be selected from each state where oppression existed in order to form a national committee that would select new homes and make arrangements for moving families to them. He further suggested that the federal government be asked to support such a migration financially. Convention members responded by passing a resolution favoring emigration from the South and another asking for half a million dollars in federal money to carry it out.[43]

The attractiveness of emigration again was evidenced a few days later

The cover of *Harper's Weekly* for January 31, 1880, depicted a mythical station called Free Soil, Kansas, with an Irishman saying to an Exoduster (who is holding a carpetbag): "An' what right have you, sure, to be after laving your native place an' coming here? Spake!" *Courtesy of Kansas State Historical Society, Topeka.*

THE REAL ESTATE & HOMESTEAD ASSOCIATION,

WILL GIVE A

FESTIVAL

AT THE

Benevolent Hall,

Cor. Spring & Bass Sts., Edgefield,

Wednesday Night, Aug. 29, 1877

OUR PLATFORM

Peace, Good Will and Harmony to all Mankind.

OUR MOTTO

Sincerity of Heart and Not many Words Loudly Spoken.

This Association was gotten up for the benefit of the Colored Laboring Classes, both men and women, to purchase them large tracts of land, peaceful homes and firesides. undisturbed by any one. To do this we must be prudent and save our little means and blend together as a band of brethren and sisters; when we do this we will then march onward to peace and prosperity.

Addresses will be delivered by Members of the Association

Prices of Admission.
Adults, 15 cts. Children 10 cts.

Houston Solomon, Supt. | Washington Antony, Marshal.
Stokely Walton, Asst. Supt.
BENJ. SINGLETON, President.
ALONZO DEFRANTZ, Secty.

LeRoi, Print.

Mass meetings, such as this one held at Edgefield, Tennessee, helped to generate the rather small colony movement that preceded the exodus. *Courtesy of Kansas State Historical Society, Topeka.*

THE ST. LOUIS
COLORED MEN'S LAND ASSOCIATION.

The object of this Association is the purchase and improvement of lands for the mutual benefit of its members. At a recent meeting BENJAMIN SINGLETON and ALONZO DeFRANZ, were appointed Land Inspectors with instructions to report as early as convenient the location, surroundings, soil and price of desirable lands that may be purchased in Kansas or other States. We therefore, in that capacity, recommend them to all whom it may concern.

J. M. M. STOKES, PRESIDENT.
P. H. MURRAY, SECRETARY.

St. Louis, Mo., May 15, 1879.

A leaflet circulated to encourage the purchase and improvement of land.
Courtesy of Kansas State Historical Society, Topeka.

COME!

To the Colored People of the United States of America:

This is to lay before your minds a few sketches of what great advantages there are for the great mass of people of small means that are emigrating West to come and settle in the county of Hodgeman, in the State of Kansas—and more especially the Colored people, for they are the ones that want to find the best place for climate and for soil for the smallest capital. Hodgeman county is in Southwestern Kansas, on the line of the Atchison, Topeka & Santa Fe Railroad.

We, the undersigned, having examined the above county and found it best adapted to our people, have applied to the proper authority and have obtained a Charter, in the name and style of "THE DAVID CITY TOWN COMPANY," in the County of Hodgeman, State of Kansas.

TRUSTEES:

The Hodgeman Colony was the western-most of these efforts, and its members suffered from drouth and frontier conditions generally. *Courtesy of Kansas State Historical Society.*

when, at one of the sessions of the convention, the Reverend T. W. Henderson of Topeka was introduced as a delegate from Kansas. He received a standing ovation. Such a reception was not due to his popularity, he later explained, but because he was from Kansas, "which to the colored man of America is the grandest, greatest, and freest of all the States of the Union." He circulated among the delegates, 140 of them representing seventeen states, and answered questions about the western promised land.

In the main, the conventioneers took the stand that American Negroes still were in the process of emerging from slavery and that their efforts to gain the political rights accorded to them by law were being met with bulldozing and terror. The additional limitation of being held in the near-thralldom of sharecropping was yet another burden to be borne. Kansas, if it offered nothing else, promised land tenure.

Southern whites were warned at Nashville that they would have to execute an about-face on the Negro question, because if they did not, the former slaves would move out, and they would continue the movement until "there was not a black face in all that country." Delegates endorsed the Vicksburg convention, which was then in session, and expressed the hope that its white sponsors fully realized the seriousness of the situation. Privately, the Nashville group may have feared that promises made at Vicksburg would not be kept, but at least the resolutions passed in Mississippi indicated a degree of concern among white planters that had never before been so plainly evinced. Their apprehensions seemed evident to delegate T. W. Henderson, who read in a Nashville paper the accusation that he was a paid agent, sent to Tennessee to induce immigration to Kansas. His denials, of course, were futile.[44]

Despite efforts on the part of the convention's leadership to tone down the excitement over emigration from the South, the delegates continued to speak of it among themselves. J. W. Cromwell, a black clerk from the federal Treasury Department and secretary to the Nashville convention, remarked at the presistence of such talk. "I was surprised to find such a unanimity of feeling on the part of the conference in favor of emigration," he admitted. "There was a positive furore about it; so much so that some of the other business for which the conference was called could not be attended to." He estimated that at least two-thirds of the delegates favored emigration.[45]

Three more colored conventions that year urged emigration. A small group of about fifty met at Richmond, Virginia, late in May, where prominent Negroes urged their countrymen to consider the move to Kansas. At Houston, in mid July, an address to Texas Negroes was formulated and adopted, one that urged them to consider favorably any opportunity to migrate to any state where the rights of all citizens would be recognized. The delegates also recommended the appointment of a commission for each county to aid those who were seeking new homes.[46] A month later a convention of blacks at Terre Haute passed a resolution urging southern members of their race to come to Indiana, promising them assistance with transportation and employment.[47]

During the weeks in which the two races debated the matter of solving their differences, the southern press continued its campaign, which was designed to show that disaster awaited foolish blacks who left home in search of better things farther north. Not only was the "promised land" portrayed as a bleak and unfriendly place, but the passage to it was said to be fraught with peril. In the southern view, the first stop on the trek, St. Louis, was a major challenge for those who sought to complete the obstacle course to Kansas. "Of all the places on earth which friendless and forlorn and afflicted people ought to avoid, St. Louis is the first and foremost," said one New Orleans paper. "We know of no community which can treat unhappy human beings with such callous and consistent cruelty." That city now was labeled as a nest of drummers, a place where men would not risk a dollar unless assured of a profit.[48]

Nor was the next stop, Kansas City, much better. A former Louisiana woman wrote that never before had she seen so many Negroes in that city, most of them huddled together in helpless clusters. When she asked them about their condition, invariably they expressed a great desire to go "home."[49]

Conditions at Wyandotte, the port of entry on the Kansas side of the river, were painted in equally gloomy terms. That little place, said the *Picayune,* of New Orleans, was swamped by the Exodusters, many of whom now went from door to door, begging for a bite of food before going back to their cold, cheerless riverbank tents. Of nearly a thousand recent arrivals at Wyandotte, more than a hundred were reported to be sick, and twenty-five had died. They had expected a warm welcome, but instead they were met with "coldness and distrust." In summing up the situation, the *Picayune* concluded that next to the grasshopper plague of recent years, Kansas regarded the latest invasion as "the worst drawback the new West has ever experienced."[50]

Having described the approaches to this great western deadfall, southern editors now painted word pictures about the pit itself. They warned that ill-advised blacks who undertook this venture were almost guaranteed an early grave under the prairie sod. "It Is Certain Death" was the title of a Texas editorial that discussed the probable effect upon Negroes who bet their very lives against a Kansas winter.[51] Even so, warned the doom sayers, some might not survive long enough to make such a wager with the grim reaper; in all likelihood, many would perish from disease or hunger before autumn. By the end of April, asserted a New Orleans paper, fully ten percent of the Exodusters had perished.[52] As an example of how a race faced extermination in Kansas, the same newspaper described how a Negro child, "farmed out" by the Kansas Freedmen's Relief Association, had died of starvation at the hands of his new master.[53]

The usual testimonials were printed to support contentions that all was not well in the promised land. Gilbert Colyer, a Texan who had visited Kansas, now warned his brother in Georgia against making such a move. "If you can earn ten cents a day where you are, stick to it," he advised, for Kansas really was a desert in his eyes. "There is no wood and no water, except when the rivers are up in the spring, when the snow melts away up in Colorado." The free-land story was held to be a myth, and calling it "all a lie," he warned against believing stories of such government gifts. Some of the Mississippi and Louisiana blacks who had gone to Kansas, said Colyer, now were stranded. Without land, farming tools, or money, they had no means of farming. Therefore, he urged his brother to forget Kansas, adding that "the country is not worth living in, anyway."[54]

Having disposed of the gloomy economic situation in Kansas, southern papers addressed themselves to blacks who were anxious to migrate in the hope of finding racial equality. He who sought this quality of life, said a Louisiana paper, would encounter in Kansas "a settled, deep and incurable antipathy against him and his race on account of their color." Whites in that part of the country obeyed the "instinct of their race" in preferring people of their own kind as neighbors. Many of these people were from eastern states and from Europe; therefore, it was contended, they did not understand the Negro.[55] The young whites among them feared a reduction of wages when faced by black competition. In such a situation, blacks were bound to suffer; and in time they would fail in the new community, after which greedy whites would take over their abandoned lands and profit from them.[56] It was the same as California's "The Chinese must go" campaign, suggested another adviser to the blacks. That cry, he said, now was being applied to arriving blacks.[57]

While southern plantation owners no doubt appreciated the efforts of the region's press in their behalf, and they must have agreed with the bad reputation that editors sought to give to the black movement, at the same time they understood that action, not words, was called for. In April, J. B. Campbell, editor of the Vicksburg *Commercial*, sent a telegram to Kansas City officials, stating that money was available to pay the return fares of all destitute southern Negroes who had left home and now were ready to return. The message also promised political and civil rights to those who would resume their old addresses.[58] All during the summer of 1879 an agent, paid by southerners, kept offices in Kansas City, where any Exoduster who wanted to go home could pick up provisions and transportation authorization for the trip. B. F. Watson, a Kansas City Negro who later testified before the Voorhees Committee, said that a state senator from Louisiana had promised that he would pay him a bonus for every family he could persuade to go back and that he would furnish travel expenses, a work contract, and a mule to any family accepting such an offer. The catch, said Watson, was that the senator intended to charge one hundred dollars for the mule, the debt to be worked off in the fields. Almost no one agreed to these terms.[59]

Southern employers were too concerned about the loss of labor to give up because their agents had failed to turn the northbound tide. During August they underwrote an excursion to Kansas, one designed to let the curious—black or white—see for themselves. The cost of each ticket was only ten dollars. Led by H. J. Hubbard, of Jaynesville, Mississippi, a racially mixed party estimated at between four hundred and six hundred made the trip. The purpose of the expedition was to demonstrate the difficulty of life in Kansas in the hope that the returning travelers would spread the good word. Upon their return, Hubbard reported that Kansas indeed was a magnificent country, but he thought that it was not at all adapted for blacks who had been born and raised in the South. Admittedly, anyone who had sufficient funds to get a start might prosper, in time, but that ruled out any hope of success for the black emigrants who had arrived there lately, for most of them were poor. Those whom Hubbard had seen were mainly in the towns, and they were far from happy. Hungry and despondent, a number of them had expressed the desire to return, but they had no money. A few of them, with fare money, had come back with the excursionists. The tour leader assured his sponsors that the experiment had been a great success. He was convinced that the influential members of the colored contingent soon would pass along an unfavorable assessment of opportunities in Kansas and that the message would be sufficient to stop the exodus.[60]

To a good many white employers Hubbard's views were those of a theoretician. Not only did they doubt the workability of his ideas, but their innate pride balked at getting down on their respective knees and begging the errant field hands to come home and to discover that all had been forgiven. What they sought was a form of substitute labor, one that would work in the fields at low wages and would raise no questions about such matters as education, social equality, or the franchise. The West Coast Chinese, who were then under particularly heavy pressure in California, appeared to be a possible solution to the problem.

The idea was not new. Ten years earlier a San Francisco newspaper had noted the arrival of the steamer *Great Republic* with nearly thirteen hundred Chinese aboard, many of whom were said to be en route to cotton and rice fields of the southern states.[61] Now, a decade later, the idea was revived, and a sum of ten thousand dollars was raised by subscription among the planters in order to send a representative to the West Coast to commence negotiations. Worried landowners were happy to note that President Hayes recently had vetoed a Chinese anti-immigration bill, because they felt that Chinese labor, already tested in the cotton fields, could provide labor more cheaply and perhaps more docilely than did the unhappy blacks.[62]

Support for the notion that Chinese laborers had desirable characteristics other than their willingness to work cheaply came from John M. Greaves, a former Mississippian who had lived in California for nine years. "They are willing to work for a very small compensation, and they take no interest in politics, religion or educational matters," he wrote to a Jackson, Mississippi, editor.[63] Planters around Natchez were interested when one of their number received an offer from a New Orleans Chinese merchant in which he offered contract labor for as low as twelve dollars a month plus one and a half pounds of rice a day and fifty cents a week in lieu of all other rations. Workers could be imported for about forty-five dollars a head, a sum to be advanced by the plantation owners and then deducted from the workers' wages at the rate of five dollars a month.[64] The prospect of replacing black with yellow labor that promised to be as servile as the former slaves and had no "uppity" notions indeed was an intriguing one.

Despite the attractiveness of supplanting one color for another in the southern fields, at bargain-basement rates, the idea of inheriting California's "yellow peril" met with opposition among civic leaders, particularly in Louisiana. In the first place, they argued, California Chinese laborers, who earned between twenty and forty dollars a month, were not apt to work for ten or twelve in the South. The agents might be able to procure these human imports directly from China on five-year contracts for as little as eight or ten dollars a month; but this was another matter, one that might well meet with congressional opposition. The Chinese "Six Companies," of San Francisco, besieged with requests for cheap contract labor, denied that they had any control over their people's labor or that they collected the workers' wages.[65]

No thoughtful man who had at heart the welfare of Louisiana would approve of the scheme, scolded a New Orleans editor. True, a few large planters would be aided, and production might be increased, but these strangers would only lower the wage scale and make it hard on white labor. Worse than that, far worse, was the indisputable fact that these people were heathens, "incapable of moral instruction." Also, they had an additionally undesirable characteristic: they multiplied. Should this tendency to proliferate be allowed free rein, the day might come when all whites would be driven from the South, and the place might be converted into a Chinese colony. Even supposing that such a disaster could be headed off, these people still posed a threat because they carried "diseases of the most fearful nature." There were better choices, concluded the editorial advisers, alternatives that should be considered before turning to the yellow peril. But first, southerners would have to control "the unmanageable mass of ignorant [black] voters who constitute the costly legacy of war and reconstruction. When that shall have been done it will be time to consider the policy of importing a race vastly more alien than the Negro was, even in his aboriginal barbarism." Hopefully, however, that day would never come, a time that might see new hordes "suffocate European civilization" and inundate the place with "Asiatic heathens."[66]

After a good deal of soul-searching and no small amount of rationalization, southerners concluded that white labor was the answer to the postwar labor problem. They wanted settlers such as the West then was getting—people who would not merely squat and then move on, but rather the permanent, hardy types that were characteristic of the frontiers. Although southern leaders laughed at the naïveté of the Negroes who imagined that Kansans would provide quarters and provender for them as they awaited access to their new farms, these entrepreneurs suggested the same reward to whites who would settle in the South. The *Daily Picayune* argued that it would be "a wise investment for the people of Louisiana to establish here [in New Orleans] a free hotel for the reception and entertainment of emigrants for a time sufficient to enable them to find homes and employers." For about $120 a day, thought the editor, plain fare and shelter could be furnished to as many as four hundred immigrants. The state needed new and preferably white blood, he continued, for these people would be the producers of wealth. To show that the idea was practicable, the case of D. M. Lyle, of Rapides Parish, was cited. As early as 1872 he had experimented with white labor, having recruited twenty-seven families in Mississippi, and since that time his little settlement had grown, now having a church, a school, and other facilities.[67]

Another New Orleans newspaper published a letter from an Englishman named Joseph Butterworth, who described opportunities for whites in the new South to his friends in Lancashire. Good farms were available, he said, farms that could raise cotton, grass, rice, sugar cane, or corn, and they could be had for as little as five to ten dollars an acre. It would be a good opportunity for white men, he thought, because southerners had not been able to adjust to free black labor. "Without slaves, they seem incapable or unable to carry on any system of labor or society which does not depend on involuntary labor." As he saw it, the war had not damaged the land, but rather it had rocked the foundations of an old society, the members of which simply had given up.[68]

If western states, so successful in soliciting immigrants, were willing to invest money in order to attract labor, there appeared to be no reason why the South could not do the same. To make money, one had to invest money. Why not insert in the new Louisiana constitution, then being formulated, a provision that fifty thousand dollars would be paid to the first company bringing in thirty thousand white settlers? asked the *Times* of New Orleans. These thrifty whites soon would show their talent for productivity, new tax receipts would pour in, and the seed money would be returned. The idea was not accepted, since it was regarded as being somewhat impractical, but by the spring of 1880 the Louisiana legislature had created a Bureau of Agriculture and Immigration, the purpose of which was to encourage white settlement. Backers of the idea expressed their approval but said that the annual appropriation intended to support the bureau was too small; the legislators were urged to think bigger.[69]

Although southerners preferred Protestant white immigrants, they were willing to settle for less. In a pinch, Irish would do, despite the infection of papism that they carried. In any case, said a New Orleans newspaper, Irish were arriving in this country in large numbers, particularly in such places as New York City, and the bulk of them were laborers. They were fairly intelligent as a class, conceded the editor, certainly of higher intellect than the Negro; and if they stayed around eastern cities, they would eke out only a bare living; certainly the South offered more.[70] No mention was made by the press about the fact that many southern field hands were barely making a living. Apparently it was assumed that the Irish would be industrious, thrifty, and consequently prosperous.

There was yet another option. If one wanted residents who were known moneymakers and hence a rich source of taxation, certainly the

Jews qualified. In an editorial entitled "Jewish Progress in the South," the *New Orleans Times* announced that no group was more warmly welcomed in Dixie. Its members, who knew the meaning of the word exodus, were promised that they had nothing to fear, for in this modern age the South was said to be a place that condemned and avoided all prejudice toward them. "The southern people, who are much opposed to ostracism and exclusiveness," unblushingly asserted the editor, "have ever extended the hand of fellowship to this race." New Orleans retail business was "strongly represented by the Israelites in this city," he explained. They were prominent among cotton factors and commission merchants, one firm alone receiving annually as many as 125,000 bales of cotton.[71] The *Times* editor did not explain how a Jewish influx would solve the labor problem; certainly those who came would not be attracted to the cotton fields.

But the spring of 1879 was not a time for contemplation or deep reasoning in the agricultural South. The chaos of Reconstruction and the thorough disruption of the laboring force brought on by emancipation simply was intensified by a lingering dissatisfaction among black laborers, some of whom had chosen to flee. Southern whites looked on with puzzlement and increasing concern, for never before had they faced a problem quite like this one.

7

THE TRUMPET-TONGUED
EDICT

The South's annoyance at the disruption of its agricultural labor force, as occasioned by the exodus, was received with grim satisfaction among northern reformers. Those whose hatred for the proud southern Bourbons burned as brightly as ever and those who suspected that a military victory had been thrown away in the political compromises that resulted from the disputed election of 1876 took comfort in any ill fortune that befell the southern white establishment. Old-time abolitionists, many of whom shared the belief that emancipation, as a war aim, had become the real "Lost Cause," were convinced that these suspicions were correct, particularly as they watched what they called the Confederate Brigadiers in the Democratically controlled Congress try to repeal the "force bills" enacted during the Republican-dominated Reconstruction years. The flight of the blacks in the spring of 1879 was yet another proof to them that the former slaves were victims of a new kind of bondage, if, indeed, they had ever escaped from the old.

Shortly after the close of the Civil War the American Anti-slavery Society terminated its operations, but that did not place these militant reformers in limbo. With the emergence of the Reform League in 1870, personnel from the old group now joined in the movement to aid the American Indians. This new interest did not mean that they had given up their fight in behalf of the Negroes. Such men as William Lloyd Garrison and Wendell Phillips, both of whom devoted a good part of their later years to the plight of the Indians, continued to be remembered first and foremost as abolitionists. Garrison died in 1879; Phillips, five years later;

but to the very end they were faithful to the original crusade, that of the American Negro.[1] It was a fitting conclusion to Garrison's career that in the final months of his life he was active in stirring his followers to espouse the cause of the Exodusters.

Boston, a place where moral nerve ends lay extraordinarily close to the surface, responded quickly to reports of fresh black discontent in the South. When Gov. Thomas Talbot called for a meeting at Faneuil Hall, to be held at noon on April 24, the concerned—both black and white—flocked to that venerable meeting place, ready once more to take up the cudgels in the cause of right. Former political luminaries occupied places of honor on the platform. Nathaniel P. Banks, one of the Civil War's better known "political" generals, was there; so was George S. Boutwell, who had served in Grant's cabinet as secretary of the treasury. Both men formerly had been congressmen and governors of Massachusetts. Banks had retired from Congress only a month earlier, having been defeated after serving nine terms.[2] Boutwell was an out-and-out Republican Radical; Banks was not, but he had come perilously close to being converted.

Boutwell, who was the main speaker at the Faneuil Hall meeting, recalled an earlier occasion in that same building, a September, 1864, gathering called to celebrate recent victories at Atlanta and Mobile Bay. "No one then foresaw or imagined that in less than fifteen years those victories would be followed by the enforced expatriation from their homes, from the scenes of their childhood, from the graves of their ancestors . . . of those who . . . gave cups of water to famished heroes by whose toils, sacrifices and suffering the victories were won," he now told an emotionally charged audience.[3]

Banks, whose public career was at an end and who stood on the precipice of a rapid slide into obscurity, must have found solace in the excitement of the moment. The old politician, who had begun his career as a Democrat and who had once shunned the Garrisonian abolitionists, now stood before them, ready to lend a hand to the former slaves. Those who were not in flight, he charged, were victims of southern cruelty and persecution, poor Americans who needed a helping hand in their quest for new and better homes. He praised these unhappy people, saying that they were a strengthening element in society, one that would contribute to any part of the land to which they might go, and he congratulated the old Slave State of Missouri, and St. Louis in particular, for helping them on their way. How could Boston fail to do any less than St. Louis in the good work at hand? he asked the cheering crowd.[4] Warming to the applause, Banks made his final gesture to the veteran abolitionists. It was true, he told them, that the former slaves had been emancipated; but they were not yet completely free. He suggested that the cause was not dead, the battle not yet decided, and he inferred that he was ready to join the troops in their continuing war on inequality.

He was a little late. Those who heard him might have remembered a time, a quarter of a century earlier, when the Massachusetts congressman had told his colleagues that with regard to slavery, "We will give it the protection it has by covenant." Perhaps some of them had not forgotten that he had opposed Eli Thayer's idea for Free State emigration to Kansas and that he had openly denied any connection with the underground railroad.[5] But now it was 1879, and the intervening years had taught the speaker much about the political potency of the abolitionist cause. He assured those who crowded into Faneuil Hall, once more to take up moral arms, that there was nothing wrong with an emigration to Kansas; it was a movement of black Americans who were following a "peculiar American example" of choosing the place in which one preferred to live, of leaving old haunts where conditions had become intolerable.[6]

Members of the audience who represented the hard-core radical group, extremists who consistently had opposed the "soft" treatment accorded to southerners and now feared that, indeed, the South was rising again, took satisfaction in the attacks leveled at the enemy. The atmosphere was reminiscent of the old days when Garrison shot his verbal thunderbolts into the Devil's camp and martyrs sprang full-blown from New England's soil. Although the aging Garrison was not present in the flesh, he was there in spirit. In a letter addressed to the gathering, he called for action. "Let the edict go forth trumpet-tongued," wrote the old agitator, "that there shall be a speedy end put to all this bloody misrule; that no disorganizing southern theory of states rights shall defiantly dominate the federal government to the subversion of the Constitution; that millions of loyal colored citizens at the South, now under ban and virtually disfranchised, shall be put in the safe enjoyment of their rights—shall freely vote and be fairly represented just where they are located."[7] Although Garrison publicly thanked individuals who had contributed relief money for those "afflicted colored refugees from southern barbarity and oppression" and personally contributed twenty dollars to the cause, he did not regard flight as the answer to the southern Negro's problem.[8] That would have been to run away from the fight and to have surrendered the ground to the white establishment. Such could never be a Garrisonian solution. A month later, on May 24, the old warrior was dead.

Absent also was John Greenleaf Whittier, whose trenchant pen had found its place in the front line of the abolitionist literary battle. Writing from his home at nearby Danvers, he had asked that his name be added to the meeting called "in aid of the colored emigrants from the bulldozed South."[9] Although he was never to take an active part in the exodus movement, he approved of Governor St. John's efforts, calling the Kansan a man of whom any nation might be proud and one who deserved "the thanks and commendation of all good and human men."[10]

Those who were disappointed by the absence of another veteran campaigner, Wendell Phillips, would have their chance to hear him soon. On the evening of June 24 he spoke to some twelve hundred whites and blacks gathered in Boston's Tremont Temple. As in days of old, he drove the crowd into a frenzy as he taunted the South, criticized a do-nothing Congress, and waved the bloody shirt. "Are the Negroes free? Was there ever a rebellion? Did Lee really drive Grant out of Virginia, and was it Jefferson Davis who pardoned Abraham Lincoln?" he asked. What of the war dead? Had their sacrifices gained anything? Did the American flag really fly over the land between the Lakes and the Gulf, or had the South won? Then, turning to what he regarded as the South's latest crime against the Negroes, he asserted that in an earlier day, New England had saved Kansas from "a pirate nation conspiring to sell her to shame," and he asked his listeners if they thought that the sons of such men would be wanting in this similar emergency. No, he answered for them, "We shall save the nation in spite of Washington. The flag does mean liberty, and the half a million men who once carried it to the Gulf still live to see that the Negro shall yet find it so."[11] It was, as a New York newspaper commented, a speech that rang "with the old eloquence that denounced the murder of [abolitionist Elijah P.] Lovejoy, and demanded the emancipation of the blacks long before the North had begun to dream that emancipation was possible."[12]

The northeastern press picked up the excitement generated by the emotional scenes at Boston, and it whipped righteous indignation into firm resolves that the flight must go on until total emancipation was achieved. Once again the New England conscience was pricked, and financial contributions began to accumulate to carry on the next campaign in bleeding Kansas. An Augusta, Maine, editor, who was still at war with the southern white establishment, editorially charged southern congressmen with holding the blacks in thralldom, and reminiscent of William Seward's "higher law," he predicted that "a wiser power than theirs is preparing the way of deliverance." Let the exodus continue, he recommended, for surely it would result in a curtailment of southern political power and wealth. In words as militant as those used by abolitionists a generation earlier, he told his readers: "This must be a free country, in fact as well as in name, and they who fight against it will be ground to

112

powder in the conflict." He recalled that in the 1850s Kansas had helped to focus national attention upon the problem of slavery, and events there tended to eliminate northern indifference to the plight of the blacks. Once again, he reminded his readers, the nation was moved by the condition of southern Negroes and their attempts to find refuge in "free" Kansas. The present movement, he concluded, "seems to be directed by the same hand that led the Israelites out of Egypt."[13]

His colleagues found no argument with such strong talk. Southern field hands indeed were fleeing from persecution and violence, from "political and social proscription," wrote another Maine editor.[14] It was a clear case of political bulldozing and a generally iniquitous treatment of the blacks, said another; but the heartless southerners had overshot their mark, and now their victims were fleeing the scene of such cruelties.[15]

In the months to come, these editorials, supplemented by lengthy news items that described various indignation meetings, stirred the soul of New England. Mrs. George L. Stearns, of Medford, Massachusetts, contributed one hundred dollars for "these victims of Southern oppression and madness." She recalled that in 1856 her husband had worked without rest eighteen hours a day to secure the soil of Kansas from the clutch of the slaveholders, "little dreaming that the day would ever come when the slaves themselves would be seeking an asylum within its hospitable borders."[16] A spinster from North Brookfield, Massachusetts, found release in the renewed crusade. Admitting that her spirit had been stirred to its depths after reading about the refugees, she offered to enlist for the duration. With reference to her home state, she told Governor St. John: "We are liberal, we are wealthy, we have strong sympathy with suffering and I feel we are ready to help." In fact, the lady already had gone to war. She haunted the offices of a local boot and shoe manufacturer, demanding that shipments of footwear be dispatched at once to Kansas for the unfortunate blacks. Philanthropic movements of such magnitude rarely came along, she thought, and this one was of the very highest order, one that bore the celestial seal of approval. "Is not the hand of the Lord in it?" she asked St. John.[17]

The Reverend Joseph Cook, of Boston, could have given her a reassuring answer. Yes, indeed, the hand of the Lord was in it, the minister had decided. All the biblical implications of the exodus made it a fit subject for one of his regular Monday-night lectures. He asked Governor St. John for documentation of the suffering then being experienced in Kansas, anything that would show "what extortions the refugees had suffered." He understood that the governor "had a bushel or so" of such papers. They would be put to good use, Cook promised, for about one hundred thousand copies of his addresses regularly appeared in news-papers.[18]

Boston's Republican newspapers readily printed any items that related to the exodus. For example, they were quick to publicize activities of local Negroes, such as the meeting of black women held at a neighborhood Baptist church late in April "for the purpose of organizing aid to the refugees."[19] Also given notice was a heavily attended gathering of Negroes at the African Methodist Church, where speakers condemned post–Civil War governmental policies that, among other things, allowed men to serve in Congress "who long since should have paid the penalty for treason at the end of a rope." When a minister from Chelsea averred that all southern lands should have been confiscated at the end of the war and then divided among soldiers and freedmen, he received a storm of applause. More cheers followed when he approved of the exodus on the ground that the outward flow of southern blacks was bound to reduce southern representation in Congress.[20]

Both critics and supporters of the movement had to admit that Boston was an excellent cockpit in which to conduct the fight. When Charlton Tandy, of St. Louis, and Richard T. Greener, the first Negro graduate of Harvard who was later dean of Howard University's law school, went to Boston to collect money for the refugees, a St. Louis paper said that they had picked the right place to start, since it was there that remnants of the old New England Anti-slavery Society still lingered. The editor men-tioned Garrison and Phillips, and he suggested that the collectors might well stop off at Brooklyn and tap "Brother [Henry Ward] Beecher" for a few dollars.[21] It was true, Boston for years had been a good hunting ground, but as a rule, it is not the orators who have money, as was now shown when H. P. Kidder of Kidder, Peabody & Company produced one thousand dollars for the cause.[22]

As the exodus continued and stories of suffering in Kansas became a steady fare for newspaper readers, there was a general response from New England and the eastern seaboard states. The action taken by a mass meeting held at Topsham, Maine, early in May, 1879, typified the concern of New Englanders. Contending that the North had an obligation to aid those whom it had set free, that group created a committee "to extend assistance to the freedmen struggling for true liberty."[23] At other meetings held in Maine, important names were brought forward to indicate the significance of the cause. Former Vice-Pres. Hannibal Hamlin and Sen. James G. Blaine were identified as officers of a society whose aim it was to "help the Negroes run away from the South and to collect money to support them in the North."[24] William Scott, identified as a black resident of the South, described conditions in his area and told a large and attentive audience of the resultant exodus.[25] The publicity and the emotional impact produced by these meetings yielded some surprising results. Ann F. Jameson, of Rockland, Maine, offered to give all of her worldly possessions to the cause. She informed Governor St. John that she had willed any money realized from her property to a fund that would be used to purchase land and homes for the Negro refugees in Kansas.[26]

Not everyone was prepared to make a philanthropic gesture of this dimension, but stout hearts marched in the ranks of the Christian soldiers, and they did their bit. William Chase, a Quaker from Salem, Massachusetts, was so moved by newspaper stories about Mrs. Comstock's efforts that he began to collect all the clothing he could lay hands on for use by the freezing blacks in the West. "I have had the great satisfaction," he told St. John, "of packing with my own hands twenty-three large sugar barrels, and six flour barrels well filled with good clothing, new and old, boots, shoes, hats, stockings, mittens, gloves etc." for the needy. In addition, he and his friends sent forward $434.[27] A contributor from New Milford, Connecticut, gave $25 to help "the poor abused people," in the hope that it would help them to "escape from the bondage they have endured."[28]

The academic world, whose normal response to any problem is the formation of a committee, was in true form at New Haven. Eugene D. Bassett wrote to St. John, saying that he and Leonard Bacon and Cyrus Northrup, of Yale, formed a group appointed to solicit aid for the Exodusters. He wanted to know how many people were to be helped, if their need was urgent, and what kind of assistance was wanted.[29] Brown University was represented in the movement by its president, who presided over a mass meeting held in the Statehouse at Providence, Rhode Island, in mid May, 1879. The effort produced a sheaf of resolutions and some promises, but no money. However, the Congregationalists of Newport, Rhode Island, later helped to rectify this deficiency by collecting $149.62, as well as nine barrels and two boxes of clothing. The Reverend Van Horn, who sent the contributions to Kansas, assured St. John that the people of New England were "in full sympathy with you and your praiseworthy efforts in looking out for these needy people."[30]

While Van Horn did not speak for all New Englanders, he represented the opinion of a militant and vocal portion of them, a group whose cause was taken up by, or at least recognized by, certain elements of the press. The *Boston Evening Transcript,* for example, seized upon the exodus as an example of southern indifference to the plight of black farmers. It warned that "the employers of labor [in] the South have, or soon may have, the alternative before them to treat the blacks as though they were whites, in respect to legal and political rights, or their fields may be left unto them desolate." It predicted that the movement "will do more to set affairs right in the bulldozed localities than anything that has occurred." To the editor the migration was explained by the fact that when conditions become intolerable, people move, in the belief that conditions can be no worse, no matter how strange the new land of their choice.[31] It was a story not confined to black Americans.

In addition to a series of pro-exodus editorials, the *Transcript* gave a prominent place to an article written by David Ross Locke, who, under the pen name Petroleum V. Nasby, had gained fame as a humorist. One of the most notable of his followers was Abraham Lincoln, who was fond of quoting Nasby. In this case, Nasby wrote from a mythical location known as "Confedrit X Roads, Kentucky," explaining that "the entire colored populashen hev been notified that they can't go and must live with us, and enjoy here the blessings of freedom. But they keep slippin' off all the time, and there is the doleful prospeck of the Corners becomin' deserted from the want uv labor." Although the *Transcript* gladly gave the piece a full column, to underscore its belief that the South was being stripped of its labor by the exodus, Kentucky was not the best place for the author to have located "Confedrit X Roads."[32] A good many Kentucky Negroes had moved to the West, but this movement owed more to the promotional efforts of "Pap" Singleton than to unhappy conditions at home. Most of those from Kentucky had money with which to buy land, and those who did so, at such places as Nicodemus, Kansas, would have resented any inferred connection with the impoverished refugees of Mississippi and Louisiana who were so heavily represented among the Exodusters.

The willingness of the Radical Republicans, particularly those in the Northeast, to espouse the plight of the Exodusters suggests the existence of a collective sponsor in search of a cause. In 1877 George W. Julian, the Indiana Radical Republican, had lamented that "there is no moral tone in either party and the spectacle is sickening." In his book *The Radical Republicans* (1969), Hans L. Trefousse quoted Julian and concluded that "it was evident that the crusade against slavery and its aftermath was over."[33] Not quite. Some of the old warriors still were around, unconvinced that the North had won the war. Their restlessness at the political resurgence of the South, as shown by events that followed the contested election of 1876, was shared by the Republicans in general. Thoughtful politicians wondered if the old abolitionist refrain might not be dusted off and played once more, this time in the election of 1880.

Moral concern, that powerful weapon so well understood by practical politicians, was resurfacing before the exodus began. That movement now was used by proponents of black civil rights as proof that a form of slavery still existed in the South. In February, 1879, J. D. Hayes, who was described as a "young colored orator and Vice President of the Young Men's Christian Association," argued the case in a lecture delivered at the Shiloh Presbyterian Church in New York City. The title of his address was "The Modern House of Bondage; or, The New Enslavement of the American Negro." While he did not advocate emigration as a solution to the problem, but rather argued that the members of his race ought to elevate themselves through education and technical training, his concern for black Americans was given a prominent place in the city's press.[34]

Those who supported the lecturer's contentions as to reenslavement openly admitted their fears of a resurgence of southern whites. The *New York Tribune* lamented the fact that in 1879 nineteen former Confederate officers sat in the United States Senate, as opposed to only four from the Union ranks. If the Union soldiers, while fighting to put down the Rebellion, could have foreseen this, how unhappy they would have been, said the editor.[35] During that spring, northern papers repeatedly alluded to the congressional power of the "Confederate Brigadiers," and they urged voters to support Republican candidates.

In effect, a militant body of northerners, led by the old-time abolitionists, for some time had been awaiting a change in order to administer an emotional recharge to their cause. The exodus provided it. In April, 1879, as stories of suffering along a new "Trail of Tears," this time to Kansas, began to be publicized in the Northeast, very little drumbeating was necessary to get a turnout at indignation meetings. That month, nearly a thousand people, most of whom were black, attended a gathering sponsored by the Zion Methodist Episcopal Church in New York City, where speakers gave their views on the hegira. Listeners heard devastating criticisms of southern conditions, of reenslavement, of bloodhounds and murder in the night. One speaker, who asked the audience to remember the Fort Pillow massacre during the war, where a number of black Union soldiers had been slaughtered, openly called the assemblage an antislavery meeting. Another urged blacks to emigrate westward—to Kansas, or even Arizona and New Mexico. In the last-named, he predicted they would find employment in railroad construction and in other fields. Black settlers, argued the speaker, not only would benefit both the race and the country to which they went, but they would help to keep out the Chinese, who were then regarded as a threat to American labor.[36]

Thus, in late April, the New York stage was set for an old-time reform gathering. Appropriately it was held at Cooper Institute, where many a cause had been launched. A New England newspaper recognized the historical import of the scene when it commented that "something of the old sympathy for the oppressed and devotion to human rights begins to make itself heard and felt throughout the loyal North, and it is inspiring to read of the great gatherings in Cooper Institute, New York . . . and Faneuil Hall, Boston . . . to give expression to public sympathy for the persecuted colored people of the South who are now fleeing from what has been to them worse than a land of bondage."

The Cooper Institute meeting was replete with performers and props. Thurlow Weed, the hardened old Republican war-horse from Albany, was on hand to "ask the assistance of the whole northern people, without regard to color, in this great struggle of the colored race to better their condition and find for themselves homes and liberty." Present also were Charlton Tandy, of St. Louis, and Professor Richard Greener of Howard University, who were then making the rounds of the East to collect money. Wendell Phillips, in poor health, sent his regrets, along with a few literary hand grenades to be tossed in battle. "Leave the tyrants and bullies to till their own soil or starve while they do nothing but wrong and rob their laborers," he wrote. "Without laborers the Southern acres are worth nothing." So far as Phillips was concerned, the tyrants and bullies were lucky to have any land to till. He thought that treason ought to have been punished by confiscation and that southern lands "should have been divided among the Negroes, forty acres to each family, and tools—poor pay for the unpaid toil of six generations on that very soil." Considering the degree to which the Negro had been reenslaved by the former Confederate, Phillips concluded that "we all see now that magnanimity went as far as it safely could when it granted the traitor his life."

A fellow trooper, William Lloyd Garrison, also was unable to attend. But in his final weeks on earth he was still waging war, and he wrote a bitter attack upon the South for the benefit of the audience. "It is clear that the battle of liberty and equal rights is to be fought over again," he predicted. "The American Government is but a mockery and deserves to be overthrown, if they are to be left without protection as sheep in the midst of wolves." This was heady stuff, and the audience loved it, as had audiences of old. Thurlow Weed, moved by the blasts from Boston, arose and told the crowd that Garrison's letter "warms my old blood."[37]

At a time when the political scene was dull, when a national election that would have no real issues lay just ahead, fire and flame from the rostrum of Cooper Institute was welcomed by the city's newspapers. The *Tribune,* in particular, was happy to report it. Unreconstructed Confeder-

118

ate bulldozers were wrecking the South, it charged. Not only were their terror tactics lining the banks of the Mississippi with blacks who were desperately anxious to escape to the North, but they were also, indirectly, driving out any prospective white settlers who might want to migrate to the cotton fields. But justice would triumph, the paper predicted, and when the persecuted blacks had left for a new land where political and civil rights were assured, southern communities would suffer for their sins though economic retrogression and decay. Beyond that, suggested the *Tribune*, lay the moral question. In an editorial entitled "The Negroes Still Slaves" it depicted southern conditions as being no better than those of ante-bellum days and wondered if southern planters were sufficiently intelligent to institute necessary reforms before it was too late.[38]

In the beginning, the *Tribune* had expressed high hopes that Kansas would provide the necessary sanctuary for the refugees. It assumed that the movement not only would aid the black immigrants but also would be highly beneficial for Kansas. In an article entitled "An Opportunity for Kansas" the editor took the view that emigration societies had made Kansas what it was and that in the present circumstance, such organizations, if well directed, could "easily secure for that State . . . a marvellous increase in population and in wealth." He called upon all readers to join the crusade and to open their hearts and their purses to this new philanthropic opportunity. In another editorial, "What the Negroes Need," he lamented that "there is no Promised Land for them; there is no pillar of fire and cloud to lead them; no bread from Heaven to feed them; but, in Heaven's name, while there are kind-hearted men and women among us who can spare a dollar from their own scanty stores, do not let it be said that God's help has failed for them out of the world!" A *Tribune* correspondent, out in Kansas, answered that the state would "not go back upon her principles nor back upon the colored man," and it would save fleeing Negroes from the horror that was the South. Months later the *Tribune* backed its appeal by sending Governor St. John five dollars "in aid of colored emigrants in your state."[39]

As time passed, the *Tribune* began to have second thoughts about Kansas as a Mecca for blacks. Realistically it admitted that "it will not do to dump them in great masses on Western prairies, even if each man is provided with land to work." Without capital or skills needed for northern farming, the newcomers would remain paupers among strangers. But if the western reaches of Kansas, then being tested by white farmers, were unsuitable, the newspaper had a solution: give the blacks land in the more-settled eastern regions of the state. It reasoned that "the Negro always succeeds better when he has the white man to imitate and to lean upon," therefore "let it be land in the neighborhood of white settlements." But when it appeared that such suggestions had not been followed, the *Tribune* editor descended from Olympus and admitted that things just were not working out. "There is scant welcome for them in any of the towns," he complained, but admitted that "naturally no struggling community wishes to be drowned in a flood of pauperism." He thought that this could have been avoided had northerners contributed more generously to the cause. "There is a great deal of windy sympathy for them among the people who make it a point of conscience to indorse the negro, right or wrong, but so far very little money or practical help has been sent from this class," he charged, adding that the accused looked "on the misery of these innocent blacks with an unaccountably chilly apathy."[40]

The barbs pricked a few consciences in New York. During the summer of 1879 one businessman challenged St. John's remark that while Cleveland had sent sixteen hundred dollars, New York had not contributed sixteen cents. St. John responded quickly, saying the letter in which he had made the statement had not been intended for publication. In fact, he admitted, some five to six hundred dollars had come in from New York in recent weeks. The Odd Fellows, for example, had made a fine contribution. And more was to come. John Dwight and Company, of New York City, sent a hundred dollars, with the request that the firm's name not be published and that the contribution not be acknowledged. Benjamin B. Sherman, president of the Mechanic's National Bank, sent a check for five hundred dollars in the name of the city's relief committee, of which he was the treasurer. Help came also from the little people. George S. McWatters, who identified himself as a working man, offered to give a dollar a month from his wages and volunteered to meet with all who would join him to discuss the wage-withholding plan.[41]

New York City donors who wished to help the Exodusters had no difficulty in finding a place to make contributions. Most of the city's important papers, such as the *Herald*, the *Times*, the *Tribune*, the *Evening Post*, and the *Mail*, expressed a willingness to receive money and forward it. The *Times* deprecated efforts by others to use the movement for partisan purposes or to encourage an indiscriminate emigration to the West, but its views rode the mainstream of eastern opinion when it attacked the conditions under which southern black labor existed. If the flow of white emigrants was toward new western lands, said the paper, it was logical that blacks, who were victims of unfulfilled promises, ought to join it. Moralizing, a reporter called the exodus "one that in its essential spirit and quality must be honored by thoughtful lovers of liberty and progress."[42]

One of those who long had advocated liberty and progress for black

Americans was Joseph Hayne Rainey, the first Negro to be elected to the House of Representatives. His tenure, dating from 1870, ended on March 3, 1879, after which he became a special agent for the United States Treasury. Described as courteous and suave, he was well known for his endorsement of black participation in politics. Early in April, 1879, he sent five dollars to J. Milton Turner at St. Louis to aid "the poor and destitute of our oppressed race, who have been compelled to seek an asylum of peace and safety in the Far West." While five dollars was only a drop in the bucket, Rainey's name was much more important, and sponsors of the refugees welcomed it. More substantial aid, as always, came from groups, and one of these, known as the Emigrant Aid Society, was organized at Washington. During 1879 its secretary, A. M. Clapp, collected about two thousand dollars, most of which was used for westward transporting of coastal blacks, principally from the Carolinas.[43]

From Philadelphia, deep in the heart of Quakerdom, came applause and substantial financial support for the courageous stand taken by those blacks who had declared independence by packing up and going west. Early in May, 1879, the usual civic meeting was called by the mayor, and a committee of twenty prominent people was appointed to get about the task of helping the refugees. Individual businessmen sent as much as fifty dollars each, but in one case it was reported that an elderly Philadelphia Quaker personally contributed ten thousand dollars to help provide western homes for fleeing blacks. G. W. Carey, vice-president of the Kansas Freedmen's Relief Association, later stated that ninety to ninety-five percent of the money that his organization at Topeka received came from Elizabeth Comstock's Quaker friends.[44]

Meetings similar to those held along the eastern seaboard were called in upper midwestern cities. During April, prominent men of Columbus, Ohio, met and formed the usual committee to raise money in aid of "the wanderers," to use their term.[45] Within a few days, William G. Deshler, of Columbus's Deshler Bank, mailed a check for $250 to St. John, promising that more would follow. He asked the governor for some details about the itinerant blacks so that he might spread the word and raise even more money in his part of Ohio.[46] George H. Eby, treasurer of the Cleveland group, sent forward a total of $1,381.50 in a period of three months. He remarked to St. John that while most of these movements were of doubtful wisdom, this one stood apart "because of its nature and the good cause it stands for." He praised St. John's state, saying, "Kansas is the heart & hope of these black men, is the historic land of freedom." Murat Halstead, the widely known editor of the *Cincinnati Commercial,* informed St. John that "we have raised over twelve hundred dollars for the fugitive slaves of the day."[47] In his remark he reaffirmed the belief, held by a good many of the old abolitionists, that slavery still existed, if only in another form.

In Illinois the Chicago *Inter-Ocean* became the leading spokesman for the Exodusters. It also took the view that the Emancipation Proclamation had become an unfulfilled promise of freedom and that, accordingly, the flight from a substitute form of slavery was both necessary and justifiable. The only alternative, asserted that newspaper, was a return to the South of federal troops in order to ensure order and justice in an unrepentant part of the land. When one of its Kansas correspondents quoted the land commissioner of the Kansas Pacific Railway as saying that there was no room for the black immigrants because they had no money with which to buy land, the editor reacted sharply. The commissioner, he said, was an Irishman with a broad brogue and less than a dozen years of residence in that sacred land of Kansas, "where these colored people first saw the light of day." He referred to S. J. Gilmore, who had written a form letter to all Negro applicants, in which he told them that there was no place for black labor in the state, that most of the work was done by machinery, and that only by going into the far-western counties, where there was no wood and little water, could they find any government land. It irritated the *Inter-Ocean* to think that the St. Louis Mullanphy fund initially had given these poor refugees a mere $100, when it had, upon occasion, awarded a single Irish family as much as $350 to continue its westward trek. Poverty should be no bar to western settlement, said the editor. These field hands surely were no poorer than the penniless multitudes arriving by the boatload from Europe. Their blackness should not be held against them; they were, according to the Kansas correspondent, far above the average immigrant in intelligence and cleanliness; to fail to help them would be evidence of nothing less than racial prejudice.[48]

Relief efforts in Chicago developed a little more slowly than in other cities. By late April the *Inter-Ocean* said that since there was, as yet, no organized movement in the city to raise money, it would serve as a repository for contributions. By then $160.97 had been collected. The newspaper was convinced, however, that among Chicago papers there was sufficient interest in the migrant blacks so as to start some kind of organized movement in their behalf.[49]

It guessed correctly. On the evening of May 1, 1879, the Exodus Aid Association was organized at Thomas's Hall, and prospective contributors were given an address to which they could send money. In the next day or so it was reported that George L. Armour, a wealthy Chicago grain dealer, had contributed two thousand dollars to assist in the colonization movement. He had just returned from the "front" in Kansas, where he had been much moved by conditions among the refugees. "It has always been considered a sort of Negro heaven since the days of old John Brown," he said in praise of Kansas. The blacks with whom he had talked said that they had fled from southern persecution, and, what was even worse in his Republican eyes, they had been forced to vote the Democratic ticket. This disturbing news moved him to make a healthy contribution, one that the *Inter-Ocean* was only too happy to publicize.[50]

The *Inter-Ocean*'s interest in the Exodusters was further stimulated by the Quaker blood that coursed through the veins of its editor, William Penn Nixon. Mixed with that heritage was the influence of his mother, who had descended from the Cherokees. Nixon, who had earned his LL.B. at the University of Pennsylvania, turned to journalism after a few years of practicing law in Cincinnati. With his brother, O. W. Nixon, he had founded the *Cincinnati Daily Chronicle,* and in 1872, William moved to Chicago, where he joined the staff of the moribund *Inter-Ocean.* Before long he controlled the paper and became its general manager and editor. Politically the journal was labeled as "reliably Republican."

Nixon himself might well have been called a "reliably Radical Republican," for he entertained the strongest of sympathies toward those whom he regarded as oppressed. In promising aid to St. John, he assured the governor: "The *Inter-Ocean* desires to aid in all good works, and it believes it to be a great and good work to help people from a land of wrong and servitude to a land of freedom and plenty."[51] Editorially, Nixon told his readers that he had no apologies for the amount of space he devoted to the Exodusters. "It involves questions of grave importance, and cannot be dismissed with a word, even if we were so inclined," he wrote. Although Nixon, along with a great many others, had no knowledge of the movement's origins, he had no trouble in fixing the blame upon southerners. In his view, these cruel, unthinking bigots had not changed one iota; Uncle Tom's people still were crossing the figurative river, pursued by whip-wielding masters. In order to seek out more details and thus, presumably, to discover the truth, Nixon sent John F. Ballantyne, of his editorial staff, on a junket to Kansas. Ballantyne did his job; he sent back a long, emotional report from Wyandotte, designed to tear at Chicago heartstrings and purses. Nixon also printed a letter from John Brown, Jr., in which the son of the martyr implored readers to help the new slaves. He asked that a latterday "New England Emigrant Aid Society" be set up at Chicago.[52]

The *Inter-Ocean* did not have a corner on Exoduster stock in Chicago. The *Tribune* also published editorials favoring the movement and, in good

Republican style, denounced southern bulldozers. When it praised Kansas as the home of black freedom, the *Missouri Republican* editorially inquired as to why the Chicago editor was so generous with Kansas lands. It was curious, remarked the St. Louis paper, that Republican journals always wanted these unfortunate people to go west. Why not invite a few blacks to Chicago? it asked.[53]

Chicago did not respond to the challenge by inviting these discontented southerners to the city, but some of its philanthropists, urged on by St. John, offered to help disperse the migration among northern states or send it deeper into the West. The objects of such kindness frequently demurred, arguing that not all places were as "natural" a home as Kansas, and it took some coaxing to get them to accept the invitations.

Despite bitter remarks from Missouri, the *Inter-Ocean* demonstrated that it pays to advertise. It not only flushed a covey of wealthy sympathizers, among whom George Armour had the fattest wallet; it also brought into the ranks the redoubtable Horatio N. Rust, who was to become a warm supporter of and constant correspondent with St. John. In mid May, 1879, he wrote to the Kansas governor, asking for information. He wanted to buy four or more sections of land to begin a colony for the emigrating Negroes, and the heading of his stationery—Horatio N. Rust & Company Warehouse—suggested that he had the means with which to purchase prairie real estate. He had in mind the cherished forty acres for each family, and he was willing to include the familiar "and a mule" for motive power. To do this, he intended to form a company in Chicago, one that would provide financial backing and would provide each section, or 640 acres, with one man who would be furnished the tools and teams necessary to break forty-acre plots as families occupied them.[54]

During the summer of 1879 Rust's campaign apparently lay dormant, for St. John heard little from him during these months. But early in September he told the governor that he had seen his latest appeal for help in the columns of the *Inter-Ocean,* and once more he was offering his assistance. Cold weather was coming on, said Rust, and warm clothing would be needed in Kansas. He agreed to receive any such items at Chicago and to use the facilities of his warehouse for storage until St. John asked that they be sent forward. Rather timidly he suggested that he wanted to be of assistance, and apparently fearing that St. John might for some reason find him suspect, Rust named the First National Bank of Chicago as a reference, adding that he knew John Brown, Jr., personally. The Chicago volunteer was enlisted in the ranks, and soon he was writing to St. John on stationery headed Southern Refugee Relief Association, of which he was the secretary and former governor John L. Beveridge was president. The stationery also announced that the organization had been formed on February 9, 1880, "for the purpose of relieving the great want growing out of the Negro Exodus."[55] Before many months had passed, Rust had become St. John's right-hand man in Chicago.

The Kansas governor's appeal was heard in faraway places, and he might be said to have acquired a small "foreign legion" in his battle for the southern refugees. For example, Louis Nagel, a pastor in Neuchâtel, Switzerland, contributed three hundred francs. He had heard Thomas Rustling, of the Jubilee Singers, talk, and he had concluded that if all blacks were as worthy as Rustling, the cause must be a good one. A response came also from Richard Allen, of Dublin, who had known Elizabeth Comstock when she worked in Ireland. While Allen did not make a monetary contribution, he congratulated St. John for his work in aid of "the liberated coloured population of the South who are fleeing from the land of oppression."[56] It would have grieved the sensitive Irishman to know that while he was extending his best wishes, his countrymen in Illinois were assaulting—even killing—blacks who were sent there to work in the coal mines. Irish labor was extremely sensitive about black competition.

Although the strident notes of Garrison's "trumpet-tongued edict" rolled across the land and were echoed from as far away as Europe, the volunteers who responded were hard-core fighters, many of whom simply had reenlisted. As in ante-bellum days, their actual numbers were less than the decibel count that they registered suggested. Among those who were not moved by the clarion call, some were openly hostile to the new crusade, but the majority of nonparticipants simply were indifferent or cautiously dubious about its merits.

As it is with many philanthropic movements, there were mixed emotions about this one in Chicago's business community. One who signed himself "Selby" wrote from that city in May, 1879, reporting that the local Board of Trade had begun a subscription to aid refugees from southern oppression. Among the heavy contributors, said Selby, was a leading Chicago packer, some of whose friends cautioned him that his generosity might have a long-range detrimental effect. Not only might it convince southern blacks that they had only to flee, and someone else would feed them, but if southern cotton and sugar fields were laid waste for want of labor, who in the South would buy meat from Chicago packers? Also, should these emigrants succeed in Kansas, surely they would raise their own hogs, and Chicago sales would suffer yet another blow.[57]

While the plea of self-interest may not have been practical, or one seriously to be contemplated, it was not unique to Chicago businessmen.

The *Boston Advertiser* warned that in New England the exodus was "beginning to arouse attention in business circles, for it is realized that if it continues the cotton, sugar, tobacco and rice crops will be jeopardized on account of insufficient labor for cultivation and harvesting." This, said the paper, would strike directly at the Northeast's economy, and it would particularly affect such an industry as the Boston shoe trade. That trade, it pointed out, "has closer relations with the thrift and steadiness of southern blacks than any other industry, and it has had occasion to note the extent of this migration by very numerous counter demand on duplicate orders for brogans and plantation shoes for Louisiana and Mississippi dealers." Additionally, cotton prices were rising in anticipation of shortages resulting from prospective southern labor difficulties, and that was going to have an influence on New England's milling industry. Even worse, cautioned another Boston newspaper, was the possible effect that the movement might have upon discontented factory employees. If, asked the editor, unhappy workers in the South were encouraged to depart, what would be the attitude of "the mill operatives of New England in case they are pushed too far?" Might they not be encouraged to head for a promised land of their own? The idea, he concluded, should be "a suggestive one to capitalists and corporations as well."[58] A Portland, Maine, editor warned that any kind of hegira, from any place dependent upon labor, "would unsettle the business of the whole country, for it would throw into complete confusion the industries of a section large enough to create serious disturbance in every branch of trade." Quite candidly he expressed the hope that there would be enough suffering in Kansas to slow the exodus and to discourage restless workers elsewhere from seeking a similar panacea for their economic problems.[59]

Chicago businessmen, who sold their goods not only to southern farmers but to western farmers as well, did not object to the westward movement so long as their city promised to be an entrepôt of plains-country trade. However, if Illinois farmers moved to Kansas and then bought their supplies from St. Louis, Chicago could be the loser. A *Tribune* correspondent visited Kansas in the spring of 1879, and although he noted that the new state's population had increased by about 150,000 in the preceding year, still the *Tribune* was forced to conclude that it was a mistake for Illinois and Indiana farmers to pull up stakes and emigrate to Kansas or Nebraska. Hard times and recent crop failures on the plains were the reasons given for staying at home. The problem of the "Kansas mania" was exacerbated by the "Leadville excitement" of 1879, and papers all the way from Chicago to New England worried about the drainage of laborers to the mines of Colorado.[60] In this respect, businessmen were cautious about applauding any kind of labor hegira, black or white. Frank Leslie, owner of New York's widely read illustrated newspaper, spoke for the eastern business establishment when he talked of the improved conditions under which Virginia Negroes lived and when he concluded that "there can be no doubt but that they are far better off than those of their race now curled up for shelter beneath the platform of the railroad depot at Wyandotte."[61] In other words, New York merchants and wholesalers were not particularly concerned about the flight of labor from Louisiana, but if Virginia farmers joined the rush, the result could touch closer to home.

Perhaps, thought New Yorkers, the idea of a black exodus might be used to solve a local white problem. Their city had accumulated a good many European immigrants who had not found places in the labor force and who had joined other people in an army of unemployed. "We have on several occasions suggested that it might be well to try the experiment of transferring them in colonies, under a system of modified guardianship, to the unoccupied lands of the South and West," suggested Frank Leslie. Already, he said, there existed a group known as the Co-operative Colony Aid Association of New York, whose object was to colonize the poor and thereby to get rid of them. He wondered if the private sector could not commit both a profitable and a philanthropic act by financing a couple of colonies of one hundred to two hundred persons, provided that the government would grant the needed land.[62] In this manner the offscourings of society could be shipped out, leaving the better class of laborers to take their places in industry. Chicago had a similar organization called the Kansas and Immigration Society, a committee of which visited Kansas and recommended Davis County, in the northeastern part of the state, as a place where land could be had on ten years' credit at four dollars an acre.[63] While the group was not organized for the purpose of getting rid of the poor, it did provide a means of controlled emigration from Chicago, and it could be used for the benefit of the city as well as for that of the individuals involved.

The notion of exporting unemployed laborers whose support troubled city fathers appealed to civic leaders in Washington, D.C. The National Emigration Aid Society of that city already had helped some southern field hands to move north, and now the *Washington Post* wondered if it could not better direct its efforts toward solving a local problem. "There is no other locality in the Union where the colored people are suffering so terribly as they are here," the paper announced, "and the only practical remedy for their manifold miseries is emigration. The supply of unskilled labor here is enormously in excess of present or prospective demand."

Why move southern farmers who were not necessarily in want? wondered the editor. "Will the National Emigration Aid society begin its work at home? Or will it prefer to waste its energies where its efforts are not needed?" he asked.[64]

Another solution to the problem of discontented southern Negroes that was talked about in eastern and northern circles during 1879 was that of establishing colonies for them. What would have happened if President Grant's desire for Santo Domingo had been realized? pondered the *Chicago Tribune*. Had it become a reality, the United States by now could have had a thriving black colony on that island. Despite Grant's frustration, thought the editor, there was no reason why the government still should not promote black colonization, but not necessarily in Kansas.[65]

Where, then? Indian Territory, or what later became Oklahoma, appeared to be a likely place. Despite the fact that Indians already had been deposited there, under the earlier removal program, it appeared to eastern journals that this should pose no problems, "for there the Government can locate freedmen by explicit provision of the treaty in the same way as Indians," in the words of one editor. This ought to be mutually satisfactory, he concluded, for "the two races fraternize easily."[66]

The idea delighted southerners. "Black men may be able to slip into Indian Territory," said the *New Orleans Picayune*. "Let the black exodus go for the red man's land."[67] Apparently the process of "slipping in" already had commenced. Early in 1879 a delegation of Negroes living among the Cherokees, in Indian Territory, appeared before the commissioner of Indian Affairs at Washington and asked for protection of their people, about three thousand in number. "The delegation described a lamentable condition of injustice, embracing the denial by the Cherokees to the blacks of a share in the orphan fund and the fund for schools for the insane," reported a New York newspaper. "They assert that they are advertised as intruders, summoned before mock courts of justice and their property threatened with confiscation if they do not remove from the Cherokee territory within sixty days."[68]

So, the races did not "fraternize easily." One answer to that problem was the establishment of an all-black colony in some western area that had not already been set aside for Indians. In the spring of 1879 a Boston organization called the National Farmers' Association obtained sixty-five alternate sections of land in northern Texas from the Dallas and Wichita Railroad at a cost of $1.50 an acre. The railroad had received the land from Texas in the form of a subsidy for construction. Shares valued at one hundred dollars each, convertible into land, now were offered to Negro families desirous of emigrating from their present homes. Some two hundred thousand men, about a third of them with families, were expected to respond to the offer. There was talk that the area would become a black state, named Lincoln, to take its place alongside other states in the union.[69]

The *New York Times* gave prominence to the story about the proposed state of Lincoln, because the idea coincided with that journal's view of southern Negro migrations. For some time, said the paper in a lengthy editorial, these people had moved from the Southeast to newer southern states, a movement within the South that the editor saw as natural. However, for these people to flee to colder climates in order to get away from their problems was looked upon as inadvisable. Comments such as "the poor blacks expect practical sympathy, and they will get very little of it in Kansas, or in any new region where every man is struggling in his own behalf," typified the argument. The Negroes, said the *Times,* simply were not equal to the trials endured by Scandinavians in such places as Kansas.[70] Those who did not favor the state of Lincoln theory might well have argued that northern Texas was no land of milk and honey. Rather, it was a place that white farmers did not find particularly attractive. That the Texans themselves were not enthusiastic about black immigration to their state was suggested in a dispatch from Mexico City a few years later, one that told of two colored emigration commissioners from Texas who had gone there to talk about procuring Mexican lands for a large colony of black cotton-raisers from Texas. If arrangements could be made for the move, said the commissioners, some ten thousand people would migrate to the new location. "There is not the same prejudice in Mexico against the colored men as there is in the United States," commented the dispatch.[71]

Democratic papers in New England tended to share the view that cold Kansas was no place for wandering southern field hands. "The money comes hard to help the Negroes deluded into Kansas," remarked one of them, charging that a few politicians who sensed the political value of the movement had made contributions, "but other people, while they pity, think it a duty to help the poor at home before sending money to agents who may let it go astray." The editor, who was from Maine, was convinced that the Exodusters were "of the idle, shiftless class who are tolerably content to live anywhere . . . if they don't have to work." His theory was that the 40th parallel was the "line of greatness" and that only those who lived in a temperate climate ever amounted to anything. If a man grew up under a tropical sun, he maintained, "you may be sure that he is not remarkably furnished in the upper story. Equatorial great men are not common."[72]

Other eastern papers indicated a similar lack of enthusiasm for the emotional endorsement accorded to the refugees by the region's liberals. A Democratic Boston newspaper expressed great sympathy for the labor problems of southern whites and chided New Englanders for contributing "their hard earned shekels for the benefit of the exodus movement." A cross-town colleague criticized the "noble, but misdirected, charity of the East," and charged that the Kansas relief committees often were in the hands of "knaves and politicians." From Washington, D.C., came the guess that nine-tenths of the Negroes then in Kansas were essentially paupers and that ninety percent of them would find the matter of making a living so difficult that they would move on.[73] The *New York Tribune,* an early supporter of the movement, stuck to its editorial guns, but confessed that in all probability the Negro never would work as hard as the German or Scottish immigrant, for "it is not in his blood." Nevertheless, thought that newspaper, the blacks could be trained to support themselves, and given a chance, they would find their own niche.[74]

As the war of emotions was fought in the nation's press and as contributions of all kinds flowed into Kansas, the contest tended to veer more and more toward the political arena. Charges and countercharges erupted with increasing frequency, to the effect that the flight of the blacks was being used for purely political purposes, at both state and national levels. Both sides looked ahead to the election of 1880, and increasingly, the Democrats charged that Republican support of the exodus was nothing more than a political ploy, an age-old device, once more dragged out to excite the fears of the voters, who would be moved to return the G.O.P. to power for yet another term. The Republicans denied all—and continued to attack the "Confederate Brigadiers" in Congress with increasing ferocity.

8

THE "BLACK" REPUBLICANS

During the spring of 1880, as the Voorhees Senate investigating committee probed the extensive and apparently unaccountable flight of southern blacks to Kansas and other places, the finger of blame for the exodus was pointed in the direction of Sen. William Windom of Minnesota. The accuser was a resident of Arlington, Virginia, named John B. Syphax, a thirty-eight-year-old black man who was a Republican justice of the peace. He charged that Windom had originated the movement or, if not, that at least he had promoted it. The senator, said Syphax, was guilty of drumming up letters from discontented Negroes so that he could wave them at his colleagues when he made a Senate speech on behalf of the former slaves. Windom's response was a sarcastic suggestion that Syphax must have escaped from a lunatic asylum, and he declined to interrogate him.[1]

While the Minnesota senator could take the lofty ground that he would not dignify the charge with a comment or a denial, his involvement with the movement was a matter of public record. On January 19, 1879, he had offered in the Senate a resolution that purported to deal with problems of black suffrage in the South. In it he recommended the appointment of a seven-man Senate committee to be "charged with the duty of inquiring as to the expediency and practicability of encouraging and promoting . . . the partial migration of colored persons from those States and Congressional districts where they are not allowed to freely and peacefully exercise and enjoy their Constitutional rights as American citizens, into such States as may desire to receive them . . . or into such Territory or Territories of the United States as may be provided for their use and occupation." His motion came on the heels of disruption occasioned by "bulldozing" of black voters in the South during the 1878 elections, disturbances that resulted in the appointment of a Senate investigating committee, headed by Henry M. Teller, of Colorado, and charged with probing political conditions in the South.

On February 7, 1879, Windom addressed his colleagues on the matter contained in his resolution, commenting that he believed black migration to be the most practical method of solving the race problem. The so-called southern question, he said, remained as the most difficult problem in American politics. In his view, slavery had laid its mark upon the slave-owners to such a degree that it had "rendered the white men of the South far less competent to deal with colored citizenship than . . . the negro to exercise it." Now southern whites refused to accept a Negro majority where it existed, and they continued to resist all laws and pressures to make them accept the new situation. Black emigration, said Windom, would help to break this deadlock.

He did not mean migration in the old sense; to transport these people to such places as Liberia was, in his view, dishonorable. It was also impractical, he added, for the black population was growing too fast to implement such an expensive plan. He preferred a local or domestic movement, one that could move significant numbers, yet keep them under the American flag. They could be transferred to some of the new territories or perhaps to a territory of their own at the cost of "only a few millions." While he did not propose to move these people at government expense, he suggested that they might be given part of the public domain and temporarily provisioned by means of governmental subsidies. The senator pointed out that the emigration idea was an old one; that Jefferson, Madison, and Clay had endorsed it; and that only a few years earlier a congressional committee, headed by Sen. Luke Poland, had talked of "exodus or extinction" for these persecuted people. Had not extinction gone far enough? he asked his colleagues. Was the time not ripe for exodus? He was convinced that the blacks were anxious to move and that all they needed was the knowledge that there was some place to go. "Let it be understood that such a place is ready for them, and the bishops and ministers of their various churches will head the exodus to the promised land," he urged. Windom assured his colleagues that it would require the removal of less than a quarter-million blacks from the South in order to dispose of "this troublesome question."[2]

In mid February, Windom was able to wave at his colleagues some of the documents to which Syphax had referred. One was a petition from the Negro Union Co-operative Aid Association and Freedmen, of Shreveport, Louisiana, alleging that its signers were "poor, friendless, dependent, defenseless, landless" people existing in a state of modern feudalism. "They urge the passage of the resolution looking to the migration of colored persons," said the senator. Another was a memorial from the Colored Western Emigration Society of Charleston, South Carolina, announcing that the time had arrived for black people of the southern states to find a new home where they could work out a better life than the postwar South offered them. They wanted to leave, peacefully.[3]

About this time the *National Republican,* of Washington, D.C., printed a letter written a few days earlier by a Port Gibson, Mississippi, Negro who endorsed Windom's proposal as being the only real and practical solution to the problems of his race. Already, said the writer, there was evidence of movement among southern farm workers, some of whom had started for Kansas. He was convinced that if transportation and accurate information about advantages available in the western states could be furnished to the former slaves of Mississippi, that state would be depopulated of blacks within two years.[4] Another southerner who was said to have supported Windom's resolution was the former Confederate general T. L. Rosser, then chief engineer for the Northern Pacific Railroad. The general was quoted as saying that the Negroes were excellent railroad builders, and he hoped that some two thousand of them could be used on his construction crews in Dakota during the coming summer. The climate and soil of Dakota, according to Rosser, were favorable, a remark meant to suggest that after their track-laying stint was over, the migrants could settle down in that new country.[5]

The entire blame for political stimulation of black emigration from the South could not be laid at the Minnesota senator's door. A colleague, John J. Ingalls, of Kansas, had introduced into the Senate what was described as a rather visionary bill proposing to set apart lands in Kansas for colored colonization. A good many of those whom it intended to aid could not read, and therefore they had no direct knowledge of the senator's intent; nevertheless, rumors spread across the South that the federal government not only was ready to give homesteads to blacks but that it was further prepared to aid them by furnishing them with mules and supplies in their efforts to get a new start.[6] Ingalls did nothing to correct such impressions.

By mid April, 1879, as Kansas began to feel the impact of southern emigration, Ingalls was asked to implement his inferred sponsorship of the blacks. Mayor J. S. Stockton, of Wyandotte, asked him to obtain federal support for those who now flooded the city, arguing that Wyandotte had exhausted its municipal resources. The senator laid the appeal before his colleagues, but at the same time he admitted that he had no explanation for this curious movement. "Whether they are fugitives from injustice and oppression, or whether they are moved by an irresistible impulse to better their condition, I do not at this time definitely know," he said. Nevertheless, he believed that western communities would welcome their fellow Americans and would absorb them without difficulty. Senate Bill No. 472, designed to aid these distressed people in their search for new homes, was referred to the Committee on Appropriations.[7]

At this point in his political career, Ingalls was willing to do no more than to support an earlier proposal; he had little enthusiasm for making a fight of it. During the Civil War period he had boasted of being the leading antislavery man in his Kansas community, and he bragged that "my colored brethren regard me as their ally and treat me with great deference." He admitted, however, that being an abolitionist carried a price, for if the Negroes thought a man to be one, "he must be the personal friend of every Nigger in the country."[8] Now, in 1879, he had other problems. Recently the Senate had received a formal complaint against him, alleging that he had been elected by means of corruption and bribery. As a result, he was fighting for his political life and needed every ally he could find. With his southern colleagues in mind, he denied that the exodus had any political overtones, claiming that it merely was a continuation of an earlier migration of blacks from such places as Kentucky and Tennessee, a natural movement westward. While he believed that the former slaves had experienced difficult times in the South, he insisted that Kansas had no need for additional Republican strength and that it had done nothing to encourage an influx of potential Republican voters.[9]

Senator Windom also denied that the movement was politically inspired. He gave a talk entitled "The Future of the Colored Race" at a Washington, D.C., church on March 21, 1879, in which he said that his proposed emigration scheme was no more than a proposition to give the blacks the same opportunity afforded to whites in settling on western lands. A few days later he enlarged upon this contention, holding that the westward movement of Negroes was not a new thing, that they had left Kentucky, Tennessee, and Missouri at a rate of from two to three thousand annually for some years. Only in the past few weeks, he argued, had the numbers become large enough to attract attention. Nevertheless, leading blacks in Washington believed that the movement of their people had been accelerated into noticeable proportions as a result of Windom's speeches in the Senate.[10] The Reverend J. O. Embry, of Kansas, claimed that he had originated the exodus in a letter written to the *Colored Citizen* (Topeka) and that the matter had come to the attention of the Senate through Blanche K. Bruce, a Mississippi Negro who had been elected to that body in 1874. Bruce, who shared Douglass's disapproval of the movement, was said to have attributed the idea to Embry. Windom may have taken an interest in it through his acquaintanceship with Senator Bruce.[11]

Early in April, 1879, a meeting attended by some thirty people was held in the Windom home in Washington; among them were Sen. Henry Teller, of Colorado; Joseph H. Rainey, the black congressman from South Carolina; the Reverend "General" Thomas W. Conway, a Republican Negro leader; and George McCrary, secretary of war. The meeting was called in order to lay plans for an organized effort to help those blacks who wanted to leave the South. Unable to reach any definite conclusions, the group cautiously appointed a committee to "carefully consider whether it was feasible to proceed," after which it adjourned.[12] Shortly the National Emigration Aid Society came into existence, with William Windom as the chairman of its executive committee. The organization, explained Windom, was "purely benevolent" in nature; it had been formed in the belief that if black migration was "governed by wise counsels, and regulated by prudence and discretion," both races would reap benefit from the movement. However, he warned, without qualified leadership or supervision such a move might "prove disastrous to the emigrant, and very injurious to the agricultural interest of the South."[13]

Windom's denials as to the political overtones of the exodus brought sarcastic remarks from Democratic papers. From St. Louis came the accusation that the Minnesota senator either misunderstood the problem or was insincere in his statements. When Windom insisted that the movement was not inspired by outside forces, and lectured his listeners on the humanitarian aspects of the southern hegira, the same paper called his remarks "highly colored" and maintained that he was a member of a congressional group that for years had taunted the South. A Jackson, Mississippi, weekly had even stronger feelings in the matter. "Unmitigated hypocrisy and cant," growled its editor, who charged that Windom and his National Emigration Aid Society executive group were feigning innocence of a movement that they themselves had instigated "and which gives them concern only as a scheme for effecting partisan results and keeping alive sectional strife."[14] Windom doggedly insisted that by removing a large number of blacks from the South, sectionalism would be eliminated from national politics; at the same time he was able to argue that his project was not politically inspired.

Even if Windom could be cleared of charges of partisan ambitions, he faced accusations of meddling with a touchy southern situation. "Senator Windom belongs to that numerous class of reformers who act on the theory that destruction is reformation," concluded the *Washington Post.* "He has used or abused his position as Senator to destroy the peaceful domestic enjoyment of hundreds of humble colored families in the South, and if he has done anything in the way of compensation for this serious and lasting injury, he has worked so quietly and secretly as to leave no mark to excite even a suspicion." The editor concluded that Windom's intemperate speeches in the Senate not only had disturbed southern agricultural life but also had resulted in great suffering by a number of recent arrivals in Kansas. A good many of those migrating blacks, he said, had received no help from the Emigration Aid Society that had been organized to assist people whom he described as "the wretched dupes of Mr. Windom's windy rhetoric." In a bitter postscript, the journalist charged that "the whole exodus business is the work of rascally demagogues, who robbed them of their little savings through the agency of the Freedmen's bank."[15]

Once the exodus came to national notice and once there was evidence of suffering among those who had made the precipitous move, members of Congress responded, but along partisan lines. On April 21, 1879, Congressman James A. Garfield introduced a bill that would have authorized the secretary of war to issue rations and tents for the refugees and would have set aside $75,000 in further aid. Congressman D. C. Haskell, of Kansas, at once notified Governor St. John of the action, remarking that the passage of the bill was very doubtful. The secretary of war was sympathetic, said Haskell, and he was personally willing to help the refugees, "but if he granted your request it would be like exposing himself to a drove of wolves. The southerners are wild over the exodus and they hope and pray (apparently) that enough of the poor creatures will come to want, to deter the rest from leaving." There was no use asking Congress to help, the congressman told St. John, because the "chief fear among the southern fellows is that they *will* receive aid sufficient to sustain them." While he did not think Garfield's bill would do any good, he was glad it came from Ohio, a place that was not directly interested in the movement. As to the origins of the movement, Haskell believed that it had resulted from "the insane acts of the Democrats." The Chicago *Inter-Ocean* agreed with Haskell's reservations and predicted that "it is not probable that southern Democrats will allow the passage of such a bill, which will be the loudest sort of a call for colored people to leave the South."[16]

Indeed, Democratic response was immediate. On that same day, Congressman Washington G. Whitthorne, of Tennessee, introduced a resolution authorizing the appointment of a joint select committee to visit the affected areas and to discover the cause of the unrest. Whitthorne's idea, said a Chicago newspaper, was to show that the migratory blacks were not fleeing from persecution but were actuated by nonpolitical motives. "Many Democrats fear that, without an investigation of this sort, it will be impossible to convince Northern people but what the blacks are driven out by persecution, and its effect on the fall elections will be very great," the editor explained. The resolution was referred to the Committee on Education and Labor and was ordered to be printed; there it died quietly.[17]

When St. John inquired of a Kansas Republican congressman as to the status of the Garfield bill, he received a prompt reply. Regretfully, said Thomas Ryan, the legislation was sleeping the sleep that knew no waking. "I hope my dear Governor is not so daft as to believe for a moment that a Democratic committee of Confederate Congressmen would be guilty of the great wrong of encouraging the exodus movement by extending relief . . . to the refugees," he added. Quite the contrary; southern congressmen would be delighted to see the migrants suffer a starvation that would make them return to the cotton fields.[18] In a newspaper interview, Ryan said that all had been done for the refugees that could be done, but that every train from the South dumped more of "these deluded people" on Kansas' doorstep, and the situation was getting out of hand. "Most of them who go to Kansas are of the more ignorant class," he added, people who would make no contribution to the state. Such opinions were popular among Kansas business leaders, who feared the economic results of imported pauperism.[19]

Republican Congressman William A. Phillips, of Kansas, also understood why Garfield's measure was destined to die aborning, and he pointed the accusing fingers at its killers. Calling the exodus an unnatural occurrence, he laid the blame squarely at the door of the southerners and the "Confederate Brigadiers" who shared Democratic control of Congress. That venerated legislative body, lamented Phillips, had fallen into the hands of a political party whose leaders had carried the nation to war eighteen years earlier; and now, unrepentant rebels were making a mockery of emancipation. Thanks to southern mental and moral rigidity on the race question, Negroes were being forced to leave their natural habitat —the sunny South—for cold, strange Kansas. "These modern children of Israel were required to make bricks without straw," he cried out. "They have gone out toward the wilderness. We see no Moses, but their cause is just, and the pillar of fire and the sheltering cloud of the Lord will be with them."[20]

Some of the voters thought that perhaps a new Moses had surfaced.

137

A couple of them from Kansas City, Kansas, wrote to St. John and thanked him for his interest in the black people of Kansas, assuring the governor that "we pledge you the entire support of the colored voters of Wyandotte County for any position you may seek."[21] Others cheered him on from afar. Former Kansas Senator Samuel C. Pomeroy, writing from New York City, praised the governor's efforts, saying, "Your position has attracted the attention of our best people & papers in the East."[22] A few even talked about "St. John for President." In general, Kansas newspapers reflected the Radical Republican view that the South had been pampered, that Democratic partisanship was ruining the black labor base in the South, that the former slaves were in danger of reenslavement. In their efforts to keep Radical reconstruction alive, Republicans, including some in Kansas, tended to praise St. John.

The governor was not unaware of the political volatility of his stand; he knew that there were dangers in it and that while he was praised nationally, the local situation could backfire. He sensed an uneasy stirring among more-conservative party members in his state, a sentiment that did not surface easily in newspaper opinion. No one wanted publicly to cast the first stone. The apparent reason that St. John was willing to take a political gamble was given by a fellow Topekan, who explained that in the past few years the Republican majority in Kansas had been declining and that even if the Democrats were as yet no real threat, the Greenbackers were growing rapidly. Faced by combined opposition, Republicans were willing to search a little more diligently for votes than had been necessary earlier.[23]

In neighboring Missouri the black migration also assumed a political coloration. Democrats defended the southerners, arguing that under President Grant the former slaves had gained the upper hand and that if Grant's policies had been carried forward another five years, it would have been the whites, not the blacks, who would now be leaving the deep South. One irritated editor asked why the emigration from the South of a few thousand blacks had been used as cheap political capital when the migration of perhaps a hundred thousand whites into Kansas caused no stir at all. Why, he asked, was it regarded as a natural movement when unemployed whites from the North and East moved westward, but when blacks followed the same course, the origin of the movement was charged to persecution?[24] Missouri Republicans denied party interest in the migration, and to divert some of the verbal blows being dealt out, they accused St. Louis's mayor, Henry Overstolz, of being a Democrat on the ground that he opposed the movement. Overstolz, who was considered to be a possible gubernatorial candidate that year, refused to admit the charge and declined to make any further statements about the exodus, an issue that burned brightly in St. Louis in the spring of 1879. The mayor, who knew political dynamite when he saw it, was more cautious than was the governor of Kansas.[25]

Similar rumblings were heard in Chicago. Republican newspapers lost no opportunity to charge that if partisan politics were at the bottom of the exodus movement, the fault lay with southern Democrats. Certainly no Republican agents were needed to inspire an emigration from the South, they argued. The instinct that prompted men to get out of the range of shotguns was sufficient inducement to leave, and this alone was held to be the reason for the movement. Correspondents to these newspapers reported that past violence, as well as the promise of more in the upcoming election of 1880, was causing deep unrest among black farmers. Meanwhile, they said, white southerners were trying to establish a system of peonage through legislative acts that would match the worst conditions then prevalent in Mexico. The use of gang labor, derived from convicts who were being contracted out, rapidly was creating a condition approaching the old slave system. "Perhaps some other Harriet Beecher Stowe may yet find employment for her pen in setting forth the miseries of the slave now made peon, and the atrocities of the overseer turned into a contractor," wrote one northern reporter.[26]

The nervousness of the Chicago Republican press was explained when, in the spring of 1879, the Democrats captured the offices of mayor and treasurer. In loud lamentations, Republican papers described the tragedy, saying that not only had the "Confederate Brigadiers" taken over Congress, but that now the disease was spreading to municipalities such as Chicago. While these papers did not directly associate the exodus with local political disasters, they gave great prominence to the movement in their columns and inferred strongly that it was at least a straw in the wind, one to be watched carefully as evidence of a national Democratic resurgence. Ruefully admitting that some blacks habitually committed the unforgivable sin of voting Democratic, the *Tribune* explained that it was because they were "honeyfugled" into it by money or whiskey.[27]

Democratic papers were quick to denounce the exodus as a Republican scheme. The *Cleveland Plain Dealer,* for example, explained its lack of sympathy for the movement on the ground that southern blacks were being used merely as Republican dupes. With a tongue-in-cheek reference to Hinton Helper's earlier book, the newspaper ran an editorial in mid April entitled "The Impending Crisis," in which it poked fun at a lightly attended meeting that had been called in behalf of the refugees. It was said to have been held for the avowed purpose of helping refugees "who are now so anxious to return to the homes from which they were seduced by small souled Republican agents sent South for that purpose." If matters kept on as they had begun, said the editor, it would be difficult to predict what "the reckless Republican demagogues who have encouraged this wild movement, will not be chargeable with."[28]

Early in August, 1879, word spread throughout Ohio that blacks were being imported into that state for the purpose of keeping it Republican. "The exodus is booming toward the Buckeye State, and the new faces of the colored brethren that are seen on the streets of a large number of the Democratic cities of the Northwest, without any visible means of support, or unable to tell from whence they came or whither they are going is causing the anxious inquiry in the minds of voters as to what it means," reported a Cincinnati newspaper.[29] A New England colleague explained the plot, recalling that in 1876 Rutherford Hayes had carried Ohio by only a few thousand votes and that in 1877 the Democrats had made considerable gains. While the Democrats had not picked up appreciable additional strength in 1878, the Greenbackers had—all of which was detrimental to the Republican cause.[30] Murat Halstead's *Cincinnati Commercial,* which was openly sympathetic to the migrating blacks, admitted that Ohio Democrats did not want the movement to be turned in their direction, for only a few thousand votes could tip the scales in favor of the Republicans. He said it was generally conceded that "whatever a black man's politics may be in Mississippi, the moment he touches Northern soil he becomes a Republican."[31]

During the spring and early summer of 1879 some of the New York papers argued that even if the exodus was not politically inspired, certainly the politicians had found it to be useful. One paper lamented the fact that the movement was stirring up "the sediment of by-gone politics," and it openly admitted that by May there was "not a single feature in the whole business which is not essentially political in character." Although public interest in the exodus faded during the summer of 1879, the political connection with it remained. Recalling an earlier day, when Kansas was said to have been bleeding, a New York editor noted that "there have been times when . . . colonization and politics were usefully allied."[32]

By autumn the Republican press revealed an increasing concern about the power of the "Confederate Brigadiers" in Congress, men who were said to "threaten the credit and prosperity, and even the life of the country." Warnings were given that a Democratic victory in New York that autumn would give great encouragement to this group. But as the year came to a close, the *New York Tribune* backed away from the notion that black emigration from the South was politically oriented. At first, said the editor, the Democratic press had represented it to be "the result of a wicked conspiracy plotted in Boston, or some other hotbed of abolitionism, between Radical politicians and grasping speculators, to entice the colored people away from their comfortable homes," but, he explained, this was nonsense; there was no need to import Republican voters into northern states, since the party already was strong in that area. By that time, results of the autumn elections had reassured Republicans, who now could assert that they no longer feared the Brigadiers.[33]

Typical of eastern reaction to the exodus, the press of New England divided itself on the question along political lines. The *Boston Daily Globe* took a deeply sarcastic line when describing efforts made in that city to support the movement. When George Boutwell and Nathaniel Banks spoke in its behalf in April, the *Globe* said that these Republicans had done no more than to expand their lungs, and little would be gained from listening to what they said. The editor bitterly criticized "Republican politicians who seek to find political profit in it [the exodus]."[34]

Eastern-based periodicals also took divergent stands when discussing the great migration. *Harper's Weekly* gave it prominent space, both in print and in illustrations. Those who had left what the magazine regarded as being a land of cruelty and oppression were lauded for their courage. In its view they were as justified in leaving as had been the slaves of an earlier day when they fled their masters. The *Nation* assumed a less emotional stance, but still it argued that the movement's origins lay in political scare tactics used by Republicans who warned the blacks that Democrats in Congress would bring them harm. The magazine was quite critical of politicians who were then using the hegira for the purpose of confirming the "bloody shirt" view of southern society or in attempts to reduce the South's representation in Congress by partially depopulating it. It asserted that reports about the excitement had been exaggerated and that blacks who remained in the South were bound to benefit from a resultant labor shortage. The sad part of the whole affair, said the *Nation,* was its detrimental effect upon relations between the two races, particularly in the South.[35]

Southerners, of course, agreed with this view. "The Republican party is responsible for all the woes that have been brought upon the colored people, who have been deluded into the belief that if they can get to Kansas they will be provided for by the Republican party of that extreme Radical state," the *Memphis Weekly Appeal* charged angrily. Actually, said that paper, the southern blacks were in a better condition than were the poor whites of the North, but unfortunately they were being misled

by the "false teachings of the Republican party." As a result, these unhappy victims were the losers, and the South was the gainer, went the
argument.[36]

From New Orleans came a harsher view of the region's Negroes.
"They grow fat and insolent," one of its journals earlier had warned
readers. "They go to the polls and defiantly vote to ruin the very man
who weakly and stupidly warms into life and strength the reptile which
he knows is stinging him. There is but one way to manage the negro.
He is, as a class, amenable to neither reason or gratitude. He must be
starved into the common perception of decency."[37] Taking a loftier view,
the New Orleans *Picayune* dismissed the Negro emigrants as being "ignorant and deluded creatures" whose reasoning powers were no greater than
those of Senator Windom who had devised this "stupid and idiotic project
to remove the Negro population from the Southern states." The Republicans, who had sent "cunning agents" into the South in order to show
the Negro how cruelly he was being treated, were assigned the responsibility for this cruel delusion. It was explained that the ordinary black was
willing to accept anything that these agents told him. "He can believe
anything he wants to believe. He pities himself and complains more as a
freedman than he did when a slave. He then had no one to tell of the
misery of the situation. Now the City of Washington will send paid
agents and lecturers to tell him about it." In defense of southern planters
the *Picayune* argued that their attachment to the Negro had not died out,
but that the former slave no longer reciprocated this feeling. The planter,
who liked the Negro, paid him as much as he could afford, ran the argument, and contrary to the situation in the North, where thousands of
northern workers were being told how to vote the "right" ticket, he rarely
tried to influence the black's decision at the polls. The editor was particularly bitter about the "Boston Republicans," who were trying to entice
some twenty thousand blacks into a colonization scheme that proposed to
erect a new state called Lincoln somewhere "between New Mexico and
Indian Territory." These poor people, he complained, were being "sold"
on an idea that was bound to end in failure, and as a result, both the
emigrants and their old home—the South—would suffer.[38]

The Jackson, Mississippi, *Weekly Clarion* represented the Democratic
white establishment of an area that had been hard hit by the exodus.
During the spring and summer of 1879 its columns were filled with editorials and slanted news items that decried the movement and fired verbal
thunderbolts at the Radical Republicans. It charged Windom and his
friends with a plot to depopulate the South for the purely political purpose
of reducing the area's congressional representations, and for this scheme

they were labeled "wretched demagogues." Republicans and Republican newspapers were attacked violently for saying that the southern Negro had been mistreated; on the contrary, said the *Clarion,* these people had been dealt with "kindly, humanely, and justly." The paper gave considerable space to the comments of Col. Edmund Richardson, of Jackson, who had some eighteen thousand acres of land under cultivation, most of it in cotton. The colonel concluded that the recent flight of blacks, some of whom were his, indeed had political overtones. The bloody-shirt business, he said, had commenced to die out, and in order to revive it, northern politicians had seized upon the most recent complaint of the former slaves in order to arouse northern voters.

According to Richardson, Mississippi field hands lived a comfortable life. They worked only about six hours a day and were well supplied with food; that, he maintained, was more than northern laboring men could say. In support of the colonel's argument, the *Clarion* published a poem, written by Guy Percival, not only to illustrate the political aspects of the exodus, but also to show that the South indeed was the black man's home. In part, it read:

I'm sittin' on de w'arf Dinah, de w'arf at Wyandotte,
De place whar Kansas darkies sit, da's all the place dey's got;
I'm mighty tired of dis place, but what's de use to pine,
Dey fotch us here—our Norther' frien's, what had an ax to grind.

I wish I could go back agin upon de ole plantation,
I'd stay dar till de angel blow'd his horn of resurrection,
I wouldn't listen to no tales from Mr. Windom's party,
I'd stay dar 'long wid old marse John, a poor, but wiser darkey.

When a New York paper quoted a "prominent citizen of Mississippi" on the flight of the field hands, the *Clarion* called his statements outspoken, and it endorsed them. According to "Citizen," emancipation had destroyed industry in the cotton fields. Meanwhile, freedom, which was presumed to be the great equalizer, was supposed to have placed blacks and whites on the same social, economic, and political plane. To ensure this the ballot box had been introduced as an instrument that would end all evils, and in it the blacks had found an Aladdin's lamp that promised to yield "the wealth of the universe in a nutshell." But then there had appeared an even greater wonder: Kansas. "Now, freedom, the ballot-box, 'forty acres and a mule,' and free horses, cigars, big dances, three work days a week and four hours a day to work, are all in the new Jerusalem— the State of Kansas," scoffed the critic. It was all a political scheme, he charged, a plot to break the southern planters; but he predicted that it would fail, for even then five-eighths of the cotton was produced by whites, and that figure would grow as the blacks left. He advocated the raising of funds in the South to ship out all the Negroes.[39]

As the exodus gained momentum, southern papers heightened the attack, repeatedly warning the blacks that theirs was a foolish and ill-advised movement promoted by fair-weather friends in the North. From the plantation country of Louisiana came the charge that carpetbaggers and scalawags, "defeated in their schemes and disappointed in their aims," now were trying to show the field hands that in order to avoid the bodily dangers in the parishes of that state, they ought to leave for Kansas and safety. This was sheer fraud, said a local editor, who explained that the South was the home of the Negroes, and if they departed for cold and unfriendly Kansas, they soon would learn of the humbuggery. "It seems that with all their experience the Negro prefers to follow the teachings instilled in him by the Radical bummers; if he cannot rule the country he will leave it," he lamented.

A Texas journal expressed parental concern for the former slaves, but it admitted that "the darkies, in the sweet credulity of their trusting natures, placed implicit faith in all the seductive tales told them of more freedom, more equality and less work in the North and West, and now they are fleeing in herds to the Yankee Canaan." The Canaanites, warned that paper, had not bargained for such a rush, and some of them, even now, were telling the southern arrivals that the northern climate might be worse than muskets and bulldozing and that inexperience in farming a new, raw land might weigh on them more heavily than the presumed persecutions of bloodthirsty southerners. "The fact is the North doesn't want the Negro in the North. It suits the purpose of a Radicalism to keep him in the South as a perpetual text for sermons on southern disloyalty," concluded the Texas editor.[40]

Southern anger reached new heights when Thomas W. Conway took up the cause and threatened to use force in "rescuing blacks from their new thralldom." Conway, referred to as "General" or "Reverend," was a militant Republican Negro who had served as an official in the Freedmen's Bureau in the closing days of the Civil War, and it was in this role that he acquired the honorary title of general. At one time he was the bureau's commissioner for the Department of the Gulf, and later for Louisiana, after which he was state superintendent of education for Louisiana. W. L. McMillen, who was New Orleans postmaster in 1879, said that far from being a general, Conway was a "political deadbeat and a religious humbug." By this time, Conway had left Louisiana and was living in New Jersey.[41]

Conway turned up at St. Louis in mid May, 1879, purporting to represent easterners interested in the exodus and bent upon investigating the obstacles placed in the way of "the free movement of our unfortunate fellow-citizens in the South." He denied that the attempted flight was in any way organized; on the contrary, he said that if there was any concerted effort, it was by the southerners who were trying to force the blacks to remain. Leading riverboat companies of St. Louis, he charged, were cooperating with southerners who were threatening to withhold patronage. "The truth is evident—the 'Father of Waters no longer runs unvexed to the sea,' and the common highway of the nation is blockaded and impeded in the interest of a class and to serve the oppressor," Conway told a St. Louis newsman. The practical answer to this, said the general, was to charter steamers, arm them if necessary, and invade enemy territory in order to rescue the beleaguered.[42]

The Conway manifesto, said a St. Louis newspaper, initiated a new phase of the exodus. It now seemed probable that the movement was to be escalated into national proportions, for here was a man who was backed by the Republican stalwarts in Washington. Conway's appearance on the scene of battle, armed with presumably significant political credentials, appeared to verify this contention. A St. Louis political figure who watched the exodus with interest concluded that "the Negro question is as big today as it ever has been."[43]

The threat of an armed invasion of the South by a former official of the Freedmen's Bureau, an honorary general, might have stirred less emotional uproar in the South if the rumor had not gone out that President Rutherford Hayes had approved the project. Although such was not the case, there had been a meeting with the president. Conway, along with the Reverend John Turner, of St. Louis, was granted an interview, at which time, according to an angry story published in a Louisiana newspaper, the men "made up quite a rawhead and bloody bones story, and said they wanted to charter Ohio River boats to go down and take off the emigrants, but threats had been made that they would be fired on." With some emotion the editor charged that "Hayes gave the fullest encouragement to all this stuff and expressed his approval of the exodus as a benefit to the Negro."

Conway's version did nothing to dissuade such beliefs. The president, he said, graciously had given the pair an audience. "He was alone and he gave us the whole evening." After hearing from them, Hayes said that he understood it was the desire of the Negroes to emigrate and that if terrorism prevailed and the boats were fired upon, they should be protected. According to Conway, he promised "that if there was any interference by armed bodies it would be a violation of the law; that the Mississippi was a national highway, and we should have protection for our boats upon it." What the "General" did not emphasize was the aftermath of the interview. It was followed by another, between Hayes and congressional representatives from Louisiana and Mississippi, in which the president was told that if he made public such an approval, it would be interpreted by the blacks and their supporters that the government wanted the exodus to continue and that the government would provide the necessary protection if not, in fact, the actual transportation. Hayes saw the point, and shortly he issued a statement to the effect that his response to Conway was based upon a condition that was only presumed to exist.

But the damage was done, and even though armed boats did not descend the great river, Conway had won his point. After his call upon the president, he visited the managers of riverboat lines at St. Louis and persuaded them that voluntary action on their part would avoid governmental intervention and embarrassment. One of the executives admitted that he had received a petition from twenty-five leading merchants of St. Louis, urging him to make passenger rates so high that the migrating blacks could not afford to book passage. Faced now by what appeared to be a higher authority, the boat companies yielded to Conway. "So the interruptions in that form ceased," Conway later recalled. "We had gone so far that we had taken steps to charter the boats; still, we discontinued them, and things have gone on easy ever since."[44]

Things may have gone on easier for Conway, but the interview was not without cost to Rutherford Hayes. The *Cleveland Plain Dealer,* of his own state, referred to him as "the impudent fraud who sits in the White House" and charged that the Associated Press story about Conway's session with the president produced nothing more than a "mess of gratuitous brimstone" on the subject of the exodus. To that paper the incident was further proof that Hayes never should have been allowed to take office. It defended the planters, saying that they had no intention of interfering with the emigration, and it remarked that, by contrast, "no Northern Black Republican manufacturer would permit a lot of mangy mischief makers to go among his workmen to array them against him, whether a presidential fraud said it was rebellion or not." The Democratic *Missouri Republican* also expressed its disapproval and maintained that even if Hayes had been misquoted, "he said something like it," and for that he should be criticized.[45]

While Hayes was assaulted by Democrats for going too far on the Negro question, some of the old Radical Republicans criticized him for not being sufficiently aggressive toward the South. Not long after the president's inauguration, in 1877, Ben Wade, living in retirement, had expressed great dissatisfaction with southern conditions. "You know with what untiring zeal I labored for the emancipation of the slaves of the South and to procure justice for them before and during the time I was in Congress," he wrote, "and I supposed Governor Hayes was in full accord with me on this subject. . . . But I have been deceived, betrayed, and even humiliated by the course he has taken to a degree that I have not language to express. . . . I feel that to have emancipated those people and then to leave them unprotected would be a crime as infamous as to have reduced them to slavery when they were free."[46]

Although Hayes did some political backing and filling when southern congressmen visited him after the Conway interview, his own personal feelings were those of sympathy for the Exodusters. He mentioned the movement in his diary, noting that "its effect is altogether favorable." He thought that it would force the better class of southerners to suppress the violence of what he termed "the ruffian class" and that, as a result, the blacks would receive better protection. "Let the emigrants be scattered throughout the Northwest; let them be encouraged to get homes and settled employment," he wrote.[47] He said much the same thing to a college president from Kingston, Jamaica; namely, that the exodus was "teaching a good lesson to the old slave-masters, and the emigration of a few would secure rights to the many who remained in their old homes."[48] Sentiments such as these infuriated the Democrats, particularly those in the South.

Democratic papers, both North and South, showered abuse upon Conway and his Republican supporters. The *Boston Daily Globe* chided that community for squandering money on such impractical projects and suggested that if there were such funds to be thrown around, they should be spent upon the Indians. The editor questioned Conway's motives, suggesting that before the affair was over, "the money contributed for this patriotic and piratical purpose will all be wasted on subsistence." Indeed, there was evidence to suggest that not all funds that had been raised were accounted for. Juliana C. Cleaveland, the widow of a Massachusetts minister, later wrote to Governor St. John, from Newburyport, complaining that in the summer of 1879 a man "styling himself Gen. Conway" was in her city, soliciting funds for the projected river armada. Interest in the exodus at that time was very great, she said, "and the money freely given, inasmuch as Gen. Conway was endorsed by two of our best clergymen. . . . A short time after he left an item in our daily paper said that he had been 'arrested for swindling' which was explained in some way but not contradicted. Since that time we have been unable to learn anything definitely of his movements." It is doubtful that any such arrest was made, for in 1880, when Conway testified before the Voorhees Committee, there seems to have been no such blot upon his record. At that time he was interested in a project to colonize a large number of blacks in New Mexico.[49]

St. Louis Democrats, caught in a crossfire of Republican activities and the reaction of southern planters who traded in that city, criticized the Republicans, the Associated Press, and eastern papers—particularly the *New York Tribune*. That eastern journal was charged with part of the responsibility "for this unnecessary and disastrous movement on the part of the blacks." Boston was sneered at for being ready to promote the excitement but unwilling to contribute much money when called upon for support. Conway was dismissed as "a fanatic of the John Brown school intending mischief," and a strait jacket was recommended as a cure for his ailment.[50]

From Cleveland came similar complaints. The Associated Press was criticized for peddling Republican campaign material, an example of which was the publicity it gave to the proposed Conway naval expedition. The press association, said a Cleveland newspaper, retailed stories "in which there is hashed up the prevailing radical gabble about the 'terrorism exercised over the Negroes by the planters and merchants along the Mississippi.'" The news service had quoted Conway as saying that only southern suppression had prevented the number of Exodusters who reached St. Louis from reaching a figure of twenty thousand. "Anything for another war for the benefit of the Republican party," growled the *Plain Dealer*. Agreeing that Conway ought to be put in a strait jacket, the editor thought another jacket should be reserved for the St. Louis agent of the Associated Press "who put the fool's vaporings into the general dispatches." He hinted that good Democratic papers who used the press service's facilities ought to register a mass protest.[51]

Southerners had nothing but the bitterest scorn for Conway and his sponsors. The New Orleans *Picayune* sarcastically called him "the new exodus angel" and charged that his plan was "fraught with danger to the entire country." Conway's honesty was questioned. That journal doubted if the invasion scheme ever could have materialized, simply because any money that reached his hands for its support would not have been used for the intended purpose. A Louisiana congressman remembered that Conway had been charged with defalcation when he lived in that state, and now, he lamented, it was a pity that such a crook should be "encouraging disturbance among peaceful citizens." The *Picayune* was worried that even though Conway's slippery ways were well known, the idea of sending boats southward to pick up dissident blacks might be adopted by more decent people, and if that happened, it feared a further upsurge in the emigration. The Jackson, Mississippi, *Clarion* blamed the "roaring, ranting, fanatical mob in Boston" for the Conway scheme. It thought that these madmen simply were using the black former administrator as a tool.[52]

The attitudes of southern political figures and businessmen varied from "good riddance" to those of paternal assurances that emigration would not solve problems facing black farmers of the cotton belt. Sen. Matthew C. Butler, of South Carolina, was one of those who professed pleasure at the movement. He harbored no doubt that it was inspired by Radical Republicans, but regardless of its origins, he rationalized that the outcome would be favorable to the South. He hoped that at least three hundred thousand blacks would leave their fields, to be replaced by white labor, on the ground that since the region depended too much upon black labor, everyone in his part of the country would benefit. A resident of West Point, Mississippi, took a similar stand, contending that blacks were leaving because they realized that, no matter how great their numbers, they could not subordinate the white race and that for this reason, many had chosen to leave. Let them go, he said, to be replaced by Swedes, Scots, Irish, and Germans; a white influx would mean increased manufacturing and a more balanced economy for the South. Meantime, he promised, southerners were determined to hold the fort, politically. Another Mississippian put it more bluntly when he complained that "there would be no trouble if the niggers would let us alone; the most of this trouble is on account of politics. If they would attend to their business and go along with their work we would settle the political question." Congressman James R. Chalmers, of Mississippi, took a milder line. He told the blacks of his district that they were free men and that they had a right to go any place they chose. But he warned them, Kansas was not necessarily the solution, because there, as elsewhere, "you will have the white man to contend with." Stay home, he urged, for "the sun is the colored man's friend. In the land where its ranges drive the white man to shelter the colored man has the advantage, but in the cold climate of the North he cannot compete with his white neighbor. Stay where your friend, the sun, aids you in the contest."[53]

Sen. Benjamin Jonas, of Louisiana, tended to discount the seriousness of the migration. He maintained that there were no more than two or three parishes in his state that were likely to be seriously affected and that the state at large would not feel the loss of labor. He admitted that cotton growing had not been particularly profitable in recent years because of generally lower prices, and if laborers had suffered, so had landowners. The blacks now were, in some cases, yielding to glowing promises from other regions, but like Chalmers, he felt that they were being misled. Congressman John F. King, also of Louisiana, argued that if any bull-dozing was evident, it was being done by Negro leaders who were driving the Negroes northward, even those who did not want to go. He blamed the leaders for spreading rumors such as the one that warned of an invasion by Indians who would kill all the blacks they could find in the South, or the story that the Queen of Spain had bought their lands and proposed to have all those who did not clear out slaughtered on the spot. W. T. Fleming, a Shreveport, Louisiana, druggist, thought that the mental condition of the blacks indeed had a lot to do with their desire to flee. He doubted that they had any material basis for their grievances; their dissatisfaction, he thought, arose from the change from Republican to Democratic state governments during the Hayes administration. "They do not know what to do," he later testified. "They had an idea, I imagine, that as long as the Republicans were in power in our State something might occur that possibly might benefit them directly. And now since the Democratic party has got into power I think they have lost that hope. There has resulted a kind of uneasiness and dissatisfaction in their minds. I think that is the entire cause of this exodus, so far as our part of the country is concerned."[54]

Although Southern politicians tended to play down the seriousness of the exodus, planters whose acreages were threatened by the sudden loss of labor displayed an undisguised concern. A hastily called meeting of cotton planters met at Greenville, Mississippi, late in May, 1879, for the purpose of considering the emigration. Many of those who gathered at Greenville consoled themselves with the idea that so far the movement was insignificant and that, indeed, some of the disillusioned blacks already were returning home. What appeared to excite the delegates most was the Conway plan. If a few hundred, or even several thousand, blacks wanted to leave, they said, no great damage would be done. But the appearance of a boat or boats, whose purpose was to furnish the disaffected with free transportation, would have a powerful effect upon credulous Negroes, and the mere presence of a rescue flotilla would confirm all the optimistic things that they had heard about Kansas and would verify all the chromos that they had seen.

Bankruptcy for the plantations loomed as a real possibility. Convention members denied that the blacks had been reenslaved. They pointed out that there were at least three contractual arrangements under which the workers operated: (1) leases payable in cotton; (2) contracts for work on shares, the landlord supplying land, teams, and forage; and (3) wages for labor. The Negro, far from being a slave, was free to choose any of these methods, went the argument. A convention memorial held that the Negro had no cause for complaint or for concern. Rather, it was the landlord who had reason to be worried, because he now faced the possibility of losing labor already contracted for and, consequently, the loss of the 1879 crop.[55]

Undisturbed—or, more probably, elated—by the cries of anguish coming out of the South, Conway continued to expand his role of "exodus angel," as the New Orleans newspaper had put it. During the spring months he played a part in caring for those who got as far as St. Louis, which city had become something of a "half-way house" for the Kansas-bound refugees. An old foundry was refurbished through the efforts of Penrose Chapman, a local restaurant owner, and James E. Yeatman, president of the Merchants' National Bank. Stoves and bunks were installed in anticipation of accommodating two to three thousand people. The old, dilapidated three-story structure was provided with new flooring on the ground level and with a new kitchen and dining facilities. It was dubbed "Hotel de Refuge" by a local reporter. Conway's name was linked to the project, but Yeatman denied this, saying that the Western Sanitary Commission was the only organization involved in it. Yeatman, being a banker and consequently being involved with businessmen who traded with southerners, drew back from any association with Conway because of the "steamboat plan," which was so unpopular in the South.[56]

Conway, meanwhile, proceeded apace, talking freely with reporters on any and all occasions about the great movement under way. In the autumn of 1879 he surveyed the results of the preceding six months and concluded that they had been a success. He was convinced that the Negroes were better off in Kansas than they had been in the South, that they were generally well employed at good wages, and that none were being supported by charity. Looking forward to the next travel season, he predicted that at least another hundred thousand more would leave the South. Despite this glowing picture, he admitted, at least by inference, that Kansas was nearly saturated. Having talked with St. John about this matter, Conway slowly backed away from his earlier position that the land of John Brown was the modern mecca. While he was willing to say that those with means to support themselves would meet with no opposition in Kansas, he thought it better that they move on to older western states where there was a demand for labor. He asserted that he had applications for farm laborers from all over the West and that he could find homes for at least twenty thousand from these sources alone.[57]

Although Conway's armada never invaded southern waters and the "General" gradually faded from sight, the idea of a physical confrontation with the old slave-masters had a powerful appeal among those northerners who remained unconvinced that the Civil War had accomplished total emancipation. Republican leaders, worried about the growing political power of the "Confederate Brigadiers" and a possible defeat in the 1880 election, were willing to use the Conway scheme as a means of dramatizing the exodus, which, in turn, was employed as proof positive that slavery was still alive. Figuratively speaking, the bloody shirt was to have been the banner under which Conway's fleet proposed to sail against an old and insulting enemy. It would have further symbolized the continuing struggle for black freedom, from the Republican point of view, and if these oppressed people once more had to be spirited out of the South by means of a new underground railroad, northern voters could be expected once again to answer the call. The destination of the blacks—Kansas— was sentimentally ideal; and if the movement could be properly exploited, John Brown country might once again figuratively be made to bleed, even if only until the votes were counted in 1880. Republicans realized that the exodus was not much of an issue, but with proper cultivation it might be made to look like one.

As events showed, Republican difficulties were not as great as some party members feared them to be, and the election of 1880 returned them to the White House. How much the exodus excitement helped them at the polls is hard to measure, but it is safe to say it did them no harm. Autumn elections, in 1879, had predicted that the Democratic resurgence was not as strong as had been feared. Writing to the *Times* (London), the secretary of the British and Foreign Anti-Slavery Society referred to these preliminary Democratic reverses and to the "heavy blow" that the party had taken. The answer to such a development, he said, was "not very far to seek." His reference was to the exodus, a movement that he believed to be politically potent enough to sway a large number of voters.[58]

When George S. Boutwell, the Massachusetts politician, spoke to a pro-exodus gathering at Boston, in the spring of 1879, he made no bones about the movement's political aspects. He told his listeners that "the struggle is for power—political power—and as was the case during the war the reliance of the South is upon the Democratic party of the North."[59] The message was clear: go out and defeat northern Democrats whose support for the new slavocracy was implicit. Toilers in the political vine-yard accepted this thesis. Amanda Way, of Philadelphia, suggested it when she told Governor St. John that she had raised some eighteen hundred dollars for the refugees. "I have been doing my best to enthuse the people to reach for their pocketbooks by speaking, visiting and writing letters," she said. "I cannot but believe that God will bless the good seed I have tried to sow, as to yet cause it to bring forth abundant fruit." With growing zeal she talked about going to Washington, D.C., where she intended to tap some of the Republican congressmen for money in support of the cause. In her view, this source ought to yield some nine thousand dollars "to help the Republican party if nothing else."[60] Amanda entertained no doubts as to the linkage between the welfare of the party and the new hegira; money raised for one cause was bound to help the other.

Aside from immediate considerations—the election of 1880—there was hope among northern Republicans and fear among southern Democrats that if enough blacks fled the South, that region would suffer a loss in congressional representation. "There is plenty of evidence that the movement is being fostered by Republican politicians and that by inducing a large number of Negroes to leave the southern states before the next census is taken the Republican managers hope to affect the representation of the states in the House and overthrow the Democratic majority in the house," reported the Democratic *St. Louis Post-Dispatch*. One of St. John's correspondents confirmed the view, saying that black colonization was the answer to breaking the power of the Democrats. He told the governor that even if it took several million dollars to get all the colored people out of the South, it would be a good buy for the North and would "secure a lasting victory over the southern conspirators." While he thought the long-range aim was to smash the Democrats, it would be even better if the transference could take place before June, 1880, to prevent what he feared might be a "Democratic triumph" that year.[61]

Meanwhile, Governor St. John attempted to weather a political hurricane that was generating force in Kansas. From all around the country came cries of encouragement and praise for his part in the movement, but at home he was under increasing attack because of problems that it was creating in his own back yard. He told Horatio Rust that he thought 1880 would see another hundred thousand Negroes flee the South and that number alone precluded the possibility of all of them coming to Kansas, that state—Topeka in particular—having cared for all that it could under the circumstances. Kansas was not just full, he said to Rust; its labor market was saturated. Could not Illinois find homes for fifty thousand refugees?[62] He hoped that it could. The governor of Kansas was beginning to get worried; politically, he feared, he had opened Pandora's Box.

9

KANSAS AT FLOODTIDE

By the early months of 1880 St. John indeed had reason to believe that, philanthropically, he was in over his head. The barracks operated by the Kansas Freedmen's Relief Association, built to accommodate two hundred, were jammed with four hundred; every available house in Topeka that could be rented for the use of refugees had been secured. Some of the children slept five to a bed while their parents sat up all night. Others shivered in cold tents, hastily erected to take the overflow. As officers of the relief association studied an empty treasury and pondered an uncertain future, the influx continued. It is no wonder that if St. John really believed that another hundred thousand would leave the South during 1880, he was anxious that few of that number would choose Kansas as their destination.[1]

At best, the governor's motives for discouraging further black immigration could be attributed to his belief that Kansas had reached a saturation point. But census figures do not argue in his behalf. In 1870, blacks composed 4.7 percent of the state's population; the 1880 figures show 4.3 percent; and those of 1890, a drop to 3.5 percent. An enormous influx of whites produced this decline in the percentages of blacks, and if the blacks had been distributed more evenly across Kansas, their presence would not have been so apparent. The problem lay in the fact that they tended to cluster in the towns, particularly in the eastern half of the state, and in those towns not only were their numbers frequently disproportionate but since these newcomers remained at the lower end of the economic scale, the candidates among them for welfare were numerous.

Political motives for shunting aside the flow of blacks were less com-

155

mendable and harder to prove, yet they existed. G. W. Carey, who became vice-president of the Kansas Freedmen's Relief Association in the fall of 1879, admitted that membership in its management no longer was sought after in Topeka. At an association meeting held in September, all the old officers resigned, after which an impromptu election was held to replace them. "I was one of those elected, and was informed of it the next morning," the surprised Carey later commented. He had doubts about the honor. "While I think it is injurious to a man in office to hold any position in that board, I felt that somebody would have to take hold of it, and I was willing to take my share," was his rationalization. So great was the pressure against further black immigration among Topeka's community leaders that association with it was becoming burdensome, if not politically dangerous.[2]

From the outset, St. John had maintained that neither he nor his state had done anything to encourage the black refugees. However, it was widely known that great efforts were being made at Topeka to care for those who did come and that an organization, at whose head stood St. John, functioned in that city. It was a matter of record that the relief association had fed thousands, had contributed to the establishment of the Wabaunsee Colony, fifty miles west of Topeka, and had provided money for those who had job offers deeper in Kansas but could not afford to get there. It is also true that St. John had sent word into the South, at a fairly early date, that only those who had means to move should do so. Yet, as a Christian, he continued to say, as he did to Horatio Rust early in 1880, that "they must find a resting-place somewhere." Again denying solicitation, he argued that "we have simply, in dealing with this question, done as we believed God would have us do." Denying that it was a political question, he maintained that "it is a question in which is involved human liberty. . . . I feel assured that the work is in the hands of true Christians, who have no other aim than to perform what they deem to be simply a duty to a much-abused people."[3] It was his obsessive Christianity, his devotion to principles, and his open-handedness to the oppressed that frustrated Kansas business leaders who felt that, one way or another, they would have to pay for the governor's philanthropies.

Business and civic leaders along the Missouri River, who were among the first to feel the deluge, took the governor at his word when he said that other states should share the burden. Farther up the river lay Nebraska municipalities that were easily reached by the cheap means of water transportation. Wyandotte, Leavenworth, and Atchison all indicated a desire to send the heavily laden river packets in that direction.

Although Nebraska newspapers praised the efforts of St. Louis to help the refugees and talked about the progress of these people toward what one paper referred to as "the happy land of Kansas," there was no great demand for them in Nebraska from anyone except members of Omaha's black community and a few philanthropists. On the contrary, the *Omaha Bee* editorially toasted the arrival of two hundred German immigrants in the spring of 1879, calling them "able and affluent." Then, to underscore Nebraska's preference, the editor commented: "This class of immigrants will form an offset to the impecunious colored immigrants from Mississippi and Louisiana." At that time, Nebraska had not yet felt any impact of the movement, but the *Bee* appeared anxious to make it known what kind of newcomers the state solicited. When an eastern correspondent spoke of opportunities for blacks in such places as Arizona, New Mexico, or Indian Territory, the *Bee* gave his account a prominent place in its columns.[4]

During the early summer of 1879 small groups of refugees arrived at Lincoln, Nebraska, destitute and in search of work. J. C. Hebbard of the Kansas Freedmen's Relief Association at Topeka had sent them on, and they were received by the local chapter of that association at Lincoln. The first contingents, being small and comprised of healthy looking specimens, posed no problems. But those who arrived during the ensuing weeks were "not as thrifty and cleanly" as their predecessors. A local paper nervously reported that a Memphis doctor had shown concern about the amount of infected baggage that was passing up river to Missouri and Kansas. The word epidemic lurked in the back of Nebraskans' minds. When a Democratic paper challenged the honesty of the Exodusters and accused them of pilfering bread, butter, eggs, coffee, salt, and other items that they needed, Lincolnites came to their defense and called such stories pure gossip. On the contrary, these were honest people, said a Lincoln newspaper, poor folks who had fled from their old masters, who did not expect anything in Nebraska more than a chance to work and to become good citizens.[5] And it was hoped that they were not bearers of any communicable disease.

The little town of Plattsmouth, Nebraska, located on the Missouri River a few miles south of Omaha, was not prepared to enlist in the cause of rescuing blacks from southern tyranny. When B. F. Watson, a Negro minister from Kansas City who represented banker A. W. Armour of that city, sent forward about two hundred refugees to East Plattsmouth, Iowa, by rail, Nebraskans across the river became alarmed. The contingent represented less than one-tenth of the number that poured into Kansas City that summer, most of whom were passed on to Topeka, but even that figure loomed large among the villagers at Plattsmouth. As Watson explained, Wyandotte would not permit any landings, so Kansas City had to bear the burden, and it became his assignment to send the new-comers anywhere that he could. Since he had received letters from individuals in Nebraska expressing sympathy and the promise of employment, he lost no time in dispatching part of his little army of refugees in that direction. When officials of the Burlington and Missouri Railroad declined to carry the group across the river and into Nebraska, because the residents of Plattsmouth would not agree to receive them, 163 of the group crossed over without permission.[6]

The arrival of the uninvited visitors produced a display of civic bad manners that sorrowed the Plattsmouth editor. "At once excitement arose, all sorts of rumors were rife, and all sorts of suggestions and many vague threats were heard," he reported. "We are sorry to recount that a great many of our people did not rise to the magnitude of the occasion and realize that a great crisis in solving one of the mightiest political problems of the days was before them. That the long talked of Negro problem was at the door, and [they] talked a good deal of baby talk about what ought to be done with them, what the authorities ought to do and especially what *they* would do if they had the power." The journalist predicted that the mayor and the city council would exercise a level of statesmanship worthy of the city's good reputation. He even suggested a course of action for those officials, one that was humane, philanthropic, and practical: send the newcomers to Omaha or to Nebraska City, a few miles down river. While he praised the arrivals, denying that they were paupers, but rather, insisting that they were people who were ready and willing to work, he felt that employment possibilities were limited in a small village such as his. He was critical of the Kansas City committee for "throwing a large and at first helpless population on an unwarned community." Sobered by the editor's scolding, community leaders abandoned harsh words and turned their efforts to raising money in behalf of the migrants, part of which was used to buy a little food, but most of which provided transportation for them to Council Bluffs, Omaha, and Nebraska City.[7]

Plattsmouth denied that it had passed on these strangers just to get rid of them. That little city merely raised money to help them reach places where they were really needed, such as Nebraska City, said the Plattsmouth editor. He was ashamed to think that 163 black transients could throw 3,000 people into such a flurry of excitement. They were a small threat to the local labor force, he argued, a threat that was only temporary.[8] A sympathetic Omaha paper explained that while Plattsmouth had few Negroes and did not feel like assuming the responsibility of caring for the unexpected arrivals, Nebraska City would have no such objections, because it had a "good sprinkling of blacks" already. The Omaha editor, who did not agree with his colleague at the *Bee,* spoke highly of the arrivals, calling the group "an exceptionally good class of blacks, willing, able and anxious to work, and will be no detriment to any community, if they are given a fair chance." He did not feel that Nebraska would suffer from the exodus. In fact, he editorialized, the state wanted black people, fifty thousand strong if that many chose to come. The men could work in the fields, while the women would help to solve the problem of domestic help. The editor asked his readers to "welcome . . . these black Waldenses" who were fleeing southern persecution.[9]

Although a segment of the Omaha press took a lofty view of the motives behind the exodus, speaking in terms that reflected the highest echelons of philanthropy, its hopes were rooted in something more tangible than principle. In competition with other western states and territories for increased population through immigration, Nebraska had discovered that advertising and other means of enticement cost money. Here, said the *Omaha Daily Republican,* "are the cheapest immigrants we can get. Every white immigrant costs 'big money' to get him; the blacks are waiting to come 'without money and without price.'" Additionally, if Nebraska could acquire ten or fifteen thousand of these bargain-basement immigrants, the state might be entitled to another congressman. The pastor of Omaha's First Methodist Episcopal Church offered yet another reason that the blacks would be useful in Nebraska. Large numbers of them would help to offset the work of the Irish Catholic Colonization Society, whose recent efforts were increasing the threat of papism in the region. Remarking that "Protestants will certainly feel that they need an element of equal strength in the state," he recommended that an organization should be set up at once to take care of the blacks in an orderly, efficient manner and to locate them in strategic places where they might effectively counter the coming Catholic invasion.[10]

E. D. McLaughlin, of an old Louisiana Creole family, who now practiced law in Omaha, had some reservations about such editorial enthusiasm for a black influx. Writing to a friend of his in Louisiana, he warned that only the "right kind" of Negro ought to think of Omaha as his future home. He was particularly suspicious of what he called the "city nigger," the man "who is generally a barber, hotel porter, waiter or cook, or swaggering, beer guzzling gambler, or impudent bawdy-house pimp." The Exodusters, he said, not only would be disappointed at failing to receive 160 acres of land, teams, food, clothing, and other forms of assistance, but "they will also find that their chances for official distinctions are exceedingly rare, and are likely to remain so for many generations." Omaha blacks, many of whom had lived there for some time, grimly agreed with him, particularly with regard to "official distinctions." In September, 1879, they met and voiced their complaints. The Republican party was accused of discrimination, of not alloting any local offices or political appointments to their race. They demanded proportionate representation in elective and appointive positions and threatened to leave the party if their wishes were ignored. This must have afforded quiet amusement to a few Nebraskans who watched Omaha with some jealousy. A Lincoln paper noted the arrival of blacks at Omaha and remarked that the *"Herald* is already figuring what the Republican majority in Douglas County will be this fall." Its concluding remark, that "it's an ill wind, etc.," proved to be somewhat prophetic when the Omaha blacks began to make demands upon the party.[11] Southerners, accused of bulldozing the blacks and of denying them any part in the region's political life, once again had reason to point fingers at northerners and to talk of hypocrisy.

There were other ironies, so far as the southerners were concerned. Kansas, the spiritual home of John Brown, now was feeling the full impact of the exodus, and some Kansans, who earlier had talked in lofty terms about helping to solve a great national problem, were on the verge of panic. In August, 1879, Congressman Thomas Ryan, of Kansas, told eastern newsmen that "when I left my home there were hundreds of freedmen on the verge of starvation, with little prospect of receiving any immediate or permanent relief. Nearly every train from the South brings more of the deluded people. Most of them who go to Kansas are of the most ignorant class. Nine-tenths reach Kansas soil without a dollar in their pockets, and become objects of charity from the day of their arrival among us." He predicted that in the coming year perhaps one hundred thousand southern blacks would move to northern states. He thought it odd that "the fever now is to go to Iowa and Nebraska, where the climate is even more severe than in Kansas."[12] There was nothing at all odd about this phase of the movement. St. John, at Topeka, and the reception committee at Kansas City, Missouri, were shipping recent arrivals out of their region as fast as they could. Nebraska's more rigorous climate was the least of their worries. That state, which was nearby and was easily reached by water or rail, was a logical target for relief committees in Kansas or Missouri.

Aside from their willingness to accept blacks because they were easily acquired immigrants whose numbers might earn for the state another congressional representative, not to mention their presumed ability to dilute the Catholic threat, Nebraskans saw these people as a potential source of inexpensive, easily controlled labor. For example, during the summer of 1879, the little town of York indicated that it could use a few "surplus" Exodusters, presumably as hired hands on nearby farms or for odd jobs in the town itself.[13] That there was some demand for labor in Nebraska was indicated when, early in 1880, the land commissioner for the A. T. & S. F. Railroad, at Topeka, shipped about two hundred Negroes to that state.[14]

J. M. Snyder, of central Nebraska's Sherman County, was one of those who thought that southern field hands would make good laborers. As a former captain of an Illinois regiment who had been in the South during the war, he watched the exodus with interest and was among those who volunteered to sponsor some of its members. "We should not object to a man with a wife and children," he told St. John. "We can furnish them work, pay them, give them good quarters, and eat at the table with them if they will keep themselves in a tidy condition." One reason for the veteran's willingness to hire the blacks, even to eat at the same table with them, was the rising cost of labor in his neighborhood. As he told St. John, both the Union Pacific and the Burlington and Missouri railroads were surveying branch lines "right through the center of the county," and one or both of the roads probably would commence construction that summer. "This has the effect to make it difficult to get hands," he explained, "as they are now paying $1.40 per day with every prospect that it will be $1.50 in a very short time."[15]

Farther west, in Colorado, labor commanded even more money. A Colorado Springs minister informed the *Colored Citizen,* of Topeka, that there was a great demand for both male and female workers in his state. Men could expect between $2.00 and $2.50 a day, while the women, usually domestics, were being paid between $16.00 and $25.00 a month.[16] The Topeka Relief Committee reported that it had received requests for labor from Colorado, one application coming from near Pueblo, were there was a place for a man and wife combination.[17] In answer to a labor request by the Union Pacific Railroad, the Relief Association sent thirty men westward in April, 1880. They were supplied with blankets provided by Elizabeth Comstock's English friends.[18]

Colorado was a young state, having achieved that status less than three years prior to the exodus, yet some of its people found time to interest themselves in a movement that must have seemed far away from the Rockies. In late April, 1879, H. I. Hale, of the mining town of Central City, sent thirty-three dollars to St. John, that sum being the proceeds of an entertainment given for the benefit of the refugees.[19] J. D. Lawson, of Colorado Springs, contributed ten dollars "for the help of destitute Negroes lately from the South."[20] However, when a public meeting was called in Denver to solicit money for the cause, the *Rocky Mountain News* reported that the gathering was very poorly attended. Impassioned speeches were made by ministers, jurists, and other interested parties, who spoke of the high motives behind their proposed efforts. Gov. Frederick W. Pitkin was appointed head of an executive committee whose task was to raise funds to aid those stranded in Kansas. Former governor John Evans, whose philanthropy was widely known, set the drive in motion with a hundred-dollar contribution. The *News* was pleased to announce that representatives from Denver's small Negro community came to the meeting and showed an interest in the cause. The blacks formed their own committee, appointed a chairman and a secretary, and pledged their assistance. The *News* promised that when the committee got to work, it would have the cooperation of the community's white membership.[21]

The Denver Committee decided against transferring funds from Colorado to Kansas for the purpose of supporting the latter state's indigent population. Rather, it concluded, the money was to be used to bring some of these people westward when they could find employment. One of the committee members made much of the fact that self-reliance was the key to freedom. Colorado, said the *Denver Tribune,* ought to tell these prospective immigrants: "We have a new State; you are entering upon a new life. There is a harmony of the two and we will help you in consequence. . . . Come out and you will breathe its fresh spirit and be strengthened." Governor Pitkin said much the same thing to St. John: "The marvelous tide of immigration toward Colorado & our mining camps brings the sick & the destitute. We are called upon to minister to the suffering emigrants in our midst & in spite of our great mineral wealth we expect to have the poor always with us." He assured St. John that if the refugees in Kansas really were suffering and if that state could not provide enough aid, Colorado would contribute; otherwise he wanted to spend funds that had been raised locally for transportation costs.[22]

This was satisfactory to St. John. He was anxious to reduce the number of blacks on hand, and he welcomed any opportunity to send some of them beyond the confines of Kansas. He told Wilmer Walton, a Denverite who was interested in the movement, that while his organization was in need of funds, it was more greatly in need of homes for his charges. He hoped that the good people of Denver could find places for at least a hundred of them. "This would not only be a great relief to our committee, but it would accomplish more from a financial standpoint than a donation of a thousand dollars in cash," he wrote in late July. The governor explained his problem: Exodusters still were arriving at Topeka faster than they could be dispatched to other points. "There are about one hundred and fifty at the barracks here, one hundred and fifty more just landed at

Kansas City and three hundred more [are on] boats between here and St. Louis and Wyandotte." He said that Kansas already had provided work and homes for a great many of the distressed, but local sources of employment were drying up.[23]

Colorado civic leaders were anxious to learn something of the Kansas situation before committing money to the cause. When "Aunt" Clara Brown, a black woman who was well known in Denver and Central City, offered to investigate the situation, Governor Pitkin agreed at once. He wrote a letter of introduction to St. John, explaining who Aunt Clara was: "She came to Colorado in 1859 & accumulated quite a large fortune, but has spent most of it for the relief of her own race. She is one of the best old souls that ever lived & is respected and loved by all who know her. She goes to Kansas to see the destitute freedmen & to report here upon their condition." Help her, said Pitkin, and give her suggestions "as you think will promote the object she has in view."[24]

Although Colorado experienced the "Leadville excitement" in 1879 and although in the immediate years that followed, there was a great demand for labor in the mining camps, only a limited number of blacks appear to have shown an interest in the area. The Exodusters primarily were farmers, and the word "Kansas" seemed to be the only one that held much magic for them. B. F. Watson, the Kansas City black man who was instrumental in distributing some of his countrymen throughout Kansas and other parts of the West, understood the attraction that John Brown country had for his people. He described an old black woman who had jumped off a Missouri River packet and cried out, "Bress God, I'se reached de land of freedom at las'." Watson admitted that these people regarded Kansas as the land of milk and honey, but, he added, "it has not flowed very freely for them lately." In 1880 he told the Voorhees Committee that "we sent a number of them to Colorado this spring, and wherever they have had this labor they desire more of it."[25] In the spring of 1879 the *New York Times* recommended such a place as Colorado, saying that the blacks were wanted there, so "let us help them wisely."[26]

In saying that the blacks were wanted in Colorado, the *Times* merely was expressing an opinion. Labor was in great demand among mine owners, and thousands of Italians, Irish, Austrians, Serbs, Slovenes, Croats, and other newly arrived immigrants answered the call. Yet, by 1880, labor conditions became so turbulent that in May the Leadville mines were shut down by strikers, and Governor Pitkin was obliged to call out the militia in order to protect property. This was not a good time or a good place for blacks to be introduced as cheap labor, and many of them undoubtedly shunned the idea as they had when opportunities had been given them to work in the Missouri coal mines. It is probable that only a relatively small number of Coloradans—a few intellectuals and some of the financial elite —had a great deal of sympathy for this minority. That these mountain people had their views about non–Anglo Saxons is illustrated in a comment made by the *Denver Tribune* in August of 1879, when the editor offered to send some Ute Indians to St. John to satisfy his humanitarian urges. "We are willing to send him job lots on long time," quipped the *Tribune*.[27] As for the blacks, a correspondent identified as "L.Q.W." warned Denverites that ever since emancipation the American Negroes had been restless and inclined toward migration. The average freedman, he said, had vague dreams of getting along without work, and he "is now an 'exoduster' by inclination, if not in act." The writer concluded that these people had become mere tools of the Republican party.[28]

There were some other possibilities for blacks in the Far West. General Conway believed that New Mexico, which as yet was not very heavily settled by Americans, was a good place to locate a large number of discontented southern Negroes. He estimated that there were approximately one hundred thousand of them in southern states with sufficient money to invest in land. Some of them, he said, already had formed a land company headed by a man named J. M. Woodward, which owned some seven hundred thousand acres of New Mexican land that was for sale in family sized plots. Conway was personally interested in southwestern real estate described by him as "ordinary valley and plateau lands, adapted to grazing, and to the methods of irrigation adopted by the New Mexicans, which can be done the same by the colored people." He thought that cotton could be raised in southern Arizona "the same as in Louisiana and Mississippi." The result? "I think the Negro, who now, for a few years having educated himself and his children, would be, I think, superior to the native New Mexicans." He planned to sell such land for fifty cents an acre less than the government price, in tracts ranging from fifty to one hundred acres.[29]

Indian Territory, or what later would be Oklahoma, was another area looked at with interest. In 1881 St. John heard from a man named George M. Jackson, who said that he was in touch with leading southern blacks who wanted Congress to open the area to the freedmen. There were some fourteen million acres of unoccupied public land in that part of the country, he said, "obtained by purchase in 1866, as the treaties recite for the purpose of settling Freedmen & Indians on—see treaties." Jackson said that he was then engaged in a movement to open these lands to settlement, and while he thought that they should be opened to the general public, "if that cannot be done let us open them to the settlement of the outraged Freedman as well as the poor &c." He asked St. John's cooperation.[30]

St. John was willing to cooperate with anyone who could help him to send Exodusters anywhere but Kansas. He had tried to stem the flow into Topeka by sending word to southern blacks, via the newspapers, that anyone who came to Kansas should have means to support himself during the transitional period. The governor's principal mouthpiece, the *Commonwealth*, was dismayed to learn that a Negro named Samuel W. Winn had written from Topeka to his friends in Mississippi, saying that in late September, 1879, only two families were being maintained at the local barracks and that they were working for a dollar a day with the prospect of being self-supporting in the near future. The writer also indicated that there was a great unsupplied demand for labor in Kansas and Colorado. The *Commonwealth* reacted sharply, calling such statements nonsense. There was no demand for labor in either of those states in the autumn, said the paper; it was wrong and even wicked to mislead southern blacks with such stories. The editor urged anyone coming to Kansas, black or white, to bring enough funds to see himself through the winter.[31]

The warnings went unheard. During the autumn days, more blacks appeared at Topeka; for example, on October 17 a group of 200 arrived, hungry and in need of shelter.[32] By the early days of 1880 the barracks were overflowing, and St. John sought relief. Once more he tried to enlist the aid of the federal government, asking that some of this surplus immigration be siphoned off to Fort Harker, in central Kansas, but again he failed to get an affirmative response from Washington.[33] Meanwhile, the influx continued. Late in January, Elizabeth Comstock commented that between 500 and 600 refugees were receiving daily rations. "The poor creatures arrive now at the rate of 600 weekly, and we ship them off to different parts of this and other states," she wrote. "It is estimated that 20,000 are now in the State. Topeka is our headquarters, is very much crowded, resulting in sickness and death. We have no city hospital or almshouse for them."

H. H. Stanton, a Topeka hotelkeeper, estimated that there were between three and five thousand Exodusters in Topeka during those early spring months. He thought that it was a heavy load for a city of between twelve and fifteen thousand to carry, and he wondered how so many blacks were able to survive under the conditions in which they lived. "I see them sitting around on the fences or standing on the corners of the street talking politics, and how they get a living is a wonder to me," he told the Voorhees Committee.[34] A correspondent to the *Commonwealth* agreed that such numbers placed a burden upon the city, but he praised

165

the local relief society for doing "a splendid work in a quiet way," in affording aid to the needy. He said that about twenty-five hundred had arrived during the last two months of 1879, and he admitted that without the assistance of "our Eastern friends" there would have been even greater suffering among Topeka's black transients. It saddened the writer, who was a local job printer, to see hungry children milling around in front of his office, begging for food, when corn was selling locally for only twenty-five cents a bushel. In an angry thrust at his fellow Kansans, he remarked that they had fed ten white tramps for every meal given to a black man.[35]

No slackening of the flow appeared to be in sight. From New Orleans came reports that large numbers of Louisiana and Mississippi Negroes were making preparations to leave. In mid January, 1880, a correspondent from Durant, Mississippi, said that about 125 blacks from that vicinity already had purchased tickets for Kansas and that with the coming of spring, hundreds of others would join them. "It is impossible to get the Negroes to make contracts for this year," he complained, "and farmers cannot get hands to work their land." The *New Orleans Times* earlier had comforted itself with the thought that the movement's force was almost spent, but now the editor decided otherwise, and he predicted that in 1880 the movement would be even larger than in 1879. Admitting that Negroes all over the South appeared to be ready to depart, the journalist turned to a familiar refrain: that over half of the 1879 cotton crop had been made by whites, that whites could work the fields as well as blacks, and that with the departure of the former slaves, southern whites would become a more industrious class, capital would flow into the area, and everyone would be better off.[36]

News stories such as this one were disturbing to Kansas readers, particularly those who lived in Topeka. Even Mrs. Comstock, who had taken up residence there to "help victims of cruelty and oppression," began to worry. Early in February she told William Penn Nixon, of Chicago's *Daily Inter-Ocean,* that the migration continued, unabated. According to her estimates, six hundred had arrived during the week preceding her letter, another hundred had turned up the night before, and she had been told that nine hundred more were on their way. Despite her bottomless reservoir of sympathy for these unfortunates, she, too, realized that Topeka was about to be engulfed and that immediate action was required. Appeals went out to the governors of Illinois, Indiana, Wisconsin, Minnesota, Iowa, Michigan, and Ohio. In response the governor of Indiana sent what she termed an insulting letter, charging her with enticing Negroes out of the South. Nixon was more sympathetic. He called a meeting at a

Chicago hotel, where, he promised, he would urge upon fellow philanthropists the urgency of economic aid to beleaguered Kansas.[37]

Although Kansas businessmen and the state's philanthropic leaders
differed sharply over the philosophic origins of the exodus and, to some
extent, over its more practical causes, they were driven to agreement on
one ground: it had become too big for Kansas alone. Through records
kept by the Kansas Freedmen's Relief Association (KFRA) and minor
local relief agencies, it was possible to get some notion as to the size of the
influx; but this could be no more than an estimate, because an unknown
percentage of the newcomers were sufficiently well off that they did not
need to seek aid from such sources. In the spring of 1880 G. W. Carey,
vice-president of KFRA, guessed that in the course of the movement
about fifteen thousand had arrived at Topeka, only about twenty-five
percent of whom were able to care for themselves.[38] John Milton Brown,
superintendent of the Relief Association, set the total number of arrivals in
the entire state, by that date, at about sixty thousand. Two-thirds of these,
he said, were in a destitute condition and had to be given help; to this end
some $68,000 had been expended. Of the total he estimated that five
thousand had gone on to other states, about thirty thousand had settled in
the country on their own or upon rented lands, or had hired out to
farmers, while the remaining twenty-five thousand were in or around
Kansas towns.[39] St. John's figures for arrivals in Kansas were somewhat
more modest. Late in 1880, while lecturing to an audience at Chicago, he
said that since 1877 some sixty thousand Negroes had left the South, forty-
thousand of whom had settled in Kansas, the remainder going to adjoining
states. He maintained that only $50,000 had been spent in Kansas to assist
these unfortunates.[40]

Topeka, the state capital and the headquarters for KFRA, by no
means funneled all the refugees through its portals, but it received more
than other towns because it housed the relief organization and because
other municipalities, which were poorly equipped to handle a sudden
influx or were unwilling to undertake such a responsibility, tended to send
the newcomers to St. John and his workers. The lack of record-keeping
on the part of other ports of entry and the fact that KFRA counted only
a portion of this immigration make it impossible to know even an approx-
imate number that entered the state during the "exodus years." However,
because there is no evidence that significant numbers returned to the South
or went on to other western states and because the 1880 census figures
show 43,107 blacks in Kansas, an increase of 26,000 since 1870, it is clear
that figures given by Brown and St. John were far too high.

For St. John and his supporters the precise number of entrants was not the most important thing. No head count was necessary to tell the governor that matters had gotten out of hand. By the spring of 1880, charges were being heard across the state that he was mainly responsible for the plight that Kansas now was in, and he struggled hard to free himself from what appeared to be a heavy political liability. He told a fellow Topekan that from the very beginning, he had opposed southern Negroes coming to Kansas as an exodus of impoverished people. On the contrary, he maintained, he had not thrown open the state's doors to indigents, but rather he had urged all immigrants to have at least a year's supply of funds on hand with which to get a start. There were better places for destitute blacks elsewhere, the governor argued, older and richer states that were better able to provide employment.[41]

One source of aid toward which St. John looked was his enthusiastic correspondent and fellow philanthropist Horatio Rust, of Chicago. During the early days of 1880 Rust wrote of his desire to "get our organization started upon so broad a basis that we can meet any demands the Exodus make from any direction." St. John lost no time in capitalizing upon the interest shown at Chicago. In a somewhat self-contradictory statement, he told Rust that while there was no difficulty at all in finding employment in Kansas for his black immigrants, money was being wasted, because once they arrived, they were being sent on at once to such places as Iowa and Illinois. It would be much more efficient to send them directly north from St. Louis. In fact, he added, in a few days a man would be sent to St. Louis to direct traffic. He liked Rust's suggestion "to land some of the refugees at Cairo and distribute them from that point," and he suggested that the people of Illinois "organize a headquarters at that point for that purpose."[42]

At a meeting of KFRA's executive board, held on March 15, it was decided unanimously to send a man named W. O. Lynch to use, as Lynch put it, "such means as I may deem prudent and expedient to turn the tide of emigration from the South into other States than Kansas." In a printed circular, presumably for use among prospective black immigrants, Lynch explained that Kansas had no objection to Exodusters but that it had done what it could for them, and now it was up to other states to lend a hand. In it he quoted a letter from Rust, in which the Chicagoan had called upon the land of Lincoln to open its arms to southern black refugees and to accept at least fifty-thousand of them. Lynch advised those who were planning to leave the South to stop at Cairo, Illinois, where representatives of KFRA would direct them onward. Already, he said, three hundred heads of families had been sent on from that point and had found homes in Illinois and Iowa.[43]

At the Voorhees Committee hearings, held during the spring months of 1880, the extent of St. John's problem was revealed. G. W. Carey, judge of a Topeka probate court, testified that while no real attempt had been made to entice the blacks into Kansas, a concerted effort then was under way to direct them elsewhere. Kansas City and St. Louis, he added, were enthusiastic partners in the project. Why? It was "to save ourselves from an overflow of this pauper emigration," said Carey. When asked if the Cairo bureau's purpose was principally to "keep the immigration off you," the witness answered affirmatively. Kansas, he explained, did not want any indigents—black or white. Sentiment throughout the state that spring definitely opposed the arrival of any more Exodusters; the judge confessed that since St. John was running for office that year, the black invasion certainly would be an election issue. St. John, of course, thought it inexpedient to admit error, and publicly he continued to argue that from a humanitarian view he had been right, maintaining that Kansas had done its duty nobly, and now it was time to let others share in the philanthropy. Carey was much more frank. He made no attempt to deny that St. John once had favored the movement, but now that it had become politically explosive, he admitted that the governor was in full retreat.[44]

Meanwhile, Lynch went about his job. At the end of March he wrote to St. John from Nashville, saying that he was hard at work persuading prospective black emigrants for Kansas to change their direction. "Some will leave this point for Illinois," he said, "and will stop at Cairo and I shall leave here for Memphis, Tennessee where a large number is going soon, thence to Cairo again and effect my plans there."

During these days, St. John continued to receive mail from various points in Illinois, the writers offering homes for small numbers of colored families. The link between St. John's temperance interests and those of his Exodusters surfaced once more when he heard from Lucia E. F. Kimball, of Chicago. Miss Kimball, who was a member of the Illinois WCTU, of which Frances Willard was president, sent the governor ten dollars and an apology that the sum could not be ten times larger. "I am deeply interested in your labor of love for these poor people," she assured the governor. "God speed the right." Less interested in labors of love were the white workingmen of Illinois. B. F. Watson, of Kansas City, complained that when he sent some blacks to the coal mines of Rock Island County, one of them was killed by strikers. He blamed it on the Irish, who, he said, generally opposed the appearance of Negroes in the labor force.[45]

Aware of Chicago's potentialities, Elizabeth Comstock had left her post at Topeka for this new mecca on the shores of Lake Michigan. Prior to her move she had received $185.70 from Nixon, to carry on the work at Topeka, and in acknowledging it, she told him how pleased she was that Chicago at last was "thoroughly aroused." Eastern cities, she added, also were awakening to the importance of the cause, Boston having sent in $2,000 during February. Mrs. Comstock attributed this partially to the work being done in Illinois, and she was thrilled to think that "the trumpet sound sent forth by Chicago has reached the Atlantic Coast."[46] It was Nixon and Rust, she told St. John, who had urged her presence in Chicago. "Canst thou not meet me there & make a speech?" she asked the governor. He would be received warmly, she thought. "Everywhere I hear Gov. St. John spoken of highly." A few enthusiasts told her that they hoped he would be the next president of the United States.[47]

Mrs. Comstock had to admit that the way of a reformer was not always an easy one. In addition to the critical letter from the governor of Indiana, referred to earlier, she was attacked by two Democratic papers in Kansas, both of which accused her of helping herself to five thousand dollars of Relief Association money. She was pleased when both Rust and St. John publicly refuted the charge. She told the latter that she was not much moved by the attacks, adding: "If the Democrats rave & the heathen rage, I shall be in good company." Undeterred by such distractions, she and Laura Haviland increased their efforts in Chicago. They visited Nixon, asking him to "send a bombshell into the Capital" that would make congressional leaders tremble, "& had a nice chat with Shelby L. Cullom the Gov. of the State."[48] In mid March Mrs. Comstock delivered what Nixon called "an eloquent speech" at Chicago's Farwell Hall, in which she charged that Chicago had not done enough and that it must be prepared for a large black immigration in 1880. The *Inter-Ocean* lamented the fact that the crowd was disappointingly small, but it said that those present represented the city's notable people, a dozen doctors of divinity being seated in the front row.[49] Chicago's excitement, of which the lady crusader earlier had spoken with such pleasure, appeared to be diminishing.

Both St. John's organization and Kansas businessmen who frequently criticized it shared the hope that Chicago's interest in black refugees had not flagged. Even "Pap" Singleton, who claimed to be the "father of the Exodus," thought that Kansas had acquired more than its share of these immigrants. When "Pap" heard that more of his people in Tennessee were ready to leave for Kansas, he advised against it. He would go back and tell them himself, he said, but he was getting too old; someone younger and more active should accept the assignment. "They should be sent to turn the tide of emigration," he said.[50]

In addition to turning back further attempted entries, the possibility existed that some of the existing surplus could be sent home. A. S. Johnson, of the AT & SF Railroad, announced that his road would return Exodusters as far as Kansas City free. When asked if this was not equivalent to sending them from the frying pan into the fire, Johnson revealed the practical side of the business community's mind. "That would get us out of our trouble and let Missouri take care of them," he responded. He offered the opinion that Missouri was much better adapted to deal with these people, meaning, perhaps, that as an old Slave State, it was accustomed to them.[51]

But few of the Exodusters accepted the offer. They, too, knew that Missouri had been a Slave State, and for that reason, as many of them stated explicitly, they did not want to live there. They wanted to live in Kansas, and Kansas it had to be. As St. John worried about his political future and the extensive philanthropy into which he and his friends had thrust the state, the movement continued, although by the end of the 1880 planting season it began to diminish, and in the following year it tapered off to a dribble. A few of the newcomers drifted on to nearby states; even more went into other upper-midwestern states, perhaps indicating that St. John's efforts to turn the tide elsewhere had been successful; and those who had come to stay in Kansas settled in and around small towns or on nearby farms and took up a new life.

10

AN AMERICAN BOTANY BAY

As it was with white settlers on the American agricultural frontier, those who were black reported varying degrees of success. Some worked hard and eked out a living; others briefly tried their hand at prairie farming and then gravitated to nearby towns; a small remnant either returned to their earlier homes or moved farther west. By comparison the blacks appear to have enjoyed fewer successes and to have suffered more than their white counterparts. Their problem lay in the difficulty of adjusting to a strange climate and an unfamiliarity with frontier crops, a condition severely aggravated by a lack of capital with which to initiate new enterprises. Unable to farm successfully, unwilling to go back home or to venture deeper into the West, and finding no place for themselves in the political, social, or more profitable economic spheres of Kansas life, a good many saw no recourse but to huddle at the edges of small towns—and hope. These were the "problem people" about whom merchants and civic leaders complained.

Typical of westward-moving people, the black settlers had left their old homes with high hopes for a new life. One of the Exoduster songs described the feeling of anticipation, mixed with regret at leaving familiar scenes:

I's going from de cotton fields, I's going from de cane,
I's going from de old log hut dat stands down in de lane;
De boat am in de ribber dat hab come to take me off,
I's gone and jined de 'exodus' dat's making for de Norf.
Dey tell me out in Kansas, dat's so many miles away,

173

De colored folks am flocking, 'cause dey're getting better pay.
I don't know how I'll find it dar, but I's bound to try,
So when de sun goes down tonight I's going to say goodbye.

CHORUS: I's going from de cotton fields,
             And ah! it makes me sigh;
             For when de sun goes down tonight,
             I's going to say goodbye.[1]

Another song told of the pull toward Kansas and the melancholy of
leaving home. Sung to the tune "Them Golden Slippers," it ran, in part:

Let de old back log give out its light
An' let us all feel good tonight,
An' hab a good time for de last time heah
'Fore we start for de land ob Kansas.[2]

By the early weeks of 1880 a good many blacks who bravely had sung
such words regretted the decision to seek greener pastures. By then the
St. Louis Relief Board had closed down for lack of funds, and KFRA at
Topeka was in serious difficulty. At one point, during the summer of 1879,
some five hundred hungry refugees had camped at the outskirts of Topeka
and were being fed by the charity of local individuals, KFRA being unable
to care for all of them. Some two hundred, who had been sent to Lawrence
and Topeka, retreated to Wyandotte because they could not find work.
At Lawrence some of the hungry gathered along the banks of the Kansas
River to beg for catfish heads from local fishermen.[3]

In the spring of 1880 the young black St. Louis attorney John H.
Johnson testified that the refugees of his group, which had been sent
forward to St. John, were "scattered out through Kansas" and "at last
reports they were doing well . . . , and nearly all of them were satisfied."
Some of those mentioned disagreed with Johnson. For example, H. H.
Roseman, a black southerner who visited the interior portions of Kansas
in mid 1879, said that he had found "thousands of the late emigrants
located along the sides of skirts of limited timber and in a region quite
destitute of good water." He charged further that "the colored people of
the state are suffering intensely—many from sickness, and nearly all for
the daily necessities of life." Warning members of his race to stay away
from Kansas, he said that at the time of his visit some 450 either were sick
or were the subjects of charitable treatment in John Brown country. Mississippi, he asserted, was a much more habitable place than "wild and
frigid Kansas." Philip Brookings, formerly of Mississippi, agreed that
his home state had its good points. "I am certain that I can make two
dollars there where I could one in Kansas," he told the Voorhees Com-

mittee. "There is nothing to do in Kansas, and nobody with any money to pay for doing it. I got a man's horse and wagon there one day; he had hired me to do some hauling; and I drove out of my way to two or three places hunting for work; I was afraid if he found it out, he would think I was stealing, but I was not; I was only trying to find something to do."[4]

Daniel Votaw, an attorney who served as agent for the KFRA at Independence, Kansas, and later was the organization's secretary, wrote to Laura Haviland early in 1880, confirming the distress. He and his wife had taken a wagonload of clothing to Coffeyville, Kansas, in relief of some refugees who were reported to be suffering from the cold. He found a portion of them camped in the woods about four miles from town, living out in the open. "Some women and children barefoot, feet frozen," he wrote. One man's hands were so frozen that the fingers came off at the knuckles. "They were mourning the death of five of their company, who were frozen to death coming through. We gave them and others the last we had of the clothes left." Most of the party, which numbered ninety-two, had not eaten for thirty-six hours, and the Votaws gave them the remnants of the food that they had brought along. Perhaps unaware of the irony of his statement, made about a group of freezing, starving, homeless blacks in snow-swept Kansas, he commented: "They intend to raise cotton."[5]

Others, who reached KFRA's headquarters at Topeka, were better off, but even there the situation left something to be desired. During the early spring days of 1880 some three hundred of them arrived weekly—on occasion the figure reached as high as five hundred—and despite all efforts to find work for them or to send them on, the number housed at the barracks rarely decreased to manageable proportions. Many of them were sick and unable to work. Those who sought employment in the neighborhood found the search unrewarding. H. H. Stanton, of Topeka, described the case of one Exoduster who, with his wife and three children, had tried to gain a foothold in Kansas. "Somebody took them up to Wamego [about thirty-five miles west of Topeka], but had nothing for them to do, and could not keep them; they got about five days' work up there, and that was all; they came very near starving; they staid [*sic*] there six weeks with nothing to do, and no place even for the family to sleep; they came back to Topeka, and landed in the barracks again." But as Stanton pointed out, the retreat provided no sanctuary: "The superintendent drove them out, saying that he had helped that family once, and they must keep away. For three nights they slept on the freight cars there, or staid on the platform." When Stanton protested to the superintendent, he was told that the refugees had been given aid once, and it was all they were going to get. Finally, the relief association board yielded, in "rather an uncivil way," and produced railroad tickets to send the family back to its southern home.[6]

Conditions were not much better in the Missouri River towns. H. C. Solomon, of Atchison, estimated that by the spring of 1880 there remained about 1,200 to 1,500 Exodusters in his city and county. The city's black population had jumped from 840 to 2,787 in 1880, much of the gain coming from the exodus. Most of those referred to by Solomon, and by census figures, lived in the town itself, with about 600 spread throughout the county. Looking at the condition of those who struggled for existence in the town, Solomon concluded that the Exodusters had not bettered their condition by coming to Kansas. He knew some who had been there for at least a year, "and they are poorer, if possible, today, and more needy, than when they landed there. They have not a cent in the world."[7]

Those who were actively soliciting funds for the Exodusters tended to boast about how much assistance had been rendered, when they talked to politicians or to fellow members of relief organizations; but when they were out on the "contribution circuit," these people admitted that there was great need among the blacks of Kansas. One newspaper quoted "a Quaker lady from Kansas" (Elizabeth Comstock), who was collecting money in New York in the autumn of 1880, as portraying grim conditions among the refugees. According to her estimate, some fifty thousand had taken part in the migration, and only about one-third of them had found any kind of work. Of these, she said, the largest part worked in coal mines, stone quarries, or public buildings, and only a very small fraction were engaged in agriculture. The remaining two-thirds were said to be in an exceedingly destitute condition.[8] Only months earlier a plantation owner at Harrison Station, Mississippi, had written to St. John, asking if he could find some laborers among the Exodusters. If they were without means and were in distress in Kansas, he offered to hire them and to treat them well.[9] If the planter obtained any such returnees, it is not a matter of record. The chances are that he did not, for there was great reluctance on the part of most Exodusters to go back. However, it is worthy of note that an unemployed black labor force of considerable size was the subject of charity in Kansas at a time when its services were being asked for in the South.

The "Quaker lady from Kansas" probably was correct when she said that only a small proportion of the Exodusters engaged in agriculture upon reaching that state. This is to distinguish them from other blacks who had filtered into Kansas for some time, people who had money with which to buy land and who earlier had farmed in such places as Kentucky and Tennessee. These were the people who, in general, made up the black colonies of Kansas and who frequently opposed the coming of the Exodusters as much as did their white neighbors—and for largely the same reasons. As St. John's correspondence indicated, a great proportion of Exodusters came from agricultural areas of the South, and as a rule, their backgrounds lay with cotton culture, or in some cases with general farming. Yet, when they arrived in Kansas, they found it difficult to continue the old way of life.

A resident of Topeka, who took a critical view of the influx, complained of the difficulty of getting the blacks onto the land. "The Negro race is clannish," he wrote, "they are never contented to live isolated, and the idea that they will take up government land and live on it like the white man is a mistaken one." He predicted that "in time they will all be in the cities and they will never forget that in Topeka they were provided for without money and without price, and they will long to be back and back they will come." Dwelling upon the ingrained characteristics of the newcomers, he remarked that "their social natures call them together where they can attend church and other gatherings. They are not content that this shall be one day in seven, but every night they will be found together, and they will not live, unless compelled to, where such cannot be the case."[10]

Anne E. Bingham, the wife of a farmer who lived near Junction City, Kansas, had much the same thing to say. When, in 1880, a group of Exodusters camped outside the town, local farmers went among them, looking for families who were in search of work. "We had a family consisting of a man and wife and four children," she later recalled. "We had no tenant house, so my husband fixed up the granary until he could provide a place for them. The man was a big, strong, burly Negro and fully able to do hard work, and was a good worker. The wife was good, too, but I only had her to do the washing and ironing." So the families lived apart, the blacks temporarily housed in the old granary, where "they would close the door and window . . . every night, although the weather was hot, to keep out the 'hants.'" The Binghams tried to improve the situation. A stone building with a good floor was built for the tenants on the side of a nearby bluff, a place that Mrs. Bingham described as comfortable. Each day she gave an hour of her time to teach the children how to read. But she said regretfully, "the family got lonesome and finally went to town."[11]

In larger towns, blacks were sufficiently numerous to constitute little subcommunities of their own. As early as 1880 "Tennessee Town" was established west of Topeka's city limits by some five hundred Exodusters. South of the city lay "Mud Town," named for its unpaved streets and for conditions that prevailed during spring floods. In north Topeka was a little community called Redmonsville, where, well into the twentieth century, remnants of the settlement still were in evidence.[12] This tendency to gather in the cities was opposed even by the black residents, those who had arrived earlier and who now found the newcomers a burden on their purses. The *Colored Citizen,* of Topeka, urged the migrants to keep moving westward. It gave prominence to a letter from A. T. Hall, Jr., of Nicodemus, who advised members of his race to settle in frontier communities if they had energy, money, and experience, but if devoid of the latter two qualifications, to go north and east. "Scatter out as did the Jews in England," he advised them. "Get all the intelligence, money and property you can, and in the process of time with you, as with the Jews, will come a favorable solution to the race problem. The more the race unites, the greater will be the pressure against it."[13]

A black minister gave similar advice. He did not favor the movement of "our promising young men or our people generally" to the cities, "for there they do not make enough to live on comfortably, as it takes all they make to dress themselves and pay house-rent." He advised those who already had made such a move to "get out of the cities and towns, stop holding up the corners and walking the streets with your hands in your pockets and a cigar in your mouth." When asked, "Where shall we go?" he answered: "Go to the country, and if you cannot buy a large piece of land, buy a small piece, or work by the month until you can buy. Or let us go West. There are hundreds and thousands of acres of land in the Western States and Territories unoccupied."[14]

There had occurred a dribbling of blacks into Kansas and other parts of the West prior to the southern exodus of 1879, but many of these, including emigrants from the North, did not appear to be agriculturally inclined. Prior to 1879, colonies had been formed in Kansas, but their general impact was small. As the *Daily Bee* of Omaha commented, "For some reason or other the colored people of the North have heretofore had but little inclination to till the soil, as a colored ranchman in the far West is something almost unheard of."[15] A resident of Atchison, Kansas, who testified before the Voorhees Committee, verified the fact that some of the earlier blacks had taken up farming in his part of the state. "We have in our county a little colony, you might call it, of colored farmers who have been there for a good many years," he said. He set the number of families at between ten and twenty, some of whom had been there for ten or fifteen years, raising corn, wheat, and vegetables. However, he added, "I think it has not proved a success by any means."[16]

Successful or not, these farmers were accepted by the white population because they were few in number. But when the influx of 1879 hit Atchison, resentment soared. "I am positive that it is the universal sentiment, not only in the city of Atchison and the county, but in the northern part of the State of Kansas . . . that they are a detriment to the State, because they are paupers; they do not produce anything, and the large portion of those who are able to work will not work," said H. C. Solomon of that river town.[17] The city fathers made every effort to scatter those people throughout western Kansas or other parts of the West.

The notion of sending on to some other point anyone—black or white—of whom "the establishments" of eastern Kansas towns did not approve had its limitations. The little towns of interior Kansas objected to being recipients of such a policy on the ground that they, too, were unable to accommodate the strangers. Yet, to push these wanderers westward even farther was recognized as being impractical. By early 1880 between eight thousand and ten thousand white settlers in far-western Kansas found it necessary to appeal for food and clothing to sustain them during the coming winter. In response to a letter from St. John, telling of crop failure and destitution at the western edge of Kansas settlement, the railroad entrepreneur Jay Gould offered to give five thousand dollars for the purchase of flour, meal, and bacon for Sheridan, Gove, and Wallace counties.[18] Faced by such conditions, the white population of such beleaguered counties strongly opposed the imposition of any further economic burdens upon them.

Western Kansas editors spoke for their readers, warning against attempts to dump helpless blacks in their midst. The *Ford County Globe,* of Dodge City, vigorously opposed the idea, suggesting that if blacks were to come to Kansas, they should be distributed throughout the state. An even happier solution, said the editor, would be to tolerate no such colonization at all. J. G. Thompson, of Dodge City, wrote to a newspaper editor in Beaufort, South Carolina, explaining that while frontiersmen were far too busy to indulge in prejudices and while his region tolerated all kinds of people, including Russian Mennonites who spoke no English, the Exodusters ought not to come there. He argued that when such people as the Irish came west, they were young and strong, but the black refugees from the South refused to leave behind the aged and the weak, who, upon arriving in Kansas, bcame public wards. White immigrants, said Thompson, often left their families behind and spent their first year in the West establishing a homestead, after which they sent for their families; he thought the blacks should do the same. Moreover, he added, anyone coming west should bring along at least five hundred dollars with which to get a start. Having said all this, the writer wondered why blacks wanted to leave South Carolina, remarking that their true land of promise lay at their very doorsteps.[19]

From other western-Kansas neighborhoods came much the same reaction. At this time, Hays City lay close to the outer fringe of agricultural settlement, and it was, in that sense, a frontier town. Through its newspaper, the *Sentinel,* townsmen voiced their objection to enforced participation in philanthropies generated in eastern Kansas. As was usually the case, the newspaper expressed sympathy to the Exodusters, but added that "we raise our voice in earnest protest against forcing them out upon the wild frontier lands without means of subsistence." Then it got to the root of the matter: "The eastern cities of Kansas in their anxiety to be rid of the Negroes are urging the short sighted policy of placing them upon the homestead lands, and have gone so far as to apply for transportation. . . . In the name of charity and compassion send them not to the West! The state can dispose of them in a better manner." The suggested alternative was to locate the black immigrants "in the older portions of the state where work may be found and where even though they gain a mere subsistence their condition is infinitely better than the one they left."[20]

Although white farmers along the Kansas agricultural frontier themselves were earning "a mere subsistence," that was not what they had come West for; they were engaged in a struggle with a tough and arid land, a contest that they hoped to win. Southern blacks, many of whom had lived above a subsistence level by cotton farming, did not always leave their old homes solely because of bad political and social conditions; they also hoped for even better times economically. Had they thought that Kansas offered nothing more than marginal living, many would not have left the South; indeed, some of the disillusioned returned when they found this to be the case.

Hays City had argued that there was no work for black immigrants in that little frontier town and that none should be sent there. Some came, however, and discovered the truth: there was no work. Learning of their plight, KFRA sent money to F. C. Montgomery, editor of the *Hays City Sentinel,* who invested it in tickets on the Kansas Pacific Railway. The donation carried the refugees eastward as far as Salina, a place that the Topeka *Commonwealth* called a growing and prosperous city, well able to absorb such surplus labor. Salina was faced with the same dilemma that had plagued other Kansas towns. At the outset of the movement it had accused southerners of "frightful wrongs and oppressions" and had promised that Kansas would do all it could to find employment for persecuted colored people who fled from such conditions. By mid summer, 1879, Salina's thinking had undergone a change. A local editor told his readers that he had no objection to helping those who already were on hand, "but when Kansas is made the poor farm for southern states, it is asking too much."

The event that generated such an outcry was the dumping of Hays City's unwanted black population at Salina's doorstep. A certain amount of charity was commendable, thought the editor of the *Herald,* but it should not be extended beyond reasonable limits. His paper was Republican in outlook, and it followed party-line thinking on the "southern question"; but the paper's circulation of 1,163 was that of a small Kansas town. Residents of Salina were not flattered by Topeka's assertions that their city was prosperous and capable of supporting a growing labor force. Nor were they happy about the actions of a Topeka-based committee in distributing minorities around the state. "We do not blame the Topeka people for desiring to rid themselves of their troublesome charges," the *Herald* remarked acidly, "but we do find fault with a self-appointed committee that takes it upon themselves to cast a burden upon towns that do not desire such a burden." In addition to the annoyance of having Hays City's rejects sent to them, Salinans were annoyed to discover that the baggage of the travelers had been impounded by the railroad in lieu of seventeen dollars still owed to the company. Local contributions were raised in order to pay the difference. Some of the refugees had been allowed to stay in the railroad's "emigrant house," and once located there, they refused to leave, even when jobs were offered. "We still do adhere to our opinion that we do not need them, that we do not want them," concluded the *Herald.* "Laborers' wages are low enough without replacing these laborers by those who are willing to work for forty or fifty cents a day." If the blacks wanted to come to Kansas, said the paper, they should pay their own way, and they should look for work in the same manner as white immigrants.[21]

The people of Ellsworth, also located in central Kansas, shared the Salinans' point of view that black immigrants would find pioneer life difficult indeed. The *Ellsworth Reporter,* a Republican journal, expressed the usual sympathy for oppressed minorities, and it praised Kansans for their good works, but at the same time the paper argued that the eastern portion of the state was better able to provide for the needy. It was wrong, said the editor, that these helpless people "should be induced to emigrate to a new country where all who come have no more than they need for their own subsistence." He agreed with other small-town Kansas editors that unless newcomers, black or white, had the means with which to get a start, they should not emigrate to the West.[22] Ellsworth County at this time had a population of only about seven thousand, a good many of whom had come from New England, and although they brought with them some traditional sympathies for less fortunate souls, they felt that they had not yet accumulated sufficient surplus capital to participate in even small philanthropies.

Opposition to a large influx of blacks into Kansas on the part of the state's business community, a high percentage of whose members voted the Republican ticket, raised questions of submerged racism. Yet, what might be termed the Kansas black establishment took much the same position. Those who had come earlier, who had brought funds with which to get a start, and whose more determined members had gained a permanent foothold objected to supporting indigents for more than a very limited period of time. Topeka's *Colored Citizen* illustrated not only the moral dilemma in which established black Kansans found themselves, but also the shift in their position as the exodus movement grew from a strong flow into what promised to be a flood. In the first days of the movement, during late March of 1879, the *Citizen* was annoyed at white-owned newspapers whose editors objected to the arrival of black paupers, and it quite correctly pointed out that thousands of white immigrants were far from well-fixed when they came West. The *Citizen* argued that its Negro countrymen were not beggars, that they would need only a reasonable time to get on their feet, and that, above all, they could not wait any longer before fleeing the South's intolerable conditions. Kansas, said that paper's editor, should be proud to be of aid in this nationally known race problem. Such arguments were little different from those found in the white press during the early stages of the movement. However, as early as the first days of May, the *Colored Citizen* had modified its position, just as would many of the nation's Radical Republican papers. At this time the paper's editor was the Reverend T. W. Henderson, a minister of the African Methodist Episcopal Church in Topeka. At this relatively early date, and at a time when Topeka's *Commonwealth* had not retreated from its original stand, Henderson publicly advised members of his race not to expect free land in Kansas should they decide to move there. Also, he cautioned them against leaving their old homes without money to support themselves while getting started in the new land and against moving before they had some definite plan as to where they wanted to settle.[23]

Other members of the Kansas black community were cautious about endorsing a mass movement of southern farmers to the state. The Reverend W. M. Twine, who had lived in Kansas since 1862 and who, in addition to his ministerial duties, had engaged in the real estate business, did not think that Kansas was the best choice for black immigrants. The state itself was not a rich one, he argued, nor was its climate suitable for southern blacks who were used to cultivating cotton. Twine showed an unabashed prejudice in favor of Tennessee and Kentucky Negroes, as opposed to those from Mississippi or Louisiana, maintaining that they were of a much higher type. Even so, he thought, there was not much room for additional labor in Kansas, regardless of qualifications, and he did not approve of the swarms of unemployed that descended upon his town of Atchison in the spring of 1879. The newcomers not only placed a burden upon the white population of little towns such as this one, but they also made demands upon the small, struggling black population that had been able to establish itself through patience and hard work.[24]

Nor was Nicodemus, in northwestern Kansas, happy about the sudden popularity of that state among southern field hands. Rather than helping to popularize black colonization in Kansas, the Exodusters appeared to have hurt it. Settlers at Nicodemus had brought with them some money and supplies, but as it turned out, such reserves were insufficient, and during 1879 the colony was obliged to ask for aid from the white residents of Kansas. The donated supplies were brought in, free of transportation charges, by the Kansas Pacific Railway, to be stored and issued, as needed, by the town's officers. To some of the residents the emergency became permanent, and rather than work, they simply depended upon the dole. Community leaders watched the development with growing concern and concluded that if it continued, not only would it be harmful to those already living at Nicodemus, but such a welfare program would attract droves of Exodusters who were arriving in Kansas by the thousands during the spring of 1879. For this reason, among others, the Nicodemus Town Company was dissolved that spring, and each resident was left to his own devices.[25] The colony, founded in 1877, was reported to have had seven to eight hundred members by 1879, but the federal census of 1880 showed only 484. Either the earlier figures were exaggerated, not an uncommon circumstance in young western communities, or a number of people were driven out in the lean years of 1879 and 1880. That times were hard in Nicodemus, as was the case in white neighboring communities, is evident. For example, H. C. Moseley of Happy Hollow, also in Graham County, wrote to St. John in the spring of 1880, asking for aid. Moseley, who once had been a slaveowner, expressed concern for the welfare of sixty-nine black men, women, and children, whose condition, he said, was pitiable.[26] Although aid was received in Graham County, it appears that the black population, which constituted only about ten percent of the total, had a difficult time getting its share. Edward P. McCabe, one of the leaders at Nicodemus who later, as state auditor, would be the first Negro to hold a major political office in Kansas, complained to St. John about the situation in the spring of 1880. "I cannot for the life of me conceive how the great number of colored people were ignored in the arrangements made for the distribution of supply for Graham County," he wrote. He accused Jay Gould and the Kansas Pacific of being interested principally in the resultant publicity gained by carrying foodstuff and supplies to beleaguered communities. "I heartily concur with you," he told the governor, "in saying that the matter of distributing aid usually is met with more curses than thanks, and when I know that political capital is being made by those having the matter in hand at this point 'tis clear to my mind that our people were destined to be ignored."[27]

Despite the difficulties, more blacks came to Nicodemus, and in the next decades the little community prospered as well as did similarly situated white settlements in that part of Kansas. The white population of Graham County, as well as the black population, however, showed discrimination when it came to admitting newcomers. The *Graham County Lever,* of Gettysburg, Kansas, indicated this when, in the spring of 1880, it described the arrival of about a hundred blacks from Kentucky. "They paid their way and seemed well supplied with clothing, and were altogether a respectable looking body of people," the editor reported proudly. "The colored people who have come and who will come from Kentucky to Kansas are not fugitives from oppression but bonafide emigrants, who are in little or no danger of becoming a burden to the State."[28] Nearly a century later, some of the few remaining residents of Nicodemus would repeat these sentiments; namely, that there was a vast difference in their minds between the Kentucky Negroes and the more "worthless" ones who came out of Mississippi or Louisiana. Nicodemus had at least one thing in common with other western communities: it did not want indigents—of any color.

More easterly portions of Kansas displayed a sharp division of opinion as to the extent of the philanthropic role that this area was expected to play. Salmon S. Prouty, editor of the *Junction City Union* and a loyal supporter of St. John, thought that Kansas should open its arms to all men who wanted to work. The state, he asserted, easily could accommodate one million blacks. A New Yorker by birth, Prouty had followed what might be called the "newspaper frontier," working his way out to Illinois and then into Kansas as a printer. In 1856, at Aurora, Illinois, he had joined an immigration group, bound for Kansas. He took up a claim near Baldwin, south of Lawrence, and there he started the *Freeman's Champion.* Later he founded the Topeka *Commonwealth,* and after his association with that paper, he moved once more, this time to Junction City. As a militant abolitionist, who had come west with the "Beecher's Bibles" crowd in the mid fifties, his active sympathy for the blacks had committed him to a political position from which he never retreated. He would not live to see the end of the 1880s, but at the beginning of that final decade he was as firmly committed to the cause as ever.

John Davis, editor of the *Junction City Tribune,* took another view. Davis, who said that he once had been an "old-line abolitionist" and who now was an ardent Greenbacker, perhaps described the reactions of Kansans to the influx of blacks with more accuracy than most of them would have admitted. He recalled that "when we heard of their coming there was a sort of bravado of hospitality that ran through our community, that was friendly to their arrival, and they felt that they were welcome to our place, as well as to other parts of Kansas. We heard that they were congregating at Topeka afterwards, and our citizens were free to say that they could take care of a few." Davis described the arrival of sixty or seventy Exodusters, who were housed in tents loaned by the commandant of nearby Fort Riley, and how he had hauled down a wagonload of supplies donated by local residents. He visited the encampment several times more before it was dissolved "by their finding places in the country and otherwheres." Up to that point the *Tribune* editor's views and his emotional response was in consonance with those of his readers. But as the burden grew, he began to rethink his position.

By the spring of 1880 Davis indicated his disillusionment with the movement. He told the Voorhees congressional investigating committee that he had talked "with men who have employed exodites, and with men generally. All agree in expressing complete disgust, and are anxious to escape or remedy the burden on some sort of humanitarian grounds." Davis had his own views as to why Kansas was being flooded by blacks: "Now, from my general judgment of the case, I cannot suppress the suspicion that while Kansas and other Northern States have been mourning over the Southern management of the freedmen, the South has been quietly favoring the exodus, that the Northern people might have a taste of the difficulties on hand, and that in making the selections they have not sent us their best specimens. In other words, that Kansas, and other States, have been a sort of Botany Bay for the town negroes and pauper classes of the South, while the better classes and field hands have been more kindly treated and retained." The small-town editor concluded, as had many of his colleagues by this time, that "Kansas is sick and tired of the past experiences and present aspects of the case. She sends out no further invitations, but begs most earnestly that the tide, if it must continue, may be diverted to other and wealthier States."[29] For one, this "old line abolitionist" had had his fill of philanthropy.

In late 1879 and early 1880, at a time when Davis and others were expressing doubts about the value of black immigration into Kansas, there were indications that the flow through St. Louis and through Missouri River towns was beginning to abate. The opposite was true in southeastern Kansas. During that period, large numbers of Texas Negroes entered the state by way of Labette County. Parsons, an important town on the Missouri, Kansas and Texas Railroad, bore the brunt of the onslaught. The "Katy," as the railroad came to be known, brought a good many of these people across Indian Territory, distributing them along its route; others came in by means of the traditional team and wagon.[30] Parsons, founded in 1871, was the product of a land boom and the coming of the railroad. During the preceding autumn the famed Horace Greeley had visited the site of the proposed town and had described the land rush then under way: "Settlers are pouring into eastern Kansas by carloads, wagonloads, horseloads, daily, because of the fertility of her soil, the geniality of her climate, the admirable diversity of prairie and timber, the abundance of her living streams, and the marvelous facility where homesteads may here be created."[31]

In general, Texas blacks were better off financially than those coming from Mississippi or Louisiana. Reports from the areas that they had vacated indicated that frequently they sold property of considerable value. One group that was brought into Kansas by the Katy paid a total of one thousand dollars in fares, many of them first-class. Others, who loaded their earthly possessions into wagons and headed north, were well supplied with healthy animals and equipment. A physician named Rockhold, who lived at Parsons, spoke of their prosperous appearance. "They would come with one, two, three, four, sometimes as high as six horses to a wagon. After landing there at Parsons, some of them bought houses in the town or vicinity, some rented, and some went right out into the country." Still others built their own homes. "I think I can safely say that fifty houses have been built there this winter," said Dr. Rockhold in the spring of 1880. By this time the town's population was estimated to be five thousand.[32]

To generalize about the relatively prosperous look of those who either passed through or stopped at Parsons was misleading. During December, 1879, conditions at that place were described as being far from satisfactory. Laura Haviland told St. John that about a thousand blacks had arrived during the preceding month and that the Parsons barracks were over-flowing. She quoted one of the recent arrivals as having said that his people were freezing and starving. Another of them, named L. S. Childs, appealed to Governor St. John for help. In a response that indicated his growing frustration, St. John told Childs that he had written hundreds of letters to Texas Negroes, urging them not to come to Kansas without funds and warning that if they did, disaster would follow. To solve the immediate problem, added the governor, those in need should apply to the Parsons branch of the KFRA or write to Elizabeth Comstock at Topeka. St. John complained that he found it impossible even to provide for those at Topeka, some fifty of whom had suffered from frostbite during a recent cold snap.[33]

Harry H. Lusk, who had purchased the Parsons *Sun* in 1878, shared the views of the paper's former owner, Milton W. Reynolds, on the question of the Exodusters. In addition to his own sympathetic editorials he published occasional pieces written by Reynolds, who now headed the newly organized local branch of the KFRA. Through the columns of the *Sun*, Kansans learned more about the problems of these people in the Parsons region. In mid December, 1879, Lusk reported that there was a good deal of talk on the streets of his town about the great suffering of the newcomers. He cited the case of three families living along Labette Creek, the men of which had been unable to find work and in which sickness was prevalent. He was somewhat defensive, pointing out that where one black man might need help, at least five "white tramps" already had been given aid by the city. Later that month, Lusk described a march of Exodusters made upon the city, calling it a pathetic sight and a "silent appeal" to the people of the town. The suppliants trudged through a driving sleet, wearing scarcely enough clothing to keep them warm; they were, said the editor, "heroic figures."[34]

As always, there were widely varying accounts as to how many black immigrants came to a given area or passed through a specified Kansas town. At the time, Kansas newspapers talked in terms of "large numbers" and "many" entering the southeastern part of the state. So many, said an Emporia newspaper, that the people of Parsons were complaining about a "Texodus." Laura Haviland's figure of a thousand during November, 1879, was possible, but it may have been somewhat exaggerated. A recent study, whose author used the figures of one thousand to thirteen hundred per week for a period of several weeks, represents an extreme on the high side. Angell Mathewson, of Parsons, Kansas, who was a member of the Kansas State Senate, testified in April, 1880, that there were about three hundred Exodusters in the city at that time and that since the fall of

1879 about one thousand had arrived, most of whom had since scattered throughout the Neosho Valley. J. B. Lamb, editor of the Democratic *Parsons Eclipse,* thought that there were more; he estimated that from September of 1879 to the spring of 1880 between fifteen hundred and twenty-five hundred Exodusters had come to Parsons, most of whom had gone into the countryside or to neighboring towns. Dr. Rockhold said that one thousand to twelve hundred was a more accurate figure. Since reports on the numbers of arrivals frequently were exaggerated by both sides—by the proponents of the movement, in order to show how great was the need for contributions, and by the opponents, to show how badly the situation had gotten out of hand—it is more reasonable to accept the lower figures when trying to make an "educated guess" as to actual numbers.[35]

Motivations for emigration among Texas Negroes resembled those of the Louisiana and Mississippi elements: they varied. One of them told St. John, in July, 1879, that Texas was a good country but that its blacks were obliged to undergo what he described as "severe treatment." He concluded that "we think it would be better to immigrate to a free country," for, as he put it, he and his people were no better than peons. Several years later, N. A. Jackson, of Mount Vernon, Texas, expressed much the same view to St. John. Texas, he said, "is not the country for colored people, for we have but little freedom in this part, and if there is any place where the colored people are free we want to know it for we are tired of living with our head & feet tied together. We want to hold our heads up and exert our liberty but we fail to do so here."[36]

The matter of political equality was, of course, a very sensitive area; Radical Republicans employed it as one of their principal weapons, and blacks who wanted sympathy in Kansas quickly learned of its volatility in John Brown country. There were, however, arguments against charges of bulldozing in Texas. In February, 1880, a black convention met at Galveston, Texas, and adopted resolutions approving an immigration of the race from older southern states, while at the same time denying that there was any necessity for blacks to emigrate from Texas. The state was described as a good place for Negroes to find new homes. St. John agreed with this, in principle, for he was not anxious to see the "Texodus" increase. However, as he had remarked earlier, he doubted that blacks from Louisiana, Mississippi, or Alabama could "be made to believe that going to Texas would materially better their condition so far as the exercise of political rights and the security to life and property is concerned."[37]

Radical Republicans lost no opportunity to aggravate the already irritated political question of equal rights. Milton W. Reynolds, founder of both the *Lawrence Daily Journal* and the Parsons *Sun,* wrote a piece

entitled "The Hegira of the Negro," which was published by the KFRA.
It was dramatic, even inflammatory. One portion of the account related
the story of a Mississippi Negro who had fled to Topeka, but who later
had returned to get his family. When he reappeared, bulldozers had surrounded him, had cut off his hands, and throwing them in his lap, had
said: "There, d— you, take them back to bleeding Kansas with you."
Reynolds later admitted that the story was hearsay, but he rationalized
that "you, of course, understand that newspaper writers do not expect
always to be as precise in their statements, as they would be in sworn
testimony." He denied that his piece was written for political purposes,
but he had consented to such a use if the Republicans so desired.[38]

As had been the case with Negroes from the deep South, the majority
of those from Texas moved to Kansas because they thought that the place
offered an opportunity to start a new life. A few of them said that they
had been badly treated in the South; others thought that something free
awaited them in Kansas; still others came because neighbors were moving,
and they responded to mob psychology by making a hasty decision to leave;
but in the main, the black Texans moved for the same reasons that had
motivated whites to settle along agricultural frontiers. When Dr. Rockhold, of Parsons, asked some of the newcomers if they expected to be given
forty acres and a mule, they laughed and said that the story was an old
one, but that they did not believe it. Rockhold was impressed by those
with whom he talked, remarking that they seemed "to be a thrifty set;
some of them have some little education." In another case a Negro
preacher named Henry Smith wrote to St. John from Marshall, Texas,
saying that while he did not believe the stories of giveaways in Kansas,
some of his parishioners did, and he wanted the governor's reassurances.
St. John obliged, and Smith responded: "You answered my letter just as
I respected [*sic*]." Then he asked for specific information as to land
costs.[39]

Typical of the whole movement, there were a few gullible ones who
listened eagerly to stories of free homes in Kansas and who responded
readily to the lures of both black and white confidence men. T. D. Duncan, a black Methodist minister from Parsons, told editor J. B. Lamb that
in 1879 two white men from Topeka were at work in the Houston, Texas,
area, distributing circulars that promised land, supplies, and pocket money
to blacks if they would come to Kansas. The circulars bore St. John's
name, said Duncan, and they caused much excitement among black
Texans. Duncan himself became enmeshed in the tangle of transportation
matters and was arrested for trying to defraud some of the Exodusters.
Some of the Kansas-bound Texans had neglected to transfer their belong-

ings to the Katy Railroad, once they reached Denison, Texas, with the result that their goods were left at that point. To straighten out the matter, Duncan took their bills of lading, for which he was given a sizeable amount of money, and went to Denison. Some of the freight bills became lost, either by their owners or by Duncan, with the result that he was accused of embezzlement and was arrested. The jury found him innocent, but he was, as Milton Reynolds put it, "bounced" from the church.[40]

Another case involved William S. Johnson, a black preacher from Florence, Kansas, who was the object of an earnest search by Stillwell H. Russell, United States marshal for the Western District of Texas. Early in March, 1880, Russell warned St. John that Johnson was selling transportation certificates that presumably gave the holder very cheap passage to Kansas and were sold under the guise that Johnson represented Governor St. John. "I am confident he is an imposter and if found will be arrested," said Russell. A few days later the marshal wrote to St. John, more fully explaining the problem. For about a year, he said, "Kansas fever" had affected the poorer class of Texas Negroes, many of whom had broken up their homes and had departed for the land of promise "under the false impression that Kansas offered every facility in bettering their condition without any effort on their part save that of going there." Russell quite frankly explained to St. John the reason that he thought this situation had developed: "Rumor for a long time has connected you with encouraging this idea and has thereby aided imposters in making easy victims." He explained further: "On the 11th [of March, 1880] a large number of colored men came into my office [at Austin, Texas] and stated that one Wm. Johnson represented himself as being a preacher . . . and among other things told them that you had sent him out to encourage the move to Kansas and upon payment of five dollars to him he would give them a free transportation ticket to Parsons, Kansas, and by a further payment at that place of $4.75 they would be entitled to free transportation to any portion of the State, etc. To further impose upon their credulity he produced various credentials, preached for them, and prayed with them and by such means so deceived them that all who could raise five dollars bought a 'Transportation Certificate' to Kansas, some of them selling all they had for a certificate." When the purchasers, thirty-five in all, presented their documents to the railroad agent at Austin, they were refused, at which time they left for the marshal's office and besieged him with a torrent of angry complaints. Johnson was nowhere to be found in Austin; however, a few days later he surfaced at San Marcos, Texas, and offered transportation certificates to Kansas at an amazingly low price. A. W. Brooks, of that city, wrote to St. John, explaining that some of his friends had taken advantage of the bargain only to discover that the local railroad agent would not honor them. Brooks now wondered if St. John possibly could furnish Elder Johnson's forwarding address.[41]

As the weather warmed in the spring of 1880, southeastern Kansas prepared itself for a renewal of black immigration from Texas. During that winter, Kansas newspapers talked about reports coming out of Texas that indicated the probability of further upheaval among discontented farmers. Such rumors were received by small Kansas communities with growing apprehension. Even Milton Reynolds, of Parsons, began to lose some of his unlimited enthusiasm for rescuing blacks from southern persecution. In late February he admitted to William Penn Nixon, of the Chicago *Inter Ocean,* that there had accumulated in his city "a surplus of colored laborers," mainly from Texas. If northern farmers were in need "of good, trusty, attentive, reliable help," the place to look was Parsons, Kansas, he said. Although he had played down the poor economic condition of those who had come in from Texas, Reynolds now complained that "most writers do not understand that the Negroes are destitute, and have no means of moving on to Wisconsin, Illinois, etc." Agents should be sent in, he suggested, to take out laborers in batches of twenty-five or more. That Parsons experienced difficulties similar to those of other Kansas towns was seen in Reynold's warning that when these laborers were moved on, they should not be allowed to gather in towns. As a people, he said, they were naturally gregarious and tended to cling together; they did not like to go far from known haunts and among strangers unless they moved in groups.[42]

Kansans who were apprehensive about the force of the exodus took solace from the fact that southern planters were increasingly concerned over the loss of their labor and were making efforts to curb the flight northward by offering better conditions at home. By the spring of 1880 Texas felt the effects of the movement and began to worry about a future diminution of its agricultural labor. E. R.Mooring, of Marshall, Texas, asked the county clerk at Topeka if arriving blacks had been able to obtain permanent employment in Kansas. He wondered if any of the recent immigrants could be persuaded to return to the South. "Some of the planters in this section are short of hands, and are thinking of making an effort to get them from Kansas," he wrote. "Do you think if transportation were offered the colored people back home *free* that any of them would return?" The Topeka *Commonwealth,* whose management had been an enthusiastic supporter of St. John and of the movement itself, but whose point of view now agreed with the governor that things were getting out of hand, admitted that the Kansas labor market was glutted. Those who migrated

191

to Kansas and who were possessed of both money with which to tide them over and of sufficient "grit" would succeed, said the editor. Where he once had talked of the state's "mission" to save these people, the journalist now grumbled that the Exodusters showed too much disposition to hang around the towns and to become public wards.[43]

Residents of Parsons understood the change in attitude at Topeka. Wilmer Walton, who now headed the local KFRA branch, complained to St. John that missionary work among the blacks in small Kansas towns had to be a labor of love. To his dismay, all efforts to improve conditions among the refugees at Parsons seemed to bear no fruit. The newcomers huddled in makeshift quarters and lived in what Walton described as "filthy, slovenly conditions as often tends to encourage immorality and vice, as well as to promote physical diseases among themselves." In desperation he called some of the black leaders together and asked them to form subcommittees whose duty it would be to inspect family living quarters and to rate their cleanliness on a scale of one, two, or three. Those who did not pass with a grade of "one" were to get no more KFRA money. Walton proposed also to go after what might be called "sanitary loafers." If the inspectors encountered any "idle, lazy persons of either sex," they were to "affix the letter *L* for 'loafer' to their names"; and even if these idlers were clean, they, too, were to be denied relief money. Those who were old and infirm were to be graded more leniently. When the city clerk at Parsons learned of Walton's proposal, he approved and suggested that it might be applied also to some of the local white people. Walton got the point. He called a meeting of local blacks who were on relief and delivered a stern lecture upon the virtues of cleanliness. The backsliding "twos" and "threes" promised to reform, and Walton sent word to St. John that he now felt better about affairs at Parsons.[44]

Despite Walton's optimism about the state of KFRA's health at Parsons and despite his determination to discipline welfare recipients, there were complaints about the way in which he administered the money that had been sent down from Topeka. A complainant named Gloss Floyd told St. John that Walton was not doing "write" by the distressed Negroes. "The people which live in the country don't get anything and the ones that lives in town gets all and some gets none," he reported. Floyd was angered when Walton refused to help the Nathan Jones family, formerly of Texas, Floyd's home state.[45]

When the white community segregated the black newcomers, its members were accused of race prejudice, a charge that they denied. They responded that the blacks were a gregarious people who did not want integration but preferred to stay with their own kind. There was general concern that the arrivals from the South, many of whom, in destitution, wore old and dirty clothes, might have brought with them some communicable disease, particularly yellow fever. An epidemic of measles broke out in Emporia that winter, and the blacks who became ill were said to be afflicted by the "niggereasles," a form of the disease that was believed to be much more serious than the variety that preyed upon Anglo-Saxons. Dr. Rockhold, of Parsons, argued that his community was more broadminded. Asked if he entertained any racial prejudice toward the newcomers, he responded: "If they behave themselves, keep themselves clean, &c., they are at least regarded as 'people.' " The doctor, who treated some of KFRA's wards, earned about one hundred dollars in all for his services during the winter of 1879–80 in southeastern Kansas. That the local blacks were treated as "people" was shown, said Rockhold, by the reception that they were given. About a hundred of the children were in school; he did not say if they were segregated, but they may have been, since that was the situation in some of the other small Kansas towns. Some of the adults were employed by local businessmen. A large grain dealer "has got nearly all his hands from the 'Exodusters,' " said Rockhold, and the owner of a large brickyard hired "a great many." The doctor was anxious to show that Parsons had done its bit.[46]

The "health problem," which was seized upon at St. Louis in the early stages of the exodus as a means of controlling a possible influx into that city, was an idea not lost upon some of the residents of John Brown country. Emporia, whose white establishment worried about the spread of "niggereasles," continued its interest in public health when considering school segregation. Salmon Prouty, of the *Junction City Union,* twitted the people of Emporia about this during the spring of 1880. At that time, he said, the question of "setting off the colored children of the city into a separate school" was being discussed, "the reason alleged being the filthy condition of the little Exodusters who are crowding into places of public instruction." Prouty was equally unhappy over the decision at Ottawa to place all black children below the seventh grade in one building "and employ a teacher for their special attention." John Davis, who edited the *Tribune* in Junction City, said that the town in which he and Prouty lived was more liberal, that Negro children attended local schools along with whites; but, he complained, "we have not a single colored man on our school board, or connected in any way with the official management of the schools."[47]

Apparently the question of school segregation agitated other Kansas communities. A tourist who visited Manhattan told his southern friends that "the school question here is looming up as a running sore, when the

Negroes are in any numbers, in any given locality. The mutterings are low and threatening, and separate schools must be had." He said that black children generally attended the regular primary schools and that, in reaction to it, some of the white parents were "keeping their little ones back from school to such an extent in some towns as to deprive their children of educational advantages." Meantime, the observer noted, "the little 'Exodusters' are victors in possession of the primary departments in some of the towns."[48]

School segregation in Kansas brought complaints from some of the black residents. A group of them from Independence, in the extreme southeastern part of the state, presented a joint appeal to St. John in the autumn of 1880. It read:

> We the collored citizens of independence Resol to inform you that whereas the school in which our children belong they have prepared a Room separated for the collored children on account of the collor and we carried our children to the school in which they belong and they was turn away on the account of they collor and we withhild our children (7) or (8) hundred yards out of the way and applied to you about it.[49]

Their charges of discrimination were echoed by the *Colored Citizen,* of Topeka, whose editor said that race prejudice was blatantly displayed through "frequent insults offered the colored women . . . by white men who openly insult the women while walking along the streets." Prejudice was also in evidence, said the editor, in the field of employment. He charged that the only blacks holding government positions in Kansas in 1879 were one postal clerk at Lawrence, a postal night clerk at Atchison, a Leavenworth mail carrier, and an appointed position at the state prison.[50]

Members of the white establishment continued to argue that there was no prejudice in Kansas because of race, that many of the newcomers were in straitened circumstances because they were shiftless and lazy, not because they were black. H. C. Solomon, of Atchison, was one of those who so argued the case. When asked by a member of the Voorhees investigating committee as to the employment status of these people at Atchison, in the spring of 1880, he replied: "Well, a great many of them have been taken charge of, as vagrants, and set to work on the rock-pile; a large portion of them are now doing that kind of work; they live around in a precarious manner that it is almost impossible to define." An observer who passed through the state that spring noted that employment prospects for blacks in Kansas were poor. He told of one with whom he had talked who had said that he was earning ten dollars a month and board. Another earned seventy-five cents a day but fed himself, while yet another earned only twenty-five cents for a day's work. Not only was employment hard to find, he continued, but Kansans showed little enthusiasm for such cheap labor. "If the poor Negro must move from the South they *all* prefer for him to go to Iowa, Indiana, Ohio, or some other State," he noted.[51]

Southerners expressed satisfaction over the dilemma in which once "bleeding Kansas" now found itself. The *New Orleans Times* gave a prominent place in its columns to a "special telegram" from Iola, Kansas, that reported labor conflicts in the southeastern part of the state. "The immigration of Southern Negroes . . . promises to become a serious evil in more respects than one," said the dispatch. "They are gradually but surely superseding white labor everywhere. The towns along the railroads south of here are crowded by them, and they are monopolizing the labor formerly done by the whites. They underbid the white and 'push in' like the Chinese. There is general complaint already among the laboring whites that they can no longer support their families at the present price they get for their services." The *Times* expressed sympathy for Kansans, and it unhesitatingly predicted that the "immigration of vast numbers of ignorant Negroes into the Western States" would hurt, rather than help, the region. It was too bad, sighed the editor, that the Republicans, in their efforts to injure the South by encouraging an exodus, now would damage another part of the country and their friends who lived there. Kansas City, openly hostile to the Exodusters, shared this view. The *Daily Times,* of that city, published a letter from a Topekan who compared the Negro to "the noble red man [whose] admirers are always among those who view him from a distance." Topeka, said the writer, was a beautiful city that had prospered and had grown naturally until the recent inundation, a circumstance he labeled "a calamity to be submitted to with Christian forbearance."[52] His complaint, coming from the heart of "St. John country," brought murmurs of satisfaction and vindication from the critics of Kansas City.

The winter of 1879–80 was one of uncertainty for Kansans. Those who had encouraged the Exoduster movement worried about its possible renewal during the coming season, fearful that the patience of the state's white community was wearing thin and that trouble might develop. These reformers realized that if the tide of public opinion turned sharply against the influx of refugees, a good many Kansans who earlier had shown no resentment toward black newcomers who arrived with funds with which to buy land now might close their hearts and their minds to the appearance of anyone who was black. One might accept the claim that Kansans were not prejudiced against the blacks because of their race, they said, but there was no guarantee that if the newcomers presented increasingly diffi-

195

cult economic problems, latent prejudices would not emerge. St. John and his intimates worried about this aspect of the problem a good deal during the winter in question.

It was difficult to guess what would happen when the weather warmed in the spring of 1880. During the late summer of 1879 a federal official who traveled through Kansas predicted that the westward movement of the blacks had just commenced and that eventually Kansas would have a half-million of them. While such a statement could be received as no more than a generalization, there was evidence of preparation in the South for a renewed emigration. For example, during December some 400 Negroes were reported to have met in Monroe County, Georgia, to perfect an organization looking toward a mass movement to Kansas. Despite a warning from St. John that Kansas could render no aid to such a movement, the group appointed committees to study the matter. Meantime, during the fall of 1879, groups of blacks continued to filter into Kansas. Late in November the "Katy" railroad delivered 220 recent residents of the Huntsville, Texas, area to Emporia. As they debarked from train cars in which they had lived for four days and nights, the newcomers revealed the unwelcome news that another 600 were on their way from that section of Texas. Although a good many people in Emporia worried about the prospect of more arrivals, they went to work with a show of energy and found homes for the 220 in the neighboring countryside. But by March, 1880, Emporia began to show signs of strain. The *Ledger* complained that the city was overcrowded with refugees and that there was much sickness and destitution. The paper bravely argued that while it was the duty of Kansas to care for these people, they should not be allowed to drift into the towns, where they became a burden. Somehow, said the newspaper, farms should be obtained for these black farmers; the cities could not support them.[53]

Members of KFRA at Topeka watched the coming of spring, 1880, with nervous uncertainty. Reports coming out of the South indicated a renewed restlessness in that part of the land. From Mississippi came word that some eight hundred blacks in Jasper and Clark counties had sold what property they owned and were readying themselves for the trek northward. A white man named Pierce had offered to transport them to the promised land for $1.50 a head, but when it came time for him to carry out his agreement, he could not be found. Determined to go, the Negroes employed J. D. McKinnon, of Jasper County, to make arrangements for them to leave by rail. He obtained a contract to get them from Meridian to St. Louis for $10.60 each, and it was estimated that seven-eighths of them had enough money to pay the fare. Others did not await

196

the coming of warmer weather. Early in February it was reported that some seven hundred, mostly from Mississippi and Louisiana, had reached St. Louis, en route to Kansas. KFRA received word that even larger numbers were ready to move, a prediction underscored by Mrs. Comstock, who urged: "Pressing need of funds; nine hundred families en route to this point."[54]

The "Texodus," of which southeastern Kansans had complained, showed renewed signs of life that spring. During the winter, blacks from Hearne, Texas, sent a committee of five into Kansas on what was described as an "exploring trip," and their report was favorable. Meantime, an Emporia, Kansas, newspaper reported driblets of black Texans arriving at that city, newcomers who had paid their own way and who appeared to have some funds. About this time, word reached Kansas that emigrating from the Lone Star State was getting to be a more difficult feat than many people imagined. R. F. Beavers told St. John that he wanted to leave the Dallas area, but the "white people says I can't sell my place until thay [his debts] are settled. I offered to sell the place for a wagon and team and thay says if I do thay will follow me and taken them away from me." He appealed to St. John for help, or at least for advice.[55]

With the approach of the 1880 travel season, St. John and his friends worried about the shape of things to come. The enthusiasms of a year earlier now became concerns; the chickens of 1879 were coming home to roost. Mrs. Comstock, who was in the East that spring, concurred with St. John and the members of KFRA in their desire to sidetrack the movement of blacks aimed at Kansas. "Some of our Friends in these eastern parts think it will be wise to send an agent down South to try & stem the tide of emigration or turn it into other states such as Ill., Iowa, & Indiana," she told the governor. "It is proposed to send John M. Watson who is well adapted to this work from his knowledge of the colored people and the state of things in Kas. & having resided in Miss. & been employed in the Friends Mission there. Our New York Friends will meet his expenses, & will be much obliged to thee if thou wilt give him a letter or a paper or some sort of a document that he can show or read to the colored people with whom thy name will have more weight than any other."[56]

As St. John, Mrs. Comstock, and others tried to apply the brakes or throw the switch that would send the influx along other routes, the national enthusiasm that they had generated for helping the refugees continued at a high level. The governor's correspondence for the spring months of 1880 was filled with letters from all parts of the East, particularly from New England, that asked questions, gave encouragement, and frequently included small donations. Mrs. William Claflin, of Massachusetts, said that she had on hand six barrels "of nice warm clothing" and wanted to know where it should be sent. She explained that she and her husband had taken a "deep interest in the colored people, and we feel more than ever that it is one's duty to do whatever we can to relieve those who have been obliged to flee from their own genial climate to escape persecution." From his sickbed a resident of Topeka, Kansas, sent a post card to the governor, at the cost of one cent, upon which he scrawled an offer of one thousand dollars for "the colored people," and an apology for not being well enough to see St. John in person.[57]

Thus, as the leaders of the movement worried about its thrust, their followers thundered forward with the faith of Christian martyrs, determined to be a part of the fight for human justice. When Crawford's Opera House, at Topeka, offered a traveling company's version of "Uncle Tom's Cabin" that spring, a turn-away crowd paid twenty-five and thirty-five cents for admission. A local paper proudly announced that the Jubilee Singers, described as "all genuine darkies," sang several plantation airs before an enthusiastic audience. So successful was the performance of the Jubilee Singers that a repeat performance was promised for those who had been turned away at the door.[58] Topeka's businessmen might have wearied from the onslaught of southern blacks, but its spiritual elements carried the banner of John Brown bravely at their forefront, determined to do their respective duties as Christian soldiers.

11

POLITICS OF THE EXODUS

From the outset, John P. St. John's enemies accused him of making political capital from the exodus. Extremists even charged that he had participated in its origination for purely political purposes. One of these was J. B. Lamb, a Democratic newspaper editor from Parsons, Kansas, who testified under oath: "I do accuse Governor St. John and that committee [KFRA] of getting up these circulars and working up that exodus of their own free will and accord." Lamb said he had talked with a number of Exodusters who said they had left their southern homes only because of their belief that St. John wanted them to come to Kansas. He cited the example of a woman who had worked for him as a domestic, who said that letters and papers originating in St. John's office had been the principal reason for her to seek out Kansas as a new home.[1]

St. John steadfastedly denied all. So did his most ardent supporters. Milton Reynolds, a Republican stalwart, argued that he never had seen any such enticing offers. "I have often, repeatedly, offered fifty dollars for a letter of his containing anything of the sort," he said, in St. John's defense. He maintained that he had not even seen a forgery of such a letter. He readily admitted, however, that the governor's enemies were trying to use the exodus against him in this election year of 1880.[2]

The Democratic press of Kansas City consistently criticized St. John for his sympathy toward the migrant blacks. During the summer of 1879, at a time when the movement was beginning to reach proportions serious enough to worry even St. John, one such paper jeeringly commented that the governor's "declaiming about the inalienable rights of man and brother to migrate from the tropics to the pole at his option is a very different thing from supplying him with hog and hominy the year round, or equipping him with a homestead to earn his own subsistence."³ Other Missouri papers used the occasion of the exodus to twit Kansans, in general, about their efforts to succor the blacks. The Democratic *Missouri Republican,* of St. Louis, reacted with a sarcastic editorial when it heard some initial mutterings of protest in Kansas. The editor recalled the days of "bleeding Kansas," when, he said, that place had bled "until Northern pockets were well nigh drained in the effort to stop the terrible hemorrhage." He quoted from Whittier:

> Upbearing, like the Ark of old,
>   The Bible in our van,
> We go to test the truth of God
>   Against the fraud of man.
>
> No pause, nor rest, save where the streams
>   That feed the Kansas run,
> Save where our Pilgrim gonfalon
>   Shall flout the setting sun!

Referring to the efforts of Garrison, Phillips, and Harriet Beecher Stowe, the journalist said that Kansas had been assigned the role of a "modern edition of Plato's Republic, specially designed for the friends of the Negro." Kansans, he thought, now were in a dilemma: they either had to carry out their announced philanthropies or bear the charge that talk was cheap.⁴ When St. John accepted the challenge, Democratic papers in Missouri and elsewhere at once accused him of grasping at a new cause, one that would benefit him politically.

Kansas City, through which large numbers of Exodusters were funneled into Kansas, continually harped on the political complexion of the movement. Its press accused St. John of encouraging such immigration, of circularizing the North for money with which to "sustain the pauper camps," and of forcing Kansans to finance his role as the Negro's friend so that he might benefit from it politically. Contributions would end one day, warned the *Times,* and when that happened, Kansans would pay a high price for St. John's personal ambitions. Meantime, said the paper, lazy blacks were lying around the barracks at Topeka, eating up rations, while any hungry white indigent who begged at the housewife's kitchen door was hauled off to jail or assigned to the chain gang. It annoyed this journal from the old Slave State of Missouri to think that in Kansas "the colored man is taken into the parlor, the best robe put on him, the fatted calf killed and a great ado made over him."⁵ St. John quickly was singled out by his detractors as the chief villain of what was regarded as a charade of social leveling, and it was he who received the brunt of their attacks.

The governor defended his position, arguing that the incoming blacks were not lazy, that they were "sober, industrious, able to see the difficulties in their way, and willing to work to overcome them." On one occasion he talked with a group that he described as being "leading colored men from the states of Mississippi and Alabama," troubled strangers who told him that they had borne their burden until it had become so oppressive that they were obliged to live elsewhere. The Republican press emphasized political difficulties in the South and repeatedly used the exodus as yet another proof that slavery had not been erased. It assigned to St. John the role of a knight in shining armor, a latter-day crusader who rode in the van of Christians as they marched against southern bigotry. Sometimes the governor was carried away by the unbounded enthusiasm of his followers. On one occasion he stated publicly, but erroneously, that of the thousands who had come, not one had returned to the land of darkness.[6]

Kansas blacks listened to the talk of political equality in the new Canaan with much interest; and not unreasonably, they sought to sample its sweetness. As early as June, 1879, political black activism was reported at Lawrence, Kansas. "There's a colored rebellion in Lawrence," reported a newspaper from southeastern Kansas. It referred to a recent meeting "at which speeches were made and resolutions passed denouncing the new city government for refusing to give colored men representation in the appointive offices." Another issue of this paper referred to the political ambitions of T. W. Henderson, editor of Topeka's *Colored Citizen*, who, it was charged, favored the new immigration because its impact might force the Republicans to nominate him as lieutenant governor.[7]

When the Republicans made their nominations in the autumn of 1880, black participants made a concerted effort to place one of their own on the ticket. When they failed, a gurgle of delight was heard from the southern press. "The Exodusters from the South are making trouble in the Kansas Republican camp," trumpeted the *Clarion*, of Jackson, Mississippi. "They claim 25,000 votes and in the Republican State Convention insisted upon having a colored man on the ticket." When a white man won the nomination for lieutenant governor, a post that the blacks had set their eyes upon, there was much discontent among the losers. "Thereupon the colored formed a separate organization and have called a State Convention to assert their 'rights,'" reported the *Clarion*. The southern editor went on to say that Republicans had held out great inducements for blacks to come to Kansas, but they drew the line at permitting political participa-

201

tion. Smugly the editor opined that these poor people would have been much better off in the South, and in the Democratic party.[8]

John L. Waller, a well-known black Kansan, confirmed the discontentment in his correspondence with St. John. "I did what I could for you and also I hoped to secure some recognition for my race upon the State ticket, but in this we failed," he told the governor. "I must in justice to yourself support the ticket as nominated at Topeka, but in doing so I will incur the condemnation of some of the leading men of my race, not that they wish to defeat you, but to call the attention of the party to the numerical strength of the Negro in Kansas." He promised to do what he could to "allay this storm of dissension," but admitted that "I expect this thing will kill me politically."[9] John M. Watson, of Columbus, Kansas, also lamented the recent stir generated by the blacks, and he tried to make the governor feel better by more or less apologizing for it. "I regret that the colored people pressed their claims so hard in convention," he wrote, "as so many of them are new settlers it would have shown wisdom to wait one more year at least as modest worth will win in the end, but seeing I am not a politician I cannot judge."[10]

If there was any alienation of the black vote that fall, it did St. John no harm. In November, 1880, he won the election by a majority of nearly 52,000 votes, as compared to 9,000 in his previous victory. However, it may have been the other arrow in his political quiver—the temperance issue—that clinched his victory over the Democratic candidate, Edmund Ross. While a good many humanitarians applauded the governor for his stand on human rights, it was the "cold water" army that provided his most consistent and most militant support. Any number of letters in the St. John correspondence attest to the fact that his most loyal followers considered Demon Rum to be the principal enemy, with southern Democrats often running a poor second. In that same election, Kansans approved a prohibition amendment, 92,302 to 84,304.

At the national level the "Exodus question" became political as soon as the first large contingents of refugees reached St. Louis during March of 1879. Although the denial of suffrage to blacks in the South generally was regarded as but one of several causes of the movement, members of the Republican party's Radical wing seized upon this as a leading reason for the flight of the blacks. Old-line abolitionists, who had watched the resurgence of southern Democrats with a growing conviction that the war had been in vain, also grasped at the exodus as a last hope in their own "lost cause." Since the approaching election of 1880 appeared to have no great issues, even those Republicans who did not believe in the political origins of the exodus were inclined to use the development as ammunition for the coming contest. As it had been in 1856, "bleeding Kansas" was far enough away to make a suitable political issue without involving matters closer to home. So convenient was the exodus as a political cause that elements of the Republican press stepped forward as unsolicited godparents at the moment of its birth.

As the ragged physical evidences of alleged southern oppression huddled along the riverbank at St. Louis during that cold, wet March of 1879, a new flame of zeal billowed from emotional torches that had grown cold during post–Civil War years. Tired old crusaders felt a reminiscent surge in their veins, and dormant emotions came to life, flashing signals for one more ride against the enemy. From Garrisonian New England to the Midwest, where once the Welds and the Lovejoys had made their sacrifices, now came cries of a renewed campaign. Good Republicans reminded themselves that it was in this cockpit of human rights that their party had been born. They recalled pledges that its struggle would continue until the issue of slavery was resolved. A St. John supporter from Kansas City praised the governor for his willingness to stand up and be counted. Predicting that the name St. John would "stand alongside the Garrisons, Giddings, Sumners and others as a friend of the oppressed," the crusader suggested the initiation of a propaganda campaign in which workers for the cause would hold meetings "and let speeches be made, songs be sung, etc."[11]

As in days of old, the hue and cry from New England was loud. "The cause of this [movement] is entirely political," shouted the Radical Republican *Daily Kennebec Journal,* of Augusta, Maine. Former slaves now were flying from oppression "as the Pilgrim Fathers fled," wrote the editor, who then assured his readership that "the heart of the North beats in sympathy with them." Another Republican editor, from Lewiston, Maine, reported that the blacks had been forced to flee from what he called "most cruel persecutions," as well as from a deprivation of all political rights.

The *Daily Eastern Argus,* of Portland, Maine, sarcastically agreed that the matter was clearly political. This Democratic paper charged that the movement had originated among the stalwart Republicans who were swaying ignorant Negroes in order to feather their own political nests.[12] The exodus was no accident, said the *Argus.* As evidence it pointed to an association in Cambridge, Massachusetts, called the Principia Club, composed of what the editor called "old abolitionists and Republicans of the most stalwart type," whose members for the past two years had prepared southern blacks for a migration. Article 3 of the club's constitution was quoted: "The object of the Association shall be to encourage the freedmen of the southern states to emigrate to northern and western states and territories, and settle upon government lands, where they can be protected, and live under laws in harmony with the constitution of the United States. ...." In the recent past, said the *Argus,* "Principia Club Papers" had been distributed by the thousands among southern black farmers. "That the object of this whole scheme is political there seems to be no room for doubt," concluded the journalist.[13]

Another Democratic paper accused the Principia Club of less-philan- thropic motives. Quoting the club's most recent tract, in which blacks were advised to leave "bulldozing country" before the 1880 census was taken, the newspaper said that the intent was to reduce southern representation in Congress. Principia members argued that if blacks were kept away from the polls and prevented from voting for their representatives, they had no recourse but to vacate such a place and create a vacuum that would weaken southern power in the House of Representatives. Northern Demo- cratic papers hoped that such an outrageous scheme would result in such a backlash among voters that it would increase their party's strength in the North.[14]

Republican newspapers seized upon the word "bulldozing" and played heavily upon southern denial of the black franchise. New Yorkers were told by the *Times* that blacks had no other choice but to leave a region where "the old slave-owning spirit still lives, and where perpetual inferiority is associated with color." The recently enfranchised blacks did not dare vote against the former master class, declared one editorial. Frank Leslie's *Illustrated Newspaper* thought that regardless of the movement's origins, it certainly substantiated Republican charges of southern bull- dozing. Leslie predicted that outraged American voters would show the world a "solid North"—Republican—in the coming election of 1880.[15]

Much the same cry was heard from Chicago. The *Tribune* agreed that while other factors may have been involved in the black emigration, it was the denial of constitutional rights to these people that finally caused many of them to pack up and leave. The editor remarked that during the days of slavery these chattels were too valuable to be killed "as a mere pastime," but after emancipation and the consequent loss of cash value, "the head of the Negro was used as a convenient target." He did not explain why, if this was true, southern landowners were so concerned about the loss of labor that was occasioned by the flight of field hands. The Republican *Globe-Democrat,* of St. Louis, echoed the *Tribune's* asser- tions, charging that southern whites were determined to keep the blacks in a condition of poverty and ignorance that was as equally degrading as slavery. This newspaper stated flatly that political terrorism was the main cause of the exodus.[16]

The southern press gave a prominent place in its columns to the notion that northern encouragement of the exodus movement was a Republican plot to reduce the South's representation in Congress. When a Milwaukee editor made this charge, a Mississippi newspaper gave the story a place on its front page.[17] Major B. H. Lanier, of Lake Providence, Louisiana, publicly expressed the conviction that the recent movement had been gotten up in Washington by Republican politicians who believed that it was possible to reduce southern congressional representation. Lanier, a native southerner who had fought in the recent war, was not one of the political losers; he was a Republican.[18] Other members of the South's white establishment were heard from. J. L. Alcorn, a former governor of Mississippi who now operated a plantation at Friar's Point, blamed recent difficulties on the "present unwise agitation in Congress." Politicians, he said, were taking advantage of ignorant black field hands who were being made to feel that they were God's chosen people, children of Israel whom the wicked Egyptians (southerners) were about to reenslave, and that their sympathetic northern sponsors were attempting to speed them to the land of Canaan. He warned the blacks that no matter where they went in the North, they would encounter the inexorable law of the white man: "Every man for himself."[19]

"Pap" Singleton, the self-proclaimed father of the exodus, indicated that he understood the "inexorable law" to which Alcorn referred. "Hyar you all is, potterin' around in politics, trying to git into office that you ain't fit for," he cautioned some of the more ambitious members of his race, "and you can't see that these white speculators from the North is simply usin' you to line their pockets, and when they git through with you they'll drop you, and the rebels will come into power, and then whar'll you be?" But this was not the kind of advice the black emigrants wanted to hear. Much more optimistic were the words of George Washington, described in testimony before the Voorhees Committee as a "very wealthy colored man," who had sold his Louisiana property and had gone to Kansas. From Wyandotte he wrote to his friend Adolphus Prince, of Madison Parish, Louisiana, advising him to come to Kansas. "They do not kill Negroes here for voting," he said. "I am living here as a lark. You can buy land at from a dollar and a half to two dollars an acre." Black leaders in Missouri also recommended the move. John H. Johnson, of St. Louis, and B. F. Watson, of Kansas City, both took the position that political oppression and a general denial of civil rights were important considerations in the move northward. The Reverend R. De Baptiste, pastor of a Negro

205

congregation in Chicago, was another of those who argued that persecution was a prime mover, and his words were given a prominent place in the *Inter-Ocean*.[20]

Promoters of the exodus used the political aspect as a powerful weapon in their argument. The highly publicized and perhaps mythical Lycurgus Jones, who advertised himself as president of the Colored Colonization Society of Topeka, Kansas, gave much attention to the subject in his inflammatory pamphlet. Directed at southern readership, the broadside announced that "your brethren and friends throughout the North" had looked on "with painful solicitude" as the "rebel masters" had heaped outrages upon the heads of the unfortunates in the cotton fields. Jones warned that the Democrats now controlled Congress, and they would attempt to reenslave those who remained in the South.[21]

Whether or not there ever existed a Lycurgus Jones—he may have been the invention of a white propagandist—the notion that Democratic control of Congress meant the negation of emancipation was a thought that probably disturbed northern voters more than it did southern black laborers. It was a matter of deep concern to Republicans, who wondered if the political complexion of Congress augured the end of their party's occupancy of the White House after the election of 1880. Warnings that dire consequences might flow from a Democratic, and hence "Rebel," Congress were not limited to pamphleteers of the Jones stripe. The *Chicago Tribune* concluded that the "purity of the ballot" was in danger due to this turn of political events. A New England editor took an even more despairing stand, lamenting the fact that a mere fifteen years after the war the "Confederate Brigadiers" had captured Congress and once more were masters of the situation. Kansas Republicans, who sat in the eye of the political hurricane, shuddered at the prospect of a national Democratic resurgence. A Topeka editor trumpeted a warning that the "Brigadiers," now encamped at Washington, D.C., were about to grasp the country by the throat for a second time. These rebels, whose hands barely were clean of bloodstains, must be ejected from Congress at all costs, he told his readers.[22]

When Gen. William Tecumseh Sherman accompanied President Hayes on a visit to Kansas, in the autumn of 1879, efforts were made by the local press to use his presence politically. As the old war hero stood on the railroad platform at Lawrence, smoking a cigar and chatting with an admiring crowd that gathered around him, a few of the local blacks came forward to shake his hand.

"Are you an exodus darkey?" he asked one of them. "I'm from Kaintuck," was the reply. "Good state," the general commented, "but I want to see a regular exodus darkey, a regular Mississippi Negro." The next handshaker said that he was from "Old Virginny," and that did not satisfy Sherman's curiosity. He wanted to see an Exoduster.

"I heard that there were thousands came to Kansas lately and a good many to Lawrence, and I haven't been able to see a single one on my whole trip to Kansas; what's become of them?" asked the general. In answer, one of the blacks said that he was from Yazoo, Mississippi. Sherman asked him why he had come north.

"Well, I tell you, Mr. Sherman; dey wouldn't let us live down thar in peace; couldn't get no pay for our work, and dey wouldn't let us vote," said the former resident of Yazoo. When the visiting dignitary assured his listeners that political rights had been provided for blacks after the war, he was told that "dey go to shootin' de darkies when dey open dar head about dar rights to vote." Typically, Sherman suggested that anyone so threatened ought to go to the polls armed, accompanied by others who were armed, and stand up for his rights. The black man from Yazoo was incredulous at such talk.

"I tell you Mr. Sherman, you know nothin' about votin' down in Yazoo," he said. As one who had lived there for twenty-five years, "I knows 'em better dan you does, and I tell you dar ain't no libben down dar for a nigger, and you don't cotch no nigger what has any sense wid a horse pistol. No sar!" Unable to suggest any other solution, Sherman lamely remarked that he hoped the newcomer would do well in Kansas.

A local paper, in reporting the conversation to its readers, gave prominent space to it, emphasizing the political difficulties under which the former slaves had lived before they had reached the land of promise.[23] No mention was made of the fact that only a few months earlier, local blacks had complained vigorously about the denial to members of their race of appointive municipal offices in the city of Lawrence. Of much more interest was political bigotry as it blossomed in more southern climes.

The alleged political aspects of the exodus movement, which were displayed so prominently in the national press, were not lost upon members of Congress. However, so long as the movement appeared to be directed toward Kansas and some of the less-populated adjoining western states, few politicians wanted to risk an involvement that might backfire and bring harm, rather than help, to their careers. Kansas was solidly Republican, and the injection of large numbers of potential Republican voters into that state could do nothing more harmful than to increase its Republicanism. By late 1879 and early 1880, as a national election approached, matters began to change. By then St. John and his followers were making great efforts to deflect the thrust of the movement to the upper Midwest, to Illinois, in particular. More alarming to northern Democrats was a move to populate Indiana with some of these black Republican voters. That state, with fifteen electoral votes, had gone Democratic by a very narrow margin in 1876. It was economically and logistically possible to change that outcome in 1880 by the importation of a relatively small number of Republican voters.

As early as April of 1879, Republican members of Congress had talked of an investigation to determine the cause of the southern exodus. Democrats, who foresaw their opponents making political capital at governmental expense, opposed the idea, calling it a waste of money. Later that year, when southern Negroes began to turn up in Indiana, it was the Democrats' turn to talk of investigations. On December 15, Sen. Daniel W. Voorhees, of Indiana, indicated the alarm felt by his fellow Democrats when he introduced into the Senate a resolution asking for the formation of a five-man committee to study the situation. Referring to the movement into his own state, he spoke of Republican allegations that blacks had been obliged to flee the South because of the "unjust and cruel conduct of their white fellow-citizens." He asked that the proposed committee "investigate the causes which have led to the aforesaid emigration."[24]

Republican leaders, themselves fearful of what a Democratically controlled committee might do with such a weapon, reacted quickly. The next day, December 16, Sen. William Windom, of Minnesota, proposed an amendment to Voorhees's resolution. It suggested that if the committee should discover that the exodus movement had been caused by cruel and unjust treatment of southern blacks, it should recommend appropriate corrective measures to Congress. Not satisfied merely to investigate the cause of the exodus, Windom proposed that the sectional issue be put at rest by a governmentally sponsored migration of blacks to other parts of the country. He further asked that the committee consider the practicability of "providing such Territory or Territories as may be necessary for the use and occupation of persons who may desire to emigrate from their present homes in order to secure the free, full, and peaceful enjoyment of their constitutional rights and privileges."

Senator Windom told his colleagues that he had been "very much gratified" when Voorhees offered his resolution. "It was gratifying to me for several reasons," he went on. "I have long wondered why the honorable Senator from Indiana, with his known sympathy for the oppressed and suffering of all countries, has failed to speak in their behalf, and when I ascertained yesterday from his resolution that at last the sufferings of that people, which have driven many of them from their homes, have moved upon the sympathies of that honorable Senator, I felt that light was dawning upon that subject." His amendment, said Windom, was designed to make Voorhees's resolution more explicit. Actually, by its very language the amendment prejudged the whole issue and indicated that Windom had long since decided about the causes of the exodus.[25]

Although Windom's amendment itself gave the resolution a definite political tint, one that Voorhees certainly could not agree with, the Indiana senator had little choice but to accept it. He was in a dilemma. He could not very well deny the implications of Windom's amendment and thereby admit his own prejudices, nor could he indicate that he lacked sympathy with the oppressed wherever they lived. In response to Windom's somewhat pious verbiage, Voorhees stated that if people were being driven from the South by cruelty, of course he was opposed to it. Then he made his own case. "If, on the other hand, there is a conspiracy on the part of disreputable people, both white and black, to disturb the condition of the black race at the South and make them discontented and unhappy, to point out to them greater advantages elsewhere which do not exist, thus spreading a delusion and a snare before them, getting them to move about, that had better be known, for the exposure of it will be the way to stop it."[26] By his reference "point out to them greater advantages elsewhere which do not exist," Voorhees meant that he was worried about a recent, and unaccountable, influx of blacks into Indiana.

What became known as the Voorhees Committee, composed of senators Daniel W. Voorhees (D, Indiana), George H. Pendleton (D, Ohio), Zebulon B. Vance (D, North Carolina), William Windom (R, Minnesota), and Henry W. Blair (R, New Hampshire), was created by a vote of the Senate on December 18, 1879. It commenced its hearings on January 19, 1880, and adjourned on April 27, during which time it examined 159 witnesses, about 50 of whom were from Kansas. Critics claimed that it wasted between thirty and forty thousand of the taxpayers' dollars.[27]

During the course of the committee's life, as the press reported day-to-day testimony given, the nation's newspapers debated the question at hand. Southerners, fearful that the publicity surrounding the investigation might increase the turmoil in their region, argued that the problem was one over which Congress had no control. As one Georgia paper remarked, the Democrats were only playing into the hands of their political opponents by giving them "an opportunity to collect bloody shirt material for northern consumption."[28] For different reasons, some northern newspapers agreed that the matter of migrations of people was not a fit subject for congressional interference. The New York *Sun* argued that if any citizen, black or white, wanted to move "from the Albemarle to the Wabash," he had a perfect right to do so "without having the national nose thrust into his domestic affairs." The Republican *Indianapolis News* took much the same position, holding that the blacks no longer were wards but were citizens, and they had a right to go where they pleased. The editor, sensitive to Democratic control of Congress, criticized what he called "the growing tendency of the legislative power in this government to feel itself called upon to regulate everything," a development that he labeled a "dangerous evil."[29]

The Chicago *Inter-Ocean,* a passionately pro-exodus Republican newspaper, fired its sharpest journalistic barbs at Voorhees, accusing him of trying to frighten the freedmen "into the notion that it is better to endure proscription and injustice in the South, rather than seek equal rights and a fair chance in life in Indiana."[30] From Topeka the *Commonwealth* shouted its angry defense of St. John and accused Voorhees of creating an expense to the taxpayers that would benefit nobody. The newspaper denied testimony given by a white Kansan to the effect that Kansas Republicans were encouraging the exodus in order to offset the effect of white immigration, which, it was said, tended to vote Democratic.[31]

Democratic papers across the North took an understandably partisan view and defended the committee's efforts. In Kansas, the Atchison *Patriot* said that Voorhees had shown what he started out to show, that the exodus was political in its origins and that sordid avarice and selfish gain were at the bottom of it. "A political party for political advantage instigated it by cruel deception and wicked misrepresentations and a grasping corporation and scheming avaricious men further it through mercenary motives and for selfish purposes," charged the *Patriot.* During the investigation the *Washington Post* made reference to some testimony given by one of the blacks and twitted Republican members for failing to wring out of him statements that would support their case. "Blair and Windom worked hard to prove by the witness that the animus of the movement was not political, and, failing in this, labored to reduce the results to insignificant proportions," said one of the January issues. "They both lost temper during the day, but gained nothing thereby."[32]

The political complexion of the issue, clear enough at the beginning of the hearings, became even more evident as a battle erupted among committee members over the selection of witnesses. Each side wanted to hear testimony that would favor its argument. Early in February, 1880, Sen. John J. Ingalls, of Kansas, indicated to St. John that the names of some selected refugees would be useful to the committee. His brother, F. T. Ingalls, made the request. "The Democrats on the Committee are endeavoring to show that the movement was instigated by Republicans for political designs and they [the Republicans] are anxious to get at the facts in the case," wrote the brother.[33] St. John responded, and a few days later Senator Windom wrote a letter of thanks. Windom said that he would like to hold the hearings in Topeka, but, "I think it will not be, as the majority has very little desire to know the real cause of the exodus." Voorhees had agreed to the use of affidavits, the Minnesota senator explained, and he suggested that St. John "could have some reliable man take the affidavits from 20 to 50 of the most intelligent emigrants showing the reasons why they left their homes, and exposing the bulldozing, and other outrages committed upon the colored people, it would be *most valuable* in the investigation."

On the face of it, there was nothing wrong in asking questions of intelligent people, but it was the better-educated blacks who, in the main, had the greatest objection to the denial of the franchise in the South. The bulk of the exodusters, who were poverty-stricken and usually uneducated, did not give this issue high priority in their reasons for moving. By making the selections that Windom recommended, a point of view favorable to the Republicans would be easy to achieve. Inferentially, Windom admitted this when, in March, he complained to St. John that Voorhees had "sent out to Kansas an officer with blank subpoenaes to select such witnesses as he may be able to find to testify in the manner desired." Windom got at the root of the matter when he commented: "The majority of the Committee being Democratic of course control its actions to suit themselves."[34]

This was not entirely true. Windom was able to bring forth witnesses who favored his cause, and they performed for him in a satisfactory manner. Dr. Rockhold and Milton Reynolds, both of Parsons, Kansas, were called to Washington, D.C., by the Minnesotan. Upon their return, Rockhold described the trip to St. John, and he commented upon the politics involved: "There was a strong effort made to connect some of the Republicans, you in particular, with the movement. That they failed to do anything of the kind is known to all. Voorhees was sick of his effort before I got there and dismissed most of the Kansas witnesses without examination." Rockhold reported to the governor that he and Reynolds were interrogated by the committee "and made our little speeches." He came away convinced that they had helped the cause, and he assured St. John: "I feel well satisfied with the results of the investigation and [we] can go before the people this fall with renewed vigor and confidence."[35]

To the surprise of no one, the final report of the Voorhees Committee showed the same division of opinion that was held by its members at the outset of its investigation. Republican senators Windom and Blair compiled a minority report, the main burden of which argued that there was great political persecution of southern Negroes, the blame for which lay with the Democrats. They derided the charge that Republicans had been trying to colonize such northern states as Indiana for political purposes, and they asked why twenty-five thousand had gone to Kansas, whose Republican majority already was over forty thousand, when only seven or eight hundred had moved to Indiana.

The committee's Democratic majority—senators Voorhees, Pendleton, and Vance—concluded that Republican political machinations lay behind the effort to persuade southern blacks to leave their homes, particularly those who were brought into Indiana from North Carolina. Their denials that these people had been prevented from voting were weak in the face of massive evidence to the contrary, as presented by a congressional committee in 1878. The majority of the Voorhees Committee lamely admitted that there had been political strife in the South, but they asked if this was not to have been expected after so bitter a civil war. All that they were able to offer was the pious hope that southern political turmoil would simmer down and that the two races simply would have to reconcile their outstanding differences. Voorhees and his fellow Democrats were on somewhat firmer ground when they maintained that southern Negroes frequently made as much money at farming as did their white counterparts in the North and West, and therefore economic pressures were not invariably a major cause of removal.[36]

The investigation, conducted in the early months of a national election year, failed to answer satisfactorily the principal question at hand. It solved no problems for either race, and it satisfied very few Americans. The same contentions and the same prejudices that existed prior to the long investigation remained after its work was concluded. About all that the hearings offered was more fodder for the newspapers of either Republican or Democratic convictions to foster the cause of their particular candidates. Rather than set at rest any questions as to the political nature of the exodus, the Voorhees Committee merely increased the intensity of the argument.

If the Democratic majority of the committee had any ground for its contention that the exodus either was politically inspired or was used for political purposes, once it gained momentum, undoubtedly the best case in point was the Indiana situation. Pretty clearly the movement of blacks into the state during late 1879 and early 1880 was not "natural." Until November, 1879, Indiana had felt the impact of the general movement only slightly; its main thrust, as well as the attendant publicity, was focused upon Kansas. After November and throughout the early months

212

of 1880, the appearance of southern blacks in Indiana was a matter of almost daily comment in the newspapers of that state.[37]

As early as the spring of 1879, Indianans had talked about the possibility that their state was to be one of the places to which black voters would be sent for the upcoming political battle of 1880, but it was not until the last days of 1879 that there seemed to be solid evidence of such activity. The arrival of some 220 thinly clad, hungry, destitute blacks at Shelbyville, on December 12, immediately generated a stir in the Indiana press, as well as in Democratic newspapers from as far away as Boston. As Shelbyville Democrats studied the political potential of the influx, they pondered the more immediate question of what to do with the indigents on hand. The mayor told his city council that like it or not, these strangers had to be fed. One member, a Democrat, so moved; a fellow Democratic councilman objected, saying that he did not want to be taxed to "support the damned nigger."[38] The tone of the proceedings sounded very much like the mutterings heard in Democratic Missouri River towns earlier that spring.

Although the hungry strangers were fed, no formal or even informal organizations, such as the group at St. Louis or KFRA at Topeka, appear to have been created for relief purposes in Indiana. From the outset, the statewide community opposed what it considered to be an artificial immigration; every effort was made to discourage it. The *Shelby Democrat* made this clear when it stated: "Negro emigrants in large bodies are not wanted and are not needed in this State. This is especially true when it is known that they are brought here for political purposes and not to advance the labor interests of the State."[39]

Indianans were much annoyed by the fact that their state had become a dumping ground. In early December, 1879, they learned that a group scheduled to arrive in Indiana a few days later had been temporarily marooned at Washington, D.C. The travelers were on charity, awaiting the raising of enough funds through contributions to get them on their way, and Indiana was the target. The National Emigration Aid Society, of Washington, was the principal instrument used to raise the necessary travel money. Although it complained about the slowness of contributions, some of the offerings came from high places, including the Rutherford Hayes family and members of the cabinet. By the spring of 1880 the Aid Society's president admitted that his organization had sent between twenty-five hundred and three thousand blacks into Indiana. Two-thirds of these had paid their own way, the remainder having been financed by the society. O. S. B. Wall, a fifty-two-year-old Washington attorney who served as the group's president, testified that the Baltimore and Ohio Railroad wanted nine dollars a head for fares between Washington and Indiana, but after a heart-to-heart talk with what he called the "grand moguls" of the company, the road offered Wall a "drawback" of a dollar a head as its contribution to a worthy cause. When asked why he had not sent these people on to Kansas, Wall explained that Indiana was closer, hence cheaper. Tickets to Kansas cost nineteen or twenty dollars, more than double the fare to Indianapolis.[40] This explanation was more satisfactory to Republican newspapers, particularly to Chicago's *Inter-Ocean,* which maintained that the movement was one made "in the direction of meat and bread," as opposed to a political motivation. When it wanted to, the *Inter-Ocean* was able to forget, for the moment, all its talk about political persecution in the South.[41]

During the early weeks of 1880, Indianans grew increasingly excited over the influx of blacks into their state. The *Shelby Democrat* described the colonizing efforts of a North Carolinian named Samuel L. Perry, who was said to be acting as an advance man for the prospective arrivals. This "short, thick-set Negro, with a pair of fine check pants, and large fashionable boots, upon an enormous pair of pedal extremities," was reported to be laying plans to locate two hundred families in Shelbyville. The newspaper accused the Baltimore and Ohio Railroad of promising to pay Perry so much per hundred head imported. The editor, who later referred to Perry as "the forger and Negro liar," said that the promoter was interested only in money, that he had no concern for his people.[42]

Perry had another interpretation for his motives. He explained that the movement had begun as far back as 1872, when he and some fellow North Carolinians had seen pamphlets issued by Oscar F. Davis, head of the Union Pacific's land department, in which both railroad and government lands that "could be got cheap" were described. Blacks in Perry's neighborhood discussed the possibility of forming a colony along the line of the road, but nothing came of it, partly because North Carolina's efforts to improve the lot of its Negroes offered them at least temporary satisfaction at home. Although Perry would not admit to the Voorhees Committee that any political inspiration lay behind the movement's revival in 1879 and 1880, the unrest experienced by the South's black population after the spring of 1877 must have had some effect. In any event, Perry, along with a preacher named Peter C. Williams, agreed to represent a group that was formed at Goldsboro, North Carolina, in 1879 in order to investigate Kansas, Nebraska, and Colorado as possible sites for a black colony. Members contributed twenty-five cents apiece, and the two men, with a total of fifty-four dollars, started off. Perry insisted that the mission had nothing to do with the exodus, that it was strictly a matter of finding land upon which to settle. By September 15, 1879, he and Williams were in Washington, D.C., trying to get assistance from the National Emigration Aid Society, but without any success. It may have been at this juncture that the focus of their venture was turned toward Indiana. Capital-city Republicans and the "grand moguls" of the Baltimore and Ohio Railroad appeared to have more interest in the Hoosier State than in Kansas at this particular time.[43]

Apparently Perry's business ventures in Indiana were less than satisfactory to him. The reception that he received, as evidenced by the attitude of the *Shelby Democrat,* and some difficulties with the Baltimore and Ohio representatives soured him on the Hoosiers. He told the Voorhees Committee that "if I owned a lot in Indiana and one in hell, I would rent out the one in Indiana and live in hell before I would live there." When Senator Voorhees asked him if he planned to continue his immigration efforts in Indiana, he replied: "No siree, boby," after which he explained that as a result of his dissatisfaction he had tried to reroute some of the Negroes who had started for Indiana. He had a very low regard for the Baltimore and Ohio Railroad, alleging that it treated no one fairly; more specifically, he charged that it had not paid money owed to him for his efforts. After failing to raise any funds for his project at Indianapolis, Perry moved on to Greencastle, where, once again, he was rebuffed. Unable to make any headway in Indiana, he and Williams returned to Washington, D.C.[44]

Some of Perry's "customers" also expressed dissatisfaction. Peter Dew said that he and four hundred others had emigrated to Indiana as a result of promises made by Perry and Williams. "They represented that I would receive for labor on farms $15 per month, provisions, and a cow and calf, and in the city would be paid $2.50 per day. They also said that each one who came would be given and furnished a house; that we could buy land in any tract that we wanted for from one dollar to a dollar and a half per acre." In a mood of bitter disillusionment, Dew concluded: "Not one of these promises is true, so far as I know."[45] Others who testified before the Voorhees Committee confirmed the charge that Perry had made some large promises. One witness said that southern Negroes were told that they would get new suits of clothes when they reached Washington, D.C., and also that they would be given free railroad tickets to Indiana or Kansas.[46]

Mingo Simmons, a former slave who lived in North Carolina, confirmed Perry's role as a promoter of southern emigration.

"Well, sir," Simmons testified, "Samuel Perry was knocking around there among some of the boys, and he said there was a circular telling us to go out to Kansas; and he said they would give us land and plenty to do; that the government wanted us to go out there; and then he began to hold meetings; some of them said they were political, and some of them said that if the government was not in it they were not going." Simmons, who later decided that Perry was a "bad fellow," explained how he was sidetracked in his efforts to get to Kansas. Perry, who had investigated Kansas, told the group to which Simmons belonged that blacks would starve in Kansas, that Indiana was a better place. Besides, Perry explained, Kansas was a long way off; he had not collected enough money to send his friends there.

Indiana was closer, but it fell far short of the glowing picture that Perry had painted of it. Mingo Simmons was in one of the first groups that left North Carolina, and he spent his first month in Indiana a hungry man. Unable to find employment, he went to work for a farmer who offered him fifty cents a day to gather corn; but when he applied for his pay, the farmer explained that deductions for board had resulted in an empty account for the employee; thus, Simmons did not get a cent for his efforts. Totally discouraged, the thirty-one-year-old illiterate black headed for home, cold, hungry, and angry.[47]

Charges by the *Shelby Democrat* that the Baltimore and Ohio Railroad was implicated in the movement of North Carolina Negroes into Indiana were more than partisan accusations made by a Democratic paper. John P. Dukehart, a fifty-five-year-old native of Baltimore, was at this time the southern passenger agent for the railroad; he had worked for the company for about thirty years. He freely admitted to the Voorhees Committee that his company was soliciting among Carolina blacks. In the spring of 1879 Dukehart was sent to Weldon, North Carolina, to look into the exodus movement. Upon arrival there, he found agents from both the Pennsylvania Railroad and the Chesapeake and Ohio Company already at work. In October of that year he was at La Grange, North Carolina, talking with Perry and Williams, after which he arranged for about forty Negroes to go to Washington, D.C. They left on cars of the Wilmington and Weldon Railroad. Since the Baltimore and Ohio did not serve La Grange, the fares were prorated between the two railroads.[48] Passage for those who were unable to pay their own fares was financed by the National Emigration Aid Society of Washington, D.C.

The appearance in Indiana of large groups of blacks, as well as the belief that they were being imported by outside interests, goaded local Democrats into a fury. "Republicans are and have been for months engaged in the nefarious business of lying to the deluded blacks of the South in order to get them to leave their peaceful homes and take up residences in Indiana where they are not wanted and where they have but few friends," wrote one editor. Arguing that Republican planners were anxious to get their black allies into the state before the first of May, so that they might qualify to vote in the presidential election, the newspaperman concluded: "The infamous purposes of the Republican party to carry Indiana this year are so plain that even the most stupid cannot be deceived." In an effort to counter the political impact of such a stratagem, he warned workingmen that "the importation of a gang of ignorant Negroes into this State is only for the purpose of compelling poor white men to stand aside in order to give place to a set of black paupers whose votes can be handled with more ease."⁴⁹

The appeal to labor was aimed at a specific group of voters. Far more inclusive was the thought that pure Hoosier blood might be tainted by an infusion of blacks, and in February, 1880, the *Shelby Democrat* turned to this political weapon.

"Exodus first; miscegenation, second," shouted that guardian of the public welfare. "Such is the dainty dish set by Indiana Republicans before the white people of the State. . . . Between the upper millstone called 'exodus' and the nether millstone called 'miscegenation' everything worth living for in this land of ours must be crushed." Then the editor provided details of the impending disaster: "The prosperity of the country cannot survive the establishment of absolute social equality. A race of hybrids would rapidly Mexicanize us. . . . In such a state of affairs the proud Republic would soon sink to the lowest level, and all the choice flowers of civilization could but wither and perish."

These were but general warnings. For fear he had not reached the darkest depths of the public's latent racism, the journalist stated as fact that "the Negro Exoduster . . . is . . . promised a white wife if he will only emigrate to the Hoosier State and dutifully support the party of great moral ideas." Considering the potency of such an incentive, the writer admitted that it was "no wonder the ebo-shins and gizzard-foots of the Tar Heel State are rapidly flooding the promised land of the West. If there is anything in this world the Negro man wants above all others, it is to have a white wife by his side."⁵⁰

As the hysteria mounted among Indiana's more rabid Democrats, conservative residents asked the germinal question: How many blacks actually had been brought in? As always, estimates varied. As of February, 1880, the best guess was 700 to 800. Such was the figure advanced by L. C. Morris, a Baltimore and Ohio passenger agent at Indianapolis. John P. Dukehart's records tended to substantiate this estimate. He testified that he had sold 763 tickets, of which 235 were half fares. "I think that I was able to capture all who went to Indiana, and the other roads got nothing," he told the Voorhees Committee. At this time the *Indianapolis Journal* said that since the inception of the movement, 1,135 blacks had arrived from North Carolina, about one-fourth of whom were men.[51]

Those who feared the political outcome of the movement brushed aside arguments that the number of arrivals was small. The fact was that poor black Carolinians were coming into the state in unusual numbers, and there was no way to predict when and if the flow would stop. Thomas P. Mills, an Indianapolis real estate agent, freely admitted to the Voorhees Committee that he wanted to see twenty thousand blacks imported into the state for the purpose of swinging doubtful areas to the Republican ranks. Testimony such as this sent Indiana Democrats into a frenzy. "To improve the civilization of Indiana with twenty thousand 'buck' Negroes is the Radical plan for carrying the State this fall," responded the *Shelby Democrat,* again warning all white workingmen to vote for their own interests by favoring the Democratic party at the fall elections.[52]

Meanwhile, prospective black allies of the Republican party found the going hard in Indiana. A group of Indianapolis Negroes formed an Aid Society which, by mid February, 1880, had raised just under three hundred dollars to help their brethren. It was far from sufficient. Horatio Rust, who left his work in Chicago to visit the newcomers to Indianapolis, wrote a sorrowful report of conditions to William Penn Nixon, of the *Inter-Ocean.* Rust and Dr. S. A. Elbert, a black physician who had been educated at Oberlin, toured the refugee quarters in Indianapolis. Observing about a hundred women and children whose men had gone out to look for work, they found conditions primitive. The blacks were cold, dressed in rags, and possessed of little bedding or furniture; many were sick.[53] J. H. Russell, an Indianapolis undertaker, reported that by the end of January he had buried nearly thirty of the migrants, mostly children. All were buried as paupers at an average cost of $5.15 per body. For this sum the deceased was entitled only to a plain box, with no religious services. Most of the deaths were caused by diphtheria or scarlet fever. Sanitary conditions, said Russell, were deplorable. "A family of nine—seven children and man and wife—had nothing at all except a pile of straw in a corner and one old comforter to cover them," he later recalled. "One of the children was taken sick and died before they let it be known."[54]

Some of Indiana's black immigrants bitterly regretted their move. "I am now in Ind. in the worst fixt I ever was in and all the days of my life," Sarah Smith wrote to her former employer, C. S. Wooten. "I am out of cloes, and I have not got no where to go and no house to sta in day and or night and no boddy wount let me in with them and I have not got nothing to eat and nothing to dow to get not a cents worth for myself nor my childdran to eat." Her sister Chloe was similarly distressed; both women wanted money for passage back to their southern homes, and Wooten sent it. Frank Jones, another of Wooten's tenants who had succumbed to the magic of emigration promoters, failed to find the good life in Indiana. Ruefully he admitted to his former landlord that "just lake you sead these pepel hare dont not like black pepel." Commenting that "Sam perry out to be hung for telling such A falshod," Jones confessed that he had been misled, and he also asked for money with which to go home.[55]

If the name of Perry gave disillusioned blacks ideas about employing the noose, there were other promoters whose efforts well may have inspired similar dark thoughts. J. H. Walker, a Terre Haute Negro, issued a circular describing the great demand for laborers in his state and the easy availability of lucrative jobs, good homes, and educational opportunities for black children. There is evidence to show that some of the Kansas-bound southerners stopped in Indiana as a result of such publicity. A. B. Carleton, who practiced law in Terre Haute and who knew the neighborhood blacks, including Walker, quite well, denied that there was any demand for labor in his city or state. Since 1874, he said, hard times had resulted in diminishing job opportunities. Even in better days, said Carleton, the demand for farm labor was minimal. James Sparks, a Shelbyville livestock dealer, agreed with this, explaining that "we have a number of Germans there [in Indiana] and they do not hire much help. What the men cannot do the women do." The black population of Indiana had no argument with statements such as those made by Carleton and Sparks. They felt that there were enough poor Negroes in Indiana already, without importing any more from the South. They scoffed at circulars promising newcomers $1.50 a day for labor, pointing out that such a figure was more than double the going rate.[56]

It was the optimism of the circulars, not the hard truth, that motivated southern blacks. As a people, they were accused by the whites of being childlike and innocent. They were all of this when it came to accepting as "gospel" the promises that were made in almost any circular. Those who had money wanted to buy land, and they believed that a newer state, such as Kansas, offered the best opportunities. Those who were poor tended to head for Illinois, Indiana, or Ohio, in the hope that they could find jobs among the farmers. In this they differed little from legions of white people who for years had been looking for a promised land of their own in less-settled parts of the country.

One of the Voorhees Committee witnesses from Indiana told the committee that he had talked with a great many of the restless blacks, and he was convinced that their motives were innocent. He believed that all they wanted was employment and that most of them had little idea that they were being encouraged to migrate for political reasons.[57] Probably this was true; if so, it helps to account for the great surprise that they felt when excited Democrats greeted them with undisguised hostility. Leonard Hackney, a Shelbyville lawyer, described the reception given to one such group of blacks who tried to settle in his town. Asked what he thought a gathering mob intended to do, Hackney replied: "They said they were going down there [to the depot] and tell the damned niggers they could not stop there." To make such impromptu action "legal," residents of Shelbyville had invoked a law of 1852 that assessed a five-hundred-dollar penalty upon anyone who brought paupers into the state. The reception committee at the depot had no difficulty in concluding that the arrivals were indigents and therefore did not qualify for residence in Shelbyville. The group moved on. Hackney, who was the county attorney, admitted that the town itself was safely Democratic but that the congressional district in which it lay was only marginally so. The infusion of any more Republican voters into the district might endanger the Democrats' tender position.[58]

Incidents such as this disturbed the Indiana press; it was not the kind of publicity desired by a state whose people liked to think of themselves as being emancipated from racial prejudice. Individuals such as Hackney could argue, in all seriousness, that they were not racially prejudiced against the "damned niggers," that the problem was political and even economic, but never racial. The *Greencastle Banner* told its readers that blacks arriving at Greencastle were pleased at the welcome they had received "in the more enlightened portions of Indiana." The local postmaster, who was much interested in the movement, was among community leaders who welcomed the strangers to Greencastle, and he helped to give the city a reputation as being one of the reception centers for migrant southern blacks. That there were relatively few "enlightened portions" of Indiana was suggested by the state auditor, M. D. Manson, who did not think that his fellow Hoosiers were ready to accept Negroes. "I do not believe that the colored people can benefit themselves by coming to Indiana," he told the Voorhees Committee. "While it is a liberal State, the people have never looked very liberally on the colored people." He then explained that "when the present constitution was adopted, there was a clause (No. 13) to prohibit colored immigration. Although the general constitution was only adopted by 20,000 votes, that clause was adopted by 80,000!"[59]

The Republican minority of the Voorhees Committee denied that the party was attempting to influence the Indiana vote by importing southern blacks, but the evidence was strong that such a scheme was afoot. Some of the better-known blacks admitted it. "General" Conway, for example, stated openly that "I have been trying to help carry Indiana by their aid." He said that the Negro was "a good Republican and a good loyal citizen" who should be allowed to vote, and "I think the Negro ought to go where he can do the most good for himself and the Republican party." Far from denying that the recent movement of blacks out of the South had political implications, Conway said: "I have not liked the idea to exclude politics from the exodus."[60]

Other black leaders were willing to admit the political implications of the movement into Indiana, but some of them were opposed to it. For example, Charles N. Otey, editor of a weekly Washington, D.C., newspaper called the *Argus,* did not want to see members of his race assigned roles as political pawns. Otey, who joined the National Emigration Aid Society, which was based in the capital city, was willing to help suffering blacks start a new life in the North. At one of the society's meetings, someone suggested that since Indiana would be a doubtful state in 1880, why not divert about five thousand northbound blacks to that state until the election was over. Otey was shocked at the suggestion and withdrew from active committee work in the society. He felt that American Negroes had been used as tools long enough.[61]

Evidence submitted to the Voorhees Committee suggested that Otey was right in his assumption that the blacks were being used. Several letters were produced to show that they were being enticed into Indiana in order to vote the Republican ticket and thus turn out the Democrats. In some cases, letters from these field hands were signed with an "X," labeled "his mark," indicating illiteracy.[62] Scott Ray, a Shelbyville, Indiana, attorney, said that Republicans had admitted complicity in such a scheme, arguing that since they had to buy votes in Indiana anyway, why not do it as cheaply as possible. This way, they said, the voter did not have to be paid every time he went to the polls.[63]

Thomas P. Mills, who was described as "an active, ardent, and prominent Republican of Indianapolis," entertained no doubts as to the origin of the black movement into his state during the early months of 1880. "I was told," he said, that "we wanted 20,000 'bucks,' buck niggers, in Indiana this year." As laborers? "No, sir, I had no idea of labor. I was looking for votes." Mills admitted that he had been disappointed in the resultant number of prospective voters. There were, he said, far too many women and children.[64]

The first test of Republican strategy in Indiana occurred in October,

1880. On the nineteenth of that month, voters went to the polls to elect state officers. The results favored the Republicans by about four thousand votes. In bitter disappointment, one Democratic newspaper attributed the outcome to the partial success of a Republican effort "to Africanize our State for political purposes" by a judicious application of "the mighty dollar and the portable Negro." It was hoped, said the editor, that Republican funds would be used up and that the Negro would be "largely needed elsewhere" by the time of the general election. However, if Indiana was to be delivered to the Democrats, greater efforts would have to be made, and this journalist, for one, was prepared to throw everything into the fight. He now announced that James A. Garfield was pro-Chinese and that if such a man triumphed at the polls, the "pauper labor of China" soon would be taking bread from the mouths of American workingmen. Should this catastrophe occur, he warned, Negro laborers, too, would feel its effects. Before long they would find "three or four almond-eyed Mongolians competing with each one of them."

By now this particular newspaper had given up the term "buck nigger" in favor of "the colored brother," when referring to black laborers. The change of heart had political origins. During September, Kansas Negro Republicans had staged a minor bolt from party discipline, complaining that they were not getting their share of offices. Indiana Democrats took new hope; perhaps they had misjudged the black electorate. If, as one of the party organs put it, "a bit of independent voting in this State by the imported Negroes" occurred, the Republican stratagem would backfire.

So, the new local policy was adopted: "Be kind to the blacks; find another point of attack." The threat to labor now became yellow, not black. In an era of increasingly heavy attacks upon Orientals the published rumor that the Chinese Six Companies, of San Francisco, had contributed to Republican coffers made delightful preelection gossip.[65] Indiana Democrats were down to the last card politically, and they had to use any weapon at hand. The general election was only days away.

Republicans acknowledged that Indiana was to be a major battleground in the 1880 election. In late August, candidate James A. Garfield admitted to Chester Arthur that, in his opinion, the election would turn on the way that Republicans managed their affairs in that state. He acknowledged that the party would have to fight against a regular Democratic majority of about six thousand votes. Division among Democrats, thought Garfield, would be the deciding factor. Understandably, he made no mention of Republican efforts to import voters; on the contrary, he charged the Democrats with such a practice, and he explained to Arthur that large numbers of trustworthy Republicans would stand guard in border counties, ready to report sudden movements of Democrats into the state.[66]

When the votes were counted in November, winner Garfield could take comfort in the fact that the doubtful state of Indiana had gone Republican by seven thousand votes. This appeared to be a small margin considering the fact that Kansas, with a much smaller electorate, had piled up a Republican majority of sixty thousand. On the other hand, a state such as New York, with thirty-five electoral votes at stake, was won with a plurality of only twenty-three thousand. It was not possible to determine how much the Indiana vote was governed by "portable blacks," as opposed to issues and a split in the Democratic party. The Democrats, of course, insisted that it was manipulation that had cost them the election in that state. The *Shelby Democrat* disconsolately concluded that "money was extravagantly used to buy and import votes to carry this State," and it called the action as "deplorable as it is shameful."

Contemporary political observers contended that the black vote, of either the imported or domestic variety, had an influence in Indiana as well as in other northern states. A postelection analysis, published in the *North American Review,* supported this contention and asserted that the subtraction of the Negro vote in Indiana and Ohio, in both the October and November elections, would have changed the outcome. The writer further asserted that the black vote was a major factor in giving Republicans their majorities in New York, Connecticut, "and perhaps other Northern States."[67] A more likely explanation would be the emotional charge provided by the exodus, as opposed to actual numbers of black voters in these northern states. New England, in particular, was given a heavy barrage of propaganda. Voters were warned again and again that the current flight of southern blacks was proof that the recent war had been in vain and that the South, indeed, had risen again, in a political sense. Workingmen might be frightened enough by the thought of a black or yellow peril that they would vote Democratic, but their forces were disorganized and inarticulate as compared to the armies of moral crusaders who marched under the colorful banner of the "bloody shirt."

Since there was no way to determine what combination of factors influenced the mind of each voter, the political influence of the exodus could not be measured. One possibility to be considered was the thrust of the movement *after* the election, when, presumably, the political issue —at least for the moment—no longer was of great consequence. If the origins had been political, presumably this pressure would have been relieved after the election and, consequently, the numbers of those fleeing the South would have fallen off. Such a premise, however, did not satisfy

223

the St. Johns, the Comstocks, or the Havilands. Although they had shouted warnings that a Democratic victory in 1880 would, in St. John's words, generate a "perfect rush from the South as soon as the coming elections are over," they would not admit that a Republican victory might calm the fears of southern blacks.[68] A Republican administration had been in power when the movement started, but as Mrs. Comstock complained, "the present [Hayes] administration have done nothing to make their [southern Negroes] condition at home more endurable." Her solution to the problem was the return to office of U. S. Grant, in whom she thought the former slaves had great confidence.[69] St. John argued that regardless of which party gained the presidency, the manner in which elections were held in the South, including the most recent one, was bound to stimulate further emigration from that region. If there was any political stimulus to the movement, he thought, it came from southern Democrats, not from members of his own party. The governor, who had been reelected in November despite predictions that his sympathy for the Exodusters would defeat him, had not changed his mind about southern social and political conditions as they affected American blacks. Even though he had confounded his critics by winning at the polls, he did not renew his earlier suggestions that there was room for all in Kansas. His state had done more than enough for persecuted southern Negroes, he thought; it was time for other northern states to share in the great national cause of completing the eradication of human slavery. From now on, concluded the governor, he would dedicate himself more completely to the emancipation of another group of enslaved Americans: the alcoholics.

12

THE FIAT TO GO FORTH
IS IRRESISTIBLE

The Voorhees Committee's inability or unwillingness to answer its own question—what caused the exodus—merely aggravated the issue and threw it as a bone to the political dogs in a presidential election year. Congress itself was criticized for creating a body that merely toyed with a politically sensitive matter and failed to make any constructive recommendations. Some years later the famed Negro educator Booker T. Washington recalled: "Thus, with its usual recklessness, congress appropriated thousands of dollars to find out what was already known to every intelligent person, and almost every schoolboy in the country, that the Negroes were leaving the South because of systematic robbery, and political cruelties. Thousands of dollars to ascertain the cause of the poor Negroes' distress, but not one cent to relieve it."[1]

The answers were not so obvious that "every schoolboy" would know them. While many members of the black community found no difficulty in placing the blame for the difficulties upon southern white bigots, there was a wide divergence of opinion among its leaders as to the wisdom of fleeing from the problem. The exodus of 1879 merely brought into focus a recognized but blurred issue that had emerged slowly since the close of the Civil War. For fifteen years the sore had festered as a newly freed race struggled for economic existence. During that period a number of blacks grew discouraged at their inability to go forward under the new rules of life, and some of them decided that the only solution to the dilemma was to leave the South. More prominent members of the race, many of whom lived in the North, argued against such a move on the ground that this was surrender to the white southern establishment. Old time abolitionists supported this view, lending their still-powerful voices to the crusade against the resurgent southern Bourbons.

It is obvious that in the immediate postwar years thousands of recently freed blacks started their new careers from point zero on the economic scale. What a good many northerners failed to appreciate was the fact that thousands of southern white farmers were in only a little better position. The devastation of war and inflation, as well as the virtual destruction of the southern economy, had left these people in serious straits. During the next decade and a half, both races showed progress. By 1880 there were Negro storekeepers, livery-stable owners, small businessmen, and successful small farmers. Some of the blacks had acquired appreciable tracts of land, which they worked and even rented out.

At the same time there were classes of both white and black people in the South who had not prospered. They formed a group of drifters, sharecroppers, and part-time laborers. Many of the footloose blacks found it relatively easy to respond to the blandishments of those who promised them a new and better life in the West or in some of the northern states. They were comparable to a good many small farmers in Europe, who, dissatisfied with their lot and dreaming of free land in the American West, pulled up stakes with no great reluctance in order to begin life anew in a land of promise.

Thousands upon thousands of southern blacks who did not respond to the exodus remained because they felt that the South was their natural home, that the climate, the cotton culture, and the agrarian system under which they had worked, even during the days of slavery, was best suited for them. A few complained about political inequities; probably the mass did not. They were more concerned over economic barriers that were put in their way by the "master race." They argued that constant impoverishment was no better than slavery, and the former masters answered that poverty was no stranger to white farmers, that it was a common problem to the agricultural classes. Such arguments did not satisfy the blacks. A poverty imposed by lack of rainfall, the boll weevil, or any other natural disaster was something that both races had to expect. But constant indebtedness through manipulated prices of both their products and the staples that they had to buy from white entrepreneurs smacked of another kind of slavery to them. They reasoned that if they ended the year no better off than they had been at the beginning of the planting season, then emancipation had not given them very much. However, there was one major difference from ante-bellum days: now the discontented could leave the South, if they chose to do so. A number of them elected to take this option.

The movement that came to a head in 1879, like most of its kind, was not as spontaneous at it appeared to be. As early as 1870 a group of blacks, led by Henry Adams, organized the Negro Union Co-operative Aid Association in Louisiana. Adams had served in the regular army from 1866 to 1869, during which time he had been taught to read and write by a white woman who ran a school for soldiers at Fort Jackson, Louisiana. After his discharge, said Adams, a group of blacks who had served in the army with him became critical of "the way our people had been treated during the time we was in service." The result was the association, whose membership was said to have reached ninety-eight thousand by 1878.

Meanwhile, in 1874, southern Negroes had begun to feel increased political pressure from the whites. As a reaction to it, Adams and some of his friends in the association had organized what came to be known as the Shreveport Committee. In all, there were nearly 500 committeemen, of which about 150 ranged around the South, looking into living and political conditions experienced by the former slaves, noting instances where exorbitant rents made the tenant farmer's situation tantamount to slavery, and at the same time scouting out places in the South to which blacks might move in order to improve their lot.

After several years of study the committeemen concluded that the only solution to the problem was migration from the region. Asked about this, Adams explained: "Well, we found ourselves in such condition that we looked around and we seed that there was no way on earth, it seemed, that we could better our condition there, and we discussed that thoroughly in our organization along in May [of 1877]. We said that the whole South . . . had got into the hands of the very men that held us slaves . . . and we thought that the men that held us slaves was holding the reins of government. . . . We felt we had almost as well be slaves under these men. . . . Then we said there was no hope for us and we had better go." Reports from committeemen who had examined the West suggested that Nebraska, Kansas, and, to some extent, Colorado formed a general area of improved working conditions where there was no bulldozing and where churches were not closed at nine o'clock at night in order to prevent meetings. In the West, thought Adams, lay equal educational opportunities for the children. Above all, the new country appeared to be a place of social acceptance. A Texas farmer named T. R. Alexander stressed this when he told St. John that in his state "colored people are looked upon by the white people with disdain and scum." He had had enough of it. "I have suffered the bukes and scums long enough down South here," he said. He and his family of seven were ready to try for a better life in Kansas.[2]

Benjamin "Pap" Singleton, who, among others, claimed to be the father of the exodus, supported the "bukes and scums" position. As he explained, he had "studied it all out, and it was cl'ar as day to me [that] my people couldn't live thar. It was ag'in nature for the masters and the slave to jine hands and work together. Nuthin' but de millenium could bring that around." Singleton, a realist, thought that his people had little with which to fight back. "The whites had the lands and the sense, an' the blacks had nuthin' but their freedom." He knew that the imposition of law had not been of much help. "Bime-by the fifteenth amendment came along, and the carpet-baggers, and my poor people thought they was goin' to have Canaan right off. But I knowed better."[3]

Singleton did not see any hope for a change of heart among white southerners: "De leopard can't change his spots. De men who used to flog their slaves ain't agoin' to ever treat 'em fair, now that they're free. Mebbe it'll be different a hundred years from now when all the present generation's dead and gone, but not afore, sir, not afore; and wha's agoin' to be a hundred years from now ain't much account to us in this present year o' de Lord." The one-time slave, described by a contemporary as "a little old man—a mulatto—over seventy years of age, with wavy, iron-gray hair, square jaws, full, quick eyes, and a general expression of courage and modesty," concluded that emigration from the South was the Negro's only salvation. When pressed and asked if he meant to include all the destitutes, the charity cases about which Kansans complained so much, he said: "Yes, I do. It is just as well for them to die here as there. It is better, in fact."[4] By the close of 1880 he had reversed himself on this point, and along with St. John, he urged the members of his race to scatter out in other parts of the North and West. Only those who were possessed of enough money with which to get a start should leave home. Singleton agreed that Kansas by then had "filled up," insofar as employment was concerned, and strangers looking for support would find life difficult.[5]

"Old Pap" stood between the ignorant, penniless field hands who drifted into Kansas and the black "establishment" represented by Douglass, Pinchback, Senator Bruce, and Milton Turner. He was very suspicious of the Nashville Convention, held in May of 1879, because he thought that men such as Douglass and Pinchback would run it, and they were opposed to the exodus. When rival Negro Aid Associations quarreled in St. Louis that same spring, "Pap" was critical. He told his followers that there were many "tonguey" men in such enterprises, men who just wanted to hear themselves talk and who were shallow seekers of publicity, as opposed to those who truly wanted to help the unfortunates of his race. Such local leaders, as well as those of national prominence, annoyed Singleton, because he thought them too ambitious. They wanted political integration, to share in the offices traditionally held by the whites, and recognition that they were in every sense equal. "Pap" argued that this was a moot point, that it was not the immediate goal. He became increasingly convinced that segregation, not integration, was the answer for his people; that separation would benefit the blacks, not injure them. There were those who agreed with this point of view. At a convention of blacks, held at Houston, Texas, in June of 1879, participants pondered the question of migrating to some unsettled area of the West where a black territory or state could be set up. Those who advocated such a move argued that somewhere there ought to be a political entity populated and controlled by none but blacks, a place where there was no white interference. Analysts interpreted this as further evidence that a vague feeling of pending reenslavement clouded the minds of many who had been emancipated only a few years back.[6]

John Henri Burch, of Louisiana, had little in common with "Pap" Singleton, but on the question of emigration the two men were of the same mind. Burch was a Negro journalist who had worked for a number of newspapers, and in the course of his career he had been afforded an opportunity to study the postwar problems of the freedmen. Also, he had served in both houses of the Louisiana legislature. As he explained to the Voorhees Committee, a large body of southern blacks still were landless and homeless, and even when they were fortunate enough to acquire homes, they had no way of knowing that they would be secure in the possession of them. Most of this floating population was highly dependent upon white landowners, said the journalist; they were obliged to work for just about any wages offered to them. "It is natural that they should desire to seek some country where their labor should secure them a home in which they would employ their children in creating at once a home and a heritage," he told the senators. At the moment—early in 1880—the West was being advertised as the place where these things could be found. Asked why the Negroes would leave their ancestral homes, Burch answered with other questions: "Have not the same causes founded and peopled America? Are any people prouder of their country than the English? Can any more adore their own land than the French?" Yet, he continued, "all these people have quitted their respective countries for the wilderness of America." Pointedly, he concluded, a good many of these white emigrants had left home because of class oppression.

Then Burch turned to the subject of social and political insecurity.

Legislatures, he said, were turning more and more to class legislation. Land laws were increasingly unfavorable to the Negroes. A recent chain-gang law, passed in Louisiana, was very disturbing to them; they feared that they would be arrested for trivial offenses and returned to slavery under the guise of public labor. The war, he said, had consumed four years and millions of dollars to "whip the southerners"; yet in 1880, southern leaders were well equipped with arms, they drilled regularly, "and their old Army associations are intact." How, asked Burch, could the newly freed black be expected to stand up to these people and demand voting and civil rights? It was no wonder to him that thousands had elected to leave for Kansas in the hope that they would encounter fewer captains and colonels who still ate, slept, and lived according to a military tradition.[7]

Another black journalist who advocated emigration from the South was George Ruby. At the time of the exodus he was editor of the *New Orleans Observer*, a journal that he had founded a year earlier. He was not a southerner by birth. Born in New York in 1841, he had worked for William Lloyd Garrison and for both the *Times* and the *Tribune*, of New York City, before going to New Orleans in 1864 to teach school. After the war he had served as an agent for the Freedmen's Bureau and had founded a newspaper (the *Standard*) in Galveston, Texas. He was deeply interested in the welfare of his people and was well aware of their increasing difficulties in the South. When a convention of blacks was called at New Orleans, in April, 1879, to consider the Negro problem, it was done at the instance of the *Observer* and similar newspapers of the region.

Ruby was chairman of one of the New Orleans convention committees, and in his report he described the political chaos and violence of Louisiana, concluding that "the fiat to go forth is irresistible." The decision to "go forth" grew out of the conviction that "slavery in the horrible form of peonage is approaching." Ruby's committee took the view that the exodus from Louisiana arose from persecutions and mob actions during 1874–75. As a result of this turmoil, said the committeemen, an organization looking toward emigration had originated in Caddo Parish.

A further cause of emigration was set forth. By 1875, said Ruby, a number of unemployed refugee blacks were huddled in New Orleans, with no means of support. Most of them had come out of the cotton parishes to the north. Part of the reason for calling the convention, he explained, was to devise some means of getting these indigents out of the state, hopefully to some place of employment. To him there was little other choice, for "they have very little if any hope from the courts." Speaking to a New Orleans mass meeting in May, the journalist again advised his people to "go forth," while at the same time cautioning them that such a move should be carefully planned and deliberately carried out. He recommended Kansas, a place where the soil was fertile and the climate, he thought, was not too cold for blacks. Moved by Ruby's rhetoric, one Louis Jones took the floor and urged his listeners to go to Kansas. He ended his plea with a vigorous attack upon Frederick Douglass, whom he called a renegade. One of the women arose and joined in the attack upon Douglass, saying that he could well afford to advise his people to stay in the South since he was safe in his sinecure at Washington, D.C. As the excitement mounted, someone cried out: "Sing the battle hymn!" and the crowd sang "John Brown's Body." It was from meetings such as this one, where the emotional pitch mounted to great heights, that many a participant who had wandered in just to listen left the gathering determined to pack up and go north with his friends.[8]

From Kansas came beckoning signals. John Brown, Jr., taking advantage of his father's name and of the new excitement in Kansas, announced that the time had come for another grand rescue of the colored race. "Young" John, now fifty-eight, announced that he was prepared to devote all his energies to the cause that had been so dear to his father. Having spent some time in Canada, he sent word south that Negroes could stand cold weather. He described fugitives who had arrived at Windsor, Ontario, broke and hungry, but had found work, had taken up government land, and had prospered. Quoting him, a New England paper assured its readers that if given a chance and if left unmolested by bulldozers, black Americans would prosper anywhere.[9]

A good many southern blacks conceded that even with the economic scales tipped against them in the cotton country, they could make a living. They objected to the inequities forced upon them by white landowners and merchants, but in a majority of cases they elected to stay—and to hope for better conditions. They objected also to the unequivocal demand by southern whites that the old establishment control state and local political machinery; but again, many of them concluded that the problem posed was not great enough to cause migration. However, if atop these two grievances was piled a burden that T. R. Alexander had labeled the "bukes and scums," it sometimes provided the proverbial straw to an already heavy emotional load carried by the former slaves. One of the Exodusters touched upon this sensitive area when he told a St. Louis newspaper reporter that he and his friends wanted to go to Kansas because he understood that they would be treated "just like white folks" there. In an editorial entitled "Just Like White Folks," the *New York Tribune* declared that in a single sentence "the poor Negro revealed the motive that under-lies this remarkable migration."[10]

There were recurring signs of restlessness in the South during these exodus years. At the beginning of the movement, committees of discon-certed southern blacks had periodically sent representatives into Kansas and other parts of the West to investigate possibilities of a move. One of them, from Alabama, called upon the editor of Topeka's *Colored Citizen* and made inquiries about prospects in Kansas. He said that times were very hard in Alabama and that it was very difficult for the former slaves to make a living there.[11] The Reverend W. O. Lynch, also from Alabama, went out to Kansas in the spring of 1879 to scout out the land for his home committee. He said that his people recently had held a meeting and had concluded that since the whites apparently were not going to accede to black demands, the aggrieved had no other choice but to leave.[12] An unhappy group from Snow Hill, Alabama, complained to St. John that "there are little respect shown to laborers down heare," and it was ready to leave for Kansas if the governor but would give the word. A colored farmer named A. M. Allen wrote to St. John from Lafayette, Alabama, stating that he had had enough of southern life under emanci-pation. "I cannot enjoy it here among the southern people," he said. "They are against them that have anything. They do not want us to have any schools and do not want us to have property, but want us to work for thirty cents per day." Before he would do that, he maintained, he would go back to Africa—or Kansas.[13]

John H. Johnson, the young black attorney from St. Louis, summed up the complaint, after having listened to a number of Exodusters who passed through his city: "They stated that they had no security for life, limb, or property; that they worked year in and year out, and, notwith-standing they raised good crops, they were at the end of the year in debt; that they were charged exorbitant prices for provisions, and all these thing kept them down and in debt." The old masters, argued Johnson, simply were not ready "to give up all control over them," and as he saw it, the former slave had no choice but to leave. He hoped every Negro in every southern state would emigrate.[14]

Johnson's belief that only partial emancipation had been achieved was shared by John Mercer Langston, named by the *Colored Citizen* as "the ablest colored man in the U.S. with the exception of Frederick Douglass." Langston, a Howard University professor who also had served as United States minister resident to Haiti, gave a public lecture on the exodus in September of 1879 in which he argued that emancipation had granted the Negro the ownership of his person but had left him otherwise devoid of property or prospects and destitute in the extreme. Harassed by the Ku-Klux, bulldozed, shotgunned, these frequently illiterate Americans were said to have been freed from very little. Langston concluded that migration from the South was the only hope for those who wanted political freedom, educational opportunities, and economic independence.[15]

Some important American blacks argued the other side of the case, holding that flight was no answer, that members of their race were wrong in surrendering what was theirs to southern whites. Stay and fight, they argued. This is your land as much as anyone's. Stay—and persevere. The contest will be long and bitter, but right is on your side. Stay, for to leave is to yield, and to yield is unmanly; it is also unnecessary.

The leading proponent of such a view was Frederick Douglass, who was, without doubt, the outstanding spokesman for his race during the nineteenth century. By 1879 he had long since achieved international fame and was enjoying its rewards at Washington, D.C., where he was a United States marshal. According to press accounts he lived in a handsome house situated on a hilltop overlooking the nation's capital. "It was built by the owner of a large tract of land who sold house lots only on condition that no plot should ever be sold to a Negro or an Irishman," said one story, whose author evidently wanted to show the extent of Douglass's success. The present owner of the home and the surrounding fifteen acres of land was described as a man whose "leonine face and head, with its mane of flowing white wool," attracted "general attention by his history, his countenance and bearing."[16] The black elder statesman, who held a federal appointment and who attended White House social functions, was the object of both envy and a certain amount of jealousy among members of his race. His stand on the exodus question brought out some of these differences of attitude toward him.

"I am opposed to this exodus, because it is an untimely concession to the idea that colored people and white people cannot live together in peace and prosperity unless the whites are a majority and control the legislation and hold the offices of the State," commented Douglass during the early stages of the movement. In a burst of the rhetoric that had made him so famous, he described the development: "Some of our race are despairing, and are rising up in darkening trains, leaving their old homes and winding up the Mississippi heartless, hopeless, ragged, hungry and destitute, leaving the South as Lot did Sodom, and going to a land without cultivation, like startled birds flying from a rock in mid-ocean which has been struck by a cannon from a passing ship."

The remarks were made to a largely black audience in a Baltimore church in May of 1879. He advised his listeners to refrain from despairing, that although there were few blacks in public office, the situation would improve in time. He wondered aloud if the franchise had not come too suddenly, if the Negro had not been thrust into politics prematurely. "Slavery was a poor school in which to develop statesmen, and colored legislatures have proved this." Social rights, too, had been slow in coming; but come they would, he predicted. It would take time. The answer, he warned, was not to be found in flight. "We have been more unsettled by schemes of colonization and emigration than from any other cause. First Hayti, then Jamaica, were our Canaan. Next came Nicaragua, and that would have been a 'Niggeragua,' while Liberia has been a standing land of Canaan." He thought that if blacks had stayed in the South under slavery, they could stay now, for the area had for them some advantages that no other place offered, not the least of which was a monopoly of the labor market. Dumping thousands of ragged blacks into northern communities would only create "that detestable class from whom we are not so free—tramps." Negroes never would change their relationships with whites until they became more economical, lived within their means, and stuck to their employment, he argued. If they did this, promised Douglass, blacks would attain the respect of all. "Other races, notably the Jews and the Quakers, worse situated than you are, have fought their way up."[17]

During the summer and autumn of 1879, as the exodus mounted in intensity, Douglass studied the phenomenon and tried to find its origins. In mid September he read a paper at a meeting of the American Social Science Association, held at Saratoga, New York, in which he discussed various theories dealing with causes of the movement. Unhappy southern blacks, he pointed out, had not tried to solve their problems by force, as had some other minorities in the past; rather, they simply had laid down their hoes and left for Kansas. He discounted the "greedy land speculator of Kansas" theory, correctly stating that speculators do not sell land to people without any money, nor do they induce groups into their area against whom there is a popular prejudice. He considered the theory that the exodus was promoted by defeated and disappointed demagogues, both black and white, who were out of power in the South and wanted to get back in. There was some truth in this, he conceded. What of the charge that Senator Windom had "set this black ball in motion"? Douglass admitted that Windom's interest in helping the blacks had offered some stimulus to the movement. However, he concluded, none of these were basic reasons. Deeper, by far, was continued harassment by southern whites. The blacks, he said, were home-loving people who feared the unknown and were not inclined to move to strange places. Only under extreme pressure, such as that exhibited by the southern white establishment, would the former slaves move. Emancipation had not brought freedom. It had seen "the lamb . . . committed to the care of the wolf," to use his words.

Having discussed probable causes of the exodus, Douglass told his listeners at Saratoga that even though his people might justify such a move, he did not agree that it was the answer to their problems. It bothered him that the Comstocks and the Havilands were going around, hat in hand, soliciting money for black unfortunates. He felt that such begging was bad for his people; that it made the public take sides in the issue. It was better, he contended, for the blacks to stay in the South, a place where there was hope for them if they persevered. The blacks should bide their time. "A Hebrew may even now be rudely repulsed from the door of a hotel," he said, "but he will not on that account get up another exodus, as he did three thousand years ago, but will quietly 'put money in his purse' and bide his time, knowing that the rising tide of civilization will eventually float him." America, said the black leader, steadily was growing more liberal and "the oppressor of the Negro is seen to be the enemy of peace." Again, he asked his people to wait patiently, pointing out that "the careless and improvident habits of the South cannot be set aside in a generation." Time, he thought, was on the side of the blacks.[18]

Democratic newspapers praised Douglass for his stand and attacked their Republican counterparts for belittling him. "There isn't a Republican editor in the North who doesn't profess to know much more about the colored people, their conditions and wants, than Fred Douglass," sneered the *Washington Post.* "They will soon doubt Mr. Douglass' 'loyalty,' and then it will not take them long to find out that he is a 'rebel sympathizer.' " Cleveland's *Plain Dealer* called the Negro leader's views "manifestly sound," and *Daily Eastern Argus,* of Portland, Maine, named him as "one of the ablest and most eloquent of his race." The Democratic *Missouri Republican,* of St. Louis, was high in its praise for the position that Douglass had assumed. It suggested that Republicans ought to listen to the words of such an authority on Negro affairs. Southern newspapers lost no time in publicizing the thoughts of this black authority. To the *Daily Picayune,* of New Orleans, he was a "noted member" of the Negro race, and it advised all Negroes to heed his words. From Memphis came more praise. The *Weekly Appeal* said that Douglass was a man of more influence and less prejudice than any of the whites, and its cross-town rival, the *Avalanche,* agreed.[19]

The Republican press found little joy in the exodus views of Frederick Douglass. Some of the editors merely ignored his stand, while others lamented the fact that he had failed to see the light. One of them mentioned that he had made a personal exodus from the country that he alleged to be so well suited to his race. The *Colored Citizen,* of Topeka, represented the views of blacks who approved of the movement. In May, 1879, editor T. W. Henderson asked Douglass to write a statement of his position, which he did, arguing that an exodus was not the proper solution to the southern question, that it was a "wretched substitute" for the fulfillment of the federal government's obligations to the race, and that it would merely fill Kansas with a "multitude of deluded, hungry, homeless, naked and destitute people to be supported . . . by alms." Unhappy with the response, Henderson editorialized: "There is not a respectable colored man in America that endorses the position Frederick Douglass has taken on the exodus question; all of them are for their race save Douglass alone." The angry editor told his readers that he had always entertained a high regard for Douglass, but now the great Negro leader was wrong. Worse, said Henderson, the famed man was feeling his elevation to power; he was no longer in touch with his people.[20]

Before many months had passed, the *Colored Citizen* would take another view. As the exodus mounted and as complaints began to be heard among both blacks and whites of Kansas that the burden was becoming too heavy, this and other newspapers backed away from their earlier support of the movement. In October of 1879 Henderson, who was a pastor in Topeka's African Methodist Episcopal Church as well as a newspaper editor, moved to St. Louis, where he took a pastorate at St. Paul's Chapel. His place at the *Citizen* was taken by W. L. Eagleson, whose views about the exodus apparently were less rigid than those of Henderson, and this, perhaps, helps to account for the shift of editorial opinion.

Black political leaders tended to agree with Douglass. Pinckney Benton Stewart Pinchback, who once had served briefly as governor of Louisiana and who in the spring of 1879 had been elected as a delegate to the Louisiana Constitutional Convention, opposed the exodus. He argued that the movement had been originated by speculators and disappointed politicians and that, as such, it could only harm his people. He was one of the principal speakers at a mass meeting held at Vidalia, Louisiana, that spring, a gathering called in order to "show up" the Kansas migration and to discourage emigration from Madison Parish. The New Orleans *Picayune* called him "an acute observer whose opportunities for forming a judgment are certainly unsurpassed." Later in the year, Pinchback had a change of heart. By then he had decided that his people had no future in the state, that there was little chance for equality before the law, and that the sooner they left, the better. The reversal of his position may have been for political reasons. He was then the editor and proprietor of the *Weekly Louisianian,* and as he wrote from the desk of that journal early in 1880, "I am on the warpath." In other words, he was back in the political arena, this time as an advocate of Grant for the presidential nomination. A good many of those who approved of the exodus, Mrs. Comstock among them, supported Grant.[21]

Sen. Blanche Kelso Bruce, another black leader, opposed the exodus. Virginia-born (1841), he became a planter in Mississippi after the war, and in 1875 he was elected to the United States Senate. Early in 1879 he wrote to Col. W. L. Nugent, of Jackson, Mississippi, giving his views on the development. He thought that it had originated from a feeling of uneasiness and insecurity on the part of the blacks, "springing from the unfortunate race collisions," and also because the former slaves "don't feel they have proper returns for their labor." Since they were in this frame of mind, he said, it was no wonder that they were attracted by "rose colored pictures" of the advantages of western life.[22] He admitted that, as Americans, his people had the right to migrate to any place they chose, but he thought that it was both injudicious and impolitic for them to leave a country in which they had been reared in order to start life anew in a strange and unfriendly climate.[23] His views, of course, were broadcast by Democratic and southern newspapers in an effort to show that sensible blacks were on the "right side" of the question.

Among those who testified before the Voorhees Committee was James E. O'Hara, who practiced law in North Carolina. He was a northerner by birth—Samuel Perry referred to him as "a carpetbag nigger from New York"—who first had taught school before being admitted to the bar. When asked how he felt about the exodus, he said that he could see no real benefit from it. As a Negro, he said he had been accorded equal privileges in his practice of law, and in general, he did not think that people of his race would benefit in this regard by going north. "For instance," he told the senators, "in the North you will seldom see a white man and a colored man eating together; in the South it is nothing unusual to see that." He went on to cite other examples of association by the two races, concluding: "The Southern man knows the Negro, the Northern man does not."

O'Hara opposed the promotional aspect of the exodus, arguing that all too often the blacks were victims of propaganda. He explained that "the Negro is of a very sympathetic nature, and will give credence to those who profess friendship before he will to others. He is very credulous, and, even though deceived from time to time, will still take to a man who tells him a good story." The American Negro, he maintained, had been a foundling and a ward too long; now he ought to be left alone to work out his own destiny. Constant uprooting, perpetual agitation to depart for some new and exciting promised land, thought O'Hara, was not in the best interest of members of his race. He agreed with Douglass, adding that "nearly all our colored people" were opposed to the principle of the exodus.[24]

Another black opponent of the exodus was Isaiah C. Wears, of Philadelphia. This long-time real estate broker called the movement "suicidal," and in order to broadcast his views, he wrote six or seven articles against it, publishing them in the *Christian Recorder*. His ideas sounded much like those of Douglass, particularly his contention that the difficulties that southern blacks were experiencing merely represented part of a revolution of which they were a part. He pointed out that neither race fully understood its role in black emancipation; that the former slaves did not always know how to handle their new liberty, a situation that tempted whites to engage in tyranny. Wears opposed colonization of any kind, holding that the South was the Negro's true home and that it was the former slave who had produced the wealth of that region. He agreed with those of his race who predicted that blacks would find little improvement in their civil rights or in social acceptance by moving north. In fact, he distrusted northern motives in the recent movement. "I mean that the North seems to be looking upon this exodus as apparently superseding the necessity of any further action on their part for the protection of the colored man," he told the Voorhees Committee. "They think that if at any time, or in any place, he is oppressed beyond what he can endure, he has this recourse—to get up and go to Kansas or somewhere else." The *Cleveland Plain Dealer* called Wears "one of the foremost writers and thinkers among the colored people of today." Born in Baltimore, Isaiah Wears never had been a slave.[25]

A variety of other black people had doubts as to the practicality of flight from the South. An example was B. F. Watson, of Kansas City, who had helped so many of his race out of their plight once they had made the commitment to go north. He told members of the Voorhees Committee that he opposed the notion of sending the destitute into Kansas, but his feelings were mixed, because he had seen so many pathetic people passing through Kansas City. Reluctantly he decided that the lesser of two evils would be to let them come.

Perhaps Malinda Harris was one of those with whom Watson had talked. She was one of the Exodusters who had made her way from Mississippi to Wyandotte, Kansas, in the spring of 1879. Shortly after her arrival she wrote to a friend in Hinds County, Mississippi, and announced that she had made a mistake. With much labor she etched out a crude description of life in the promised land and concluded that a change of scenery had not provided the answer to her problems. "Dear Sister Mary

Percein," she began, "i Write you a few lines to let you know that I am
weell and family are very weel. I am Just tollible weell. I don't like the
country a tall. if you doing well dont you Break up. dont study a Bout
coming away. if I knowed what I know no Body could not Pull me a way.
look for me next fall. for Just as soon as I get hold enough money I am
coming back. . . . Pray for me for I kneed Prayers."[26]

As Malinda Harris and her kind sought heavenly intervention in time
of trouble, the American black community continued to debate the issue
at hand. At a conference of the African Methodist Episcopal Church, held
at Washington, D.C., in the spring of 1879, the Reverend W. H. Chambers
advised his followers to "hasten slowly." He looked at his troubled people
to the south and sympathized with them, yet he had doubts about the
move northward. "Senator Windom says that the United States Government would protect them in Kansas," he commented. Yet, he thought,
"It is folly to say the Government could protect them there when they
could not do it in Louisiana." Listeners at the conference approved of
such caution, and amidst applause for his stand, one of them shouted:
"Brother Chambers, the last wine is the best."[27]

The thinking of Chambers was in line with that of Douglass, Pinchback, Bruce, and former senator Hiram R. Revels, of Mississippi, all of
whom urged the black warriors to stay in the trenches and fight. "Pap"
Singleton continued to disagree. He thought that these men were out of
touch with the ordinary blacks, that they had more or less gone over to
the white establishment as a result of their recognition and success. "They
had good luck," he would tell his listeners, "and now are listening to
false prophets; they have boosted up and got their heads a whirlin', and
now they think they must judge things from where they stand, when the
fact is the possum is lower down the tree—down nigh to the roots."[28]

John Milton Brown, of Topeka, was one who could say that he had a
grass-roots view of the matter and that he knew the thinking of those
members of his race who had left the South. By the time he appeared
before the Voorhees Committee, Brown said that he had talked with a
great many of the twenty-five thousand refugees who had passed through
his city. On occasion he had spoken before groups as large as five hundred,
at which times he had asked the reason for their flight. "They said there
was no security for life, liberty, or property," Brown reported. That this
was the reason for the departure of many cannot be doubted. But the response may have been given by a smaller percentage of the refugees than
Brown inferred, for he was "establishment," was a faithful worker in the
St. John camp, and probably was one of the "selected" witnesses that F. T.
Ingalls was looking for in response to the request for such people from the

pro-exodus camp at Washington. Brown later was head of the KFRA headquarters of Topeka. His image was somewhat damaged when he was charged with using some of the donations received to buy a farm for himself.[29]

Booker T. Washington was highly critical because the congressional committee had failed to discover a cause for the exodus that was satisfactory to him. As was the case with so many Americans at the time, he was convinced that he knew the answer, and it disturbed him that others were unable to understand the problem. Closer to the matter itself were such people as John Milton Brown, who thought that he also knew the reason for the movement. Both men were convinced of southern perfidy. But of the thousands of blacks who filtered through St. Louis, on up the Missouri River to Wyandotte and its sister cities along the river, and then inland into Kansas, only a few understood the deeper implications of the move. Interrogators who wanted to prove that social, economic, and political life in the South was absolutely intolerable for the former slave could find any number of refugees who would willingly give a satisfactory answer to a properly slanted question. Those who wanted to prove the contrary also could find witnesses who would confirm their preconceived views. In some respects the situation resembled the white man's questioning of the American Indian, who often tried to produce a certain answer, hoping perhaps for a present or some favor, or just to be agreeable.

Newspaper reporters invariably quizzed arriving Exodusters as to the reasons they had left the South, and depending upon the political complexion of the newspaper that they represented, the desired answers were found if enough people were questioned. For example, when a St. Louis reporter, accompanied by a member of the Sells & Sells shipping firm, interviewed a recent arrival named William Chapman, the questioning appeared to be aimed at showing readers that there was no political motivation behind the movement and that the trip to Kansas was a foolish venture. Chapman seemed anxious to say the right things to the reporter and in front of Miles Sells, whose company did a great deal of business with southern planters.

Why had the newcomer left his southern home, asked the reporter?

"Well'n," said Chapman, "I dunno. I wuz a hyearin' de people all talkin' about comin', an' a gittin' ready fur to come and dey wuz a sayin' wat a nice place Ka-ansas wuz, an' so I jes' bundled up my things and come along." Then the reporter asked, "Was that the only reason?" And Chapman answered: "Da's de only reason I know for it." The reporter's next question was: "No one threatened you?" And the answer was: "Oh, no, no; no, indeed. Bless you, no white man ever ha'med me." So went the dialogue, as written by the newspaper reporter.

Another recent arrival was interviewed. Henry Watson, who was described as looking like a creeping hospital—his eyes were watery, and he appeared to have a cold—told of his motivations for migration. "They said dat we wuz to get land, and $300, and hosses an' plows, an' we all thought we was goin' right straight to fo'tune; but I tell you I'm mighty sick of it. I ain't bin a day well since I got hyere, an' I believe ef I was to stay hyere 'nuther week I'd be a dead nigger." Wondering if Watson's debilitated appearance might have been caused by a change of drinking water at St. Louis, the reporter asked if the traveler's bowels had been affected. Yes, said Watson, the results were so catastrophic that "I tell you, I'm afraid to set my foot down *hard!*"

Watson and Chapman were joined by Nathan Robinson, and all three of them agreed that they had been overcharged for goods in the South, that they always ended the year broke; nevertheless, they agreed, they were going back, because they could live more easily, even lazily in that warmer, leisurely climate.[30]

Those who talked with the Exodusters, newspapermen in particular, invariably asked about the causes of the movement. The answers were less than satisfactory, unless one takes into account responses to leading questions put by those who knew what answer they wanted. As a rule, the run-of-the-mill field hand who was queried along the way to the Promised Land was vague about the reasons for his departure and even about the new life that he expected to find in Kansas or other parts of the West. Negro leaders who adhered to the Radical Republican view entertained no doubts as to the origins of the migration: persecution and racial prejudice had caused it. Bad luck, poor management, laziness, drouth, pestilence, or just a normal desire to migrate to a fresh part of the country—all such reasons were swept aside by those who had a preconceived notion of the problem. The argument among black intellectuals was not so much one over causations as that of how their people ought to respond to the development. To stay and fight, or to leave the southern whites stranded, without a labor base, was the question to be settled.

In Kansas, as well as across the nation, a great number of people from different walks of life and representing various political points of view, accepted the fact of the movement but wondered why it had occurred. As it was with the black leadership, various prejudices emerged in any attempt to answer the question—prejudices, or at least preconceptions, that made it very difficult to determine the real reason that these people had left their homes in such great numbers, so suddenly.

13

A BLEAK
AND ARDUOUS LAND

White supporters of the exodus idea expressed their conviction that 1880 would see an even larger outpouring from the South. They were hopeful that southern landowners would feel an increasingly serious economic pinch as more labor fled northward, leaving behind miles of unmanned and desolated plantations. Most of these extremists did not live in Kansas, but rather were residents of eastern cities, particularly of New England. Generally speaking, they had no economic interest in the matter, had little knowledge of southern conditions other than stories they had seen in the press, and represented what might be called the "unreconstructed abolitionists."

Such anticipations were not realized. The flow did continue in 1880, particularly out of Texas and into southern Kansas, but with nowhere near the degree of intensity experienced in the spring of 1879. By early 1880 St. John and his supporters were making desperate efforts to sidetrack the onrush and to deflect it into other northern states. Conditions in Kansas in that year were unfavorable for prospective settlers, and as word of that situation spread throughout the South, the movement began to subside. A cold autumn followed a poor crop year on the high plains. Wilmer Walton wrote to St. John, from Parsons, saying that in late November, nighttime temperatures were below zero. "I find many of the colored men, women and children around here are shivering for want of sufficient warm clothing," he told the governor. Fortunately, he added, the numbers arriving lately had dwindled steadily, and now they represented only a trickle.[1]

Meantime, between eight and ten thousand white settlers in western Kansas were obliged to appeal for donations of food and clothing to get them through the winter. Economically stranded, this beleaguered army of farmers clung to its tenuous position, hoping against hope that utter defeat would not be the ironic reward for venturing westward. It is hard to determine whether or not reports of such conditions were circulated among restless southern blacks with the same thoroughness that earlier stories about the "land of plenty" had been told to them. By the spring of 1881 the black flood that had washed westward across Kansas had ceased.

Thus, almost as quickly as it had come, the exodus faded and died. People who had asked each other about the movement's causes also wondered why it had withered so suddenly. For two years, politicians, humanitarians, and community leaders—both black and white—had tried to find out what had generated all the excitement in the spring of 1879, and depending upon their political, moral, and even economic positions, they found different answers. More difficult of solution was the question of whether the phenomenon had ceased because whatever had set it off no longer operated to keep it going. If the origin was political persecution by southern whites, had they now reformed? If the cause was economic, one might ask if these conditions in the South suddenly had improved. Or had the word spread to the effect that Kansas indeed was no promised land?

As has been the case with many developments, there was no identifiable single cause for the exodus. But if the answer was multiple, the different forces that generated it could not have had an equal amount of influence upon those who fled the South; something must have predominated. No one ever is going to discover the precise reason for the flight, because hundreds upon hundreds of those who made the hegira did not themselves know why they had left. This is equally true of the white legions who moved westward, but in the main, the underlying reason for the movement of both races was a desire to better one's condition, principally in the economic sector as well as in other spheres of daily life.

Economic causation was accepted by a good many people, both black and white. But not everyone interpreted it in the same manner or used it for the same purpose. Although St. John talked a great deal about political persecution, he also laid emphasis upon economic matters, usually stressing the unfairness of southern planters as opposed to built-in conditions that faced both races in the South. "All the refugees agree substantially that the cause of their leaving the South exists in the fact that they have been unfairly dealt with, really robbed year after year of their earnings, and also not only deprived of their political rights, but for years have been insecure in both life and property," he wrote in answer to questions put to him by the Philadelphia *Times*.[2] He added that the blacks for years had contemplated movement; however, they had waited, hoping for improved conditions. When better times did not materialize, they moved.

Strictly speaking, St. John was on the right track; but simply to suggest that after an indeterminate period of waiting, thousands "just moved" is a considerable oversimplification. Something triggered a movement that might well have been on the verge of developing. There are several possible explanations for the immediate causes, among them a poor crop in 1878, the probable return of yellow fever to the river-bottom regions, stories handed around by word of mouth and in church periodicals about a land of promise, and predictions of increased bulldozing on the part of the whites. But to these must be added the excitement of the moment. Wild rumors danced across the southern countryside and fired the minds of a restless, suspicious, and credulous people. There were whispered stories to the effect that Louisiana's new constitution would contain a clause providing for the reenslaving of Negro children for a period of twenty-one years. Another terrifying report stated that Jefferson Davis was on the loose again, this time in command of ten thousand troops, supported by a flotilla of four gunboats, and he had threatened to send back into slavery every black who tried to go up the river. Countering this discouraging news was a rumor that "General Grant has ordered us to go to Kansas and he will take care of us." To carry out his plans, Grant was said to have stationed his old friend General Sherman at New Orleans in order to protect the former slaves, who, if they wished, now could go to Kansas, which recently had been set aside as a Negro state, and every family making the move would be given free land, free housing, and five hundred dollars. The offer was limited, warned one of the more colorful versions of the rumor; after March 15, 1880, all blacks found in the South were to be exterminated upon orders of President Hayes, who, unaccountably, had turned Democrat. As if this were not frightening enough, yet another story was spread, this one to the effect that any who escaped the net thrown out by Hayes would be put to death by the Indians, who were to be sent out on a grand scalping spree among southern blacks. Filled with thoughts as horrifying as these, it is easy to imagine the responses of emotionally aroused listeners who were told that the last boat was on its way out, that it was now or never.[3] White planters, who may not have followed events closely, found it hard to explain the presence of hundreds of highly excited blacks lined along the banks of the Mississippi, frantically hailing passing steamboats.

Landlords did not understand, or professed not to understand, what all the uproar was about. One of them, who signed himself "Planter," wrote from Warren County, Mississippi, saying that he thought that black farmers had no real basis for complaint. "From the Gulf Coast of Louisiana to the Arkansas line, and I presume above there, the rate of wages paid field hands varies from 50 to 60 cents per day, or $10 to $12 per month and rations," he said. "When a Negro rents land he usually takes twenty acres, for which he pays four bales of cotton of 400 pounds each. He has, also, to purchase his supplies which can easily be done for $150, and which will supply him liberally, to which we can add $50 for contingencies, making a total expense of four bales of cotton and $200 to make his crop." Such a farmer, said "Planter," could expect a crop of fourteen bales, as well as enough corn to feed himself and his mule for a year. "Deduct the rent and the Negro has ten bales wherewith to pay his supply bill, which will sell for $350, leaving a profit of $150. Where can you find a better paid labor than that?" he asked.[4]

The problem was, said "Planter," that the black farmer tended to be improvident. Thomas Sturges, who had fought in the war on the Union side, but who now lived at Jackson, Mississippi, shared this feeling about the attitude of the former slave. Ever since freedom, said Sturges, the Negro had been getting worse about working. Since the days of slavery, production had declined, yet he thought that the average farmer easily could produce twice as many bales as he did. The Negro sharecropper, it was charged, refused to do any such outside labor as ditching, fencing, and other necessities of upkeep, thus forcing the plantation owner to do it. Few of the former slaves wanted to work for wages, because it did not leave them as their own masters, but rather it subjected them to orders, and they did not like that. But when they farmed on shares, their lack of attention to detail resulted in bad management practices. Despite this discouraging development, said Sturges, blacks generally were treated well by the whites with whom, or for whom, they worked.[5]

The southern press, representing, as it did, the white establishment and the business community generally, subscribed to the "shiftless" theory as applied to Negro farm labor. The *Picayune,* of New Orleans, for example, argued that during several years prior to 1879, cotton prices had suffered a decline, and the South itself was in the midst of a general depression. Given these agricultural conditions, the newspaper could understand why there was unrest in the cotton and sugar-cane fields. At best, it thought, the black farmer was not very adept at planning and management. "The Negro is shiftless and rarely begins a season with any means, no matter how favorable the preceding year may have been," commented the editor in May of 1879. "He must then purchase all that he may need through the spring and summer on credit. The country storekeeper deals with a customer who has no property, and who depends upon the growing crop for the means to pay his debts. He therefore takes the risk of his customer's honesty, besides the chances of a failure of the crops. His profits must necessarily be large." Admittedly, said the *Picayune,* such a credit system had its dangers, but they involved white borrowers also. Blacks invariably accused their creditors of cheating them, and no matter how clearly the black farmer's account was explained to him, he would claim that he had been cheated.[6] One of the heritages of slave days was the continuing distrust between the races.

Despite all disclaimers by southerners that the average black farmer was a happy man and that his labor brought him rewards that compared favorably to those of agricultural workers elsewhere, the question of land tenure remained as an irritation between the races. A Chicago newspaper touched upon this tender point when it said that southern landowners "must open their eyes to the inevitable fact that free labor must own the land it cultivates, and that if this is impossible in one locality, then labor will seek out some other locality where it is possible." The editor explained that at the end of the war, cotton planters had tried to hire black labor, but that the practice had been abandoned after a few years because the owners frequently did not have the required cash and because those who loaned it to them risked the loss of their investment if the crop failed. He reiterated the criticism that Negroes had for the wage system: namely, that its gang-labor characteristics reminded them too much of slavery.[7]

Charles L. Howe, who owned plantations in Louisiana and Arkansas, tried a combination rental and wage system. He hired men for seventy-five cents a day, and women for sixty, paying them by the week. To others, who preferred a contract arrangement, he rented mules, plows, clothing, provisions, and land at eighty pounds of cotton per acre farmed. As a rule, living quarters and a garden were thrown in. About 150 Negroes worked for him, some on a wage basis, the rest on shares. Those who received wages bought their own provisions.

Howe's main complaint touched upon laziness and improvidence, said to be so common among the former slaves. He thought that they did not work enough. That the hands avoided the fields on Saturday was not a new development; many had done so under slavery. But, said Howe, Saturday now was spent in town, if there was one nearby, "having a 'whoop' and a 'hurrah,' and getting drunk,—a good many of them." Some of the employees would not work even a full week, he charged. At most they would give only four days of their time, and they spent every cent they earned. E. B. Borden, a Goldsboro, North Carolina, planter, supported the contention that those who worked for wages saved almost none of them. Under this system, he said, laborers developed very little attachment to any locality, and therefore they found little to hold them when new attractions beckoned from places such as Kansas.[8]

Many of the Negroes who migrated to Kansas admitted freely that they had saved little money. It was not so much due to improvidence, they argued, as it was to the ever-tightening economic vise in which they were pinched. St. John had remarked that these people were "really robbed" of their earnings year after year. The victims explained the method by which such extractions were made. First, the credit system, as operated under the "store order" arrangement, provided a heavy drain. Some of the Mississippi Negroes said that they had paid as high as $18 to $20 a barrel for pork that sold in St. Louis for half that amount. Land that would not sell for $25 was reported to be renting for as much as $10 an acre, an amount that left tenants with very little when crops were poor, as was the case in 1878. The *Clarion,* of Jackson, Mississippi, denied that rent came to anywhere near $10 an acre, but rather, it averaged about $6.40 in the richer parts of Mississippi. In addition to the land, said the newspaper, normally went a cabin, a garden, a pasture, and frequently the use of a cotton gin—all free. In the upland country, lands could be rented for as little as $1 to $3 an acre. No matter, countered the *New York Tribune,* rent was a fixed cost, and a poor crop could mean that many a black family was without money to buy clothing and provisions for the coming year. Under such circumstances, said the newspaper, it was small wonder that impoverished cotton farmers were attracted by promises of better returns in other regions.[9]

Assuming that economic discontent was one of the main underlying problems for post–Civil War southern blacks, it still would take some kind of inducement to make many of them pack their things and leave. Fear, of course, was a "push" factor; promises of a more pleasant life provided the "pull." As the movement swelled to alarming proportions, a number of accusations filled the air, each charging this or that "interest" with having propagandized uneducated, gullible Negroes. Since western railroads were in bad repute during these years and rapidly were becoming targets of reformers, it is not surprising that they were accused of trying to lure the blacks away from the South with promises of free or cheap land.

Charges against the railroads came from all sides. One New Orleans newspaper was convinced that a "ring of ever-cunning railroad speculators in Kansas" who wanted to bilk the innocent Negroes had triggered the exodus. The newspaper inferred that the ploy was not very successful when it admitted that the "sharpers and speculators soon got tired of this exodus business and abandoned it." But by then, said the editor, the ease with which unhappy blacks had made their way northward had captured the attention of the politicians who saw great possibilities in colonizing these people in Democratic northern states.[10] A St. Louis paper examined what it called the "Kansas Pacific theory," one that charged Jay Gould with being at the bottom of the exodus plot; and it suggested that if the accusation had any foundation in fact, the railroad company should take care of the paupers whom it had induced to go to Kansas.[11]

Less hostile observers admitted that the roads might have had something to do with the movement indirectly, but not through any active propaganda campaign aimed at any specific group. W. J. Buchan, of Wyandotte, said that some of the refugees whom he talked with had an out-of-date circular from the Leavenworth, Lawrence and Galveston Railroad, issued in 1868. "That paper was old and dirty, as if they had had it a long time" he said, explaining that apparently the holders of it thought that railroad land was easily available in Kansas, and perhaps that it was offered under special terms. In fact, the advertisement simply offered land for sale along the line of the road; no promises of any kind were included.[12]

In other instances, railroads were accused of offering jobs, as an allurement to black workers. A Democratic paper in Boston reported that the chief engineer of construction for the Northern Pacific Railroad had promised attractive wages to Negro laborers, that Jay Gould wanted at least a thousand of them for the Union Pacific, and that Huntington would take an equal number on the Southern Pacific. In this instance the roads hardly could be charged with intentionally encouraging the exodus; what they wanted was cheap labor, regardless of color. Nevertheless, the editor of the *Memphis Appeal* used reports of such recruitment as further evidence that "railroad agents" were luring away southern labor and were thus contributing to the southland's problems.[13]

Less publicized were the charges leveled at steamboat lines, whose business was said to be on the decline in the new age of railroading. The *Star,* of Kansas City, later recalled that these companies tried to stimulate traffic by distributing lurid posters throughout the black belt, advertisements that held out promises of forty acres and a mule as well as other rewards. "The deluded creatures came up the river in droves," said the *Star.*[14]

That the influence of propaganda was important appears to be indisputable, yet it is the hardest of all the accusations to pinpoint. Any number of people said that they had seen chromos, handbills, and posters, but very few of these documents could be produced. Sen. Benjamin F. Jonas, of Louisiana, is a good example of one who referred to the propaganda but had not seen it. "I learn that in many of their [the black farmers'] cabins can be seen highly-colored pictures representing the Western prairies as dotted with beautiful cabins, just ready for occupation, around which the buffalo and other game animals are feeding, and just waiting to be shot," he reported to the *New York Times*. "Glowing stories of this country have been told them by the agents of Western railroads having land to sell, and they naturally want to leave their present homes, where there is hard work and small pay, for this land of peace and plenty."[15]

Arriving Exodusters told Kansans that such inducements had influenced their decision to leave the South. A. A. Harris, a Fort Scott attorney, told of one such conversation: "One man from Texas told me that a white man came down through that country, selling railroad tickets; the white man had a chromo, on which was a picture of a colored man on a farm in Kansas, with a two-story white house, with pianos, and carpets, and things of that kind, and white servants." However, admitted Harris, "I never saw one of these pictures, but this is what this colored man told me."[16]

Another reporter who had tried to find one of the elusive documents described his efforts to St. John. "Only yesterday I was informed that circulars had been sent from Ohio to leading colored men here and elsewhere informing them that lands would be given them in Ohio and Kansas in exchange for their homes here," wrote S. A. Hackworth from Brenham, Texas. "I have sent some of my colored friends here in search of one of these circulars and hope to get one," he added.[17] Now and then, men who had seen or had possessed one of the much-publicized tracts described their contents. "We got papers down South stating the government had furnished land for us in Kansas, and was giving us free transportation from Saint Louis, and that some railroads in Kansas would furnish us land and allow us four payments, and the government would allow us five payments," wrote James Brown, of Madison Parish, Louisiana.[18]

Information such as this was exaggerated, but only to a degree, when one considers other inducements that caused discontented southern blacks to leave home. Promises ranged from fares as cheap as one cent a mile, better wages, and more-favorable living conditions, to outlandish assurances that almost everything was free in the new Canaan. In the latter category was the offer of little flags, no larger than the palm of one's hand, that were said to be passports, "and the Negroes think that with these they can pass anywhere without money and without price." Some of the flag salesmen modified their claims, asserting that one of their products, stuck into Kansas soil, earned title to sixty acres of land. Unfortunately, some of the purveyors of such happiness were Negroes who understood the credulous nature of their customers and preyed upon them unmercifully. The blacks who innocently put up their hard-earned cash for "passports" were easy marks for the hucksters. As one St. Louis paper put it, the Negroes, who for some time had been emancipated and enfranchised, were "so utterly ignorant that they believe stories a white boy of twelve would laugh at." These people had learned almost nothing during Reconstruction years, thought the editor, who said that in 1879 they were merely grown-up children.[19]

The credulity of the former slaves was recognized by southerners, who had used it to their own advantage for some time, but who now discovered that it was being used against them. From Mississippi came the comment that the blacks had "enjoyed the delights of a Utopian state of existence" briefly after they had gained freedom; then came the realization "that there could be no exemption from the irreversible decree of the Almighty that man must live by the sweat of his face." Hard labor and hard times brought on a disquietude among them that made stories about faraway Kansas sound like the promised land, and in their distress, they wanted to believe what they heard.[20] A Warren County landowner attributed the reason for the flight to Kansas to the natural excitability of the Negroes and to the fact that they had been "most gloriously" lied to. [21] From adjoining Hinds County came agreement. Plantation owner Henry C. Pike said that for months, unsigned handbills had circulated among the Negroes who appeared anxious to believe all that the literature promised. Bitterly he commented that the "Negro's idea of liberty is to have all he wants to eat and wear and to have no work to do. He cares for nothing else."[22]

North Carolinians admitted that blacks in their state were in a mood to believe promises of a better life elsewhere. Julius A. Bonitz, editor of the *Goldsboro Messenger,* thought that many of the freedmen were naturally of a roving disposition and therefore that they were easily disposed to move. "They look upon the prospect of a journey north as a grand excursion," he said. Lewis H. Fisher, a Negro merchant from Kinston, confirmed what Bontiz had to say. He agreed that many of the local blacks were attracted by the prospect of better wages and living conditions in the North and by the rumor that rail fare from Goldsboro to Washington, D.C., could be purchased for as little as one cent a mile.[23]

Texans of both races were disturbed by propaganda that quietly filtered through their neighborhoods, leaving in its wake restless and excited Negroes. Some of the more concerned residents wrote to St. John asking him how much credence should be put in these printed rumors.

C. W. Porter, pastor of the Brazos, Texas, A.M.E. church, said that many of the blacks in his neighborhood were "laboring under the impression that land, provisions and everything essential to their prosperity will be given them free." He asked for the governor's opinion of the movement, how those who had made the trip were getting along, and if land and provisions actually were being furnished to arriving southern refugees. J. M. Curd, of Cold Springs, Texas, also had questions for the Kansas governor. Was it true, he asked, that black people were not welcome among the Jawhawkers? He wondered how freedmen got along in Kansas and if it was true that the government allowed a homestead to every colored man who wished to have land in that state. C. P. Hicks, of Brenham, Texas, requested that St. John spread the word across the entire South, as he had done in a circular letter to Texas, to the effect that Kansas was not a land of milk and honey. Hicks, who said that too many ignorant blacks believed propaganda leaflets, thought it only fair that prospective emigrants from southern states know what they might encounter in Kansas. Although he appeared to be concerned that the freedmen would leave his neighborhood in large numbers, he admitted that the weekly church meetings that these people attended had to be protected by armed guards.[24]

In addition to social and political pressures, Texas Negroes complained that in their poverty they were little better off than in ante-bellum days. Bad crop years simply accentuated the conviction. As one of the Voorhees Committee witnesses put it: "Most of those who left Texas left because they had a short crop there last year; they did not raise any corn nor wheat, and but very little cotton." Another witness admitted that Texas was losing black farmers to Kansas, but at the same time it was trying to induce others in such states as Louisiana and Mississippi, even those as far north as Tennessee, to migrate to Texas. Early in 1880 a colored convention was held at Dallas, to consider the exodus question. One of the resolutions that was adopted declared that there was no necessity for any such movement from Texas, "whatever may be the condition of affairs east of the Mississippi," and that those who were in search of a better life were invited to come to the undeveloped northwest part of the state "with the assurance that all men there are treated according to their merits."[25]

While Texans promoted the Lone Star State as the land of promise for blacks living in less enlightened portions of the land, southern plantation owners continued to discuss the exodus movement and to puzzle over its origins. Texas was not the only southern latitude that had experienced agricultural depression in recent times. W. K. Ingersoll, a Vicksburg, Mississippi, planter, said that in 1878 local Negroes had harvested only half a crop. He thought that this went a long way to account for their restlessness and was the reason that some had left. Crop failure in that area, said Ingersoll, was quite unusual; it happened about once in fifty years. He admitted that landowners were not as sensitive to the situation as they might have been, for rents were not reduced in less abundant years.[26] A news note from New Orleans pointed to poor harvests and the low price of cotton as disturbing elements among southern farmers, and it noted that although political considerations were being advanced as the cause of the hegira, nevertheless it was economic uncertainty that actually had set in motion the rush northward.[27]

It is not surprising that the southern press should argue against political explanations for the exodus and that it would seek answers in the less-controversial field of economics. Considering the source of its support and the nature of its readership, such a stance is entirely understandable, if somewhat suspect. However, others, whose prejudices were on the opposite side of the question, shared the view that the inability of southern blacks to prosper under white financial control had led to the idea of migration. One of these was Professor Richard T. Greener, who was a black graduate of Harvard and was dean of the law school at Howard University in 1879 and 1880. In sharp disagreement with Douglass, he argued that the solution to the problem of the former slaves was emigration from the South. Greener thought that the situation of the Negro tenant farmer in the South now was worse than at any time since slavery and that the only hope was the prospect of a better life elsewhere. He saw no reason that American Negroes could not get along just as well in the West as Swedes, Norwegians, Icelanders, and Poles.

Greener discounted any political plot to distribute blacks around northern states in order to influence key elections. Speaking in May, 1880, he said that such a plan would cost at least two million dollars, and even if such money were made available, it was too late to do any good for the election of that year. Rather than lay all the blame on southerners, Greener assessed part of it to northerners, holding that they had bungled reconstruction and that as a result of that program's failure, the Negro had become the chief sufferer.[28]

In retrospect the causes of the exodus appear to differ little from the incentives that attracted millions of immigrants to the American West. Students of the movement generally agree that economic discontent, a sense of personal insecurity, and attractive propaganda combined to start more than one unhappy black southern farmer on his way to a vaguely defined promised land characterized by the simple word "Kansas."[29] While these causes are not always assigned the same priority, economic discontent invariably is found near or at the top of the list. Other attractions and other pressures simply were contributing factors, more colorful or spectacular aspects of the excitement.

Although the denial of political rights to postwar southern blacks and the extreme lengths employed to carry out such a program are historical fact, the connection between this dark side of American history and the hegira of 1879 has not been proved. Old-line abolitionists tried to make a case for flight as a result of bulldozing during the time of the movement itself, and others later were drawn toward that explanation, particularly during the resurgence of the 1960s, when a great deal of literature concerning the history of the American Negro appeared. But despite the sentimental attractions of sympathy for an oppressed race, the "bulldozing" theory did not fit a majority of those who made their way to John Brown country in 1879 and 1880. "To better my condition" was the inevitable answer that white frontier farmers gave when asked why they had pulled up stakes and moved; despite the relative failure of the black farmers in Kansas, as regards the exodus movement, the answer for them generally was the same. While to better one's condition also could mean improvement in the realm of political participation, it almost always dealt with dollars and cents, as opposed to ideologies, even for the Exodusters.

More immediate motivations, those closer to the surface and hence more easily noticed, arose out of the emotional nature of the people involved. Contemporary observers were aware that cotton-belt field hands, a good many of them former slaves, were impressionable souls and that frequently they found an outlet in religious exhilaration. In the spring of 1879 the *Chicago Tribune* remarked that "some of the more ignorant and enthusiastic Negroes undoubtedly believe that the entire Negro race will leave the South as the Jews left Egypt, and [they] regard the movement rather as a religious than as a political or material improvement." *Appleton's Annual Cyclopedia* for 1879 supported this contention, maintaining that one of the principal reasons for the flight was religious enthusiasm. Some students of Negro history, writing in more recent times, have accepted this force as one of the important causes of the phenomenon.[30]

There were additional emotional reactions that made black men decide to leave their ancestral homes. For example, a North Carolina newspaperman remarked that when Democrats advised blacks in his state not to leave, they immediately assumed that this meant there was something good about the exodus, and they began to look into the matter more closely, some of them deciding to join the hegira. On the other hand, there were negative "convincers" that helped to make up the minds of the doubtful. A notice posted in Mississippi about this time was food for thought. It read: "Calvin Ostin: This is to notify you that you can't stay here innay longer than fifteen days; its nothing that we have against you, as you have a good name with white and black. Now, if not gone within fifteen days you will receive buckshot soop."[31] In Kansas, upon arriving, some of the Exodusters told of such pressures, but they were a decided minority. Those who either had experienced threats or had been told of them found Republican newspaper reporters more than ready to hear their stories. The consequent publicity, laid before a readership that was anxious to read about southern atrocities, tended to exaggerate the charges insofar as this group of migrants was concerned.

Frequently the attitudes of former slaves were hard to define. Occasional threats of "buckshot soop" were easy for them to comprehend, and responses to these threats were not complicated; but beneath these surface irritations lay a feeling of uncertainty and insecurity among a newly freed people that even they were unable to explain. As previously mentioned, both races had difficulty in adapting to the new condition of employment, and suspicions on both sides were not easily set aside. If the whites had trouble in their new role as landlords, as opposed to being masters, the blacks were in an even greater dilemma, for many of them were very poorly equipped to take on the responsibility of managing even a few acres for themselves. The demands of the competitive system and the complexities of coping with their former owners in a sharecropping system often defeated the new free black farmers. It does not require a deep understanding of human nature to appreciate their desire to avoid problems at home by moving to another location where much better conditions were promised. Thousands of European immigrants had taken a similar course. Exaggerated written promises, blown into absolutely ludicrous proportions when passed along by word of mouth, were seized upon hungrily by a people in search of a black Canaan. To them it meant final emancipation.

Kansas was a doubtful Canaan, and the hegira was a general failure. Subsequent history would reveal that relatively few black homesteaders took up farms in the American West, and while it would be difficult to prove, it is worth at least some speculating that the lack of success attained by those who rushed northward in 1879 may have discouraged others from trying their hands at farming government lands on the high plains.

The reasons why the Exodusters of 1879 generally did not succeed as farmers in Kansas, or in neighboring states, are several—and they are not entirely black. While not all of these people were indigents, a high percentage of them were, and even those who had money, had very little. White farmers discovered that free farms did not mean free living, and many of them were driven back from their homesteads, unable to outlast climatic extremes, early crop failures, and other reverses in what a St. Louis paper described as a "bleak and arduous land." A certain amount of capital was necessary in order to get settled in a new country. Unfortunately, the black army that invaded the plains in 1879 faced abnormally difficult conditions, for it was not composed of first-line agricultural troops. Far too many of them were old men, women, and small children. Sickness and the inability to participate in productive labor meant that the many were a drag upon the few who were able-bodied. A good many of those who fled to Kansas were members of a family group: children, grand-parents, in-laws, and relatives. Just as in a day when these members were terrified at the thought of being "sold down the river" to deep-South slave markets, so now they clung together, afraid of a new land, strange people, and a hostile climate. They had a particular distaste for the isolation and the distances of the West, and loneliness added to the discouragement generated by meager crops and cold weather. Before long, those who had ventured out to live on a farm of their own retreated to small towns, where they accepted menial labor or charity in preference to isolation and marginal crops. In this instance the retreat from the frontier farm was motivated by the additional element of a racial characteristic: gregarious-ness. This was one of the few cases where black and white experience at homesteading differed.

Another reason that the black frontiersmen of 1879 found little success in the plains country of western Kansas lay in their inability to adapt to a change of crop and the use of unfamiliar implements. Those who entered the southern part of the state tried to stay with the old familiar crop: cotton. The others, who found themselves in an arid climate and subjected to unknown extremes of temperature, had great difficulty in trying to raise wheat or corn under new conditions. In addition to the normal difficulties faced by all who went west, the black farmer often was reduced to battling nature with his bare hands. More than one of the Exodusters tried to dig out little circles of sod with hand shovels and to plant potatoes in the unfriendly soil below. Even white settlers who watched the pathetic efforts sympathized with their black neighbors. As it was, the odds against success were high, but the futile effort to tame the West by hand appeared to be downright foolhardy. There was little surprise in white circles when former field hands from the deep South gave up and moved to the nearest town; many of the whites themselves were starved out and were obliged to go back East in defeat.[32]

The blacks who were driven away from their farms were far more reluctant to go back where they came from than were the white homesteaders. Instead, they huddled in small western towns and accepted charity so readily that the donors soon became very critical of them. Herein lay the basis for the defense, by Kansans, that they were not prejudiced against the newcomers for reasons of color, but rather because they imposed a heavy burden upon small, struggling frontier towns. These little municipalities not only were new and unused to the demands made upon older cities, such as that of charity, but their founders took pride in their creations and thought it a reflection upon the growing town that any group had to be supported by others. Handouts to those who were unwilling or unable to join the labor force appeared to argue against claims that the new country was a land of opportunity for all. The Protestant ethic—the notion of work and save—ran strong in these communities, many of whose origins had a noticeable New England cast. The admixture of willingness to lend a helping hand to any and all in need, tempered by the dollars-and-cents cost of such gestures, provided a dilemma to the residents of these frontier settlements that was not entirely unique in the human experience. The fact that the objects of the argument were black people who had sought out John Brown country as a land of hope and promise merely sharpened the moral struggle in the hearts and minds of Kansas villagers. In the beginning the moral battle was one-sided, because the number of Exodusters was relatively small, and it was easy to insult the haughty southerners by offering unfortunate blacks an elaborately open-handed welcome. But as the flood grew and as increasingly unwieldy numbers threatened to dissipate the small financial resources of west-country towns, the tide turned. Before long, newly arrived blacks found the social climate as frigid as Kansas winters, and a good many of them wondered if the move northward had materially improved the "scums and bukes" situation.

As it was with many a white immigrant, the decision to move now was almost irreversible. Despite cold, poverty, and prejudice, the black immigrants frequently had no choice but to hang on and hope for the best. Either they did not want to go back, or as happened frequently, they simply did not have the funds with which to return. Some of their old employers were willing to furnish fare money to bring these wanderers back to the cotton and sugar fields, but such offers were made to only a small percentage of those who had migrated. In a good many cases, southerners took the "good riddance" attitude, feeling that they had rid themselves of some unproductive, trouble-making members of society, and they had no desire to see them again. In this, the black frontier farmers shared something with many a white neighbor who also would not have found the welcome flag out had he returned to scenes of earlier strife and contention. Again, as was the case with the white settlers, Kansas blacks dug in and did the best they could, or they moved along to Nebraska, Colorado, or other places in the West where they thought they could make a living. Some of those who stayed succeeded. In proportion to their white counterparts, they were fewer in number; but in their success, perhaps they had found more satisfaction, for the ascent through the economic, political, and social strata of Kansas often was impeded by difficulties that were attributed to racial origins. In this, Kansas differed little from other western states, if that thought made it any easier for those who were subjected to such restrictions.

14

THE AFTERGLOW

By the spring of 1880 Kansans could look back upon a year of black migration from the South. During those eventful twelve months they had seen the exodus swell to alarming proportions and then subside as winter settled upon the state. With the approach of spring there were numerous predictions that warm weather would bring another and perhaps even larger group of disillusioned freedmen seeking new homes on the prairies.

By now, Gov. John St. John felt that he had done his turn philanthropically and that it was time for others to step forward in aid of the cause. During the early months of the year he and his Topeka associates urged Horatio Rust, at Chicago, to encourage a redirection of the movement toward Illinois. The faithful Rust was more than willing to carry out such orders from his chief, but as he told St. John, "the mass of the people are very ignorant of the Exodus as yet, and all are astonishingly indifferent." Nevertheless, Rust and Mrs. Comstock conducted a meeting at Chicago at which a resolution was adopted that invited fifty thousand Negroes to settle in Illinois. That these newcomers might not be the kind of immigrants who would be welcomed by members of the business community was evidenced in the creation of an executive committee, whose task it was to make arrangements "for receiving and distributing refugees" throughout the state. When St. John spoke at Chicago later in the year, he was annoyed at the lack of enthusiasm shown for his program of peopling Illinois with unfortunate southern blacks. Less than two hundred people turned out to hear him. The *Chicago Tribune* admitted that after the governor had talked for forty minutes to a small and unresponsive audience, the Kansan switched to the discussion of another and more exciting form of bondage in which men found themselves helpless victims: the slavery of alcohol. Unhappy with his reception at Chicago, St. John moved on to New York, where he told his listeners that he thought a number of the Exodusters would be willing to return to their southern homes if they were guaranteed the protection of life, livelihood, and their right to vote. He said nothing about welcoming them to Kansas.[1]

Even as St. John urged Rust to beat the drums of philanthropy in Illinois, he dispatched Mrs. Comstock to Nebraska. That kindly soul, described as "an elderly lady with white hair and benevolent face, and dressed in the style of the Quakers," admitted to Rust that recently she and Laura Haviland had had "an earnest consultation" with St. John concerning the "prospective difficulties in our work" and that he had advised both of them to "repair at once" to Lincoln, to see how many refugees that part of the country was willing to accept. Mrs. Haviland, who was then in her seventy-third year, at this time was secretary of the Kansas Freedmen's Relief Association at Topeka. Obediently, she and Mrs. Comstock journeyed northward, in response to their leader's command.[2]

Efforts to divert the influx to other states could provide only a partial solution to the problem. In addition to the driblets that arrived during the late spring of 1880, there remained a number of holdovers who had to be fed and housed by the KFRA at Topeka. In June, 1880, that organization designated three men to scour the East for more contributions to accomplish this end. G. W. Carey, a probate-court judge at Topeka who earlier had been a vice-president of KFRA, now joined with two of his fellow Topekans in protest to such a move. In a public letter the men argued that there was no need for such a solicitation, that only a handful of Exodusters now were entering the state, and that Kansans in general were unwilling that any more begging be carried out in their names. "There is great want among the whites on our frontier," wrote the complainants, "but in their name no one proposes to go east for aid. Neither should anyone go east or west to raise aid for a prospective influx of colored refugees."[3]

Judge Carey's reversal typified the thinking of a good many of his contemporaries. Frank Wilkeson, a correspondent for the *New York Sun,* wrote that "the majority of the citizens of Topeka are strongly opposed to this influx of poverty-stricken blacks from the southern states." He qualified his statement, saying that strangers with money rarely were the victims of hostility, except from the most ignorant of the whites, but "in the case of the pauper blacks, openly expressed hostility is general." More-sophisticated Topekans, thought Wilkeson, were able to detect dialects, and armed with the information gained from listening to the newcomers, they concluded that a lot of "town Niggers" had been sent their way. In fact, he said, some Kansans suspected that "Confederate brigadiers" had scoured southern towns, "collecting the blind, the halt, the old and the imbecile black paupers" for export. The purpose of such a policy, it was alleged, was to rid the South of its unwanted members in the belief that rail and boat fares were cheaper than a long-drawn-out welfare program. Northerners, who had expressed so much sympathy for the freedmen, could provide the necessary welfare programs.[4]

Those who had rather unwillingly submitted to the notion of welcoming the Exodusters to Kansas and later had openly opposed the movement justified their switch on the ground that a reasonable amount of philanthropy might be expected, but that the whole thing had gotten out of hand and now threatened to bankrupt John Brown's former stamping grounds. That, in turn, led to the inevitable argument as to how many blacks had invaded Kansas, and depending upon the source of the claim, figures tended to be widely disparate.

As mentioned earlier, there were assertions that sixty thousand Exodusters had entered the state, a figure that, with an exception or two, represented the high in various estimates. In January, 1880, St. John himself said: "I am of the opinion that, since last April, from 15,000 to 20,000 colored refugees have arrived in Kansas." Of these he admitted that about twelve thousand were destitute, and of that number, KFRA found employment for some ten thousand. Other reliable sources tended to agree with St. John's guess as to how many had entered Kansas. Henry King, the Topeka journalist, said that by the fall of 1879 there were approximately fifteen thousand Exodusters in Kansas and that perhaps four thousand had gone on to such places as Nebraska and Iowa. The *Commonwealth*, a St. John mouthpiece, guessed that in the spring of 1880 there were between twenty and twenty-five thousand of these immigrants scattered around Kansas, a good many of whom were in the southern part of the state. Writing from Topeka on the last day of 1879, a correspondent for the Chicago *Inter-Ocean* said that between fifteen and twenty thousand had come, of which only about one-fifth were able to buy any land. At that time, KFRA was housing and feeding nearly seven hundred at Topeka, and its treasury was empty.[5]

Despite these more-modest assessments, exaggerated figures continued to be handed out. When Elizabeth Comstock went out on the fund-raising circuit in the fall of 1880, it was reported that she was making the journey in behalf of "50,000 Negroes more or less destitute." A former

261

Kansan, then living in New York, objected when that figure was published by the *Herald*.

Remarking that its magnitude was "cruelly exaggerated," he suggested that if conditions really were that poor in the South and if so many were obliged to leave, then the entire North, and not just Kansas, should share the burden. Even St. John did not think that there were that many Exodusters in his state. However, at the end of 1880 he talked of forty thousand on hand with another twenty thousand having been sent on to other places. Earlier that year he had set the figure at twenty to twenty-five thousand; but even accepting the larger figure, it is doubtful that another fifteen thousand entered the state during 1880; the evidence does not support such a contention.[6]

While it is difficult to determine how many Exodusters entered Kansas during 1880, the indications are that the flow was much less than that of 1879. Despite St. John's public statements about the size of the 1880 immigration, his private correspondence indicates a falling off in numbers. Late in the year, Daniel Votaw, who represented the KFRA at Independence, in southeastern Kansas, wrote to him that "it appears from thy letters to New York and other places that new arrivals of Refugees are few & that there is little need just now." Votaw admitted that since August only about five hundred had arrived in his town. During that month, Wilmer Walton, of Parsons, reported that only a few at a time had drifted into that little southeastern Kansas town in recent weeks. Both Votaw and Walton said that recent arrivals were cold and in sad need of food and clothing. On November 22 the temperature at Parsons dropped to eight degrees below zero.[7]

Despite dwindling numbers the problem of supply remained great. Most of those arriving at Independence were "old, worn out men, widow women & children"; not more than one in ten of them had teams, according to Votaw. Thinly clad and without shoes, they suffered greatly. Even when a supply of shoes was dispatched to Kansas, the problem was not solved, for, as the *Commonwealth* explained, nearly all of the donations were too narrow to be of any use because the needy, having worked in the fields all their lives, required large, broad-soled footwear known as "plantation shoes." At this time Mrs. Comstock was in Philadelphia, begging for cast-off suits from policemen, firemen, and college students. With much satisfaction she reported that between two and three carloads of clothing would be sent on to Kansas at once.[8]

As the *Inter-Ocean* had remarked, not all of the arrivals were charity cases, some of them having money with which to buy farms and get started. John Milton Brown, who played a prominent role in the Topeka welfare operation, said that a few members of his race bought lands along the Neosho River and settled down in the new country with a minimum of difficulty. Uplands could be had for $1.25 an acre, with bottom lands costing a little more. Prices ranged between $3 and $5 an acre for railroad land, but it could be obtained on an eleven-year credit arrangement, or one-third off for cash. Those who could not buy land hired out as laborers, either on farms or in the towns. Farm work brought between $15 and $20 a month, including board, and frequently with free housing and a garden plot thrown in, much as they had been furnished in the South. Those who worked at regular jobs in the towns—in the packing houses of Kansas City, for example—earned about $1.25 a day.

Laura Haviland, who operated KFRA's employment bureau at Topeka, was active in her efforts to find work for her charges. Printed circulars appealed to the consciences of prospective employers, urging them to take whole families and to avoid separating them, as had been done in an earlier day of "accursed bondage." She reminded businessmen that most of these people could neither read nor write, so "communication by mail is practically denied them." Mrs. Haviland urged employers in outlying portions of Kansas to hire some of these workers, promising that an undue number would not be sent and that therefore they would not "be felt as a disturbing element in the social or business life of our people."[9]

Kansans living in the western part of the state paid little attention to such appeals. The newspapers of the little towns along that agricultural frontier gave almost no space to the exodus or even to Negro colonies such as Nicodemus, so great was their preoccupation with the daily fight for survival that faced them. Drouth and consequent crop failure hit the more arid regions of the plains hard in 1879 and 1880. Rather than offering aid to the less fortunate, these people themselves asked for assistance, arguing that it would be hard to find anyone in worse circumstances. They were in a do-or-die fight for survival, and if anyone had accused them of a lack of sympathy for the unfortunate southern blacks who had fled to Kansas, they would have regarded the charge as just one more irritation among many that plagued them in their efforts to hang onto the tenuous toe hold that they had established in a barren, unfriendly, and even hostile land. Accusations of racism merely would have mystified them.

By the early months of 1881 a good many residents of more-settled portions of Kansas had thrown in the towel and had retired from the battle to save the black refugees. Drouth and crop failures in the more recently developed western part of the state were giving Kansas a bad name nationally. The statewide business community, but more particularly its membership in the eastern counties, feared that additional rumors of difficult economic conditions brought on by heavy demands for charity might further cloud the young commonwealth's image.

Then the *Huntington Advertiser*, of West Virginia, plunged a dagger into the hearts of Kansas merchants. "The people of Kansas wonder why emigration passes that state by," remarked the newspaper. "The reason is their confounded chronic beggary. If they would not cry for charity for a whole year it would be good for the State." This is exactly what Kansans had feared would be said, moaned the *Topeka Weekly Times,* and it commented bitterly that in any other state an organization such as the KFRA long since would have been thrown out. Angrily the *Times* suggested that concerned Kansans should "rotten egg every man, woman or child found asking aid for Kansas, and give them fifteen minutes to get out of town. . . . All such beggars are the vilest frauds."[10]

Two of the accused already were worried about the recent course of events. One of them, Elizabeth Comstock, admitted to the other—Horatio Rust—that she was much perplexed about what to do with the "refugee things" that she had collected; she wondered if Rust could find a storage place for them. At the same time, she admitted that "our money is nearly all gone." As determined as ever, she redoubled her efforts to raise funds; but faced by a rising criticism of "beggary," from Kansans, she had to admit that the going was getting tougher all the time. In May, 1881, she wrote to St. John that "funds are dropping off for refugee work, while demands for money are increasing." Even so, some twenty-five thousand dollars worth of supplies and thirteen thousand dollars in cash had arrived from England in the preceding four months, making a total contribution valued at about eighty thousand dollars provided by the lady's workers in Great Britain, three of whom were her sisters.[11] However, as she said to Rust, the donated funds had been expended, and the prospect of getting more had dimmed.

Not only were contributions to KFRA drying up during the spring of 1881, but dwindling interest among Kansans was beginning to turn into a hard-core resistance toward the remnants of the exodus movement. At Chicago, Horatio Rust pressed Elizabeth Comstock for more money to aid his Southern Refugee Relief Association, whose announced purpose was to aid "the colored refugees in Kansas." At the same time he indicated that the end of the Kansas project was in sight when he told St. John that in Chicago "there is a plan on foot to send a colony of refugees to the Sandwich Islands." As he told the governor, sugar planting showed promise for former cotton raisers, and he thought that the Hawaiian proposal sounded like "a good scheme." Down in southern Kansas, Wilmer Walton still was on the battlefield, waging his fight against destitution among arriving blacks. He praised St. John and expressed his belief that the governor's heart was still beating in sympathy for the oppressed of his state. He promised that God would reward the chief executive.[12]

Walton, at his Parsons outpost, was somewhat out of touch with events transpiring at headquarters. St. John's heart might be beating in time with the ideals of the movement, but realities suggested that the tempo, and perhaps the tune itself, had changed. On April 15, 1881, KFRA closed its Topeka headquarters; six weeks later the barracks and other elements of the operation in the city were shut down. This did not mean that relief work in Kansas had come to an end, but rather that Topeka no longer was the nerve center.

For some months Mrs. Comstock had been aware that the Topeka command post of KFRA would have to be evacuated in the foreseeable future. In July, 1880, she asked St. John if he did not agree that the main effort ought to be shifted to the southeastern part of the state, a section that now was experiencing a heavier influx than eastern Kansas. Candidly she admitted that there was "much dissatisfaction in Topeka, among the citizens, many of who think that our doing so much there has increased the refugees there," but she wondered if it would be "wise or right" to shift the focus of their efforts to southeastern Kansas. Another alternative was for her group to secede from KFRA. "I confess, I am unwilling to do that," she told the governor. "I fear that our doing so would tend to lessen public confidence & the funds and supplies would fail in consequence."[13]

By late March of 1881, shortly before KFRA closed its Topeka offices, Mrs. Comstock had made a decision about her relationship to that organization. In the future she would work independently of it. On the eleventh she told St. John that she and the Kansas Friends "had pretty much decided" to aid the unemployed freedmen by putting them to work on agricultural lands that the group intended to purchase in southeastern Kansas and for which three thousand dollars had been raised. Optimistically they proposed to employ any and all refugees who wanted to learn practical farming. In connection with the project there would be established what she described as a training institute in agricultural and domestic arts "that men & women, boys & girls can all be employed & taught." The reason that she was ready to abandon welfare in favor of a project that would involve employment was explained in a letter of March 26. "Owing to the fact that so many of the refugees congregate in and around Topeka where aid has been so largely distributed, many more being here than can possibly find employment, and it being positively necessary that they should scatter to other parts where they can find work as spring advances, I am urgently advised by Governor St. John and the best friends of the colored people here, to abandon those headquarters at once," she informed the *Daily Capital,* of Topeka, whose editor cheered both the idea and the governor.[14]

When Mrs. Comstock and Friends selected southeast Kansas as the site of their next endeavors, they chose a part of the state that was relatively infertile so far as sympathy for the Exodusters went. Editor Frank C. Scott, of Independence, Kansas, argued that "the illiterate beggar, the world over, is a curse to society he infests. He is a debased, degraded, debauched wretch, whose presence in any community is an unhealing ulcer; he is of the class to which a large majority of the Exodus Negroes belong, and we indignantly protest against these miserable wretches being thrown upon the society of southern Kansas." W. S. Newlin, whose home was Lawrence, tried to engage in missionary work for St. John at Oswego, a few miles east of Independence. It did not take him long to agree with Scott that blacks were not very welcome in that neighborhood. "The cause of the refugee down here is unpopular," he reported to the governor. "Sleek, well clad & fed Pharisees let these poor ulcer clad Lazeruses pick no crumbs from their tables & care nothing for them & know nothing of them & despite us who work among them." Newlin had written a plea for aid to the Chicago *Inter-Ocean,* which local whites feared would hinder white immigration to the area. St. John's field worker admitted that as a result of his letter "I unfortunately am suffering great persecution here. . . . The Land Agents & Democrats are most exercised by it."[15]

Even some of the enthusiasts among St. John's following were losing interest in the region. Albion W. Tourgee, who became so well known for his novels about the conditions among blacks in the postwar South, decided to sell his quarter-section of land in Butler County. He thought it was worth eight dollars an acre, but he told the governor that he was willing to sell the property at cost, or five dollars an acre, on ten years' time. Perhaps he thought the investment had been "A Fool's Errand," to borrow the title of one of his better-known books. In any event, he now wanted to dispose of land that he never had seen.[16]

Aside from Mrs. Comstock's defection, there were other signs that the day of KFRA was over. In an early period, blacks of the "Pap" Singleton variety had promoted colonies, selling land to members of their race who had funds enough to move. The rush to Kansas in 1879 and 1880, heavily subsidized by Mrs. Comstock's Quakers and St. John's humanitarian army, had provided stiff competition for those who wanted to continue the colony-founding business. But now, in the spring of 1881, such promotions reappeared. On March 23 the South Kansas Colony Company was founded at Topeka, with Columbus Johnson as president and A. D. De Frantz as secretary. Both of these men were old hands in the business.[17] During the next month, leading black men of St. Louis, led by J. Milton Turner, founded the Freedmen's Oklahoma Association. They intended to settle the part of Oklahoma known as the ceded lands, or lands relinquished in 1866 by Creek, Choctaw, Chickasaw, and Seminole Indians "for the purpose, as stated in the treaties, of locating thereon other Indians and freedmen."[18] Turner had played a prominent, if somewhat controversial, role in the exodus movement as it affected St. Louis in its earliest days.

Even Laura Haviland, formerly secretary of the KFRA at Topeka, admitted that the welfare program had revealed a weakness. "I am satisfied *continual giving* has its demoralizing effect," she told St. John in the autumn of 1881. "Yet it could not be avoided last winter, and when they were coming by hundreds."[19] She wrote from Columbus, Kansas, as secretary to a new organization known as the Agricultural and Industrial Institute, a school chartered in late April of 1881 by Mrs. Comstock and some of her Quaker supporters. It was situated on four hundred acres of land, to which Mrs. Comstock referred in her letter of April 11, located in the extreme southeastern part of the state. Although Elizabeth Comstock listed herself as "Foundress," the president of the board was a Quaker, an old-time abolitionist named Jonathan E. Pickering. His son L. M. Pickering, who once had been in charge of an Indian farm on the Sac and Fox Reservation, was appointed to superintend farming operations and instruction. The chief clerk was a man named S. W. Winn, whom the *Commonwealth* described as "an educated and competent refugee from Mississippi." Although Mrs. Comstock had complained about an increasing difficulty in raising funds for refugee relief, by mid May of 1881 she had gathered up eighteen thousand dollars for the new project near Columbus, Kansas.[20] Within another six weeks she had shipped nearly seven thousand dollars worth of supplies to her friend Laura Haviland at the new institute, where already fifty-two refugees were employed. At that time Mrs. Haviland said that her group could accommodate at least 150 in the school.[21]

The Friends were enthusiastic about the establishment of educational facilities for the blacks of Kansas, but they admitted that financial support was hard to come by. S. W. Winn, the acting secretary of the Kansas Yearly Meeting Committee of Friends, praised the Agricultural and Industrial Institute and tried to get St. John to use his influence to procure railroad passes for the school's officers. He said that the educational program was much liked by the colored people "who are gradually coming in to work," but that as of early June, 1881, the school had no money with which to pay them. Elizabeth Comstock suggested that the financial burden could be lightened if the state would take over the school. Or if not, she said, perhaps it would match funds raised by the Friends. She expressed the hope that the training center would become a "second Hampton" Institute.

Meantime, the tireless Quaker lady had been to see President Garfield, to solicit his aid, and she reported that their conversation had been satisfactory. She urged the president to support a program that would both protect blacks in the South and at the same time provide means to distribute them around the North, or as an alternative, to furnish them with a large tract of land of their own. In a half-hour interview, she said, the president had exhibited a keen interest in the Exodusters.[22]

Despite a shift in direction by Mrs. Comstock and the Friends, from support of charity to that of the educational ideal, there was rising dissatisfaction within the ranks of those who were dedicated to the alleviation of suffering among black refugees. September of 1881 found Elizabeth Comstock hard at work raising money for the cause among easterners, but by now her efforts had begun to generate criticism. James B. Chase, of Sherwood, New York, told St. John that while much was still being done in his state to help blacks in Kansas, it troubled him that stories were making the rounds to the effect that Mrs. Comstock was not trustworthy and that "what may be sent her may never be applied as intended." He asked the governor if the Agricultural and Industrial Institute was worthy of assistance. He wondered if one could depend upon Mrs. Comstock's statements about the condition of the refugees. F. C. Stanley, of Cardington, Ohio, made similar inquiry, asking St. John if aid to Mrs. Comstock might not be "misplaced charity."[23] Before long the answer to questions about the lady's personal problems would be provided by Wilmer Walton, who told St. John, early in 1882, that she was in a sanitarium in Dansville, New York, under treatment for an ailment that he described as "mental and physical debility."[24]

Meanwhile, even the Kansas blacks complained about the manner in which the relief and rehabilitation program was being carried out. In June, 1881, a group of them at Topeka charged that KFRA had been dissolved not so much because its mission was regarded as accomplished as from a feeling that there had been mismanagement of the organization. They charged that funds, clothing, tools, and so forth had been diverted to the institute. This, said the complainants, was not the purpose for which many a donor had made his gift to the needy. Mrs. Comstock took offense at the accusations, arguing to St. John that the dissolution of KFRA had been a good thing. "I wish the colored people in South Kansas could feel the same," she wrote, adding a sorrowful comment about the "commotion they are making." Even more distressing to her were the attacks the Topeka blacks made upon Jonathan Pickering and his son, charging them with misappropriation of funds "& various other charges without any foundation." She swore to the governor that she had not spent a cent of KFRA funds on the institute. Topeka Negroes, she continued, demanded control of the boxes and bales of relief supplies arriving at the capital city. "They claimed them as a right, refused to go to places offered them to work & said 'We've worked for white people long enough, we are going to work for ourselves now.'" The gentle Quakeress, now alarmed, predicted that St. John would "have great trouble with this element," and in a surprisingly aggressive statement she recommended that they be "put down."[25]

Despite Mrs. Comstock's protestations that all was well at the institute, charges of irregularities could not be silenced. Daniel Votaw, who represented the KFRA at Independence, Kansas, reported to St. John, in June, 1881, that Kansas black leaders were "dreadfully dissatisfied with the doings" at the school. He suggested to the governor the importance of keeping the state's colored community happy: "And as they and their Friends have a strong balance of power in the state and we want thee to fill a senator's place next term, we want them to have their votes and thee can have them as easy as to turn thy hand." S. W. Winn, writing from the institute, assured the governor that there were no real problems at the establishment, even though Votaw recently had passed around a petition there, which had been signed by a "few ignorant, deluded, colored people around him." This was no more than an indication of Votaw's prejudice and jealousy, said Winn. But Votaw persisted, charging that officials at the institute were selling thousands of dollars worth of clothing that was badly needed by near-naked blacks in order to get money enough to run the place. Unhappy refugees had asked him if St. John had ordered Jonathan Pickering "to take all our money & all our clothes & buy the land & put up them bildens and make us work for to pay for what was ours, and did he say that we needed no more help and does he know that Pickering sold our clothing by wagon loads to the Missourians who used to whip our backs?" By May of 1882 Votaw was able to report to St. John that on the seventeenth both Pickering and Winn had been convicted of embezzling about eleven thousand dollars worth of goods intended for distribution among the Exodusters.[26]

Despite opposition by those who preferred the KFRA welfare program to training schools for impoverished, unemployed blacks, the Quakers pressed forward their educational plans. The idea of self-help, as envisaged by Mrs. Comstock in her Agricultural and Industrial Institute, was neither new nor unique. As early as February, 1880, there was originated at Topeka a proposal for free industrial night schools to train girls and women for household work "and fitted for the duties of cooks, chambermaids, seamstresses, and housekeepers." By then, one already was functioning at Lawrence. The organization, called the Freedmen's Educational Society, was headed by James E. Gilbert and F. W. Giles, of Topeka; and St. John gave his endorsement. Giles wanted to go even further: he proposed the creation of a joint stock company with sufficient capital to buy lands, agricultural implements, and housing, all of which would be rented to Exodusters. He had a theory that if southerners could make money out of Negro labor, surely northern whites could do the same. Why not, he asked, combine business with philanthropy?[27]

A variation of the scheme that Giles proposed was the establishment of colored colonies, something that KFRA had dabbled with earlier. While organizing a colony did not necessarily involve training, as did the A. and I. Institute, neither was it out-and-out charity. The Little Coney Colony, located in Chautauqua County, which was presided over by a black politician named the Reverend Alfred Fairfax, tried to get money originally intended for KFRA diverted to it. By May of 1881 the colony's officers complained that Mrs. Comstock's promises of such aid had been violated and that instead she had poured some thirty thousand dollars into a "swindle upon the freedmen" that would benefit only a few, namely the A. and I. Institute. They asked for and received the assistance of Daniel Votaw, of Independence, who led the attack upon the institute.[28] In the autumn of 1882 Wilmer Walton visited the colony—he called it the "Fairfax Settlement"—and reported to St. John that the black colonists were hard at work, raising cotton, sweet potatoes, corn, and sorghum. Some of them had laid in a good stock of supplies for winter, while the more shiftless had set aside nothing. He said that the white neighbors, who also were poor, were generally well disposed toward the newcomers except in a few cases where he admitted that there was a lingering prejudice against the "descendants of Ham."[29]

Apparently the colonists in southern Kansas fared better than the unorganized blacks who drifted into the region, looking for work or for contributions to their support. In the spring of 1882 Daniel Votaw confessed to St. John that he was weary, that he was getting but four hours of sleep a night, and that despite heroic efforts, his charity cases were starving to death. He said that there were about a hundred families in the neighborhood, but that they had no teams and had nothing with which to break ground except mattocks and spades. All their horses but one had starved to death during the winter, and that lone survivor, explained Votaw, had been killed by a "siclone" that also "blowed down" houses, dugouts, and other dwellings. His discouragement was compounded by the fact that little help was arriving from outside sources. One of the Friends, a Reverend Lydia Sexton, told Votaw that she could get all kinds of relief funds from Boston, but St. John would not endorse her. The governor's unwillingness to involve himself further added to Votaw's deepening gloom over the situation.[30]

W. T. Yoe, the postmaster at Independence, was not as pessimistic as Votaw. He thought the blacks were doing as well as could have been expected, although he thought that they might have done better working as in days of old under an overseer. Some did well by themselves, but others, without someone to direct them, were "practically useless." Even so, some of the newcomers already had comfortable homes and were doing reasonably well, considering how poor they had been upon arrival. It was the more improvident group that worried Yoe. These people, he said, did not seem to know how to provide for winter; so, when cold weather came, they would have to "root hog or die like white people." He did not think local whites could afford to give up any more food; they had done all they could. So had Votaw, said the postmaster, who called the KFRA man good hearted and so generous that he had mortgaged his own home to help feed the needy. He did not blame Votaw for wanting to get out of the relief business; in fact, he said, "our people are very tired of it."[31]

There were other indications that during 1881 and 1882 philanthropic zeal was fading in Kansas. For example, E. D. Bullen, of Dunlap, found that participation in the program of relief for arriving blacks was not without its problems. He complained to St. John that while he had served willingly as one of the governor's faithful soldiers in the cause, he had acquired a few scars. His role as treasurer for the local Freedmen's Aid Association had proved to be "very detrimental to my business [and] very detrimental to my social & political standing." Looking at the future, he wondered if standing by the association was his duty or even if it was a wise thing to do. "I will say the Association is doing a good work for the colored people," he admitted, "but so very obnoctious [*sic*] to the whites. I am about the only one who is here that could be made available to act as treasurer."[32] Meanwhile, Wilmer Walton had given up his KFRA outpost at Parsons. He continued to help local Negroes by getting clothes from the eastern Friends and by furnishing seed and advice for farming, but this was a more or less private philanthropy, carried out individually.[33] "Pap" Singleton agreed that the movement was slowing down. In the fall of 1881 he remarked that sailors tended to leave the craft when the rats boarded it. "I have been looking at the sign and the mice are leaving and now and then a half grown rat," he told a Topeka newspaper. However, he maintained, "I am yet upon the old vessel but discontented." The old man, who was seventy-three, had become embittered. He felt that others had taken from him his true role as leader of blacks into the western wilderness.[34]

Despite St. John's efforts to shed some of the political garments that he had acquired in consequence of the movement, he could not shake off its associations. The rumor that thousands of refugees were starving to death in Kansas haunted him, as well as hurting him politically. Doubts as to the validity of the program continued to crop up, and as the 1882 election neared, such stories were most unwelcome at the Kansas Statehouse. That spring, for example, one of the clothing contributors wrote to St. John from Monroe, Wisconsin, expressing doubts as to the philanthropy in which he and the governor were engaged. He said that a young gentleman in his city was passing around the story that the alleged suffering among the refugees in Kansas was "the greatest humbug ever palmed off upon a generous public." Although the story had given the writer doubts so disturbing that he questioned Daniel Votaw's reliability, nevertheless he renewed his pledge to the cause, and he promised to stay with the commitment.[35]

It was the undying loyalty of his followers that troubled St. John. Echoes of praise for him floated across the Kansas countryside long after the governor had concluded that he would just as soon not hear them. G. S. Bascom, of Vermillion, Dakota Territory, represented the zealous band of non-Kansas admirers who continued to swear their loyalty to him. The Dakotan expressed admiration for the manner in which Kansas was trying "to solve reconstruction questions" by accepting Exodusters. He gave St. John much credit for his efforts to "solve social and moral problems by Prohibition." Bascom, who sent in a one-dollar contribution and demanded a receipt for it, expressed a sentiment held by many of the Kansas governor's followers when he said, "You are fighting a battle for all the world." He added that he was then reading Albion Tourgee's *Brick's without Straw,* and he wondered if Nimbus was "one of your dusky immigrants."[36]

St. John's "battle for all the world" was a more ambitious program than Kansans cared to undertake, and they retired him from office in the autumn election of 1882. His interest in the exodus movement had been a contributing factor to the movement of thousands of blacks from the South to Kansas, but there the campaign for betterment of these people slowed to a halt. Relief measures were taken, employment for considerable numbers was found on farms and in the towns, and others were assisted in migrating farther west, but resistance against integration and particularly against political participation made many a southern black wonder if his move had in any way opened the franchise to him. A black man's convention, held at Emporia in August of 1883, went on record as opposing the political ostracism practiced against blacks in America and in Kansas. A Topeka paper scoffed at demands for political equality, saying that "when properly stated in plain language [it] means that 'we colored people propose to demand a portion of the offices because we are colored.'" The newspaper contended that blacks in Kansas had been treated most liberally, in a political sense, one of them having been elected as state auditor—the reference was to E. P. McCabe—and that it was nonsense for them to talk about setting up a politically oriented organization based solely on color.[37] Further criticism was heard following a convention of blacks held at Lawrence on August 30. The *Commonwealth,* once the spokesman for St. John and the champion of the politically oppressed blacks arriving from the South, called the meeting "one of the noisiest and most discreditable conventions ever held by a colored people of Kansas." The confusion was so great, said the paper, that passers-by on the street stopped to listen. Before the meeting adjourned, resolutions were passed condemning discrimination against blacks in accommodations theaters, and in the schools.[38]

Within a few years even the Negroes were beginning to question the validity of trying to establish a black political force within the state. Referring to a convention held at Salina in 1890, one of them suggested that efforts to force major political parties to include his people in nominations had failed and that a new tack should be tried. "The idea that we must remain in a 'black phalanx' is un-American," he commented. "If we are to succeed at all it must be by individual effort and not move along in a 'herd.'"[39]

The phenomenon that momentarily diverted the attention of Kansans from the routine of daily life and the promotion of that young state, in the spring of 1879, was of fairly short duration. The failure of the federal government, rightly or wrongly, to foster the hegira of blacks from the South, the difficult conditions under which these impoverished strangers tried to get a start in a new land, and the general inability of what was in many respects still a frontier community to support a large number of refugees—all meant that the movement could not sustain itself for any length of time.

Aside from the moral aspects of southern mistreatment of former slaves and the righteousness of the blacks' cause, almost everything else about the exodus was wrong, or at least unfortunate, from the Kansas viewpoint. That thousands of southern blacks had been deluded by false promises made by individual interests is difficult to deny. Accordingly, this disillusioned multitude of southerners, ready to break and run from an increasingly trying situation, responded to what appeared to be the clarion call. As a result, Kansas had to bear an unexpected burden, not only of an army of hungry refugees, but also of the heritage bestowed upon it by the fanatic John Brown, one that pointed a moral gun at this recently settled western state. Traditionally the frontier communities advertised heavily for settlers, and they were not always careful with the truth when extolling the virtues of their newly discovered Edens; therefore it was somewhat of an irony that one of them—Kansas, in this case—reaped an unexpected harvest from publicity that it had helped to disseminate about its agricultural and other attributes.

EPILOGUE

When John Milton Brown testified before the Voorhees Committee in the spring of 1880, he had predicted that the exodus would go on for twenty years until all, or most, of the members of his race had vacated the South. He believed that they would go into Indian Territory, into western states other than Kansas, into as yet unorganized western territories, and they would be scattered "all over the Northern States."[1] At that time there was a good deal of speculation as to the probable extent of the movement out of the South and as to the direction that these migrants would take. Cynics maintained that a large part of them would find the world outside of Dixie to be cold and unfriendly and that before long, large numbers of the discontented would be only too glad to return home. Supporters of the movement, who agreed with Brown, were sure that the movement would reach flood proportions, that both North and West would vacuum out enormous numbers of former slaves from the southland. Both groups guessed wrong.

Some of the fleeing blacks went home, but how many did so cannot be determined. The best guess is that a relatively small number of the total chose to take this course. Scattered newspaper references indicate the return of occasional small groups and, less frequently, of larger numbers. Early in May, 1879, newspapers from Maine to Missouri gave prominent space to an account of one of these return trips. On the afternoon of May 6 the *James Howard* left St. Louis for down-river ports; aboard was a "large number" of returnees—the size of the group varying from 48 to 140, depending upon which newspaper one read. The reason

275

for their descent of the river also depended upon one's choice of newspaper. The *St. Louis Post-Dispatch* explained that it was impossible for the Negroes to do anything but starve in Kansas, while in the South they had plenty to eat and wear. Readers of the *New York Times* learned that the turnaround had been instigated by southern planters who, fearing a loss of labor, now were using their influence to get back the absent workers. The *Chicago Daily Tribune* agreed. The Democratic *Washington Post* reported that hundreds had gone home and that many more would have done so had they possessed the funds; it was an anti-exodus newspaper. The New Orleans press painted a dismal view of Kansas, asserting that those aboard the *Howard* were glad to escape from such a place. A passenger aboard the vessel said that he had asked one old lady if the government had helped them in Kansas. "Lord bless you, honey," she replied, "we never see'd no Gov'ment out dar. Nobody give us nuffin,'" An old man spoke up, explaining: "Boss, I is got enuf of Kansas. This makes three times we colored folks is been fooled—fust, 'tas de forty acres and de mule, which we didn't git; then dars de Freedmen's Bank, which busted all to smashes, then here is de Kansas oxidus, which might near killed us all. Well, 'tis de last button on Gabe's coat; and if them lying niggers and them poor white trash up in de Nort ever fools dis darkey agin, de angels of de Lord will git up and cut de piggin wing, while devil plays de fiddle."[2]

Most of those who came up river early in 1879 did not return. John A. Scudder, president of the Anchor Line, whose vessels carried so many of the Exodusters northward, said in late June, 1879, that fully ninety percent of the Negroes who went to Kansas stayed there or moved on to other western or northern states. He admitted that a few who were ill or were afraid of the Kansas winter had returned.[3] In March, 1880, John Milton Brown testified before the Voorhees Committee that he knew of only five families whose members had elected to go back home.[4] Other figures suggest that Brown, who was deeply involved in the KFRA and the relief movement in general, was too conservative in this estimate. A. S. Johnson, of Topeka, said that by April of 1880 about a hundred had accepted the offer of the Atchison, Topeka and Santa Fe Railroad to give free rides back to Kansas City to those who wanted to go home.[5] Some of the Texas blacks, who had crossed Indian Territory and had tried to settle in southern Kansas, returned. A recent study concludes that the number of returnees from this group amounted to about ten percent.[6] One of the southbound wagons bore the sign:

Farewell to Kansas,
Farewell forever,

I may go to hell,
But back to Kansas, never.[7]

The difficulty of determining how many of the Exodusters gave up and went back home is matched by the problem of discovering where they went after leaving the packet boats at various Missouri River ports or after their arrival by train or wagon from places such as Texas. Even contemporaries had but a vague notion as to where those who had come to the state during the exodus movement had located. When W. J. Buchan, of Wyandotte, testified before the Voorhees Committee in the spring of 1880, he was asked where the newcomers were to be found. "They are mostly scattered through the State," he answered. Buchan, who had not welcomed these people and who said that they were "a great injury to us," was very little interested in their whereabouts.[8] Roy Garvin, a Kansas City attorney who wrote about the movement much later, could offer only generalizations as to where the black immigrants finally had settled. He said that by 1881 they had almost disappeared from public notice, many of them having "moved elsewhere," while those who remained "became integrated into the life of their communities and achieved varying degrees of security."[9]

Some of the more successful blacks, such as "Pap" Singleton, Columbus Johnson, and others, stayed on and continued to pursue their real estate interests. E. P. McCabe, of Nicodemus, who became the highest black office holder in Kansas when he was elected state auditor, went on to engage in colonizing efforts in Oklahoma. In 1891 he was trying to develop a place called Langston, described as "a distinctively Negro city," located twelve miles from Guthrie, Oklahoma. A Topeka paper, in reporting difficulties that the early comers were having at Langston, rang a familiar bell when it said: "There is no room here for paupers. The country is new and poor. Those who can support themselves have no money to keep their dependent neighbors, and for the same reason there is little labor outside the family employed on the farms."[10]

A few of the arriving blacks who stayed achieved a degree of success that surpassed that of many of their white counterparts. Perhaps one of the most notable examples was Junius G. Groves, of Edwardsville, Kansas. Born a slave in Kentucky, in 1859, he came out to Kansas in 1879 with a large group of black immigrants. Starting off with less than a dollar in his pocket and then working on a farm at forty cents a day, he progressed to share cropping and finally to the position of landowner. By 1900 he possessed one of the largest potato farms in the Kaw Valley, had land upon which one thousand fruit trees grew, and owned town property that, a few years later, was valued at eighteen thousand dollars. In 1903 Groves produced 72,150 bushels of potatoes, enough that Booker T. Washington dubbed him "the Potato King."[11]

Another of the seventy-niners was Henry Carter, a Tennessee refugee who was so poor, upon arrival, that he started out from Topeka for Dunlap on foot, his wife carrying the bedding and Carter carrying a few hand tools. By 1880 he had cleared forty acres, had made his first payment, and was the owner of a small cottage, a good horse, and two cows. The money for these things came from labor that he performed on nearby ranches.[12] Several other black farmers, most of them in the Topeka area, also succeeded quite well. Robert and William Turner became market gardeners. So did Benjamin Vance and Robert Keith. When Vance arrived in the early eighties, he had a team of horses and fifty cents; by 1900 he was recognized as one of the area's prosperous farmers. Keith, who was born in Georgia, came to Kansas in 1884 via Ohio. By 1900 he was worth twenty-five thousand dollars and was said to be the richest Negro in Shawnee County. John M. Brown, who was very active among the Exodusters at Topeka, settled on a 100-acre farm north of that city, raising potatoes and fruit. During the eighties he was elected county clerk for Shawnee County on the Republican ticket.[13]

In 1889, ten years after the exodus movement, a Topeka newspaper summed up the phenomenon and made an assessment of its long-range results. The *Daily Capital* said that of those coming in during 1879 and after, a portion undoubtedly had bettered their conditions, but a large number had undergone severe hardships through destitution and sickness, a good many had died, and of the survivors a considerable number remained in a poverty-stricken condition. Of those who came, most remained in or near the towns, working as unskilled laborers and earning between $1.25 and $1.50 a day. Generally they were able to find employment for only about two-thirds of the year.[14]

The exodus movement, which was born out of misapprehension as to the rewards offered in Kansas and out of a moment of panic as to the probable penalty for remaining in the South, was a phenomenon in the frontier movement. It was confused with an older and more orderly migration of black farmers, and it tended to diminish the chance for success of those who tried to move west to find new homes in the more traditional manner. While earlier movements had caused little or no animosity in places such as Kansas, the exodus—by its very definition a mass movement—upset both the societal and economic balance of a new and as yet not well established community.

Black migration to Kansas, prior to 1879, caused very little stir in that state, but the problems generated by an unexpected and unexpectedly large influx both frightened and confused some of the Kansans of that day. Their reaction frequently was one of withdrawal and a display of latent racism that many of them would just as soon have submerged. Others displayed an irritation at the noisy philanthropy of eastern well-wishers who played a heavy part in caring for the refugees, while still others, unsung and often anonymous, accepted the burden thrust upon them and gave rather freely of both money and time. After these farmers and townspeople had made an effort to alleviate the suffering experienced by strangers who had arrived so precipitously and had done what they could to find employment for them, they turned their eyes once more to the practical tasks at hand, that of survival in their portion of the old American Desert.

The exodus blacks, who had been unknown and unheralded prior to the flight in 1879, gradually faded from public notice and quietly melded into the Kansas scene or moved to neighboring states. A few of them succeeded economically, while others probably were no worse off financially than they had been in the South; but a very high percentage of the total suffered. In all, their appearance on the Kansas scene constituted, for both black and white residents of that place, an unusual episode in the state's history.

NOTES

Unless otherwise indicated, all correspondence of Governor St. John is in the Papers of Governor John P. St. John at the Kansas State Historical Society in Topeka, either in "Correspondence Received, 1879–83," or in "Correspondence Sent, 1879–83." In these notes, such correspondence will indicate only the names of the corresponders and the date.

PROLOGUE

1. Thomas D. Clark and Albert D. Kirwan, *The South since Appomattox* (New York: Oxford University Press, 1967), p. 23.
2. Ibid., p. 29.

CHAPTER 1

1. *St. Louis Globe-Democrat,* March 12, 1879. Although the newspaper contains the word "Democrat" in its title, it was Republican; on the question of the Negro, however, it was not "Radical," as were some of the New England and eastern papers of the day. To further confuse matters, the *Missouri Republican* was Democratic.
2. *Missouri Republican* (St. Louis), February 21, 23, March 6, 1879.
3. Ibid., March 13, 1879.
4. Testimony of Charlton H. Tandy, *Report and Testimony of the Select Committee of the United States to Investigate the Causes of the Removal of the Negroes from the Southern States to the Northern States, Senate Reports,* no. 693, 46th Cong., 2d sess., 1880 (serials 1899 [pt. 1] and 1900 [pts. 2 and 3]), pt. 3, pp. 36–37. Hereinafter cited as Voorhees Committee Report.

5. *St. Louis Globe-Democrat,* March 13, 1879; Testimony of Charlton H. Tandy, Voorhees Committee Report, pt. 3, p. 37.
6. *St. Louis Globe-Democrat,* March 14, 1879.
7. John Thomas Scharf, *History of Saint Louis City and County,* 2 vols. (Philadelphia: Louis H. Everts & Co., 1883), 1:714.
8. *St. Louis Globe-Democrat,* March 16, 1879; *Missouri Republican* (St. Louis), March 16, 1879.
9. *Missouri Republican* (St. Louis), March 16, 1879; *St. Louis Globe-Democrat,* March 16, 1879; *Omaha Daily Bee,* March 16, 1879.
10. *St. Louis Globe-Democrat,* March 14, 1879.
11. Ibid.
12. Ibid., March 13, 1879.
13. *New York Times,* May 10, 1879.
14. *Missouri Republican* (St. Louis), March 15, 1879.
15. Testimony of John H. Johnson, Voorhees Committee Report, pt. 2, pp. 289–92; *St. Louis Globe-Democrat,* March 18, 1879.
16. Irving Dilliard, "James Milton Turner: A Little Known Benefactor of His People," *Journal of Negro History,* vol. 19, no. 4 (October, 1934), pp. 372–411.
17. George Everett Slavens, "The Missouri Negro Press, 1875–1920," *Missouri Historical Review,* vol. 64, no. 4 (July, 1970), p. 428. Wheeler edited a paper named the *Palladium.*
18. *Missouri Republican* (St. Louis) and *St. Louis Globe-Democrat,* both for March 21, 1879.
19. *St. Louis Globe-Democrat,* March 21, 1879.
20. Ibid., March 19, 1879.
21. Ibid., March 20, 1879.
22. Ibid., March 21, 22, 1879.
23. Glen Schwendemann, "Negro Exodus to Kansas: First Phase, March–July, 1879" (Master's thesis, University of Oklahoma, 1957), p. 81. Hereinafter cited as Schwendemann thesis.
24. *St. Louis Globe-Democrat,* March 23, 1879. See also Glen Schwendemann, "St. Louis and the 'Exodusters' of 1879," *Journal of Negro History,* vol. 46, no. 1 (January, 1961), pp. 32–46.

CHAPTER 2

1. *Missouri Republican* (St. Louis), March 24, 1879. For a more-complete description of the St. Louis situation see Glen Schwendemann, "St. Louis and the 'Exodusters' of 1879," *Journal of Negro History,* vol. 46, no. 1 (January, 1961), pp. 32–46.
2. *St. Louis Globe-Democrat,* March 31, 1879. Testimony of John H. Johnson, Voorhees Committee Report, pt. 2, p. 289.
3. *St. Louis Globe-Democrat,* April 9, 13, 14, 17, 1879.
4. Ibid., April 17, 18, 1879.

5. *Times* (London), April 17, 1879. From a *Times* correspondent at Philadelphia.
6. *Missouri Republican* (St. Louis), April 18, 1879.
7. *St. Louis Globe-Democrat,* April 15, 17, 1879.
8. Ibid., April 30, 1879.
9. Testimony of John W. Wheeler, Voorhees Committee Report, pt. 3, p. 11. The Colored Refugee Relief Board, which succeeded the Committee of Twenty-five, published a pamphlet dated April 22, 1879, stating that by that date 4,004 persons had been transported westward by the group. It also stated that 50,000 rations had been issued and that $3,341.42 had been raised to aid the refugees. Pamphlet reprinted in Voorhees Committee Report, pt. 2, pp. 121–22.
10. *St. Louis Globe-Democrat,* April 15, 16, 1879; *New York Times,* April 19, 29, 1879.
11. *St. Louis Globe-Democrat,* April 20, 22, 1879. Appeal for financial aid by the Colored Immigration Aid Association, April 22, 1879, reproduced in Voorhees Committee Report, pt. 2, p. 121. See also Moses Dickson to Gov. John St. John, May 1, 1879. A southern view of Turner may be found in *New Orleans Daily Democrat,* April 4, 1879.
12. Testimony of John H. Johnson, Voorhees Committee Report, pt. 2, pp. 121, 295, 296. J. Milton Turner's interests were primarily political. When he later visited President Hayes, presumably to make yet another plea for the Exodusters, he stressed the fact that while the black vote in Missouri totaled 40,000 and controlled two or three districts, no Negroes were given responsible appointive positions in that state. The president simply said that he was in favor of doing all he could for the race. *Omaha Daily Republican,* April 2, 1880.
13. *Missouri Republican* (St. Louis), April 10, 14, 17, 1879.
14. Estimates in *New York Times,* April 29, May 10, 1879; *Harper's Weekly,* May 17, 1879.
15. *New York Times,* April 29, 1879.
16. *St. Louis Globe-Democrat,* April 21, 1879.
17. Testimony of John H. Johnson, Voorhees Committee Report, pt. 2, p. 299.
18. *St. Louis Globe-Democrat,* June 11, 1879. At that time Johnson was secretary of the Relief Board, Moses Dickson its president.
19. Testimony of Charles Tandy, Voorhees Committee Report, pt. 3, p. 68. John H. Johnson, also testifying, estimated the figure to be between 15,000 and 20,000. See his testimony, ibid., pt. 2, p. 290.
20. *St. Louis Globe-Democrat,* May 7, 1879.
21. Ibid., April 28, 1879.
22. Ibid., May 16, 1879.
23. Ibid., June 28, 1879.
24. *Missouri Republican,* July 7, 1879.
25. *Weekly Clarion* (Jackson, Miss.), July 30, 1879. The Western Sanitary Commission was created by Gen. John Fremont, September 5, 1861, to

improve sanitary conditions among his troops. Women nurses, under the direction of Dorothea L. Dix—then in St. Louis—assisted in the work. It was a privately supported organization, assisted by the government, which provided free transportation and a certain amount of supplies. Another of its services was to lend aid to refugees in the Mississippi Valley. New England, in particular, responded generously, supplying $500,000 in contributions by 1864.

CHAPTER 3

1. Testimony of B. F. Watson, Voorhees Committee Report, pt. 2, p. 339.
2. *Kansas City Times,* March 28, April 3, 4, 1879.
3. The "African immigration" comment was by A. N. Moyer, of Wyandotte, Kans., in a letter to Gov. John P. St. John, April 7, 1879. The "alm house" comment was made by V. J. Lane in testimony before the Voorhees Committee. See Voorhees Committee Report, pt. 3, pp. 325–29. See also *Wyandotte* (Kans.) *Gazette,* April 4, 1879, and Schwendemann thesis pp. 84, 87.
4. Stockton to St. John, April 12, 1879; *Wyandotte* (Kans.) *Herald,* April 3, 10, 1879; *Atchison* (Kans.) *Daily Champion,* April 10, 1879.
5. *Missouri Republican* (St. Louis), April 3, 1879; *Omaha Daily Bee,* April 10, 12, 1879; *Wyandotte* (Kans.) *Herald,* April 10, 1879. The burial controversy is mentioned in Lee Ella Blake, "The Great Exodus of 1879 and 1880 to Kansas" (Master's thesis, Kansas State University, Manhattan, 1942), p. 25.
6. *Commonwealth* (Topeka), April 17, 1879, quoting *Journal*; *Wyandotte* (Kans.) *Herald,* April 17, 1879.
7. *St. Louis Globe-Democrat,* April 17, 1879; *St. Louis Post-Dispatch,* April 17, 1879; *Commonwealth* (Topeka), April 18, 1879.
8. *Commonwealth* (Topeka), April 18, 1879; *Daily Picayune* (New Orleans), April 22, 1879. Roy Garvin, "Benjamin, or 'Pap,' Singleton and His Followers," *Journal of Negro History,* vol. 33, no. 1 (January, 1948), pp. 7–23, has a good description of the small Negro settlements that grew around Kansas City.
9. *Wyandotte* (Kans.) *Herald,* April 24, May 1, 1879; *Wyandotte* (Kans.) *Gazette,* April 25, 1879. See *Commonwealth* (Topeka) of April 25 for further political accusations.
10. Testimony of V. J. Lane, Voorhees Committee Report, pt. 3, p. 326.
11. *Kansas City Times,* April 17, 1879; *Leavenworth* (Kans.) *Times,* April 19, 1879; *St. Louis Post-Dispatch,* April 17, 1879; *St. Louis Globe-Democrat,* April 20, 1879; *Daily Picayune* (New Orleans), April 22, 1879.
12. *New York Tribune,* April 24, 1879; *Daily Picayune* (New Orleans), April 22, 1879; *Weekly Clarion* (Jackson, Miss.), April 23, 1879; *Iowa State Press* (Iowa City), April 23, 1879.

13. *Wyandotte* (Kans.) *Gazette,* April 26, 1879; Blake, "The Great Exodus," p. 32; James G. Dougherty to Gov. John P. St. John, April 22, 1879.

14. *Commonwealth* (Topeka), April 25, 1879. See also the testimony of W. J. Buchan, of Wyandotte, in Voorhees Committee Report, pt. 3, p. 474.

15. *Wyandotte* (Kans.) *Gazette,* May 2, 1879; *Wyandotte* (Kans.) *Herald,* April 24, 1879.

16. *Wyandotte* (Kans.) *Gazette,* April 25, 1879. The *Memphis Weekly Appeal* (April 30, 1879) was quick to publish the rumor that Wyandotte's Rifle Club was ready to prevent the landing of any more of the black plague, "and threats are made that they will sink any boat with a cargo of Negroes which attempts to land."

17. *St. Louis Globe-Democrat,* April 28, 1879.

18. *Wyandotte* (Kans.) *Gazette,* May 2, 9, 1879.

19. *Leavenworth* (Kans.) *Times,* March 19, 30, 1879; *Omaha Daily Bee,* March 31, 1879, quoting *Times.* (Kans.) *Appeal.*

20. *Missouri Republican* (St. Louis), May 1, 1879, quoting *Leavenworth*

21. *Leavenworth* (Kans.) *Times,* April 25, 1879. The statement by Waller is found in John L. Waller to John St. John, April 22, 1879.

22. W. M. Fortescue to Governor St. John, May 2, 16, 1879; *Leavenworth* (Kans.) *Times,* April 26, 1879; *Wyandotte* (Kans.) *Herald,* May 1, 8, 1879.

23. Testimony of Edward S. Mills, Voorhees Committee Report, pt. 3, p. 29; *Missouri Republican* (St. Louis), May 2, 1879.

24. *Atchison* (Kans.) *Daily Champion,* March 11, 21, 22, April 1, 2, 20, 24, 26, 29, 1879.

25. Testimony of H. C. Solomon, Voorhees Committee Report, pt. 3, p. 23.

26. *Inter-Ocean* (Chicago), May 16, 1879.

27. Testimony of H. C. Solomon, Voorhees Committee Report, pt. 3, p. 23.

28. Testimony of H. C. Park, H. C. Solomon, and Edward S. Mills, Voorhees Committee Report, pt. 3, on pages 21, 24, and 31, respectively; cited passage on p. 22.

29. Testimony of Green Smith, Voorhees Committee Report, pt. 3, pp. 223–24.

30. Testimony of H. C. Solomon, Voorhees Committe Report, pt. 3, p. 25.

31. Testimony of H. C. Solomon and Edward Mills, Voorhees Committee Report, pt. 3, pp. 24 and 29, respectively.

CHAPTER 4

1. *New York Tribune,* June 7, 1879. For further details about St. John's background see Schwendemann thesis, p. 117.

2. Earl Howard Aiken, "Kansas Fever" (Master's thesis, Louisiana State University, 1939), p. 19.

3. Isaac O. Pickering, "The Administrations of John P. St. John," in *Trans-*

actions of the Kansas State Historical Society, 1905–1906, vol. 9 (Topeka, 1906), pp. 378–94.

4. *New York Times,* April 22, 1879; *Atchison* (Kans.) *Daily Champion,* April 22, 1879.

5. Testimony of F. M. Stringfield, Voorhees Committee Report, pt. 3, p. 329; *Commonwealth* (Topeka), April 24, 25, 1879. See also *St. Louis Globe-Democrat,* April 22, 1879. Reference to Susan Anthony's contribution is found in Susan B. Anthony to John P. St. John, April 2, 1879.

6. Testimony of M. H. Case, Voorhees Committee Report, pt. 3, pp. 15–19.

7. *Commonwealth* (Topeka), April 19, 1879.

8. Testimony of George S. Irwin, Voorhees Committee Report, pt. 3, pp. 315–16.

9. Testimony of John Milton Brown, Voorhees Committee Report, pt. 2, p. 358.

10. *Commonwealth* (Topeka), May 1, 1879.

11. Testimony of F. M. Stringfield, Voorhees Committee Report, pt. 3, p. 329.

12. *Commonwealth* (Topeka), April 24, 1879.

13. Testimony of A. S. Johnson, Voorhees Committee Report, pt. 3, p. 126. See also the Testimony of H. H. Stanton, M. Bosworth, and G. W. Carey, found in part 3, on pages 98, 290, and 406.

14. Testimony of A. S. Johnson, Voorhees Committee Report, pt. 3, p. 118.

15. Leland George Smith, "The Early Negroes in Kansas" (Master's thesis, University of Wichita, 1932), p. 69. Smith is here quoting a Mrs. J. Whitted of Wichita.

16. *Commonwealth* (Topeka), May 7, 1879, and *New York Times,* May 7, 1879, both gave May 6 as the date of incorporation. The organization's stationery, however, as of 1881, used the date of May 8 on its heading to indicate time or origin. See also the Testimony of J. C. Hebbard, Voorhees Committee Report, pt. 3, pp. 216–19, and the Testimony of M. Bosworth, ibid., pp. 287–90. In addition to his clerkship in the Kansas legislature, Hebbard was something of a local historian. The Topekan was one of the contributors to the monumental Andreas history of Kansas that appeared in 1883. He ran for secretary of state in 1884 and came in a poor third.

17. *Commonwealth* (Topeka), May 8, 1879.

18. Ibid., May 14, 15, 1879.

19. Testimony of Joshua Barratt, Voorhees Committee Report, pt. 3, pp. 208–13.

20. Cook's lecture is mentioned in *Missouri Republican* (St. Louis), May 29, 1879. For comments on Brown see *Commonwealth* (Topeka), May 17, 1879, and the Testimony of John Milton Brown, Voorhees Committee Report, pt. 2, p. 359.

21. *Commonwealth* (Topeka), April 25, 1879.

22. *Missouri Republican* (St. Louis), May 24, 1879.

23. *Commonwealth* (Topeka), May 10, 1879.

24. Letter of May 5, 1879, from St. John, published in *Philadelphia Times* and reprinted in *St. Louis Globe-Democrat,* May 13, 1879.
25. *Wyandotte* (Kans.) *Gazette,* May 9, 1879.
26. *Commonwealth* (Topeka), May 8, 1879.
27. John P. St. John to John Sims of Oskaloosa, Iowa, and to J. M. Adams of Washington, D.C., both on June 9, 1879.
28. John P. St. John to Charles Dodge, June 9, 1879.
29. John P. St. John to Joseph M. Kern, June 9, 1879.
30. *Commonwealth* (Topeka), July 10, 1879.
31. *Missouri Republican* (St. Louis), July 22, 1879.
32. Quoted in *Weekly Clarion* (Jackson, Miss.), July 30, 1879.
33. *Commonwealth* (Topeka), July 20, 22, 30, 1879; *Wichita City Eagle,* July 17, 24, 1879.
34. *Commonwealth* (Topeka), July 30, 1879.
35. *New York Tribune,* June 7, 1879.
36. *Missouri Republican* (St. Louis), April 20, 1879; *Kansas City Times,* April 17, 1879; *Mirror and News Letter* (Olathe, Kans.), May 8, 1879.
37. Elizabeth L. Comstock to John P. St. John, August 31, 1879. See also *Inter-Ocean* (Chicago), August 21, 1879, and March 13, 1880; clipping (n.d.) from West Chester, Pennsylvania, *Daily Republican,* entered in testimony, Voorhees Committee, April 17, 1880, in Voorhees Committee Report, pt. 3, pp. 366–67.
38. John P. St. John to H. C. Weeden of Louisville, Kentucky, September 12, 1879.

CHAPTER 5

1. *New York Times,* March 25, 1879.
2. *Missouri Republican* (St. Louis), April 1, July 15, 1879; *St. Louis Post-Dispatch,* April 25, 1879.
3. See also *St. Louis Globe-Democrat,* February 21, 1879.
4. *New York Tribune,* March 24, 1879; *Commonwealth* (Topeka), April 4, 1879.
5. *Kansas City Times,* April 11, 1879.
6. *Cincinnati Commercial,* May 4, 1879.
7. *Emporia* (Kans.) *Ledger,* September 5, 1879.
8. *Evening Standard* (Lawrence, Kans.), July 3, 1879.
9. *Mirror and News Letter* (Olathe, Kans.), March 13, 1879.
10. Testimony of A. A. Harris, Voorhees Committee Report, pt. 2, pp. 419–23; Testimony of John Milton Brown, ibid., p. 359.
11. *Memphis Weekly Appeal,* April 2, 1879; see also *Missouri Republican* (St. Louis), March 27, 1879.
12. Testimony of John Davis, Voorhees Committee Report, pt. 3, p. 225; *St.*

Louis Post-Dispatch, April 17, 1879; David M. Emmons, *Garden in the Grasslands: Boomer Literature of the Central Great Plains* (Lincoln: University of Nebraska Press, 1971), pp. 88–89.

13. Testimony of H. H. Stanton, Voorhees Committee Report, pt. 3, pp. 97–98.

14. Testimony of F. M. Stringfield, ibid., p. 330.

15. T. C. Henry to Governor St. John, May 14, 1879; *Junction City* (Kans.) *Union,* April 2, 1881.

16. Wendell H. Stephenson, *The Political Career of General James H. Lane,* Publications of the Kansas State Historical Society, vol. 3 (1930), p. 132. Lane was one of the first United States senators elected from Kansas. He served from 1861 until he died by his own hand in 1866.

17. Testimony of M. H. Case, Voorhees Committee Report, pt. 3, p. 17.

18. *Daily Picayune* (New Orleans), May 16, 1879; *New York Tribune,* April 11, 1879.

19. *Times* (London), April 23, 1879.

20. *St. Louis Globe-Democrat,* March 14, 21, 1879.

21. Thomas Nickerson to Governor St. John, September 10, 1879. Also see reference to this in *Inter-Ocean* (Chicago), May 6, 1879.

22. Testimony of A. S. Johnson, Voorhees Committee Report, pt. 3, pp. 121–22.

23. *New York Times,* July 12, 1879.

24. Quoted in *Weekly Clarion* (Jackson, Miss.), February 4, 1880.

25. *Washington Post,* February 6, 1880.

26. *Commonwealth* (Topeka), August 30, 1879.

27. Leland George Smith, "The Early Negroes in Kansas" (Master's thesis, University of Wichita, 1932), pp. 39B, 40A, 62. See also Carroll D. Clark and Roy L. Roberts, *People of Kansas* (Topeka, 1936).

28. W. R. Hill to John St. John, April 10, 1879; Glen Schwendemann, "Nicodemus: Negro Haven on the Solomon," *Kansas Historical Quarterly,* vol. 34, no. 1 (Spring, 1968), p. 12. Hill's statement about Negro political participation is found in *Graham County Lever* (Gettysburg, Kans.), September 4, 1879, quoted in Orval L. McDaniel, "A History of Nicodemus, Graham County, Kansas" (Master's thesis, Kansas State College, Fort Hays, 1950), p. 74.

29. Testimony of Benjamin Singleton, Voorhees Committee Report, pt. 3, pp. 379–80; *Colored Patriot* (Topeka), May 4, 1882, clipping in Singleton Scrapbook, Kansas State Historical Society, Topeka (hereafter referred to as KSHS). Schwendemann ("Nicodemus: Negro Haven on the Solomon," p. 11 n) mentions 1873 and 1876 as possible dates for the founding of the Baxter Springs Colony. I have used Singleton's testimony before the Voorhees Committee and a reference in a Negro newspaper published in Topeka as my evidence concerning the founding date. See also Nell Blythe

Waldron, "Colonization in Kansas from 1861 to 1890" (Ph.D. diss., Northwestern University, 1932), p. 127. Reference to the denial of white cemeteries to the blacks is found in *Junction City* (Kans.) *Union,* March 6, 1880.

30. Lee Ella Blake, "The Great Exodus of 1879 and 1880 to Kansas" (Master's thesis, Kansas State University, Manhattan, 1942), p. 56.

31. *St. Louis Globe-Democrat,* May 31, 1879, quoting a correspondent of *Cincinnati Gazette; Weekly Clarion* (Jackson, Miss.), June 25, 1879, quoting correspondent of *Boston Herald;* Blake, "The Great Exodus," p. 52; Waldron, "Colonization in Kansas," p. 127.

32. Waldron, "Colonization in Kansas," p. 130; *Weekly Clarion* (Jackson, Miss.), June 25, 1879; Testimony of John Milton Brown, Voorhees Committee Report, pt. 2, p. 392.

33. Blake, "The Great Exodus of 1879," p. 52.

34. Waldron, "Colonization in Kansas," p. 128.

35. *Daily Picayune* (New Orleans), April 19, 1879; *New York Times,* May 3, 1879.

36. *Atchison* (Kans.) *Daily Champion,* quoted in *New York Times,* May 3, 1879.

37. *Commonwealth* (Topeka), quoted in *New Orleans Times,* April 23, 1879.

38. *Daily Picayune* (New Orleans), April 12, 1879; see also Testimony of H. H. Stanton, Voorhees Committee Report, pt. 3, p. 97.

39. Lawrence D. Rice, *The Negro in Texas: 1874–1900* (Baton Rouge: Louisiana State University Press, 1971), p. 200. Rice believes that the story was intentionally exaggerated to defeat the purpose of the hegira, but when laid against other evidence of this sort, as revealed by the Voorhees Committee, I am not inclined to agree with him. Another explanation as to why a paper would print such a letter four times lies in the theory that many southern community leaders believed that the movement would drain off the dissident and therefore "no good" Negroes; thus they encouraged it.

40. Earl Howard Aiken, "Kansas Fever" (Master's thesis, Louisiana State University, 1939), pp. 21–22; *Weekly Clarion* (Jackson, Miss.), July 2, 1879.

41. *New Orleans Times,* May 16, 1879; *Evening Standard* (Lawrence, Kans.), July 18, 1879. See also *New Orleans Daily Democrat,* May 28, 1879.

42. *Louisiana Capitolian* (Baton Rouge), January 31, 1880, quoted in Aiken, "Kansas Fever," p. 23.

43. *Daily Picayune* (New Orleans), January 24, 1880.

44. *Missouri Republican* (St. Louis), May 7, 1879.

45. Quoted by a correspondent of *Boston Herald,* from Topeka, June 1, 1879. Reprinted in *Weekly Clarion* (Jackson, Miss.), June 25, 1879.

46. *Louisiana Capitolian* (Baton Rouge), May 1, 1880, quoted in Morgan Dewey Peoples, "Negro Migration from the Lower Mississippi Valley to Kansas, 1879–1880" (Master's thesis, Louisiana State University, 1950), p. 82.

47. *St. Louis Globe-Democrat,* April 9, 1879.

48. Testimony of Henderson Alexander, Voorhees Committee Report, pt. 2, pp. 558–61.

49. Testimony of Philip Brookings, Voorhees Committee Report, pt. 3, pp. 108–13.

50. Testimony of Washington Walker, Voorhees Committee Report, pt. 2, pp. 578–82; *Shreveport* (La.) *Standard* (n.d.), quoted in Voorhees Committee Report, pt. 2, p. 139.

51. *Missouri Republican* (St. Louis), May 6, 1879; Citizens of Nicodemus to Governor St. John, March 22, 1880.

52. *Kansas Herald* (Topeka) (n.d.), quoted in Voorhees Committee Report, pt. 2, p. 253.

53. Washington, D.C., correspondent to *St. Louis Globe,* quoted in *Weekly Clarion* (Jackson, Miss.), August 20, 1879; *Evening Standard* (Lawrence, Kans.), December 2, 1879.

54. *Commonwealth* (Topeka), April 5, June 26, 1879; *Evening Standard* (Lawrence, Kans.), July 18, 1879; *Missouri Republican* (St. Louis), May 4, 1879.

55. *Commonwealth* (Topeka), August 29, 1879.

56. The story of sight-restoring Kansas is found in the *New Orleans Daily Democrat,* May 28, 1879. The account of the Negro who preferred to die in Kansas is found in the *St. Louis Globe-Democrat,* May 7, 1879.

57. *Weekly Clarion* (Jackson, Miss.), June 2, 1880.

58. Testimony of John Milton Brown, Voorhees Committee Report, pt. 2, p. 364.

CHAPTER 6

1. *Memphis Weekly Appeal,* March 19, 1879.

2. *Mobile Register,* quoted by *New York Times,* March 27, 1879; *Weekly Clarion* (Jackson, Miss.), April 30, 1879; *State Guard* (Austin, Tex.), April 26, 1879; *Galveston Weekly News,* July 31, 1879.

3. *Daily Picayune* (New Orleans), August 3, 1879.

4. *Memphis Daily Avalanche,* April 22, 1879; *Daily Democratic Statesman* (Austin, Tex.), May 7, 1879.

5. *Weekly Clarion* (Jackson, Miss.), February 12, 1879. This comment actually preceded the migration; it was written in connection with a prediction that a black exodus was in the offing.

6. *Peoples' Vindicator* (Natchitoches, La.), April 5, 1879.

7. *Weekly Clarion* (Jackson, Miss.), April 16, July 2, 1879. See also *New Orleans Times,* June 27, 1879.

8. *Daily Picayune* (New Orleans), June 11, 1879.

9. Ibid., August 28, 1879.

10. *Commonwealth* (Topeka), May 15, 1879, quoting a St. Louis dispatch. See also *New York Tribune,* May 15, 1879, and the *Louisiana Capitolian* (Baton Rouge), July 26, 1879.

11. *Daily Picayune* (New Orleans), April 16, 1879.

12. Testimony of Henry Adams, Voorhees Committee Report, pt. 2, p. 149.

13. Testimony of Phillip Joseph, ibid., p. 404.

14. *New York Times,* May 22, 1879, quoting a Memphis dispatch.

15. Testimony of Alexander Yerger, Voorhees Committee Report, pt. 3, p. 509.

16. Testimony of L. L. Tomkies, ibid., p. 337.

17. *St. Louis Globe-Democrat,* May 24, 1879.

18. *Weekly Clarion* (Jackson, Miss.), April 23, 1879.

19. *St. Louis Post-Dispatch,* April 9, 1879.

20. *Cincinnati Commercial,* July 19, 1879.

21. *Missouri Republican* (St. Louis), May 14, 1879.

22. *Daily Picayune* (New Orleans), May 6, 1879.

23. Quotation from *Daily Picayune* (New Orleans), May 6, 1879.

24. *Memphis Evening Herald,* March 21, 1879.

25. *Memphis Weekly Appeal,* March 26, 1879.

26. *Daily Picayune* (New Orleans), March 27, 1879; *Missouri Republican* (St. Louis), April 1, 1879.

27. *St. Louis Globe-Democrat,* March 22, April 5, 1879.

28. Letter of W. W. Mangum of Refuge, Miss., April 11, 1879; *St. Louis Post-Dispatch,* April 17, 1879.

29. *New Orleans Times,* April 20, 1879.

30. *New York Times,* April 20, 22, 1879.

31. *Daily Picayune* (New Orleans), May 8, 1879.

32. Morgan Dewey Peoples, "Negro Migration from the Lower Mississippi Valley to Kansas, 1879–1880" (Master's thesis, Louisiana State University, 1950). Most of his information on this point came from *New York Tribune,* May 6, 7, 1879; *Times* (London), May 8, 1879.

33. *Weekly Clarion* (Jackson, Miss.), April 23, May 7, 1879.

34. "The Proceedings of a Mississippi Migration Convention in 1879," *Journal*

of Negro History, vol. 4, no. 1 (January, 1919), pp. 51–54; *Weekly Clarion* (Jackson, Miss.), May 14, 1879; *New York Times,* May 7, 1879.

35. *Weekly Clarion* (Jackson, Miss.), May 14, 1879.
36. *New York Times,* September 23, 1879. William Murrell, a participant in the convention, at first thought that its work had been effective, because during the summer of 1879 the movement tended to diminish, but by early 1880 he decided that since political bulldozing had not ceased in Louisiana, for example, the movement was bound to continue. Testimony of William Murrell, Voorhees Committee Report, pt. 2, pp. 513–14.
37. *Times* (London), May 9, 1879; *New York Tribune,* May 7, 1879; *Daily Picayune* (New Orleans), May 18, 22, 1879; *New Orleans Times,* May 23, 1879.
38. *Missouri Republican* (St. Louis), June 4, 1879; *St. Louis Globe-Democrat,* June 10, 1879; *Daily Picayune* (New Orleans), June 12, 1879.
39. *Times* (London), April 17, 1879, quoting, in a New York dispatch, *St. Louis Globe-Democrat,* April 16, 1879.
40. Testimony of George T. Ruby, Voorhees Committee Report, pt. 2, p. 38; *New York Times,* April 19, 1879; *New Orleans Daily Democrat,* May 28, 1879. George Ruby, New York–born, had gone south as a schoolteacher. Later he became editor of *New Orleans Observer* and a correspondent to *New York Times.* The New Orleans colored convention of April 17, 1879, was called at the behest of *Observer* and other area newspapers. Ruby founded *Observer* in 1878.
41. Earl Howard Aiken, "Kansas Fever" (Master's thesis, Louisiana State University, 1939), p. 27; Lee Ella Blake, "The Great Exodus of 1879 and 1880 to Kansas" (Master's thesis, Kansas State University, Manhattan, 1942), p. 11. See also *New York Times,* April 22, 1879; *Daily Picayune* (New Orleans), April 19, 20, 22, 1879. For more about Pinchback see James Haskins, *Pinckney Benton Stewart Pinchback: A Biography* (New York: Macmillan Publishing Co., 1973).
42. *New York Times,* February 12, 1879.
43. *New Orleans Times,* May 7, 1879; *New York Times,* May 6, 7, 1879; *St. Louis Globe-Democrat,* June 7, 1879; Voorhees Committee Report, pt. 2, pp. 244, 246.
44. *Commonwealth* (Topeka), May 16, 1879.
45. Testimony of J. W. Cromwell, Voorhees Committee Report, pt. 1, p. 5.
46. *Iowa State Register* (Des Moines), July 15, 1879; *New York Times,* May 20, 21, 1879.
47. *Omaha Daily Republican,* August 15, 1879.
48. *New Orleans Times,* March 18, 1879.
49. *Louisiana Democrat* (Alexandria), May 21, 1879.

50. *Daily Picayune* (New Orleans), April 22, 1879.
51. *Daily Democratic Statesman* (Austin, Tex.), April 9, 1879.
52. *New Orleans Daily Democrat,* April 26, 1879.
53. Ibid., quoted by *Weekly Clarion* (Jackson, Miss.), June 4, 1879.
54. The Colyer letter, written May 21, is found in *Daily Picayune* (New Orleans), July 6, 1879. See also the issues of July 31 and August 21. Other evidence is found in *Weekly Clarion* (Jackson, Miss.), April 30, 1879, and *New Orleans Democrat,* May 8, 1879.
55. *Daily Picayune* (New Orleans), August 16, 1879, and March 6, 1880.
56. *Daily Democratic Statesman* (Austin Tex.), April 16, October 5, 1879; *Galveston Weekly News,* July 10, 1879.
57. *Weekly Clarion* (Jackson, Miss.), April 2, 1879.
58. *Atchison* (Kans.) *Daily Champion,* April 15, 1879.
59. Testimony of B. F. Watson, Voorhees Committee Report, pt. 2, pp. 339–40.
60. Ibid., pp. 348–49; *New Orleans Times,* August 21, 1879.
61. *Daily Morning Chronicle* (San Francisco), June 20, July 2, 1869.
62. *Natchez* (Miss.) *Democrat,* quoted by *Weekly Clarion* (Jackson, Miss.), April 30, 1879.
63. *Weekly Clarion* (Jackson, Miss.), May 14, 1879.
64. Ibid., August 13, 1879.
65. *Daily Picayune* (New Orleans), May 4, 1879; *Memphis Daily Avalanche,* April 24, 1879; letter from Chinese Six Companies, found in *St. Louis Globe-Democrat,* April 12, 1879.
66. *Daily Picayune* (New Orleans), April 26, 1879; *New Orleans Times,* March 11, 1880.
67. *Daily Picayune* (New Orleans), July 1, November 1, 1879.
68. *New Orleans Times,* September 7, 1879.
69. Ibid., July 1, 1879, and March 25, 1880.
70. *New Orleans Times,* June 10, 1879; *Louisiana Capitolian* (Baton Rouge), January 17, 1880, as quoted in Aiken, "Kansas Fever"; *New Orleans Times,* September 7, 1879.
71. *New Orleans Times,* September 7, 1879.

CHAPTER 7

1. For a full discussion of the relationship between the causes of abolition and Indian rights see Robert Winston Mardock, *The Reformers and the American Indian* (Columbia: University of Missouri Press, 1971).
2. Fred Harvey Harrington, *Fighting Politician: Major General N. P. Banks* (Philadelphia: University of Pennsylvania Press, 1948).
3. *Daily Kennebec Journal* (Augusta, Maine), April 26, 1879; *New York*

Times, April 25, 1879. For more about Boutwell and Radical Republicans in general see Hans L. Trefousse, *The Radical Republicans* (New York: Alfred A. Knopf, 1969).

4. *Boston Evening Transcript,* April 24, 1879.
5. Harrington, *Fighting Politician,* p. 20.
6. *Boston Evening Transcript,* April 24, 1879.
7. *Daily Kennebec Journal* (Augusta, Maine), April 26, 1879. For further information about Garrison see Walter M. Merrill, *Against Wind and Tide: A Biography of Wm. Lloyd Garrison* (Cambridge, Mass.: Harvard University Press, 1963).
8. *Boston Evening Transcript,* April 25, 1879; *Times* (London), April 23, 1879.
9. *Boston Evening Transcript,* April 23, 1879.
10. Quoted in a letter from Elizabeth Comstock to John P. St. John, August 10, 1881.
11. *St. Louis Globe-Democrat,* June 26, 1879.
12. *New York Tribune,* June 25, 1879.
13. *Daily Kennebec Journal* (Augusta, Maine), April 8, 26, 1879.
14. *Bangor* (Maine) *Daily Whig and Courier,* April 9, 1879.
15. *Lewiston* (Maine) *Evening Journal,* March 29, 1879.
16. Mrs. George L. Stearns to John P. St. John, February 21, 1880.
17. Abbie W. Johnson to John P. St. John, February 16, 1880.
18. Joseph Cook to John P. St. John, February 18, 1880.
19. *Boston Evening Transcript,* April 23, 1879.
20. Ibid., May 6, 1879.
21. *Missouri Republican* (St. Louis), April 19, 1879.
22. The source of this contribution was H. P. Kidder, who made it through the Atchison, Topeka and Santa Fe Railroad. He did so "on the strength of Mrs. Comstock's letter received . . . , as to the suffering of the colored refugees." Letter to Gov. John P. St. John, February 27, 1880. The source of the Emigrant Aid Society material is found in Testimony of A. M. Clapp, Voorhees Committee Report, pt. 1, p. 35.
23. *Daily Kennebec Journal* (Augusta, Maine), May 5, 1879.
24. *Daily Eastern Argus* (Portland, Maine), May 21, 1879.
25. *Lewiston* (Maine) *Evening Journal,* May 3, 1879.
26. Ann F. Jameson to John P. St. John, July 29, 1881. The letter refers to a previous action, taken sometime in 1880 or early 1881.
27. William Chase to Governor St. John, March 9, 1880.
28. C. E. Boardman to John P. St. John, February 3, 1880.
29. Eugene D. Bassett to John P. St. John, May 15, 1879.
30. *Chicago Daily Tribune,* May 14, 1879; *Inter-Ocean* (Chicago), May 14,

1879; *Omaha Daily Republican,* May 14, 1879; M. Van Horn to John P. St. John, March 6, 1880.

31. *Boston Evening Transcript,* April 5, 18, 21, 23, 24, May 10, 1879.

32. *Boston Evening Transcript,* May 1, 1879; *Wyandotte* (Kans.) *Gazette,* May 2, 1879.

33. Trefousse, *Radical Republicans,* p. 470.

34. *New York Times,* February 28, 1879.

35. *New York Tribune,* March 21, 1879.

36. *St. Louis Globe-Democrat,* April 13, 1879.

37. *New York Tribune,* April 24, 1879; *Bangor* (Maine) *Daily Whig and Courier,* April 26, 1879. The comments that Phillips made about treason and traitors were written for *North American Review* in response to questions asked various northern leaders about Negro suffrage. See James G. Blaine et al., "Ought the Negro to Be Disfranchised? Ought He to Have Been Enfranchised?" *North American Review* 128 (March, 1879): 260.

38. *New York Tribune,* March 26, May 8, October 31, 1879.

39. *New York Tribune,* April 14, 15, May 10, 1879; *Commonwealth* (Topeka), quoting the *Tribune,* April 19, 1879. The five-dollar contribution is found in New York Tribune Office to St. John, February 25, 1880.

40. *New York Tribune,* March 18, May 2, 28, 1879.

41. John Dwight & Company to St. John, April 26, 1879, and Benjamin B. Sherman to St. John, January 17, 1881; John St. John to E. C. Johnson, August 18, 1879; *New York Tribune,* April 30, 1879.

42. *New York Times,* April 21, May 20, September 23, 1879.

43. *St. Louis Globe-Democrat,* April 9, 1879.

44. *Bangor* (Maine) *Daily Whig and Courier,* April 28, 1879 (story of the elderly Quaker and $10,000); *Boston Evening Transcript,* May 3, 1879; *Omaha Daily Republican,* May 3, 1879; Thomas Elkinton to Governor St. John; Testimony of G. W. Carey, Voorhees Committee Report, pt. 3 p. 396.

45. *Missouri Republican* (St. Louis), April 22, 1879; *Memphis Daily Avalanche,* April 22, 1879.

46. William G. Deshler to St. John, May 1, 1879.

47. George H. Eby to St. John, April 23, 1879, and Murat Halstead to St. John, May 11, 1879; *New York Times,* April 25, 1879.

48. *Daily Inter-Ocean* (Chicago), March 22, 28, April 23, 1879, and January 2, 1880; David M. Emmons, *Garden in the Grasslands* (Lincoln: University of Nebraska Press, 1971), p. 89. The Mullanphy fund later gave the Exodusters additional funds.

49. *Daily Inter-Ocean* (Chicago), April 18, 29, 30, 1879; letter from William Penn Nixon, of the *Inter-Ocean,* to St. John, April 28, 1879.

50. *Daily Inter-Ocean* (Chicago), April 10, 21, May 2, 1879; *Commonwealth* (Topeka), May 8, 1879; *Missouri Republican* (St. Louis), May 3, 1879.

51. William Penn Nixon to St. John, June 19, 1879.

52. *Daily Inter-Ocean* (Chicago), May 5, 1879.

53. *Chicago Daily Tribune,* various issues, spring, 1879; *Missouri Republican* (St. Louis), April 24, 1879, quoting the *Chicago Tribune.*

54. Horatio N. Rust to St. John, May 17, 1879.

55. Horatio N. Rust to St. John, September 3, 1879, and in the St. John correspondence for 1880.

56. Louis Nagel to St. John, April 26, 1880, and Richard Allen to St. John, March 9, 1881.

57. Letter of Selby from Chicago, Ill., May 6, 1879, in *Daily Picayune* (New Orleans), May 9, 1879.

58. *Daily Eastern Argus* (Portland, Maine), April 12, 1879, quoting the *Advertiser; Boston Evening Transcript,* June 14, 1879.

59. *Daily Eastern Argus* (Portland, Maine), April 12, 1879.

60. *Chicago Daily Tribune,* March 21, April 2, 8, 21, 1879.

61. *Frank Leslie's Illustrated Newspaper,* May 10, 1879.

62. Ibid.

63. *Chicago Daily Tribune,* April 7, 1879.

64. *Washington Post,* April 15, 1879.

65. *Chicago Daily Tribune,* March 20, 1879.

66. *Boston Evening Transcript,* May 24, 1879.

67. *Daily Picayune* (New Orleans), May 30, 1879.

68. *New York Tribune,* February 22, 1879; see also Testimony of John Milton Brown, Voorhees Committee Report, pt. 2, p. 393.

69. *New York Times,* April 7, 1879.

70. Ibid., April 4, 1879.

71. *Evening Telegram* (Portland, Oreg.), July 5, 1889.

72. *Daily Eastern Argus* (Portland, Maine), April 25, 30, 1879.

73. *Boston Daily Globe,* July 9, 1879; *Boston Herald,* quoted in *Weekly Clarion* (Jackson, Miss.), June 25, 1879; *Washington Post,* April 12, 21, 1879.

74. *New York Tribune,* April 25, 1879.

CHAPTER 8

1. Testimony of John B. Syphax, Voorhees Committee Report, pt. 1, pp. 391–93.

2. Resolution of Senator Windom, January 16, 1879, *Senate Miscellaneous Documents,* no. 34, 45th Cong., 3d sess. (serial 1833), p. 1; Senate, *Congressional Record,* 45th Cong., 3d sess. (1878–79), vol. 8, pt. 1, p. 483;

ibid., pt. 2, pp. 1077–82. The Poland Committee Report that Windom referred to was dated February, 1872, and was called "Affairs in the Late Insurrectionary States." *House Report,* no. 22, 42d Cong., 2d sess. (serials 1529 to 1541 inclusive).

3. *Congressional Record,* Senate, 45th Cong., 3d sess., February 17, 18, 1879, vol. 8, pt. 2, pp. 1430, 1510.

4. *Weekly Clarion* (Jackson, Miss.), February 19, 1879, quoting *National Republican.*

5. *St. Louis Globe-Democrat,* February 13, 1879, in a story datelined Bismarck, D. T., February 12.

6. *New York Tribune,* March 18, 1879.

7. *Congressional Record,* 46th Cong., 1st sess., April 22, 1879, vol. 9, pt. 1, p. 661.

8. Burton J. Williams, *Senator John James Ingalls: Kansas' Iridescent Republican* (Lawrence: University Press of Kansas, 1972), p. 48.

9. *Chicago Daily Tribune,* April 25, 1879.

10. *Washington Post,* March 24, 1879; *Memphis Evening Herald,* March 31, 1879.

11. *Weekly Louisianian* (New Orleans), March 22, 1879; *New York Times,* April 7, 1879; Nell Irvin Painter, *Exodusters: Black Migration to Kansas after Reconstruction* (New York: Alfred A. Knopf, 1977), p. 243.

12. *Washington Post,* April 7, 1879.

13. *New York Daily Tribune,* April 11, 1879.

14. *Missouri Republican* (St. Louis), April 17, 1879; *Weekly Clarion* (Jackson, Miss.), April 16, 1879.

15. *Washington Post,* December 18, 1879.

16. *Congressional Record,* 46th Cong., 1st sess., April 21, 1879, vol. 9, pt. 1, p. 260; D. C. Haskell to John P. St. John, April 22, 1879; *Inter-Ocean* (Chicago), April 22, 1879. Haskell's response to St. John, dated April 28, 1879, is found in Lee Ella Blake, "The Great Exodus of 1879 and 1880 to Kansas" (Master's thesis, Kansas State University, Manhattan, 1942), p. 29. See also *Wyandotte* (Kans.) *Gazette,* May 9, 1879.

17. *Congressional Record,* 46th Cong., 1st sess., April 21, 22, 1879, vol. 9, pt. 1, p. 625; *New York Times,* June 23, 1879.

18. Thomas Ryan to St. John, June 20, 1879.

19. *Boston Evening Transcript,* August 4, 1879.

20. *New York Tribune,* April 2, 1879. Scottish-born Phillips came to the United States in 1838 and was admitted to the bar in 1855, after which he practiced law at Lawrence. He was a member of the first Kansas Supreme Court. In 1858 he founded the town of Salina. He entered Congress in 1873.

21. A. Bigman and Leroy Jackson to St. John, May 28, 1882.
22. S. C. Pomeroy to St. John, June 27, 1879. Pomeroy had gone to the Senate in 1860 upon the admittance of Kansas to the Union. He served until March, 1873. Earlier he had been an organizer and financial agent of the New England Emigrant Aid Company. He arrived in Kansas in 1854, living first at Lawrence, then at Atchison, where he was mayor.
23. Testimony of Dr. F. M. Stringfield, Voorhees Committee Report, pt. 3, p. 331.
24. *Missouri Republican* (St. Louis), March 24, April 1, 2, 1879.
25. *St. Louis Globe-Democrat,* March 26, June 27, 1879.
26. *Chicago Daily Tribune,* May 4, 5, 1879; *Missouri Republican* (St. Louis), April 9, 1879, quoting *Tribune*; *St. Louis Globe-Democrat,* June 27, 1879, quoting *Tribune*; *Inter-Ocean* (Chicago), March 13, 1880.
27. *Inter-Ocean* (Chicago), April 2, 1879; *Chicago Daily Tribune,* May 2, 1879.
28. *Cleveland Plain Dealer,* April 16, 22, May 5, July 25, 1879.
29. *Daily Picayune* (New Orleans), August 8, 1879, quoting *Enquirer*.
30. *Boston Daily Globe,* July 18, 1879.
31. *Cincinnati Commercial,* May 7, August 1, 1879.
32. *New York Tribune,* May 8, 1879; *New York Times,* July 12, 1879.
33. *New York Tribune,* October 4, December 11, 1879.
34. *Boston Daily Globe,* April 24, July 10, 1879; *Boston Herald,* quoted by *Weekly Clarion* (Jackson, Miss.), June 25, 1879.
35. *Harper's Weekly,* May 17, 1879; *Nation,* April 10, 1879.
36. *Memphis Weekly Appeal,* April 9, 1879.
37. *New Orleans Bulletin,* July 2, 1874, quoted in Voorhees Committee Report, pt. 2, p. 172.
38. *Daily Picayune* (New Orleans), March 18, April 17, May 8, June 2, August 3, 1879.
39. *Weekly Clarion* (Jackson, Miss.), February 26, April 30, July 2, August 6, December 3, 1879.
40. *People's Vindicator* (Natchitoches, La.), March 22, April 19, 1879; *Fort Worth Democrat,* quoted by *Missouri Republican* (St. Louis), April 22, 1879.
41. Testimony of Thomas W. Conway, Voorhees Committee Report, pt. 3, p. 435; Truett King Grant, "The Negro Exodus, 1879–1880" (Master's thesis, Baylor University, 1952), pp. 71–75; *Missouri Republican* (St. Louis), May 18, 1879.
42. *St. Louis Globe-Democrat,* May 16, 1879; *New York Times,* May 13, 1879.
43. *Missouri Republican* (St. Louis), May 16, 1879.
44. Testimony of Thomas W. Conway, Voorhees Committee Report, pt. 3,

pp. 438–42; *Daily Picayune* (New Orleans), May 26, 28, 1879; *New York Times,* May 20, 1879; Grant, "The Negro Exodus," p. 73.

45. *Cleveland Plain Dealer,* May 26, 1879; *Missouri Republican* (St. Louis), May 30, 1879.

46. Hayes to Uriah Painter of the *New York Times,* quoted in Hans L. Trefousse, *The Radical Republicans* (New York: Alfred A. Knopf, 1969), p. 469.

47. *Diary and Letters of Rutherford Birchard Hayes,* ed. Charles Richard Williams, 5 vols. (Columbus: Ohio State Archaeological and Historical Society, 1924), 3:553–54.

48. *New York Times,* May 24, 1879, quoting the Reverend D. J. East, president of Calabar College, Kingston, Jamaica.

49. *Boston Daily Globe,* June 21, July 31, 1879; Juliana C. Cleaveland to Governor John St. John, August 21, 1880; Testimony of Thomas Conway, Voorhees Committee Report, pt. 3, p. 437.

50. *Missouri Republican* (St. Louis), May 6, 17, 1879.

51. *Cleveland Plain Dealer,* May 12, 20, 1879.

52. *Daily Picayune* (New Orleans), June 8, 14, 1879; *Weekly Clarion* (Jackson, Miss.), July 2, 1879. The Louisiana congressman was quoted by *Bangor* (Maine) *Daily Whig and Courier,* May 30, 1879.

53. Senator Butler, quoted by *Daily Eastern Argus* (Portland, Maine), May 28, 1870; *Weekly Clarion* (Jackson, Miss.), January 28, 1880; Testimony of B. F. Watson, Voorhees Committee Report, pt. 2, p. 341; *Missouri Republican* (St. Louis), July 18, 1879.

54. Jonas, quoted by *New York Times,* April 19, 1879; King to *New York Herald,* as quoted by *Daily Eastern Argus* (Portland, Maine), April 30, 1879; Testimony of W. T. Fleming, Voorhees Committee Report, pt. 3, p. 175.

55. *St. Louis Globe-Democrat,* June 10, 1879; *Daily Picayune* (New Orleans), June 12, 1879.

56. *Missouri Republican* (St. Louis), May 17, 1879.

57. *New York Times,* September 21, 1879; *Bangor* (Maine) *Daily Whig and Courier,* September 22, 1879; *Weekly Clarion* (Jackson, Miss.), October 8, 1879; *Inter-Ocean* (Chicago), October 10, 1879.

58. *Times* (London), November 8, 1879.

59. *Daily Kennebec Journal* (Augusta, Maine), April 26, 1879.

60. Amanda M. Way to Governor St. John, June 30, 1879.

61. *St. Louis Post-Dispatch,* April 8, 1879; S. A. Hackworth to St. John, May 31, 1879.

62. St. John to H. N. Rust, January 16, 1880, quoted by Lee Ella Blake, "The Great Exodus of 1879 and 1880 to Kansas," pp. 73–79.

CHAPTER 9

1. St. John to Horatio N. Rust, January 16, 1880, in Voorhees Committee Report, pt. 3, p. 293; letter of Mrs. Caroline De Greene, of Topeka, January 26, 1880, submitted to Voorhees Committee, April 14, 1880, in Voorhees Committee Report, pt. 3, pp. 292–93; Testimony of G. W. Carey, vice-president of the KFRA, Voorhees Committee Report, pt. 3, pp. 391–93.
2. Testimony of G. W. Carey, Voorhees Committee Report, pt. 3, pp. 406–8.
3. St. John to Horatio N. Rust, January 16, 1880, given in testimony before the Voorhees Committee, April 14, 1880, Voorhees Committee Report, pt. 3, p. 293.
4. These comments are found in the issues of April 3 and 9, 1879.
5. *Daily Nebraska State Journal* (Lincoln), July 11, 15, 16, 20, 1879. See also *Nebraska Herald* (Plattsmouth), July 10, 1879; *Kansas City Daily Times,* July 8, 1879.
6. *Daily Nebraska State Journal* (Lincoln), July 15, 18, 20, 27, 1879; *Nebraska Herald* (Plattsmouth), August 7, 1879; Testimony of B. F. Watson, Voorhees Committee Report, pt. 2, p. 338.
7. *Nebraska Herald* (Plattsmouth), July 17, 24, 1879.
8. Ibid., July 24, 1879.
9. *Omaha Daily Republican,* July 22, August 15, 1879.
10. Ibid., July 23, 1879.
11. *Weekly Louisianian* (New Orleans), July 26, 1879; *Omaha Daily Republican,* September 12, 1879; *Daily Nebraska State Journal* (Lincoln), July 22, 1879.
12. Datelined New York, August 2, 1879, and quoted by *Weekly Clarion* (Jackson, Miss.), August 13, 1879.
13. *Daily Nebraska State Journal* (Lincoln), July 24, 1879.
14. Testimony of A. S. Johnson, Voorhees Committee Report, pt. 3, p. 119.
15. J. M. Snyder to Governor St. John, March 14, 1882.
16. *Colored Citizen* (Topeka), April 19, 1879.
17. *Commonwealth* (Topeka), May 9, 1879.
18. Ibid., April 8, 1880.
19. H. I. Hale to St. John, April 29, 1879.
20. J. D. Lawson to St. John, May 3, 1880.
21. *Daily Rocky Mountain News* (Denver), May 9, 1879.
22. *Commonwealth* (Topeka), May 14, 1879; Frederick W. Pitkin to St. John, May 14, 1879.
23. St. John to Wilmer Walton, July 30, 1879; *Commonwealth* (Topeka), August 5, 1879.
24. Frederick W. Pitkin to St. John, August 16, 1879. For further information about "Aunt" Clara see Kathleen Bruyn, *"Aunt" Clara Brown: Story of a Black Pioneer* (Boulder, Colo.: Pruett Publishing Co., 1970).
25. Testimony of B. F. Watson, Voorhees Committee Report, pt. 2, p. 343.

26. *New York Times,* May 10, 1879.
27. *Commonwealth* (Topeka), August 9, 1879, quoting *Tribune.*
28. *Daily Rocky Mountain News* (Denver), January 10, 1880.
29. Testimony of T. W. Conway, Voorhees Committee Report, pt. 3, pp. 439–40; *Kansas City Daily Journal,* November 17, 1880.
30. George M. Jackson to St. John, January 1, 1881.
31. *Commonwealth* (Topeka), October 31, 1879.
32. *New York Tribune,* November 8, 1879.
33. J. A. [?] Anderson to St. John, December 15, 1879.
34. Letter of Mrs. Comstock, submitted in testimony, April 14, 1880, Voorhees Committee Report, pt. 3, p. 292; Testimony of H. H. Stanton, in ibid., p. 96. Nell Painter, in *Exodusters,* agreed that it is very difficult to determine the number of migrants. She speaks of 6,000 blacks moving from Louisiana, Mississippi, and Texas "in the space of a few months" (p. 184), but also quotes Tandy as saying that 20,000 moved through St. Louis in 1879–80 (p. 184 n).
35. *Commonwealth* (Topeka), January 13, 1880.
36. *New Orleans Times,* January 19, 1880.
37. *Daily Inter-Ocean* (Chicago), February 7, 1880.
38. Testimony of G. W. Carey, Voorhees Committee Report, pt. 3, pp. 391–93.
39. Norman B. Wood, *The White Side of a Black Subject: A Vindication of the Afro-American Race* (Chicago, 1896), p. 275.
40. *Weekly Clarion* (Jackson, Miss.), December 16, 1880.
41. Testimony of A. S. Johnson, Voorhees Committee Report, pt. 3, p. 120.
42. H. N. Rust to St. John, January 20, 1880; St. John to Rust, February 14, 1880; *Daily Inter-Ocean* (Chicago), February 28, 1880.
43. Circular signed by W. O. Lynch, entered in testimony before the Voorhees Committee, April 17, 1880, Voorhees Committee Report, pt. 3, pp. 368–69.
44. Testimony of G. W. Carey, Voorhees Committee Report, pt. 3, pp. 393, 407–8.
45. D. Adams to St. John, February 2, 1880; Lucia E. F. Kimball to St. John, March 16, 1880; and W. O. Lynch to St. John, March 27, 1880; Testimony of B. F. Watson, Voorhees Committee Report, pt. 2, p. 343.
46. Elizabeth Comstock to W. P. Nixon, February 20, 1880; *Daily Inter-Ocean* (Chicago), February 28, 1880.
47. Elizabeth Comstock to St. John, March 8, 1880.
48. Elizabeth Comstock to William Penn Nixon (n.d.), entered into testimony before the Voorhees Committee, April 17, 1880, in Voorhees Committee Report, pt. 3, pp. 376–78; Elizabeth Comstock to St. John, March 13, 1880.
49. *Daily Inter-Ocean* (Chicago), March 16, 1880.
50. Quoted in *Daily Capital* (Topeka), March 13, 1880.
51. Testimony of A. S. Johnson, Voorhees Committee Report, pt. 3, p. 119.

CHAPTER 10

1. Quoted by Norman B. Wood, *The White Side of a Black Subject: A*

Vindication of the Afro-American Race (Chicago, 1896; reprinted by the Negro Universities Press, New York, 1969), p. 285. The song was written by Thomas P. Westendorf.

2. *Wa-Keeney* (Kans.) *Weekly World,* September 3, 1881.

3. *Kansas City Daily Times,* July 23, 27, 1879; *Evening Standard* (Lawrence, Kans.), May 2, 10, 1879.

4. Testimony of John H. Johnson, Voorhees Committee Report, pt. 2, p. 293, and Testimony of Philip Brookings, ibid., pt. 3, p. 110. Roseman's account is found in *Missouri Republican* (St. Louis), July 6, 1879.

5. Daniel Votaw to Laura Haviland, March 7, 1880, quoted in *Daily Inter-Ocean* (Chicago), March 15, 1880; also submitted in testimony to the Voorhees Committee, April 14, 1880, Voorhees Committee Report, pt. 3, p. 292.

6. Testimony of H. H. Stanton, Voorhees Committee Report, pt. 3, p. 99; Testimony of A. S. Johnson, ibid., p. 125.

7. Testimony of H. C. Solomon, Voorhees Committee Report, pt. 3, p. 25.

8. Quoted in *Weekly Clarion* (Jackson, Miss.), November 25, 1880.

9. W. S. Brett to St. John, February 10, 1880.

10. Topeka citizen to Brooklyn *Eagle,* quoted in *Kansas City Daily Times,* July 9, 1879.

11. Anne E. Bingham, "Sixteen Years on a Kansas Farm, 1870–1886," *Collections of the Kansas State Historical Society, 1919–1922,* vol. 15, p. 520.

12. Roy Garvin, "Benjamin, or 'Pap,' Singleton and His Followers," *Journal of Negro History,* vol. 33, no. 1 (January, 1948), p. 13; Lee Ella Blake, "The Great Exodus of 1879 and 1880 to Kansas" (Master's thesis, Kansas State University, Manhattan, 1942), p. 49.

13. *Colored Citizen* (Topeka), July 26, 1879.

14. From the Reverend William H. Yeocum's lecture "The Exodus Movement" (1879), quoted in Robert Lee Chartrand, "The Negro Exodus from the Southern States to Kansas: 1869–1886" (Master's thesis, University of Kansas City [now University of Missouri at Kansas City], 1949), p. 46.

15. *Omaha Daily Bee,* April 3, 1879.

16. Testimony of H. C. Park, Voorhees Committee Report, pt. 3, p. 22.

17. Testimony of H. C. Solomon, ibid., p. 23.

18. *Graham County Lever* (Gettysburg, Kans.), January 30, 1880.

19. *Ford County Globe* (Dodge City, Kans.), May 13, 20, 1879.

20. *Hays City* (Kans.) *Sentinel,* May 2, 1879.

21. *Saline County Journal* (Salina, Kans.), April 17, 1879; *Salina* (Kans.) *Herald,* July 5, August 2, 1879; *Hays City* (Kans.) *Sentinel,* August 1, 1879.

22. *Ellsworth* (Kans.) *Reporter,* April 24, May 8, 1879.

23. *Colored Citizen* (Topeka), March 22, 29, April 5, 12, 19, May 3, June 28, July 12, 1879.

24. Testimony of W. M. Twine, Voorhees Committee Report, pt. 3, pp. 318–25.

25. Glen Schwendemann, "Nicodemus: Negro Haven on the Solomon," *Kansas Historical Quarterly,* vol. 34, no. 1 (Spring, 1968), p. 17.
26. H. C. Moseley to St. John, May 1, 1880.
27. E. McCabe to St. John, February 26, 1880.
28. *Graham County Lever* (Gettysburg, Kans.), March 26, 1880. John Milton Brown, who was black, testified that most of those coming from Kentucky brought with them some means of temporary support. Testimony of John Milton Brown, Voorhees Committee Report, pt. 2, p. 359.
29. Testimony of John Davis, Voorhees Committee Report, pt. 3, pp. 224–33.
30. Vincent Victor Masterson, *The Katy Railroad and the Last Frontier* (Norman: University of Oklahoma Press, 1952), contains a good deal of information about Parsons. In 1875 Kansas required corporations operating in that state to maintain general offices there, and the Katy responded by locating its main office at Parsons (p. 216).
31. Ibid., p. 90; *St. Louis Post-Dispatch,* February 22, 1879.
32. Testimony of Dr. C. Rockhold, Voorhees Committee Report, pt. 3, pp. 310–11; Lawrence D. Rice, *The Negro in Texas: 1874–1900* (Baton Rouge: Louisiana State University Press, 1971), p. 202; *Emporia* (Kans.) *Ledger,* December 11, 1879. See also Alwyn Barr, *Black Texans: A History of Negroes in Texas, 1528–1971* (Austin, Tex: Jenkins Publishing Co., 1973), p. 96.
33. *Sun* (Parsons, Kans.), December 6, 1879; John P. St. John to L. S. Childs of Chetopa, Kans., January 9, 1880. See Laura Haviland's comments, quoted in *Daily Inter-Ocean* (Chicago), January 2, 1880.
34. *Sun* (Parsons, Kans.), December 6, 13, 27, 1879.
35. For general comments about "many" coming, see, for example, *Emporia* (Kans.) *Ledger,* January 22, 1880, and *Junction City* (Kans.) *Union,* February 3, 1880. See also *Weekly Clarion* (Jackson, Miss.), February 11, 1880, with a story datelined Parsons, Kans., February 3. Rice, *The Negro in Texas,* p. 203, provides the 1,000–1,300 per week figure. For the lower figure see Testimony of Angell Mathewson, Voorhees Committee Report, pt. 3, p. 431. Both Lamb and Rockhold gave their figures in testimony before the Voorhees Committee. See pt. 3, pp. 267–73, 310.
36. Frank D. Vaughan, of Millican, Tex., to St. John, July 19, 1879, and N. A. Jackson, of Mt. Vernon, Tex., to St. John, July 2, 1882.
37. *Indianapolis News,* February 17, 1880; St. John to S. A. Hackworth, of Brenham, Tex., June 13, 1879.
38. Testimony of M. W. Reynolds, Voorhees Committee Report, pt. 3, pp. 304–5.
39. Testimony of C. Rockhold, Voorhees Committee Report, pt. 3, p. 312; the Reverend Henry Smith to St. John, May 17, 1879.
40. Testimony of J. B. Lamb and M. W. Reynolds, Voorhees Committee Report, pt. 3, pp. 273–75, 300. See also *Emporia* (Kans.) *Ledger,* January 15, 1880.

41. Stillwell H. Russell to St. John, March 11, 15, 1880, and A. W. Brooks to St. John, March 18, 1880.

42. For one example of stories in Kansas newspapers about renewed migration see *Saline County Journal* (Salina), January 15, 1880; letter of M. W. Reynolds to William Penn Nixon, February 21, 1880; *Daily Inter-Ocean* (Chicago), February 28, 1880.

43. *Commonwealth* (Topeka), March 12, 1880.

44. Wilmer Walton to St. John, April 27, 1880.

45. Gloss Floyd to St. John, from Parsons, Kans., March 22, 1880.

46. *Emporia* (Kans.) *Ledger,* February 5, 1880; Testimony of C. Rockhold, Voorhees Committee Report, pt. 3, pp. 312, 313.

47. *Junction City* (Kans.) *Union,* May 1, 1880; Testimony of John Davis, Voorhees Committee Report, pt. 3, p. 231.

48. *Weekly Clarion* (Jackson, Miss.), June 2, 1880, quoting a letter from Manhattan, Kans.. dated May 22.

49. Blake, "The Great Exodus of 1879 and 1880 to Kansas," p. 44.

50. *Colored Citizen* (Topeka), May 31, July 26, 1879; *Times* (Baxter Springs, Kans.), April 10, 1879, quoting *Colored Citizen*.

51. Testimony of B. J. Waters (a Fort Scott attorney), Voorhees Committee Report, pt. 3, p. 2; Testimony of H. C. Solomon, ibid, pp. 27–28; Testimony of A. S. Johnson, ibid., p. 125; letter of a tourist from Mississippi, written from Manhattan, Kans., May 22, 1880, in *Weekly Clarion* (Jackson, Miss.), June 2, 1880.

52. *New Orleans Times,* January 25, 1880, quoting a dispatch in *Kansas City Daily Times; Kansas City Daily Times,* July 9, 1879, quoting a dispatch to the Brooklyn *Eagle.*

53. The federal official was First Assistant Postmaster General Tyner. His comments were carried in *Cincinnati Commercial,* August 3, 1879. For comments about the possible resurgence of blacks to the North, see *Saline County Journal* (Salina, Kans.), December 25, 1879; *Emporia* (Kans.) *Ledger,* December 4, 11, 1879, and March 11, 25, 1880.

54. *Weekly Clarion* (Jackson, Miss.), January 7, February 4, 1880, given in testimony before Voorhees Committee, April 14, 1880, Voorhees Committee Report, pt. 3, p. 293.

55. *Galveston Weekly News,* September 18, 1879; *Emporia* (Kans.) *Ledger,* December 18, 1879, and March 18, 1880; R. F. Beavers to Governor St. John, February 16, 1880.

56. Elizabeth Comstock to St. John, June 9, 1880.

57. Mrs. William Claflin to St. John, November 13, 1880. The post-card sender was Philena Lawrence, who wrote on August 9, 1880.

58. *Commonwealth* (Topeka), April 15, 1880.

CHAPTER 11

1. Testimony of Dr. J. B. Lamb, Voorhees Committee Report, pt. 3, pp. 267–76.

2. Testimony of Milton W. Reynolds, ibid., p. 300.
3. *Kansas City Daily Times,* July 24, 1879.
4. *Missouri Republican* (St. Louis), March 28, 1879.
5. *Kansas City Daily Times,* July 9, 13, 1879.
6. St. John to Laura Haviland, August 18, 1879; *Daily Inter-Ocean* (Chicago), August 18, 1879; *Omaha Daily Republican,* May 29, August 27, 1879.
7. *Times* (Baxter Springs, Kans.), June 5, 12, 1879.
8. *Weekly Clarion* (Jackson, Miss.), September 8, 1880.
9. John L. Waller to St. John, September 3, 1880, from Lawrence, Kans.
10. John M. Watson to St. John, September 6, 1880.
11. D. Shelton to St. John, April 21, 1879.
12. *Daily Kennebec Journal* (Augusta, Maine), April 8, 1879; *Lewiston* (Maine) *Evening Journal,* April 3, 1879; *Daily Eastern Argus* (Portland, Maine), April 15, 1879.
13. *Daily Eastern Argus* (Portland, Maine), April 12, 1879.
14. *Missouri Republican* (St. Louis), April 10, May 2, July 8, 1879; *Evening Standard* (Lawrence, Kans.), May 15, 1879.
15. *New York Times,* April 24, 1879; *Frank Leslie's Illustrated Newspaper,* April 26, 1879.
16. *Chicago Daily Tribune,* March 20, 29, April 21, 1879; *St. Louis Globe-Democrat,* March 24, 1879.
17. *Weekly Clarion* (Jackson, Miss.), April 30, 1879.
18. *Missouri Republican* (St. Louis), June 2, 1879.
19. Ibid., May 21, 1879; *Weekly Clarion* (Jackson, Miss.), June 4, 1879.
20. Singleton's statement is found in Leland George Smith, "The Early Negroes in Kansas" (Master's thesis, University of Wichita, 1932), p. 67. See also Testimony of William Murrell, Voorhees Committee Report, pt. 2, pp. 527–28; Testimony of John H. Johnson, ibid., p. 292; Testimony of B. F. Watson, ibid., p. 341; *Inter-Ocean* (Chicago), May 16, 1879.
21. *Washington Post,* April 17, 1879.
22. *Chicago Daily Tribune,* April 14, 1879; *Daily Kennebec Journal* (Augusta, Maine), April 7, 1879; *Kansas Farmer* (Topeka), April 23, 1879.
23. *Daily Journal* (Lawrence, Kans.), October 8, 1879.
24. Resolution of Senator Voorhees, December 15, 1879, *Senate Miscellaneous Documents,* no. 15, pt. 1, 46th Cong., 2d sess. (serial 1890), p. [1].
25. Amendment of Senator Windom to a resolution submitted by Senator Voorhees, *Senate Miscellaneous Documents,* no. 15, pt. 2, 46th Cong., 2d sess. (serial 1890), p. [1]; *Congressional Record,* Senate, December, 1879, 46th Cong., 2d sess., p. 124.
26. *Congressional Record,* Senate, December, 1879, 46th Cong., 2d sess., p. 156.
27. Voorhees Committee Report, pt. 1, pp. iii–viii.
28. Augusta, Ga., *Chronicle,* quoted by *Indianapolis News,* December 27, 1879.
29. *Sun* (Parsons, Kans.), quoted in *Indianapolis News,* December 27, 1879; *Indianapolis News,* December 10, 1879.

30. *Daily Inter-Ocean* (Chicago), February 25, 28, March 11, 1880.
31. *Commonwealth* (Topeka), April 23, 1880. See also the issue for December 30 for another reference to the Voorhees Committee.
32. *Atchison* (Kans.) *Daily Patriot,* February 27, 1880; *Washington Post,* January 31, 1880.
33. F. T. Ingalls to St. John, February 6, 1880.
34. William Windom to St. John, February 26, March 22, 1880.
35. C. Rockhold to John P. St. John, April 30, 1880.
36. Voorhees Committee Report, pt. 1, pp. iii–ix. Nell Painter, in *Exodusters,* decided that the Republican committee members were "accurate" in their findings while the Democrats were "wrong-headed" (p. 254).
37. Testimony of M. D. Manson, Voorhees Committee Report, pt. 1, p. 337. Manson was the Indiana state auditor.
38. Story datelined Shelbyville, Ind., December 13, 1879, in *Cincinnati Commercial,* December 14. See also *New York Tribune,* December 14, 1879. Leonard J. Hackney, a Shelbyville attorney, also described the arrival of the first black contingent, as well as the city council's response. Testimony of Leonard J. Hackney, Voorhees Committee Report, pt. 1, p. 265.
39. *Shelby Democrat* (Shelbyville, Ind.), December 4, 1879.
40. Testimony of O. S. B. Wall, Voorhees Committee Report, pt. 1, pp. 20–26, 32–38, 42.
41. *Inter-Ocean* (Chicago), December 8, 1879.
42. *Shelby Democrat* (Shelbyville, Ind.), January 1, February 19, 1880.
43. Testimony of Samuel L. Perry, Voorhees Committee Report, pt. 1, pp. 280–83.
44. Ibid., pp. 296–97.
45. Testimony of J. W. Dodd, Voorhees Committee Report, pt. 1, p. 385. Dew made his deposition before Dodd, a former auditor for the state of Indiana, who in turn testified before the Voorhees Committee.
46. Testimony of John P. Dukehart, ibid., p. 76. See also *Philadelphia Record,* January 31, 1880.
47. Testimony of Mingo Simmons, Voorhees Committee Report, pt. 1, pp. 371–74.
48. Testimony of John P. Dukehart, ibid., pp. 71–72.
49. *Shelby Democrat* (Shelbyville, Ind.), January 8, 15, 22, 1880.
50. Ibid., February 5, 1880.
51. Testimony of L. C. Morris, Voorhees Committee Report, pt. 1, p. 348; Testimony of J. P. Dukehart, ibid., p. 73; *Indianapolis Journal,* February 12, 1880.
52. Testimony of Thomas P. Mills, Voorhees Committee Report, pt. 1, p. 205; *Shelby Democrat* (Shelbyville, Ind.), February 26, 1880.
53. Rust to Nixon, February 27, 1880; *Daily Inter-Ocean* (Chicago), February 28, 1880.
54. Testimony of J. H. Russell, Voorhees Committee Report, pt. 1, p. 318.
55. Testimony of C. S. Wooten, ibid., pp. 220–22.

56. Testimony of J. W. Cromwell (who told of Walker's efforts) and of A. B. Carleton, both in ibid., pp. 12–20. The testimony of James W. Sparks is found in pt. 2, p. 288, of the Voorhees Committee Report.

57. Testimony of J. W. Cromwell, ibid., pt. 1, p. 10.

58. Testimony of Leonard J. Hackney, ibid., p. 270; *Junction City* (Kans.) *Union,* February 9, 1880.

59. *Greencastle* (Ind.) *Banner,* September 25, 1879, as quoted in the Voorhees Committee Report, pt. 1, p. 167. Testimony of M. D. Manson, ibid., p. 338.

60. Testimony of Thomas W. Conway, ibid., pt. 3, pp. 443–47.

61. Testimony of Charles N. Otey, ibid., pt. 1, pp. 101–3; see also testimony of James O'Hara, ibid., p. 70.

62. Testimony presented to the Voorhees Committee, ibid., pp. 332–33.

63. Testimony of Scott Ray, ibid., pp. 321–23.

64. *Shelby Democrat* (Shelbyville, Ind.), April 1, 1880.

65. Ibid., September 16, October 21, 28, November 11, 1880.

66. James A. Garfield to Chester Arthur, August 30, 1880, Garfield Letter-books, Division of Manuscripts, Library of Congress, Washington, D.C.

67. H. H. Chalmer, "The Effects of Negro Suffrage," *North American Review* 132 (March 1881): 239–48; *Shelby Democrat* (Shelbyville, Ind.), November 11, 1880.

68. St. John to Horatio Rust, October 4, 1880, Horatio N. Rust Scrapbook, KSHS.

69. Mrs. Comstock's remarks are found in *Commonwealth* (Topeka), June 6, 1880. For St. John's comments on the outcome of the election see *Commonwealth,* December 23, 1880.

CHAPTER 12

1. Booker T. Washington, *A New Negro for a New Century* (Chicago: American Publishing House, 1900), p. 290.

2. The comments of Henry Adams are found in his testimony before the Voorhees Committee. See Voorhees Committee Report, pt. 2, pp. 101–18, 154, 198. Also, *New Orleans Times,* April 22, 1879. Alexander's comments are found in T. R. Alexander to St. John, July 27, 1879.

3. *St. Louis Globe-Democrat,* April 21, 1879; *Frank Leslie's Illustrated Newspaper,* May 17, 1879.

4. *St. Louis Globe-Democrat,* April 21, May 2, 1879.

5. Unidentified newspaper clipping of November 18, 1880, in Singleton Scrapbook, KSHS.

6. *St. Louis Globe-Democrat,* April 16, 21, May 2, 1879. See also Walter L. Fleming, " 'Pap' Singleton, the Moses of the Colored Exodus," *American Journal of Sociology* 15 (July, 1909): 61–82.

7. Testimony of John Henri Burch, Voorhees Committee Report, pt. 2, pp. 218–45.

8. Testimony of George Ruby, ibid., pp. 37–39, 51, 63; *Daily Picayune* (New Orleans), May 23, 1879.
9. *Lewiston* (Maine) *Evening Journal,* April 16, 21, 1879.
10. *New York Tribune,* April 2, 1879; *Times* (London), April 17, 1879.
11. *Colored Citizen* (Topeka), March 15, 1879.
12. *Missouri Republican* (St. Louis), May 17, 1879.
13. W. M. Milner et al. to St. John, July 29, 1882, and A. M. Allen to St. John, August 12, 1882.
14. Testimony of John H. Johnson, Voorhees Committee Report, pt. 2, pp. 290, 294.
15. "The Exodus," in John Mercer Langston, *Freedom and Citizenship: Selected Lectures and Addresses* (Washington, D.C.: Rufus H. Darby, 1883; reprinted in 1969 by Mnemosyne Publishing Co., Inc., Miami, Fla.), pp. 232–58.
16. From two unidentified and undated newspaper clippings in Benjamin Singleton Scrapbook, KSHS.
17. *Daily Memphis Avalanche,* May 8, 1879; *Daily Picayune* (New Orleans), May 14, 1879.
18. Frederick Douglass, "The Negro Exodus from the Gulf States," *Journal of Social Science* 11 (May, 1880): 1–21. See also an interview with Douglass in *Frank Leslie's Illustrated Newspaper,* December 13, 1879.
19. *Washington Post,* September 19, 1879; *Cleveland Plain Dealer,* May 14, 1879; *Daily Eastern Argus* (Portland, Maine), May 7, 1879; *Missouri Republican* (St. Louis), April 30, May 16, 1879; *Daily Picayune* (New Orleans), September 19, 1879; *Memphis Weekly Appeal,* May 7, 1879; *Daily Memphis Avalanche,* February 21, 1879. See also *Vicksburg* (Miss.) *Commercial Daily Advertiser,* May 7, 1879.
20. *Colored Citizen* (Topeka), April 21, May 24, 31, 1879. For the "personal exodus" remark see *Bangor* (Maine) *Daily Whig and Courier,* May 6, 1879.
21. *Daily Picayune* (New Orleans), April 24, 25, June 10, December 9, 1879; *New Orleans Weekly Democrat,* March 15, 1879; James Haskins, *Pinckney Benton Stewart Pinchback: A Biography* (New York: Macmillan Publishing Co., 1973), p. 244.
22. *Memphis Daily Avalanche,* April 29, 1879; Nell Irvin Painter, *Exodusters: Black Migration to Kansas after Reconstruction* (New York: Alfred A. Knopf, 1977), p. 243.
23. *New Orleans Times,* April 6, 1879; *Missouri Republican* (St. Louis), April 20, 1879; Lee Ella Blake, "The Great Exodus of 1879 and 1880 to Kansas" (Master's thesis, Kansas State University, Manhattan, 1942), pp. 10, 11.
24. Testimony of James O'Hara, Voorhees Committee Report, pt. 1, pp. 52–69, and of Samuel Perry, ibid., p. 302.
25. Testimony of Isaiah Wears, ibid., pt. 3, pp. 151–60; *Cleveland Plain Dealer,* October 30, 1879.
26. *Colored Citizen* (Topeka), September 6, 1879; Testimony of B. F. Watson,

Voorhees Committee Report, pt. 2, p. 339; Malinda Harris to Mary Peercern, April 6, 1879, in *Weekly Clarion* (Jackson, Miss.), April 30, 1879.

27. *Chicago Daily Tribune,* May 9, 1879.
28. Fleming, " 'Pap' Singleton, the Moses of the Colored Exodus," p. 72.
29. Testimony of John Milton Brown, Voorhees Committee Report, pt. 2, p. 361; Blake, "The Great Exodus," p. 81.
30. *St. Louis Globe-Democrat,* April 9, 1879. Although the *Globe* was Republican, its readership and advertisers frequently had strong commercial connections with down-river firms, and generally speaking, the newspaper did not take a Radical Republican view of the exodus. By April 9, its earlier stand (for example, see issue of March 24) had been softened, possibly by pressure from St. Louis business interests.

CHAPTER 13

1. Wilmer Walton to St. John, November 22, 1880.
2. Quoted in *Topeka Daily Blade,* May 17, 1879.
3. *New Orleans Democrat,* May 28, June 8, 1879; *Weekly Clarion* (Jackson, Miss.), July 2, 1879; *Louisiana Capitolian* (Baton Rouge), January 10, 1880.
4. *St. Louis Globe-Democrat,* March 21, 1879.
5. Letter of April 11, 1879, by Thomas Sturges, in *Missouri Republican* (St. Louis), April 15, 1879.
6. *Daily Picayune* (New Orleans), May 18, 1879.
7. *Chicago Daily Tribune,* May 2, 28, 1879.
8. *Cincinnati Commercial,* June 1, 1879; Testimony of E. B. Borden, Voorhees Committee Report, pt. 1, p. 215.
9. Pork prices and rent figures were given in *St. Louis Globe-Democrat* for April 18, 1879, and were denied in *Weekly Clarion* (Jackson, Miss.), April 30, 1879. Complaints about the "store order" system are found in the Testimony of J. W. Cromwell, Voorhees Committee Report, pt. 1, p. 16; see *St. Louis Globe-Democrat* of November 21, 1879, for its quotation of *New York Tribune*'s opinion. *Chicago Daily Tribune,* May 2, 1879, also talked about high prices charged Negro sharecroppers.
10. *New Orleans Times,* December 10, 1879.
11. *St. Louis Post-Dispatch,* April 29, 1879.
12. Testimony of W. J. Buchan, Voorhees Committee Report, pt. 3, p. 481.
13. *Boston Daily Globe,* April 18, 1879, quoting *Appeal.*
14. *Kansas City Star,* July 11, 1912.
15. *New York Times,* April 9, 1879.
16. Testimony of A. A. Harris, Voorhees Committee Report, pt. 2, p. 422.
17. S. A. Hackworth to St. John, July 31, 1879.
18. Deposition of James Brown, entered in testimony, Voorhees Committee Report, pt. 3, p. 49.
19. The flag story is related in *Weekly Clarion* (Jackson, Miss.), July 2, 1879;

see also *Weekly Advocate* (Baton Rouge), May 2, 1879. Related stories appeared in *Washington Post,* June 23, 1879, and *Missouri Republican* (St. Louis), March 22, 1879.

20. *Weekly Clarion* (Jackson, Miss.), May 14, 1879.
21. *St. Louis Globe-Democrat,* March 21, 1879.
22. *Daily Picayune* (New Orleans), March 24, 1879.
23. Testimony of Julius Bonitz, Voorhees Committee Report, pt. 1, pp. 133–34; Testimony of Lewis H. Fisher, ibid., p. 311.
24. C. W. Porter to St. John, June 23, 1879; J. M. McCurd to St. John, July 23, 1879; C. P. Hicks to St. John, July 30, 1879.
25. Testimony of A. A. Harris, Voorhees Committee Report, pt. 2, p. 425; Testimony of J. W. Cromwell, ibid., pt. 1, p. 7; *Graham County Lever* (Gettysburg, Kans.), February 27, 1880.
26. *Chicago Daily Tribune,* May 1, 1879.
27. A New Orleans dispatch in *Democratic Daily Eastern Argus* (Portland, Maine), April 2, 1879.
28. R. T. Greener, "The Emigration of Colored Citizens from the Southern States," *Journal of Social Science* 11 (May, 1880): 22–32; *Chicago Daily Tribune,* April 9, 1879.
29. For example, see John G. Van Deusen, "The Exodus of 1879," *Journal of Negro History,* vol. 21, no. 2 (April, 1936), pp. 111–29; Truett King Grant, "The Negro Exodus of 1879–1880" (Master's thesis, Baylor University, 1952); Rayford W. Logan and Irving S. Cohen, *The American Negro: Old World Background and New World Experience* (Boston, 1967), p. 142. See also Henderson H. Donald, "The Negro Migration of 1916–1918," *Journal of Negro History,* vol. 6, no. 4 (October, 1921), pp. 394–95, where the author refers back to the movement of 1879. Arvarh E. Strickland, in his article "Toward the Promised Land: The Exodus to Kansas and Afterward," *Missouri Historical Review,* vol. 69, no. 4 (July, 1975), pp. 376–412, laments the fact that writers and scholars "have not been able to move beyond a rather narrow economic interpretation" of the exodus (p. 377), and he goes on, not very convincingly, to show the importance of social causes. Nell Painter, in *Exodusters,* leans heavily upon political persecution as a cause.
30. *Chicago Daily Tribune,* May 23, 1879; *Appleton's Annual Cyclopedia, 1879,* p. 634. For more recent support of the view see Vernon L. Wharton, *The Negro in Mississippi, 1865–1890* (Chapel Hill: University of North Carolina Press, 1947), p. 116.
31. Testimony of Julius Bonitz, Voorhees Committee Report, pt. 1, p. 141. The notice is from the *Sentinel* (Summit, Miss.), for February 6, 1878. Entered in the Testimony of R. B. Avery, Voorhees Committee Report, pt. 2, p. 270.
32. Morgan Dewey Peoples, "Negro Migration from the Lower Mississippi Valley to Kansas, 1879–1880" (Master's thesis, Louisiana State University, 1950), p. v.

CHAPTER 14

1. Horatio N. Rust to St. John, February 12, 1880; *Commonwealth* (Topeka), April 1, 1880; *Chicago Tribune,* December 11, 1880; *New York Tribune,* December 8, 1880.
2. Horatio N. Rust Scrapbook, p. 81, KSHS; see also *Commonwealth* (Topeka), March 31, 1880.
3. *Commonwealth* (Topeka), June 19, 1880.
4. Quoted in *Shelby Democrat* (Shelbyville, Ind.), March 11, 1880.
5. A Kansas preacher named G. W. Benning later claimed that as many as 100,000 had entered the state, a figure that was hotly denied by the *Burlingame* (Kans.) *Chronicle* in its April 18, 1881, issue. For late 1879 and 1880 estimates see John P. St. John to Horatio N. Rust, January 16, 1880, Horatio N. Rust Scrapbook, KSHS; *Commonwealth* (Topeka), March 18, 23, 1880; a quotation from *Inter-Ocean* (Chicago), in Laura Haviland, *A Woman's Life-Work: Labors and Experiences of Laura S. Haviland* (Cincinnati, Ohio, 1881), p. 486. Carter G. Woodson, in his book *A Century of Negro Migration* (Washington, D.C., 1918), erroneously stated that by April, 1879, some 60,000 had arrived in Kansas. Almost certainly no such number came, even during the entire movement.
6. For comments about Mrs. Comstock's figure of 50,000 see *Shelby Democrat* (Shelbyville, Ind.), November 25, 1880. St. John's claim of 40,000 is found in the *Chicago Tribune,* December 11, 1880. The Kansan living in New York City was George A. Crawford. See George A. Crawford to St. John, November 11, 1880.
7. Daniel Votaw to St. John, November 25, 1880, and Wilmer Walton to St. John, November 22, 1880.
8. Votaw to St. John, November 25, 1880, and Elizabeth Comstock to St. John, November 20, 1880; *Commonwealth* (Topeka), April 14, 1880.
9. Testimony of John Milton Brown, Voorhees Committee Report, pt. 2, p. 360, and of B. F. Watson, ibid., p. 345. See Haviland's printed brochure in vol. 1, Negro Clippings, Manuscript Division, KSHS.
10. *Topeka Weekly Times,* May 13, 1881, quoting *Advertiser.* See also the issue of February 11, 1881, for a similar charge.
11. E. L. Comstock to H. N. Rust, from Rollin, Michigan, May 11, 1881, H. N. Rust Scrapbook, KSHS; Elizabeth Comstock to St. John, May 13, 1881. See also *Topeka Daily Times,* March 11, 1881, and *Topeka Daily Capital,* March 9, 1881.
12. H. N. Rust to St. John, December 10, 1880, and Wilmer Walton to St. John, February 7, 1881.
13. Elizabeth Comstock to St. John, July 25, 1880. For the closing of KFRA at Topeka see Lee Ella Blake, "The Great Exodus of 1879 and 1880 to Kansas" (Master's thesis, Kansas State University, Manhattan, 1942), p. 59; and Nell Blythe Waldron, "Colonization in Kansas from 1861 to 1890" (Ph.D. dissertation, Northwestern University, 1932), p. 130.

14. Elizabeth Comstock to St. John, April 11, 1881; letter of March 26, 1881, addressed to *Capital,* in *Topeka Daily Capital,* April 5, 1881. *Topeka Daily Times,* April 8 issue, expressed sorrow that the KFRA was leaving. Comments about Mrs. Comstock continuing her work independently are found in H. N. Rust to St. John, June 24, 1881. See also Norman B. Wood, *The White Side of a Black Subject: A Vindication of the Afro-American Race* (Chicago, 1896; New York, 1969), p. 276 of 1969 edition.
15. *Independence Kansan,* August 3, 1881; W. S. Newlin to St. John, February 26, March 11, 1881.
16. Albion W. Tourgee to St. John, July 29, 1881.
17. *Commonwealth* (Topeka), March 23, 1881.
18. *Kansas City Journal,* April 14, 1881.
19. Laura Haviland to St. John, from Columbus, Kansas, September 7, 1881.
20. *Commonwealth* (Topeka), May 14, 1881.
21. *Columbus* (Kans.) *Courier,* n.d., found in vols. 5–6 of Negro Clippings, KSHS. The story refers to a June 30, 1881, report by Laura Haviland.
22. S. W. Winn to St. John, June 2, 1881, and Elizabeth Comstock to St. John, June 4, 1881, and September 11, 1882.
23. James B. Chase to St. John, September 2, 1881, and F. C. Stanley to St. John. See also Elizabeth Comstock to St. John, September 20, 1881.
24. Wilmer Walton to St. John, February 20, 1882.
25. *Topeka Daily Capital,* June 15, 1881; Elizabeth Comstock to St. John, June 16, 1881, from Portland, Maine.
26. Daniel Votaw to St. John, June 10, November 28, 1881, and May 5, 21, 1882. Winn's letter is lated June 7, 1881. For complaints about cheating at the institute see also *South Kansas Tribune* (Independence), June 1, 1881.
27. *Commonwealth* (Topeka), February 20, April 3, 1880. See also Mary E. Griffith to St. John, April 20, 1880. Mrs. Griffith listed herself as superintendent of the Topeka office of the Freedmen's Educational Society.
28. *Topeka Weekly Times,* May 27, 1881. For more about Fairfax, a former slave who rose to prominence in Louisiana before migrating to Kansas, see Nell Irvin Painter, *Exodusters: Black Migration to Kansas after Reconstruction* (New York: Alfred A. Knopf, 1977), pp. 134, 163 n, and 163–70.
29. Wilmer Walton to St. John, October 6, 1882.
30. Daniel Votaw to St. John, April 19, May 21, 1882.
31. W. T. Yoe to St. John, September 11, 1882.
32. E. D. Bullen to St. John, May 5, 1882.
33. Wilmer Walton to St. John, February 20, 1882.
34. *Kansas State Journal* (Topeka), September 23, 1881.
35. E. R. Gillett to St. John, March 28, 1882.
36. G. S. Bascom to St. John, March 2, 1881. For St. John's denial that blacks were starving see *Topeka Daily Capital,* September 23, 1882, quoting *St. Louis Republican.* See also *Commonwealth* (Topeka), August 22, 1882, for comments about the destitute in Kansas.

37. *Commonwealth* (Topeka), August 3, 1883, referred to the Emporia meeting; see also *Topeka Daily Capital,* August 5, 1883.
38. *Commonwealth* (Topeka), September 7, 1883.
39. *Topeka Daily Capital,* August 14, 1890.

EPILOGUE

1. Testimony of John Milton Brown, Voorhees Committee Report, pt. 2, p. 364.
2. *Lewiston* (Maine) *Evening Journal,* May 7, 1879; *St. Louis Post-Dispatch,* May 6, 1879; *New York Times,* May 7, 1879; *Washington Post,* May 8, 1879; *Chicago Daily Tribune,* May 7, 23, 1879; *Wyandotte* (Kans.) *Gazette,* May 16, 1879. The long quotation comes from *Daily Picayune* (New Orleans), May 16, 1879.
3. *St. Louis Globe-Democrat,* June 28, 1879.
4. Testimony of John Milton Brown, Voorhees Committee Report, pt. 2, p. 364.
5. Testimony of A. S. Johnson, Voorhees Committee Report, pt. 3, p. 126.
6. Lawrence D. Rice, *The Negro in Texas: 1874–1900* (Baton Rouge: Louisiana State University Press, 1971), pp. 203–4.
7. Morgan Dewey Peoples, "Negro Migration from the Lower Mississippi Valley to Kansas, 1879–1880" (Master's thesis, Louisiana State University, 1950), p. 81, quoting *New Orleans Picayune,* August 20, 1879.
8. Testimony of W. J. Buchan, Voorhees Committee Report, pt. 3, pp. 483–84.
9. Roy Garvin, "Benjamin, or 'Pap,' Singleton and His Followers," *Journal of Negro History* 33 (January, 1948): 22.
10. *Topeka Capital,* March 18, 1891.
11. *Mail and Breeze* (Topeka), February 2, 1900; Booker Washington, "A Negro Potato King," *Outlook* 77 (May, 1904): 115–18. See also *Kansas City Star,* May 28, 1909, for mention of Groves's town property.
12. Norman B. Wood, *The White Side of a Black Subject: A Vindication of the Afro-American Race* (Chicago, 1896; reprinted in 1969 by Negro Universities Press, New York), p. 275.
13. *Mail and Breeze* (Topeka), February 2, 1900.
14. *Topeka Daily Capital,* May 2, 1889.

BIBLIOGRAPHY

The principal federal document dealing with the black exodus of 1879 is the Voorhees Committee Report of 1880, a three-part work (see Public Documents) that details the extensive testimony taken from both blacks and whites who were immediately concerned with the movement. Although it was much maligned at the time as a partisan effort and later by scholars who tended to question its credibility for the same reason, it contains a great deal of useful information if one understands that both sides quite naturally called up witnesses who might say things favorable to a particular point of view. Assuming that each party had an opportunity to call those witnesses whom it desired, and there is no evidence that such was not the case, the reader must then strike his own balance, make his own conclusions and judgments. To say, as one recent scholar has, that the findings of the committee members representing one party were accurate and that those of the members representing the other were wrong-headed is a position that is extremely hard to defend, one that in itself suggests bias.

A great deal has been written about the conditions of southern life in the post–Civil War era, some of which is based upon reports such as the Teller Committee findings of 1878. This extensive Senate document (see Public Documents) provides testimony concerning the turmoil that was created when the "redeemers" took control of southern polling stations. It is helpful to those trying to understand the political aspects of the exodus that took place in the following year.

The most important single source in Kansas is the St. John collection housed at the Kansas State Historical Society (KSHS) in Topeka. Letters received and copies of those sent give a detailed picture of events as they unfolded in what once had been John Brown country. Much of the passion of

315

the former abolitionists is felt in the correspondence of those who now supported the cause of blacks whom they regarded as having been reenslaved by southerners. Historians have argued, and still do, that the black side of the story is weakened because it is written by whites using white sources. While this is frequently true and while there is much room for argument in it with regard to the Exodusters, it is not completely the case in this instance. Governor St. John's files contain a good many letters of inquiry written by southern blacks who wanted to confirm glowing stories that they had heard about Kansas. The efforts often are painfully illiterate, but their meaning is clear, and the obvious labor with which their authors wrote them make these documents all the more meaningful and certainly poignant.

Other remnants of the movement that are held at the Topeka depository are illuminating. While "Pap" Singleton was neither an Exoduster nor a leader of the movement, despite his claims, his story is one that is closely related, and his surviving scrapbook therefore is both interesting and useful. The unknown and unheralded Horatio N. Rust—who was, in a sense, "Horatio at the Bridge" for St. John—also left a scrapbook, now housed in the quarters of KSHS. I found much of his material fresh and meaningful. Closely related are records of the Kansas Freedmen's Relief Association, especially the minutes of the board of directors; these, too, are in Topeka. When the Comstock and Haviland materials held by KSHS are added to the above, a pretty complete record of the exodus story is available. What is not a matter of record, or is unavailable if extant, is the account of what happened to these migrant blacks in the years immediately after their arrival.

UNPUBLISHED SOURCES

Correspondence and papers of John P. St. John. General correspondence sent and received, 17 boxes, 2 volumes; see immigration, Negro Exodus, March–September, 1879. KSHS.
Correspondence and Papers of William Windom, Minnesota Historical Society, St. Paul.

PUBLISHED DOCUMENTARY SOURCES

Comstock, Elizabeth L. *A Statement by Mrs. E. L. Comstock, Correspondent of the Kansas Freedmen's Relief Association.* Topeka: Commonwealth Steam Printing Office, 1880. KSHS.
Kansas Freedmen's Relief Association. Second Semi-annual Report, April, 1880. Topeka: Daily Capital Steam Printing House, 1880. KSHS.
Kansas Freedmen's Relief Association, Topeka, Kansas. Minutes of the Board of Directors. KSHS.
"The Proceedings of a Mississippi Migration Convention in 1879." *Journal of Negro History,* vol. 4, no. 1 (January, 1919), pp. 51–54, originally in *Vicksburg* (Miss.) *Commercial Daily Advertiser,* May 5, 1879.
Rust, Horatio N., Scrapbook. KSHS.

Singleton, Benjamin, Scrapbook. Newspaper clippings, KSHS Library.

Williams, Charles Richard, ed. *Diary and Letters of Rutherford Birchard Hayes.* 5 vols. Columbus: Ohio State Archaeological and Historical Society, 1924.

PUBLIC DOCUMENTS

U.S., Congress. *Congressional Record,* 46th Cong., 1st sess., 1879.

U.S., Congress, House. Memorial of National Convention of Colored Persons (December, 1873, at Washington, D.C.). *House Miscellaneous Documents,* no. 44. 43d Cong., 1st sess. (serial 1617), 4 pp.

U.S., Congress, Senate. Address of the Convention of Colored Americans, Convened in the City of Washington, D.C., February 3, 1890. *Senate Miscellaneous Documents,* no. 82. 51st Cong., 1st sess. (serial 2698), 3 pp.

————. *Report and Testimony of the Select Committee of the United States Senate to Investigate the Causes of the Removal of the Negroes from the Southern States to the Northern States* [Voorhees Committee Report]. *Senate Reports,* no. 693. 46th Cong., 2d sess., 1880 (serials 1899 [pt. 1] and 1900 [pts. 2 and 3]).

————. *Report of the United States Senate Committee to Inquire into Alleged Frauds and Violence in the Election of 1879, with the Testimony and Documentary Evidence. Senate Reports,* no. 855. 45th Cong., 3d sess. (serial 1840). Committee chairman Sen. Henry M. Teller, Colorado.

————. Resolution of Sen. Daniel W. Voorhees, December 15, 1879. *Senate Miscellaneous Documents,* no. 15. 46th Cong., 2d sess. (serial 1890), 1 p.

————. Resolution of Sen. William Windom, January 16, 1879. *Senate Miscellaneous Documents,* no. 34. 45th Cong., 3d sess. (serial 1833), 1 p.

THESES AND DISSERTATIONS

Aiken, Earl Howard. "Kansas Fever." Master's thesis, Louisiana State University, 1939.

Blake, Lee Ella. "The Great Exodus of 1879 and 1880 to Kansas." Master's thesis, Kansas State University, Manhattan, 1942.

Chartrand, Robert Lee. "The Negro Exodus from the Southern States to Kansas: 1869–1886." Master's thesis, University of Kansas City (now University of Missouri at Kansas City), 1949.

Gift, Elmer Birdell. "The Causes and History of the Negro Exodus into Kansas, 1879–1880." Master's thesis, University of Kansas, 1915.

Grant, Truett King. "The Negro Exodus of 1879–1880." Master's thesis, Baylor University, 1952.

McDaniel, Orval L. "A History of Nicodemus, Graham County, Kansas." Master's thesis, Kansas State College, Fort Hays, 1950.

Peoples, Morgan Dewey. "Negro Migration from the Lower Mississippi Valley to Kansas, 1879–1880." Master's thesis, Louisiana State University, 1950.

Schwendemann, Glen. "Negro Exodus to Kansas: First Phase, March–July, 1879." Master's thesis, University of Oklahoma, 1957.

Smith, Leland George. "The Early Negroes in Kansas." Master's thesis, University of Wichita, 1932.

Waldron, Nell Blythe. "Colonization in Kansas from 1861 to 1890." Ph.D. dissertation, Northwestern University, 1932.

Williams, Corinne Hare. "The Migration of Negroes to the West, 1877–1900, with Special Reference to Kansas." Master's thesis, Howard University, 1944.

NEWSPAPERS

Argos (Washington, D.C.)
Atchison (Kans.) *Daily Champion*
Atchison (Kans.) *Daily Patriot*
Bangor (Maine) *Daily Whig and Courier*
Boston Advertiser
Boston Daily Globe
Boston Evening Transcript
Boston Herald
Burlingame (Kans.) *Chronicle*
Chicago Daily Tribune
Chronicle (Augusta, Ga.)
Cincinnati Commercial
Cincinnati Daily Chronicle
Cincinnati Enquirer
Cincinnati Gazette
Cleveland Plain Dealer
Colored Citizen (Topeka)
Colored Patriot (Topeka)
Columbus (Kans.) *Courier*
Commercial (Vicksburg, Miss.)
Commonwealth (Topeka)
Daily Democratic Statesman (Austin, Tex.)
Daily Eastern Argus (Portland, Maine)
Daily Fort Scott (Kans.) *Monitor*
Daily Kennebec Journal (Augusta, Maine)
Daily Morning Chronicle (San Francisco)
Daily Nebraska State Journal (Lincoln)
Daily Picayune (New Orleans)
Daily Republican (West Chester, Pa.)
Daily Tribune (Lawrence, Kans.)
Denver Tribune
Eagle (Brooklyn)
Edwards County Leader (Kinsley, Kans.), a weekly

Ellsworth (Kans.) *Reporter,* a weekly
Emporia (Kans.) *Ledger*
Enterprise (Pawnee City, Nebr.)
Evening Standard (Lawrence, Kans.)
Evening Telegram (Portland, Oreg.)
Ford County Globe (Dodge City, Kans.)
Fort Worth Democrat
Frank Leslie's Illustrated Newspaper (New York City)
Freeman's Champion (Baldwin, Kans.)
Galveston Weekly News
Goldsboro (N.C.) *Messenger*
Graham County Lever (Gettysburg, Kans.), a weekly
Greencastle (Ind.) *Banner*
Hays City (Kans.) *Sentinel,* a weekly
Houston Daily Post
Huntington (West, Va.) *Advertiser*
Independence Kansan
Indianapolis Journal
Indianapolis News
Inter-Ocean (Chicago)
Iowa State Leader (Des Moines)
Iowa State Press (Iowa City)
Iowa State Register (Des Moines)
Junction City (Kans.) *Tribune*
Junction City (Kans.) *Union,* a weekly
Kansas City Daily Journal
Kansas City Daily Times
Kansas City Star
Kansas Farmer (Topeka), a weekly
Kansas Herald (Topeka)
Leavenworth (Kans.) *Times*
Lewiston (Maine) *Evening Journal*
Louisiana Capitolian (Baton Rouge)
Louisiana Democrat (Alexandria)
Mail and Breeze (Topeka, Kans.)
Memphis Daily Avalanche
Memphis Evening Herald
Memphis Weekly Appeal
Mirror and News Letter (Olathe, Kans.), a weekly
Missouri Republican (St. Louis)
Mobile Register
Natchez (Miss.) *Democrat*
Nebraska City News
Nebraska Herald (Plattsmouth)
New Orleans Daily Democrat

319

New Orleans Observer
New Orleans Times
New Orleans Weekly Democrat
New Orleans Weekly Louisianian (P. B. S. Pinchback's paper)
New York Times
New York Tribune
North Topeka Times
Omaha Daily Bee
Omaha Daily Republican
Parsons (Kans.) *Eclipse*
People's Vindicator (Natchitoches, La).
Public Ledger (Memphis)
Rocky Mountain News (Denver)
St. Louis Globe-Democrat
St. Louis Post-Dispatch
Salina (Kans.) *Herald,* a weekly
Saline County Journal (Salina, Kans.), a weekly
Sentinel (Summit, Mass.)
Shelby Democrat (Shelbyville, Ind.)
Shreveport (La.) *Standard*
Sioux City (Iowa) *Daily Journal*
South Kansas Tribune (Independence)
State Guard (Austin, Tex.)
Sun (New York City)
Sun (Parsons, Kans.)
Texas Capital (Austin, Tex.)
Times (Baxter Springs, Kans.), a weekly
Times (London)
Times (Philadelphia)
Topeka Daily Blade
Topeka Daily Capital
Topeka Daily Times
Topeka Weekly Times
Vicksburg (Miss.) *Commercial Daily Advertiser*
Wa-Keeney (Kans.) *Weekly World*
Washington Post
Weekly Advocate (Baton Rouge, La.)
Weekly Banner (Brenham, Tex.)
Weekly Clarion (Jackson, Miss.)
Weekly Louisianian (New Orleans)
Western Star (Hill City, Kans.), a weekly
Wichita City Eagle
Wyandotte (Kans.) *Gazette,* a weekly
Wyandotte (Kans.) *Herald*

Bibliography

ARTICLES

Athearn, Robert G. "The Promised Land: A Black View." *Record,* vol. 34, pp. 5–21. Pullman, Wash.: Friends of the Library, Washington State University, 1973.

——. "Black Exodus: The Migration of 1879." *Prairie Scout* 3 (1975): 86–97. Abilene, Kansas: Kansas Corral of the Westerners, Inc.

Bentz, Donald N. "Nicodemus—the Promised Land?" *Golden West,* vol. 5, no. 1 (November, 1968), pp. 24–27, 60–63. Mistakenly associates Nicodemus with the Exodusters.

Bingham, Anne E. "Sixteen Years on a Kansas Farm, 1870–1886." *Collections of the Kansas State Historical Society, 1919–1922,* vol. 15, pp. 501–23.

Blaine, James G., et al. "Ought the Negro to Be Disfranchised? Ought He to Have Been Enfranchised?" *North American Review* 128 (March, 1879): 225–83.

Chalmer, H. H. "The Effects of Negro Suffrage." *North American Review* 132 (March, 1881): 239–48.

Chamberlain, D. H. "Reconstruction and the Negro." *North American Review* 128 (February, 1879): 161–73.

Dilliard, Irving. "James Milton Turner: A Little Known Benefactor of His People." *Journal of Negro History,* vol. 19, no. 4 (October, 1934), pp. 372–411.

Donald, Henderson H. "The Negro Migration of 1916–1918." *Journal of Negro History,* vol. 6, no. 4 (October, 1921), pp. 383–498. A Yale University Master's thesis, May, 1920, revised and augmented.

Douglass, Frederick. "The Negro Exodus from the Gulf States." *Journal of Social Science* 11 (May, 1880): 1–21. A paper read before the American Social Science Association at Saratoga, N.Y., September 12, 1879.

Fleming, Walter L. " 'Pap' Singleton, the Moses of the Colored Exodus." *American Journal of Sociology* 15 (July, 1909): 61–82. Singleton was not an exodus leader.

Garvin, Roy. "Benjamin, or 'Pap,' Singleton and His Followers." *Journal of Negro History,* vol. 33, no. 1 (January, 1948), pp. 7–23.

Greener, R. T. "The Emigration of Colored Citizens from the Southern States." *Journal of Social Science* 11 (May, 1880): 22–35. Paper read before the American Social Science Association at Saratoga, N.Y., September 12, 1879.

King, Henry. "A Year of the Exodus in Kansas." *Scribner's Monthly* 20 (June, 1880): 211–18.

Moore, N. Webster. "James Milton Turner: Diplomat, Educator and Defender of Rights, 1840–1915." *Bulletin,* Missouri Historical Society, vol. 27, no. 3 (April, 1971), pp. 194–201.

Peoples, Morgan D. " 'Kansas Fever' in North Louisiana." *Louisiana History,* vol. 11, no. 2 (Spring, 1970), pp. 121–35.

Pickering, Isaac O. "The Administrations of John P. St. John." In *Trans-*

321

actions of the Kansas State Historical Society, 1905–1906, vol. 9, pp. 378–94. Topeka: State Printing Office, 1906.

Savage, W. Sherman. "The Negro in the Westward Movement." *Journal of Negro History,* vol. 25, no. 4 (October, 1940), pp. 531–39.

Schwendemann, Glen. "Wyandotte and the First 'Exodusters' of 1879." *Kansas Historical Quarterly,* vol. 26, no. 3 (Autumn, 1960), pp. 233–49.

———. "St. Louis and the 'Exodusters' of 1879." *Journal of Negro History,* vol. 46, no. 1 (January, 1961), pp. 32–46.

———. "The 'Exodusters' on the Missouri." *Kansas Historical Quarterly,* vol. 29, no. 1 (Spring, 1963), pp. 25–40.

———. "Nicodemus: Negro Haven on the Solomon." *Kansas Historical Quarterly,* vol. 34, no. 1 (Spring, 1968), pp. 10–31.

Slavens, George Everett. "The Missouri Negro Press, 1875–1920." *Missouri Historical Review,* vol. 64, no. 4 (July, 1970), p. 428.

Strickland, Arvarh E. "Toward the Promised Land: The Exodus to Kansas and Afterward." *Missouri Historical Review,* vol. 69, no. 4 (July, 1975), pp. 376–412.

Van Deusen, John G. "The Exodus of 1879." *Journal of Negro History,* vol. 21, no. 2 (April, 1936), pp. 111–29. Most of this came from Senate Document no. 693, the Voorhees Committee Report.

Washington, Booker. "A Negro Potato King." *Outlook* 77 (May 14, 1904): 115–18.

BOOKS

Barr, Alwyn. *Black Texans: A History of Negroes in Texas, 1528–1971.* Austin, Tex.: Jenkins Publishing Co., 1973.

Bontemps, Arna, and Conroy, Jack. *They Seek a City.* Garden City, N.Y.: Doubleday, Doran & Co., 1945. Republished as *Anyplace But Here.* New York: Hill & Wang, 1966.

Brawley, Benjamin. *A Social History of the American Negro.* New York: Macmillan Co., 1921; paperback, 1970.

Bruyn, Kathleen. *"Aunt" Clara Brown: Story of a Black Pioneer.* Boulder, Colo.: Pruett Publishing Co., 1970.

Clark, Carroll D., and Roberts, Roy L. *People of Kansas.* Topeka: Kansas State Planning Board, 1936.

Clark, Thomas D., and Kirwan, Albert D. *The South since Appomattox.* New York: Oxford University Press, 1967.

Cutler, William G., ed. *History of the State of Kansas.* Chicago: A. T. Andreas, 1883.

Emmons, David M. *Garden in the Grasslands: Boomer Literature of the Central Great Plains.* Lincoln: University of Nebraska Press, 1971.

Fehrenbach, T. R. *Lone Star: A History of Texas and the Texans.* New York: Macmillan Co., 1968.

Bibliography

Harrington, Fred Harvey. *Fighting Politician: Major General N. P. Banks.* Philadelphia: University of Pennsylvania Press, 1948.

Haskins, James. *Pinckney Benton Stewart Pinchback: A Biography.* New York: Macmillan Publishing Co., 1973.

Haviland, Laura S. *A Woman's Life-Work: Labors and Experiences of Laura S. Haviland.* Cincinnati, Ohio: Walden & Stowe, 1881. Reprint, New York: Arno Press and the New York Times, [1969].

Henri, Florette. *Black Migration: Movement North, 1900–1920.* Garden City, N.Y.: Doubleday & Co., 1975.

Katz, William Loren. *The Black West.* Garden City, N.Y.: Doubleday & Co., 1971.

Langston, John Mercer. "The Exodus." In *Freedom and Citizenship: Selected Lectures and Addresses of Hon. John Mercer Langston.* Washington, D.C.: Rufus H. Darby, 1883. Reprinted in 1969 by Mnemosyne Publishing Co., Inc., Miami, Fla. A lecture delivered in Washington, D.C., September, 1879, at the invitation of O. S. B. Wall, president, Emigrant Aid Society.

Logan, Rayford W., and Cohen, Irving S. *The American Negro: Old World Background and New World Experience.* Boston: Houghton Mifflin Co., 1967.

Mardock, Robert Winston. *The Reformers and the American Indian.* Columbia: University of Missouri Press, 1971.

Masterson, Vincent Victor. *The Katy Railroad and the Last Frontier.* Norman: University of Oklahoma Press, 1952.

Merrill, Walter M. *Against Wind and Tide: A Biography of Wm. Lloyd Garrison.* Cambridge, Mass.: Harvard University Press, 1963.

Painter, Nell Irvin. *Exodusters: Black Migration to Kansas after Reconstruction.* New York: Alfred A. Knopf, 1977.

Porter, Kenneth Wiggins. *The Negro on the American Frontier.* New York: Arno Press, 1971.

Quarles, Benjamin, ed. *Frederick Douglass.* Englewood Cliffs, N.J.: Prentice-Hall, Inc., 1968.

Rice, Lawrence D. *The Negro in Texas: 1874–1900.* Baton Rouge: Louisiana State University Press, 1971.

Savage, W. Sherman. *Blacks in the West.* Westport, Conn.: Greenwood Press, 1976.

Scharf, John Thomas. *History of Saint Louis City and County, from the Earliest Periods to the Present Day, . . .* 2 vols. Philadelphia: L. H. Everts & Co., 1883.

Smith, Samuel Denny. *The Negro in Congress, 1870–1901.* Port Washington, N.Y.: Kennikat Press, Inc. Copyright, 1940; reissued, 1966.

Stephenson, Wendell Holmes. *The Political Career of General James H. Lane.* Publications of the Kansas State Historical Society, vol. 3. Topeka, 1930.

Trefousse, Hans L. *The Radical Republicans: Lincoln's Vanguard for Racial Justice.* New York: Alfred A. Knopf, 1969.

Washington, Booker T. *A New Negro for a New Century.* Chicago: American Publishing House, 1900. Reprinted in 1969 by Mnemosyne Publishing Co., Inc., Miami, Fla., and by Arno Press, New York.

Wharton, Vernon L. *The Negro in Mississippi, 1865–1890*. Chapel Hill: University of North Carolina Press, 1947.

Williams, Burton J. *Senator John James Ingalls: Kansas' Iridescent Republican*. Lawrence: University Press of Kansas, 1972.

Wood, Norman B. *The White Side of a Black Subject: A Vindication of the Afro-American Race*. Chicago: Donohue, Henneberry & Co., 1896. Rev. ed., New York: Negro Universities Press, 1969.

Woodson, Carter G. *A Century of Negro Migration*. Washington, D.C.: Association for the Study of Negro Life and History, 1918. Reprinted by Russell & Russell, New York, 1969, and by AMS Press, Inc., New York, 1970. Chapter 7: "The Exodus to the West."

Zornow, William Frank. *Kansas: A History of the Jayhawk State*. Norman: University of Oklahoma Press, 1957.

INDEX

Index

Central City, Colo., 161
Central Immigration Board of Kansas, 44
Central Relief Board (Topeka), 44
Chalmers, James R., 150; his advice to blacks, 149
Chambers, H. W.: his advice to emigrants, 239
Chapman, Penrose: aids Exodusters, 151
Chapman, William: on causes of exodus, 240
Charleston, S. C., 133
Chase, James B.: criticizes Elizabeth Comstock, 268
Chase, William: collects clothing, 115
Chautauqua County, Kans., 270; colony located in, 79
Chelsea, Mass., 114
Cherokee Colony (Kans.): founded, 76. *See also* Baxter Springs Colony (Kans.)
Cherokee Indians, 123; Negroes living among, 128
Chesapeake and Ohio Railroad: agents of, 216
Chicago, Ill., 43, 124–27 passim, 137, 139, 166, 167, 170, 191, 204, 206, 210, 214, 218, 247, 260–66 passim; relief efforts at, 122, 168; meetings at, 259
Chicago Daily Tribune, 128, 139, 206, 254, 259; on Kansas population growth, 126; on origins of exodus, 204; on causes of exodus, 276
Chicago *Inter-Ocean,* 124, 136, 166, 170, 191, 206, 210, 214, 218, 261, 262, 266; as spokesman for Exodusters, 122, 123
Chickasaw Indians, 267
Childs, L. S.: appeals to St. John, 187
Chinese, 106, 117, 195, 222; of California, 103; as possible cotton growers, 105
Choctaw Indians, 267
Christian Recorder, 238
Cincinnati, Ohio, 45, 99, 123, 140
Cincinnati Commercial, 121, 140
Cincinnati Daily Chronicle, 123
Circulars, 250; use of, in South, 80, 81
City of Vicksburg. See Riverboats
Civil War, 3, 19, 38, 51, 54, 99, 109, 110, 114, 117, 134, 152, 225
Claflin, Mrs. William: sends clothing, 197–98
Clapp, A. M.: and Emigrant Aid Society, 121
Clark County, Miss.: black emigrants from, 196
Cleaveland, Juliana C.: on Conway, 147

Cleveland, Ohio, 28, 64, 148; contributes to Exodusters, 120
Cleveland Plain Dealer, 148, 235, 238; on Exodusters as dupes, 139; criticizes Hayes, 146
Coffeyville, Kans.: Exodusters at, 175
Cold Springs, Tex., 252
Colorado. See Riverboats
Colorado (state), 75, 103, 126, 132, 135, 161–65 passim, 214, 227, 258; Exodusters sent to, 163
Colorado Springs, Colo., 161
Colored Colonization Society (Topeka): and Lycurgus Jones, 206
Colored Immigration Aid Society, 31; organization of, 29
Colored Refugee Relief Board (St. Louis), 32, 33; organization of, 30, 174; report of, 283 n.9
Colored Western Emigration Society: of Charleston, S.C., 133
Columbus, Kans., 202, 267
Columbus, Ohio: and committee formed at, 121
Colyer, Gilbert: warns against migrating, 103
Committee of Fifteen (St. Louis): proposal for, 18
Committee of Twenty-five (St. Louis), 28, 29, 30; work of, 27
Comstock, Elizabeth, 74, 115, 121, 161, 165, 166, 169, 170, 176, 187, 197, 224, 235, 237, 259–70 passim; volunteers services, 66; asks for funds, 197
Confederate Brigadiers, 109, 117, 130, 137, 139, 140, 141, 152, 206, 261
Connecticut (state), 223
Conway, the Reverend Thomas W., 147–52 passim, 164, 221; as Negro leader, 135; plans to rescue blacks, 144, 145, 146, 150
Cooke, the Reverend Joseph: lectures on exodus, 60, 113
Co-operative Colony Aid Association (New York City), 127
Cooper Institute: meeting at, 118
Council Bluffs, Iowa, 158
Crawford's Opera House (Topeka): entertainment at, 198
Craxton, Sylvia Ann: claims she was raped, 33
Creek Indians, 267
Cromwell, J. W.: at Nashville convention, 101

327

Cullom, Shelby L., 170
Curd, J. M.: queries St. John, 252

Dakota (territory), 133
Dallas, Tex., 197; convention at, 252
Dallas and Wichita Railroad, 128
Dansville, N.Y., 268
Danvers, Mass., 111
Davis, Jefferson, 79, 112, 245
Davis, John, 186, 193; on objections to
  black immigrants, 71; on Exodusters, 185
Davis, Oscar F. (Union Pacific land agent),
  214
Davis County, Kans.: recommended for
  immigrants, 127
Dayton, Ohio, 28
De Baptiste, the Reverend R.: visits
  Atchison, Kans., 47; on persecution, 205
Decatur, Ill., 28
De Frantz, A. D., 77; as colony founder, 55,
  267
Democrats, 47, 48, 49, 52, 80, 97, 99, 109,
  110, 123, 129, 130, 135–41 passim,
  146–53 passim, 157, 170, 199–213 passim,
  216, 218, 220–23 passim, 235, 237, 245,
  249, 254, 266, 276
Denison, Tex., 190
Denver, Colo., 162; meeting at, 161
Denver *Rocky Mountain News*: reports
  meeting, 161, 162
Denver Tribune, 164; on exodus, 162
Deshler, William G.: sends contribution, 121
Dew, Peter: criticizes Perry and Williams,
  215
Dickson, the Reverend Moses, 30, 32, 44;
  collects funds, 28
Dix, Dorothea L., 284 n.25
Dodge City, Kans., 179
Douglass, Mrs. Anna: sends clothing, 28
Douglass, Frederick, 45, 99, 135, 228, 231,
  232, 236, 238, 239; declines to aid Tandy,
  34; as U.S. marshal, 233; his position on
  exodus, 233–35; reads paper at meeting,
  234
Dukehart, John P., 217; as agent for
  Baltimore and Ohio Railroad, 216
Duncan, T. D., 190; on black circulars, 189
Dunlap, Kans., 271, 278
Dunlap Colony (Kans.): founding of, 77
Durant, Miss.: blacks from, 166

Eagleson, W. L.: and *Colored Citizen,*
  236

East Plattsmouth, Iowa, 157
Eby, George H.: treasurer of aid committee,
  121
Edwardsville, Kans., 277
E. H. Durfee. See Riverboats
Elbert, Dr. S. A. (a black physician), 218
Election of 1880: an exodus movement, 116
Ellis, Kans.: receives Exodusters, 43
Ellsworth, Kans.: on exodus, 181
Ellsworth County, Kans., 182
Ellsworth Reporter: on Exodusters, 181, 182
Embry, J. O.: claims to have originated
  exodus, 134
Emigrant Aid Society: organized, 121
Emigration and Relief Committee: addressed
  by Henry Foote, 97
Emporia, Kans., 197; press of, on land
  settlement, 70; epidemic at, 193;
  complaints of, 196; convention at, 273
Emporia Ledger: on Exodusters, 196
England: contributions from, 264
Espenschied, Philippine (wife of Henry
  Overstolz), 14
Evans, John: contributes to Exodusters, 162
Exodus: politics of, 11, 17, 18, 21, 40, 73,
  129, 130, 152, 153, 155, 199, 202, 203,
  204, 208, 209, 212, 216–25 passim, 240,
  244; causes of, 244, 245, 249
Exodus Aid Association: founded at
  Chicago, 122
Exodusters, 7, 33; early arrivals at St. Louis,
  9, 11, 16; and Mullanphy Board, 11, 12;
  of concern to St. Louis, 14; offered
  employment in Kansas, 39; at Wyandotte,
  Kans., 40; criticized by editor, 41;
  problems of, at Leavenworth, Kans., 44,
  45; reception of, at Atchison, Kans., 46;
  treatment of, at Topeka, 55, 57, 165;
  receive national support, 61; numbers in
  Topeka, 67; Kansas opinion of, 71; their
  difficulties in Kansas farming, 78, 83, 85,
  86, 104; efforts to entice them from South,
  81, 82; expectations of, 88; ignored by
  steamboat captains, 91, 92; supported by
  old abolitionists, 110; aid offered to, 119,
  120; support of, from Chicago, 123;
  integrity of, challenged, 157; arriving
  numbers of, 167, 176, 187, 257, 261–62;
  reception of, at Nicodemus, Kans., 183;
  complaints about, 192; segregation of,
  194; as worry to Kansans, 195; and
  Indiana prejudice against, 217; quizzed
  on origins of exodus, 240; Kansas prejudice
  against, 266; complaints of, 268–69;

Index

Lewiston, Maine, 203
Liberia, 19, 132, 234; movement to, 6
Lincoln, Abraham, 112
Lincoln, Nebr., 160, 260; refugees at, 157
Lincoln, proposed state of, 129, 142
Lindell Hotel (St. Louis), 29
Literary and Business Academy: location of, in Dunlap Colony, 77
Little Coney Colony (Kans.), 270; location of, 79
Little Rock, Ark., 100; convention at, 98
Lloyd, George W.: on southern blacks, 91
Locke, David Ross [pseud. Petroleum V. Nasby]: on exodus, 116
Logan Black Law, 53
Louisiana (state), 9, 84, 89, 90, 94, 98–106 passim, 116, 126, 127, 144–48 passim, 157, 159, 164, 166, 183–88 passim, 205, 227, 229, 230, 246, 247, 250, 252; immigration bureau created, 107; flow of blacks from, 197; new constitution of, 245
Lovejoy, Elijah P., 203; murder of, 112
Lusk, Harry H. (Parsons, Kans., editor): sympathizes with Exodusters, 187
Lyle, D. M.: experiments with white labor, 106
Lynch, John R.: on blacks leaving the South, 100
Lynch, W. O., 169; tries to divert Exodusters, 168; visits Kansas, 232

McCabe, Edward P., 273, 277; success of, 184
McCrary, George, 135; as secretary of war, 39
McFarland, Judge N. C., 55, 57, 58; appointed to committee, 53; defends exodus, 56
McKelly, A. K.: arrested, 93
McKennan, Daniel (emigration "agent"), 82, 83
McKinnon, J. D.: employed by black emigrants, 196
McLaughlin, E. D.: on Exodusters, 159
McMillen, W. L.: critical of Conway, 144
McWatters, George S.: offers aid, 120
Madison Parish, La., 21, 205, 236, 250
Maine (state), 113, 114, 129, 275
Manhattan, Kans., 193; receives Exodusters, 42, 88
Manson, M. D.: on prospects for blacks, 220
Marshall, Tex., 189, 191

Massachusetts (state), 110, 111, 147, 197
Mathews, William D.: on exodus, 45
Mathewson, Angell: testifies on exodus, 187
Mechanic's National Bank (New York City), 120
Medford, Mass., 113
Memphis, Tenn., 89, 157, 169, 235; press opinions of, 94
Memphis and St. Louis Packet Company: sued, 35. See also Anchor Line
Memphis Daily Avalanche, 235
Memphis Weekly Appeal, 141, 235, 249; on lynching in Kansas, 71
Mennonites, 4, 179
Merchants' National Bank (St. Louis), 151
Meridian, Miss., 82, 196
Mexico, 139, 217; possible emigration of Negroes to, 129
Michigan (state), 166
Mills, Edward: comments on Exodusters, 48
Mills, Thomas P.: wants blacks in Indiana, 218; on origins of exodus, 221
Milwaukee, Wis.: on reduction of southern representation, 205
Minnesota (state), 131, 133, 135, 166, 209, 211
Mississippi (state), 9, 48, 79, 81, 86–90 passim, 95–107 passim, 116, 119, 126, 133, 140, 143, 146, 148, 149, 157, 164, 165, 166, 174, 183–89 passim, 196, 201, 205, 207, 233, 237, 238, 239, 248, 251, 252, 254, 267; flow of blacks from, 197
Mississippi River, 25, 86, 146, 245, 252
Mississippi Town (a Kansas black community), 40
Mississippi Valley, 37, 98
Mississippi Valley Labor Convention: held at Vicksburg, 96
Missouri (state), 19, 42, 44, 61, 69, 70, 76, 92, 93, 110, 124, 134, 138, 157, 160, 164, 171, 200, 269, 275
Missouri, Kansas and Texas Railroad, 189; transports blacks, 186, 196
Missouri Pacific Railroad: carries Exodusters, 45; complaints about, 73
Missouri River, 26, 27, 32, 55, 74, 75, 156, 157, 163, 176, 186, 213, 240, 277
Missouri River Packet Company, 28, 32, 35
Mitchell, Simon (an Exoduster), 26
Mobile, Ala., 5
Mobile Bay, battle of, 110
Monroe, Wis.: contributions from, 272
Monroe County, Ga.: meeting in, 196
Montgomery, Ala., 5

332

Index

Nixon, William Penn, 166, 170, 191, 218; background of, 123; as editor, 123
North American Review: on politics of exodus, 223
North Brookfield, Mass., 113
North Carolina (state), 6, 209, 212–18 passim, 237, 248, 251, 254
Northern Pacific Railroad, 95, 249
Northrup, Cyrus: aids Exodusters, 115
Northrup Brothers (Wyandotte bankers), 40
North Topeka Baptist Church: meeting at, 58; history of, 59
North Topeka Methodist Episcopal Church: meeting at, 60
North Topeka Times, 55
Nugent, Col. W. L.: presents resolutions, 96; on exodus, 237

Oberlin, Ohio, 28
Oberlin College, 19, 218
O'Hara, James E., 238; on exodus, 237
Ohio (state), 136, 140, 166, 195, 209, 219, 223, 250, 278
Oklahoma (state), 128, 164, 267; colonies in, 277
Olathe, Kans., 52; and John St. John, 51; press opinions of, 70
Omaha, Nebr., 157–60 passim
Omaha Bee, 159, 178; on immigration, 157
Omaha Daily Republican: on black immigration, 158
Oswego, Kans., 266
Otey, Charles N.: on politics of exodus, 221
Ottawa, Kans.: school segregation at, 193
Overstolz, Henry C.; 138; responds to Exodusters, 14, 15, 16

Painter, Nell Irvin, 5; on exodus numbers, 301 n.34, 306 n.36
Park, H. C.: objects to Exodusters, 48
Parsons, Kans., 188–93 passim, 199, 243, 262, 265, 271; founding of, 186; branch of KFRA at, 187, 192
Parsons Eclipse: on numbers of Exodusters, 188
Parsons *Sun*: on Exodusters, 187
Patterson, Corvine: on Exodusters at Wyandotte, 40
Pendleton, George W., 212; as member of Voorhees Committee, 209
Pennsylvania (state): type of immigrants from, 70

Pennsylvania, University of, 123
Pennsylvania Railroad: agents of, 216
Percival, Guy: poem by, 143
Perry, Samuel L., 216, 219, 237; aids migrants, 214; unhappiness of, 215
Philadelphia, Pa., 28, 32, 152, 238, 262; aids Exodusters, 121
Philadelphia *Times,* 245
Phillips, Wendell, 109, 114, 118, 200; speaks at Boston, 112
Phillips, William: Kansas Congressman, 137; background of, 297 n.20
Pickering, Jonathan E., 269; of Agricultural and Industrial Institute, 267
Pickering, L. M. (of Agricultural and Industrial Institute), 267
Pike, Henry C.: on circulars, 251
Pinchback, P. B. S., 228, 239; speaks at convention, 99; opposes exodus, 236; shifts position, 236–37
Pitkin, Gov. Frederick W., 163; raises Exoduster funds in Colorado, 162
Plankinton & Armour (packing plant), 42
Planters' House Hotel (St. Louis), 93
Plattsmouth, Nebr., receives Exodusters, 157
Plumb, Sen. Preston B.: opposes black influx, 73
Poland, Sen. Luke: heads congressional committee, 132
Pollard, Curtis, 22; as southern refugee, 21
Pomeroy, Samuel C.: as former Kansas senator, 138; background of, 298 n.22
Pool Line (riverboat company), 91
Porter, C. W.: on exodus myths, 252
Port Gibson, Miss., 133
Portland, Maine, 126, 203
Portland (Maine) *Daily Eastern Argus,* 235, charges Republicans, 203, 204
Prince, Adolphus: advised to migrate, 205
Principia Club (Cambridge, Mass.): on black migration, 203–4
Prohibition: St. John's support of, 52
Protestants, 107, 158, 257
Prouty, Salmon S., 193; approves exodus, 184
Providence, R.I.: meeting at, 115

Quakers, 77, 115, 121, 123, 176, 197, 234, 260, 265–71 passim; aid Exodusters, 74
Quindaro, Kans.: and Freedmen's University, 38

Rainey, Joseph Hayne, 135; contributes to black migrants, 121

334

Index

Rapides Parish, La., 106
Rattlebone Hollow (a Kansas black
 community), 40
Ray, Scott: on politics of exodus, 221
Raymer, T. W. (emigrant agent), 17
Redmonsville (Topeka suburb), 178
Red River Valley, 91
Reed, Henry: on Exodusters at Wyandotte,
 40
Reform League, 109
Republicans, 49, 52, 54, 55, 62, 73, 99,
 109, 110, 114–18 passim, 121, 124,
 130–53 passim, 160, 164, 181, 182, 188,
 189, 195, 201–23 passim, 235, 241, 255;
 on causes of exodus, 18; black party
 members of, and 1880 election, 201
Revels, Sen. Hiram.: opposes exodus, 239
Reynolds, Milton W., 190, 191; on exodus,
 187; founds newspapers, 188; writes
 article on exodus, 189; supports St. John,
 199; testifies, 211
Richardson, Col. Edmund, 143; promises
 lower rents, 95
Richardson, Isey (Mississippi planter), 83
Richmond, Va.: as site of convention, 101
Riverboats:
 Annie P. Silvers, 27; arrives at St. Louis, 25
 Belle of Memphis: lands blacks at St.
  Louis, 11
 City of Vicksburg, 27; arrives at St. Louis,
  20
 Colorado, 16, 22; brings blacks, 9, 14;
  additional trips of, 26
 E. H. Durfee, 26, 32, 37, 38; transports
  Exodusters, 25, 26, 42
 Fanny Lewis: carries Exodusters, 38
 Grand Tower, 21, 22, 27, 92; brings
  Exodusters to St. Louis, 13, 15, 17;
  additional trips of, 26
 Halliday, 27; arrives at St. Louis, 25
 James Howard, 275, 276; early trip of, 92
 Joe Kinney, 32, 38, 43, 44, 46, 47; its
  trips to Wyandotte, 22, 23, 25, 42
 John B. Maude, 22, 27; arrives at St.
  Louis, 21
Robinson, Nathan: on southern conditions,
 241
Rockhold, Dr. C., 188, 189, 193; quoted,
 186; testifies, 211
Rockland, Maine, 115
Rollin, Mich., 66
Roseman, H. H.: visits Kansas, 174
Rosenblatt, Meyer: comments on Exodusters,
 33, 34

Ross, Edmund: defeated by St. John, 202
Rosser, T. L.: and Northern Pacific
 Railroad, 133
Ruby, George, 231; as black journalist, 230
Russell, J. H.: buries black migrants, 218
Russell, Stillwell H. (U.S. marshal), 190
Rust, Horatio N., 153, 156, 168, 170, 259,
 260, 264; as Chicago philanthropist, 75;
 plans colony, 124; visits Indiana, 218
Rustling, Thomas, 125
Ryan, Thomas: as Kansas Congressman,
 137; on condition of Exodusters, 160

Sac and Fox (Indian) Reservation, 267
St. John, John P., 38, 45, 49, 52–67 passim,
 72–76 passim, 112–25 passim, 160–71
 passim, 174–79 passim, 183–92 passim,
 195–203 passim, 207, 210, 211, 224, 227,
 228, 232, 239, 243–52 passim,
 259–73 passim; early career of, 51, 53;
 receives letters on exodus, 61; on southern
 prices, 64; asked to aid Nicodemus, 87;
 as potential presidential candidate, 170;
 complaints about segregation to, 194;
 election of, 1880, 202; on dwindling
 exodus funds, 264
St. Landry Parish, La.: emigration clubs,
 of, 82
St. Louis, Mo., 7, 12–17 passim, 20–38
 passim, 42, 43, 44, 55, 61–66 passim, 71,
 83, 89, 91, 93, 95, 102, 110, 114, 121,
 124, 126, 135, 139, 145, 146, 148, 151,
 156, 162, 168, 169, 174, 186, 193, 197,
 200–205 passim, 213, 231–36 passim, 240,
 241, 248–51 passim, 256, 267, 275; and
 early exodus arrivals, 9, 11, 13; health
 board of, 15; local blacks of, 18; responds
 to Exodusters, 18, 21, 22, 26; pro-exodus
 meeting at, 20
St. Louis Globe-Democrat: on numbers of
 Exodusters, 28; on politics of exodus, 204;
 newspaper's politics, 281 n.1, 309 n.30
St. Louis *Missouri Republican,* 61, 124, 146,
 200, 235; comments on exodus, 31; on St.
 John, 65; politics of, 281 n.1
St. Louis Post-Dispatch, 276; on politics of
 exodus, 153
St. Paul, Minn., 28
St. Paul's Chapel (St. Louis), 30, 236; as a
 refuge, 20, 21
Salem, Mass., 115
Salina, Kans., 273; and migrant blacks,
 180, 181

335